Muslims
AROUND THE WORLD

RAVINDRA PADALKAR

ISBN
Paperback 979-8-89475-356-0
Hardcase 979-8-89519-540-6

Disclaimer

This book is based on the various references available on websites, mostly on Wikipedia which is available to everyone. This author has utilized his time to collect the data available on Wikipedia which is based on various references. The author of this book shall not be responsible for any content, information and correctness of such information in the book. The Author shall not be prosecuted for any such content, information, pictures, references, etc, The author has not expressed his opinion in this book.

The book is all about the collection of various references, dates, incidents, pictures, stories, news and data etc available on websites, books, and other sources only.

The reader shall not read this book unless agreed upon above.

– Author

Contents

Contents

Chapter 1

Opening Remarks

There are three major religions based on the population in the world.

1. Christian Religion

2. Islam Religion

3. Sanatan Dharma (also known as Hindu Religion)

Considering the present situation all over the world, Islamic Religion is the fastest growing religion. Muslim population is increasing faster than any other religion in the world. Since majority decides the fate of any country, every country is worried about this increasing population of Muslims.

More babies were born to Christian mothers than to members of any other religion in recent years, reflecting Christianity's continued status as the world's largest religious group. But this is unlikely to be the case for much longer: Less than 20 years from now, the number of babies born to Muslims is expected to modestly exceed births to Christians, according to new Pew Research Center demographic estimates.

Muslims are projected to be the world's fastest-growing major religious group in the decades ahead, as Pew Research Center has explained, and signs of this rapid growth already are visible. In the period between 2010 and 2015, births to Muslims made up an estimated 31% of all babies born around the world – far exceeding the Muslim share of people of all ages in 2015 (24%).

PEW Research Center explains –

The Changing Global Religious Landscape

Babies born to Muslims will begin to outnumber Christian births by 2035; people with no religion face a birth dearth

The world's Christian population also has continued to grow, but more modestly. In recent years, 33% of the world's babies were born to Christians, which is slightly greater than the Christian share of the world's population in 2015 (31%).

Babies born to Muslims will begin to outnumber Christian births by 2035

Estimated number of babies born, by mother's religion, during each five-year period

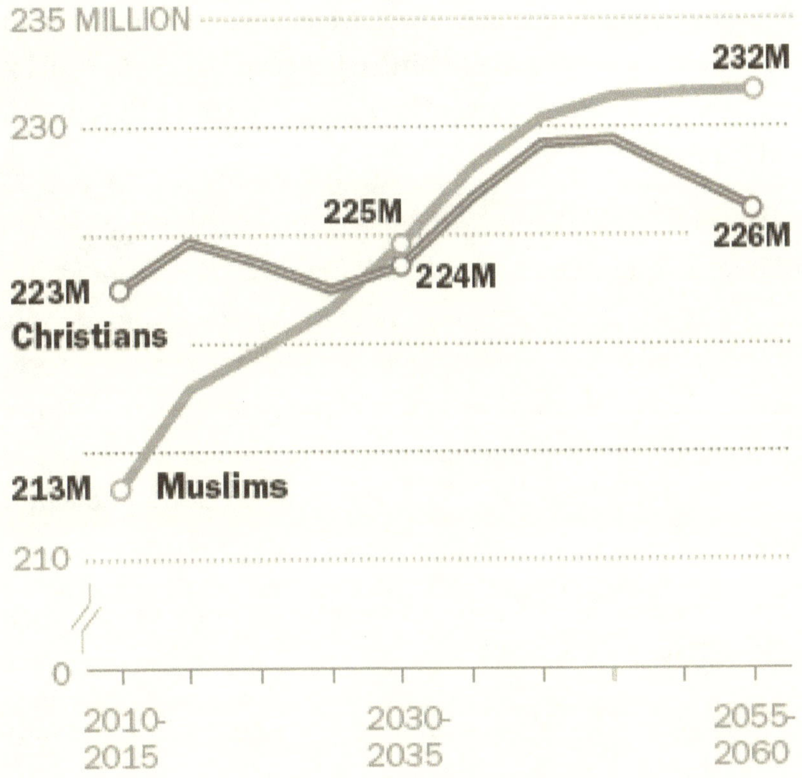

Source: Pew Research Center demographic projections. See Methodology for details.
"The Changing Global Religious Landscape"

PEW RESEARCH CENTER

While the relatively young Christian population of a region like sub-Saharan Africa is projected to grow in the decades ahead, the same cannot be said for Christian populations everywhere. Indeed, in recent years, Christians have had a disproportionately large share of the world's deaths (37%) – in large part because of the relatively advanced age of Christian populations in some places. This is especially true in Europe, where the number of deaths already is estimated to exceed the number of births among Christians. In Germany alone, for example, there were an estimated 1.4 million more Christian deaths than births between 2010 and 2015, a pattern that is expected to continue across much of Europe in the decades ahead.

The problems that arise due to increased population are manifold. Muslims ask to introduce Sharia in the country. Many Muslims (particularly refugees) migrate to the countries where they are in minority so that their population increases in those countries. Many Muslims believe that the people who worship the idols (मूर्तिपूजक) are Kafirs and it is their right to kill these Kafirs which is their religious duty. Such acts spoil the atmosphere in that country.

It is believed that finally, Muslims want to spread Islamic religion all over the world.

It will have a lot of social implications and will have political complications.

Let us see the position with respect to Islam in major countries of the world.

Chapter 2

USA

Islam is the third largest religion in the United States (1%), behind Christianity (63%) and Judaism (2%), and equaling the shares of Buddhism and Hinduism. A 2017 study estimated that 1.1% (or 3.45 million Americans) of the population of the United States are Muslim. In 2017, twenty states, mostly in the South and Midwest, reported Islam to be the largest non-Christian religion. In 2020, the U.S. Religion Census found there to be 4.45 million Muslim Americans, or roughly 1.3% of the population.

The first Muslims to arrive in America were enslaved people from West Africa (such as Omar ibn Said and Ayuba Suleiman Diallo). During the Atlantic slave trade, an estimated 10 to 20 percent of the slaves brought to colonial America from West Africa were Muslims, however Islam was suppressed on plantations. Nearly all enslaved Muslims and their descendants converted to Christianity during the 18th and 19th centuries, though the Black power movement of the 20th century would later influence the revival of Islam among descendants of slaves. Prior to the late 19th century, the vast majority of documented Muslims in North America were merchants, travelers, and sailors.

From the 1880s to 1914, several thousand Muslims immigrated to the United States from the former territories of the Ottoman

Empire and British India. The Muslim population of the U.S. increased dramatically in the second half of the 20th century due to the passage of the Immigration and Nationality Act of 1965, which abolished previous immigration quotas. About 72 percent of American Muslims are immigrants or "second generation".

In 2005, more people from Muslim-majority countries became legal permanent United States residents—nearly 96,000—than there had been in any other year in the previous two decades. In 2009, more than 115,000 Muslims became legal residents of the United States.

American Muslims come from various backgrounds and, according to a 2009 Gallup poll, are one of the most racially diverse religious groups in the United States. According to a 2017 study done by the Institute for Social Policy, "American Muslims are the only faith community surveyed with no majority race, with 26 percent white, 18 percent Asian, 18 percent Arab, 9 percent black, 7 percent mixed race, and 5 percent Hispanic". The Pew Research Center estimates about 73% of American Muslims are Sunni and 16% are Shia; the remainder identify with neither group, and may include heretical movements such as the Nation of Islam, Ahmadiyya, or non-denominational Muslims. Conversion to Islam in large cities has also contributed to its growth over the years.

History

Historical overview

The early history of Muslims in the New World is the subject of debate. Historians argue that Muslims first arrived in the Americas in the early 16th century in what is now New Mexico and Arizona. All analysts agree that the first large population of Muslims consisted of

African slaves. Most slaves who tried to maintain Islamic religious practices after their arrival were forcibly converted to Christianity. In the mid-seventeenth century, Ottoman Muslims are documented to have immigrated with other European immigrants, such as Anthony Janszoon van Salee a merchant of mixed origin from Morocco. Immigration drastically increased from 1878 to 1924 when Muslims from the Balkans, and Syria settled in modern-day Illinois, Ohio, Michigan, Iowa, North Dakota and South Dakota. During that era, the Ford Company employed Muslims as well as African-Americans, since they were the most inclined to work in its factories under demanding conditions. By the 1930s and 1940s, Muslims in the US built mosques for their communal religious observance. At present, the number of Muslims in the US is variously estimated at 3-4 million, and Islam is soon predicted to become the second-largest religion in the US.

Early records

One of the earliest accounts of Islam's possible presence in North America dates to 1528, when a Moroccan slave, called Mustafa Azemmouri, was shipwrecked near what is now Galveston, Texas. He and three Spanish survivors subsequently traveled through much of the American southwest and the Mexican interior before reaching Mexico City.

Historian Peter Manseau wrote

Muslims' presence [in the United States] is affirmed in documents dated more than a century before religious liberty became the law of the land, as in a Virginia statute of 1682 which referred to "negroes, moores, molatoes, and others, born of and in heathenish, idolatrous, pagan, and Mahometan parentage and country" who "heretofore and hereafter may be purchased, procured, or otherwise obtained, as slaves."

American Revolution and thereafter

Records from the American Revolutionary War indicate that at least a few likely Muslims fought on the American side. Among the recorded names of American soldiers are "Yusuf ben Ali" (a member of the Turks of South Carolina community), "Bampett Muhamed" and possibly Peter Salem.

The first country to recognize the United States as an independent nation was the Sultanate of Morocco, under its ruler Mohammed ben Abdallah, in the year 1777. He maintained several correspondences with President George Washington. On December 9, 1805, President Thomas Jefferson hosted a dinner at the White House for his guest Sidi Soliman Mellimelli, an envoy from Tunis.

Bilali "Ben Ali" Muhammad was a Fula Muslim from Timbo, Futa-Jallon, in present-day Guinea-Conakry, who arrived at Sapelo Island during 1803. While enslaved, he became the religious leader and Imam for a slave community numbering approximately eighty Muslim men residing on his plantation. During the War of 1812, Muhammad and the eighty Muslim men under his leadership protected their master's Sapelo Island property from a British attack. He is known to have fasted during the month of Ramadan, worn a fez and kaftan, and observed the Muslim feasts, in addition to consistently performing the five obligatory prayers. In 1829, Bilali authored a thirteen-page Arabic Risala on Islamic beliefs and the rules for ablution, morning prayer, and the calls to prayer. Known as the Bilali Document, it is currently housed at the University of Georgia in Athens.

Between 1785 and 1815, over a hundred American sailors were held for ransom in Algiers. Several wrote captivity narratives of their experiences that gave most Americans their first view of the Arab World and Muslim ways, and newspapers often commented on them. The views were generally negative. Royall Tyler wrote The Algerine Captive (1797), an early American novel depicting the life of an American doctor employed in the slave trade who himself is captured and enslaved by Barbary pirates. Finally, Presidents Jefferson and Madison sent the American navy to confront the pirates, and ended the threat in 1815 during the First Barbary War.

Nineteenth century

On the morning of April 5, 1865, near the end of the American Civil War, Union troops commanded by Col. Thomas M. Johnston set ablaze the University of Alabama; a copy of the Quran known as The Koran: Commonly Called The Alcoran was saved by one of the university's staff.

Estimates ranging from a dozen to two hundred and ninety-two Muslims served in the Union military during the American Civil War, including Private Mohammed Kahn, who was born in Persia, raised in Afghanistan, and emigrated to the United States. The highest-ranking Muslim officer in the Union Army was Captain Moses Osman. Nicholas Said (born 1836), formerly enslaved to an Arab master, came to the United States in 1860 and found a teaching job in Detroit. In 1863, Said enlisted in the 55th Massachusetts Colored Regiment in the United States Army and rose to the rank of sergeant. He was later granted a transfer to a military hospital, where he gained some knowledge of medicine. His Army records state that he died in Brownsville, Tennessee, in 1882. Another

Muslim soldier from the Civil War was Max Hassan, an African who worked for the military as a porter.

During the American Civil War, the "scorched earth" policy of the North destroyed churches, farms, schools, libraries, colleges, and a great deal of other property. The libraries at the University of Alabama managed to save one book from the debris of their library buildings. On the morning of April 4, 1865, when Federal troops reached the campus with an order to destroy the university, Andre Deloffre, a modern language professor and custodian of the library, appealed to the commanding officer to spare one of the finest libraries in the South. The officer, being sympathetic, sent a courier to Gen. Croxton at his headquarters in Tuscaloosa, Alabama asking permission to save the Rotunda, but the general refused to allow this. The officer reportedly said, "I will save one volume as a memento of this occasion." The volume selected was a rare copy of the Qur'an.

Alexander Russell Webb is considered by historians to be the earliest prominent Anglo-American convert to Islam in 1888. In 1893, he was the sole representative of Islam at the first Parliament of the World's Religions. The Russian-born Muslim scholar and writer Achmed Abdullah (1881–1945) was another prominent early American Muslim.

In the 1891 Supreme Court case In re Ross, the Court referred to "the intense hostility of the people of Muslim faith to all other sects, and particularly to Christians". Scores of Muslim immigrants were turned away at U.S. ports in the late 19th and early 20th centuries. Christian immigrants suspected of secretly being Muslims were also excluded.

Slaves

Many enslaved people brought to America from Africa were Muslims from the predominantly-Muslim West African region. Between 1701 and 1800, some 500,000 Africans arrived in what became the United States. Historians estimate that between 15 and 30 percent of all enslaved African men and less than 15 percent of the enslaved African women were Muslims. According to 21st century researchers Donna Meigs-Jaques and R. Kevin Jaques, "these enslaved Muslims stood out from their compatriots because of their resistance, determination and education."

It is estimated that over 50% of the slaves imported to North America came from areas where Islam was followed by at least a minority population. Thus, no less than 200,000 came from regions influenced by Islam. Substantial numbers originated from Senegambia, a region with an established community of Muslim inhabitants extending to the 11th century.

Through a series of conflicts, primarily with the Fulani jihad states, about half of the Senegambian Mandinka were converted to Islam, while as many as a third were sold into slavery to the Americas through capture in conflict.

Michael A. Gomez speculated that Muslim slaves may have accounted for "thousands, if not tens of thousands", but does not offer a precise estimate. He also suggests many non-Muslim slaves were acquainted with some tenets of Islam, due to Muslim trading and proselytizing activities. Historical records indicate many enslaved Muslims conversed in the Arabic language. Some even composed literature (such as autobiographies) and commentaries on the Quran.

Some newly arrived Muslim slaves assembled for communal salat (prayers). Some were provided a private praying area by their owner. The two best documented Muslim slaves were Ayuba Suleiman Diallo and Omar Ibn Said. Suleiman was brought to America in 1731 and returned to Africa in 1734. Like many Muslim slaves, he often encountered impediments when attempting to perform religious rituals and was eventually allotted a private location for prayer by his master.

Omar ibn Said (c. 1770–1864) is among the best documented examples of a practicing-Muslim slave. He lived on a 19th Century North Carolina plantation and wrote many Arabic texts while enslaved. Born in the kingdom of Futa Tooro (modern Senegal), he arrived in America in 1807, one month before the U.S. abolished importation of slaves. Some of his works include the Lords Prayer, the Bismillah, this is How You Pray, Quranic phases, the 23rd Psalm, and an autobiography. In 1857, he produced his last known writing on Surah 110 of the Quran. In 1819, Omar received an Arabic translation of the Christian Bible from his master, James Owen. Omar converted to Christianity in 1820, an episode widely used throughout the South to "prove" the benevolence of slavery. However, many scholars believe he continued to be a practicing Muslim, based on dedications to Muhammad written in his Bible.

Religious freedom

Views of Islam in America affected debates regarding freedom of religion during the drafting of the state constitution of Pennsylvania in 1776. Constitutionalists promoted religious toleration while Anti-constitutionalists called for reliance on Protestant values in the formation of the state's republican government. The former group won out and inserted a clause for religious liberty in the new state constitution. American views of Islam were influenced by favorable Enlightenment writings from Europe, as well as Europeans who had long warned that Islam was a threat to Christianity and republicanism.

In 1776, John Adams published "Thoughts on Government", in which he mentions the Islamic prophet Muhammad as a "sober inquirer after truth" alongside Confucius, Zoroaster, Socrates, and other thinkers.

In 1785, George Washington stated a willingness to hire "Mahometans", as well as people of any nation or religion, to work on his private estate at Mount Vernon if they were "good workmen".

In 1790, the South Carolina legislative body granted special legal status to a community of Moroccans. In 1797, President John Adams signed the Treaty of Tripoli, declaring the United States had no "character of enmity against the laws, religion, or tranquillity, of Mussulmen".

In his autobiography, published in 1791, Benjamin Franklin stated that he "did not disapprove" of a meeting place in Pennsylvania that was designed to accommodate preachers of all religions. Franklin wrote that "even if the Mufti of Constantinople were to send a missionary to preach Mohammedanism to us, he would find a pulpit at his service".

President Thomas Jefferson defended religious freedom in America, including those of Muslims. Jefferson explicitly mentioned Muslims when writing about the movement for religious freedom in Virginia. In his autobiography Jefferson wrote "[When] the [Virginia] bill for establishing religious freedom... was finally passed,... a singular proposition proved that its protection of opinion was meant to be universal. Where the preamble declares that coercion is a departure from the plan of the holy author of our religion, an amendment was proposed, by inserting the word 'Jesus Christ', so that it should read 'a departure from the plan of Jesus Christ, the holy author of our religion'. The insertion was rejected by a great majority, in proof that they meant to comprehend within the mantle of its protection the Jew and the Gentile, the Christian and Mahometan, the Hindoo and infidel of every denomination." While President, Jefferson also participated in an iftar with the Ambassador of Tunisia in 1809.

However, not all politicians were pleased with the religious neutrality of the Constitution, which prohibited any religious test. Anti-Federalists in the 1788 North Carolina ratifying convention opposed the new constitution; one reason was the fear that some day Catholics or Muslims might be elected president. William Lancaster said:

Let us remember that we form a government for millions not yet in existence... In the course of four or five hundred years, I do not know how it will work. This is most certain, that Papists may occupy that chair, and Mahometans may take it. I see nothing against it.

In 1788, Americans held inaccurate, and often contradicting, views of the Muslim world, and used that in political arguments. For example, the anti-Federalists compared a strong central government to the Sultan of the Ottoman Empire and the American army to Turkish Janissaries, arguing against a strong central government. On the other hand, Alexander Hamilton argued that despotism in the Middle East was the result of the Sultan not having enough power to protect his people from oppressive local governors; thus he argued for a stronger central government.

Small-scale migration to the U.S. by Muslims began in 1840, with the arrival of Yemenis and Turks, and lasted until World War I. Most of the immigrants, from Arab areas of the Ottoman Empire, came with the purpose of making money and returning to their homeland. However, the economic hardships of 19th-century America prevented them from prospering, and as a result the immigrants settled in the United States permanently. These immigrants settled primarily in Dearborn, Michigan; Paterson, New Jersey; Quincy, Massachusetts; and Ross, North Dakota. Ross, North Dakota is the site of the first documented mosque and Muslim Cemetery, but it was abandoned and later torn down in the mid-1970s. A new mosque was built in its place in 2005. Construction of mosques sped up in the 1920s and 1930s, and by 1952, there were over 20 mosques. Although the first mosque was established in the U.S. in 1915, relatively few mosques were founded before the 1960s.

- 1893: Alexander Russell Webb starts the first Islamic Mission in the United States called the American Muslim Propagation Movement.

- 1906: Bosniaks (Bosnian Muslims) in Chicago, Illinois, started the Džemijetul Hajrije (Jamaat al-Khayriyya) (The Benevolent Society; a social service organization devoted to Bosnian Muslims). This is the longest lasting incorporated Muslim community in the United States. They met in Bosnian coffeehouses and eventually opened the first Islamic Sunday School with curriculum and textbooks under Bosnian scholar Sheikh Kamil Avdich (Ćamil Avdić) (a graduate of al-Azhar and author of Survey of Islamic Doctrines).

- 1915: What is most likely the first American mosque was founded by Albanian Muslims in Biddeford, Maine. A Muslim cemetery still exists there.

- 1920: The Ahmadiyya Muslim Community was established by the arrival of Mufti Muhammad Sadiq, an Indian Ahmadi Muslim missionary, he later purchased a building in south Chicago and converted it to what is today known as the Al-Sadiq Mosque which was rebuilt as purpose-built mosque in 1990s.

- 1929: The Ross Masjid in North Dakota was founded by Syrian Muslims, there is still a cemetery nearby.

- 1934: The oldest continuously and still standing building built specifically to be a mosque was established in Cedar Rapids, Iowa. The mosque is where Abdullah Igram a notable Muslim veteran would teach the Quran, Abdullah Igram later wrote a letter to President Eisenhower persuading him to add the M option (for Muslims) on military dog tags.

- 1945: A mosque existed in Dearborn, Michigan, home to the largest Arab-American population in the U.S.

"Since the 1950s," many notable political activists and socialites with influence over politicians have come from the American Muslim community.

The Muslim population of the U.S. increased dramatically after President Lyndon B. Johnson signed the Immigration and Nationality Act of 1965 into law. The act abolished former immigration quotas, and expanded immigration opportunities from countries with significant Muslim populations.

Approximately 2.78 million people immigrated to the United States from countries with significant Muslim populations between

1966 and 1997, with some estimating 1.1 million people of that population being Muslims. One-third of those immigrants originated from North Africa or the Middle East, one-third originated from South Asian countries, with the remaining third originating from across the entire world. Immigration to the United States post-1965 favored those deemed to have specialized educational and skills, thus impacting the socio-economic makeup of American Muslims. The United States began seeing Muslim immigrants arrive in the late 20th century as refugees due to such reasons as political unrest, war, and famine.

Subgroups of Muslim Americans

According to the Pew Research Center, approximately 55% of Muslims in the United States are Sunni Muslims, with Shia Muslims representing roughly 16% of the American Muslim population. The remainder identify with neither group, including some who consider themselves to be non-denominational Muslims.

United Nation of Islam

The United Nation of Islam (UNOI) is a group based in Kansas City, Kansas. It was founded circa 1978 by Royall Jenkins, who continues to be the leader of the group and styles himself "Royall, Allah in Person".

Conversion to orthodox Sunni Islam

After the death of Elijah Muhammad, he was succeeded by his son, Warith Deen Mohammed. Mohammed rejected many teachings of his father, such as the divinity of Fard Muhammad, and saw a white person as also a worshiper. As he took control of the organization, he quickly brought in new reforms. He renamed it the World

Community of al-Islam in the West; later it became the American Society of Muslims. It was estimated that there were 200,000 followers of W. D. Mohammed at the time.

W. D. Mohammed introduced teachings which were based on orthodox Sunni Islam. He removed the chairs in the organization's temples, and replaced the entire "temple" concept with the traditional Muslim house of worship, the mosque, also teaching how to pray the salat, to observe the fasting of Ramadan, and to attend the pilgrimage to Mecca.

A small number of Black Muslims however rejected these new reforms brought by Imam Mohammed. Louis Farrakhan, who broke away from the organization, re-established the Nation of Islam under the original Fardian doctrines, and remains its leader.

Shia Islam

An estimated 386,000 to 900,000 Shia Muslims live in the United States. They originate from South Asia, Europe, Middle East, and East Africa; and are often from the countries of: Islamic Republic of Pakistan, India, Islamic Republic of Iran, Lebanon, Iraq, Afghanistan, Syria, Yemen and East Africa; Shiites in the United States also make up about 16 percent of the country's total Muslim population.

The "heart of Shiism in the U.S." is placed in Dearborn, home to the Islamic Center of America. The North American Shia Ithna-Asheri (Twelver Shi'ism) Muslim Communities Organization (NASIMCO) is the largest umbrella group for North American Shias.

Sufism

Some Muslim Americans adhere to the doctrines of Sufism. The Islamic Supreme Council of America (ISCA) is a small body representing Sufi teachings, which, according to adherents, is the inner, mystical dimension of Islam. The ISCA's stated aims include providing practical solutions for American Muslims, based on the traditional Islamic legal rulings of an international advisory board, many of whom are recognized as the highest-ranking Islamic scholars in the world. ISCA aims to integrate traditional scholarship in resolving contemporary issues affecting the maintenance of Islamic beliefs in a modern, secular society. It has been linked to neo-traditionalist thought.

Quranic movement

The largest Quranist movement in the United States is the United Submitters International. This movement was founded by Rashad Khalifa. His movement popularized the phrase: "The Qur'an, the whole Qur'an, and nothing but the Qur'an". Although he was initially well received by many, his subsequent claims of divine inspiration caused friction between him and others, and he was assassinated in 1990. Notable Americans influenced by Rashad Khalifa include his son, Sam Khalifa, a retired professional baseball player, and Ahmad Rashad, a sportscaster and retired football player.

Non-denominational Muslims

Research by Pew in 2011 found that Non-denominational Muslims make up roughly one in seven of all American Muslims, at 15%. Non-denominational Muslims, do not have any specific affiliation with a religious body and usually describe themselves as being "just a Muslim". Muslims who were born in the US are more likely to be non-denominational than immigrant Muslims. 24% or one in four US-born Muslims are non-denominational, versus 10% of immigrant Muslims.

Ahmadiyya

The Ahmadiyya Community was established in 1920 in the United States. Ahmadi Muslims were among the earliest Muslim missionaries in America, the first being Mufti Muhammad Sadiq, who arrived in America on February 15, 1920, and between 1921 and 1925 alone they converted over 1000 people to Islam. Although at first their efforts were broadly concentrated over a large number of racial and ethnic groups, subsequent realization of the deep-seated racial tensions and discrimination made Ahmadi missionaries focus their attention on mainly African Americans and the Muslim immigrant community and became vocal proponents of the civil rights movement. Officially incorporated in Illinois in 1948 as the Ahmadiyya Movement In Islam, Inc. and commonly referred to as the Ahmadiyya Muslim Community since 2006. Many Ahmadi Muslims fled countries like Pakistan due to persecution in recent times.

Other Muslims

There are some mosquegoers who adhere to sects and denominations that form very small minorities. Examples of such small branches include progressive Muslims, Mahdavi Muslims, Ibadi Muslims, and Ismaili Muslims.

Conversion to Islam

Some of the earliest Islamic missionary activities were undertaken by Alexander Russell Webb, who in 1893 established a mission in Manhattan, although it faltered due to lack of funding. From 1910 to 1912, Inayat Khan toured major American cities preaching Islam; he attracted large audiences though not as many converts. More successful in converting Americans to Islam was Mufti Muhammad Sadiq, who established a mission in Chicago in 1920. The converts Sadiq attracted tended to be African American. Soon after, African-American Muslim groups began to form: the Moorish Science Temple was established in Chicago in 1925, and the Nation of Islam formed in 1930.

According to an article in 2001, 25,000 Americans convert to Islam per year.

In more recent years, there has been significant conversion to Islam in the state, federal, and local prisons of the United States. According to J. Michael Waller, Muslim inmates constitute 15–20% of the prison population, or roughly 350,000 inmates in 2003. Waller states that these inmates mostly come into prison as non-Muslims. He also says that 80% of the prisoners who "find faith" while in prison convert to Islam. These converted inmates are mostly African American, with a small but growing Hispanic minority.

Demographics

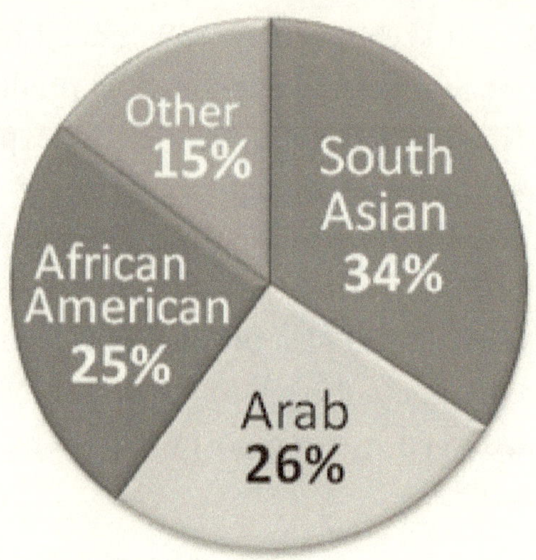

According to the U.S. Department of State (2009), the largest ethnic groups of American Muslims are those of South Asian, Arab and African-American descent.

According to a Pew Forum estimate, in 2017 there were 3.45 million Muslims, constituting about 1.1% of the total U.S. population, compared with 70.6% who follow Christianity, 22.8% unaffiliated, 1.9% Judaism, 0.7% Buddhism, and 0.7% Hinduism.

Mosques are usually explicitly Sunni or Shia although there are over 55 Ahmadiyya mosques as well. There are 2,769 mosques in the United States as of 2020, and the nation's largest mosque, the Islamic Center of America, is in Dearborn, Michigan. It caters mainly to the Shia Muslim congregation; however, all Muslims may attend this mosque. It was rebuilt in 2005 to accommodate over 3,000 people for the increasing Muslim population in the region. More than half (55%) of the religious affiliations of Muslims is Sunni, 16% Shia, 22% non-affiliated and 16% other/non-response.

Muslims of Arab descent are mostly Sunni (56%) with minorities who are Shia (19%). Muslims of South Asian descent including Bangladeshis (90%), Indians (82%) and Pakistanis (72%) are mainly Sunni, other groups such as Iranians are mainly Shia (91%). Of African American Muslims, 48% are Sunni, 34% are unaffiliated (mostly part of the Community of W. Deen Mohammed), 16% other (mostly Nation of Islam and Ahmadiyya) and 2% Shia.

Education and income

The household income levels of American Muslims are about as evenly distributed as the general American population.

When it comes to education, the Institute for Social Policy and Understanding reported in 2017 that across the board, American Muslims, Protestants, and Catholics have similar education levels. It has also been found that Muslim women (73%) are more likely than Muslim men (57%) to go on to pursue higher education beyond high school, and they are also more likely to report being in the middle class.

45 percent of immigrant Muslims report annual household income levels of $50,000 or higher. This compares to the national average of 44 percent. Immigrant Muslims are well represented among higher-income earners, with 19 percent having annual household incomes of $100,000 or higher (compared to 16 percent for the Muslim population as a whole and 17 percent for the U.S. average). This is likely due to the strong concentration of Muslims in professional, managerial, and technical fields, especially in information technology, education, medicine, law, and the corporate world.

Muslim population By state

There were estimated to be about 4.5 million Muslim adherents across the United States in 2020.

Amongst highest are

New York 724,475

California 504,056

Illinois 473,792

And lowest are

North Dakota 540, South Dakota 535, West Virginia 849, Alaska 400,

Wyoming 226, Montana 200, Hawaii 145

The Islamic Center of Passaic County in Paterson is the epicenter of Muslim culture in New Jersey, the U.S. state with the third-highest Muslim population concentration.

In 2020, the US Mosque Survey identified 2,796 Islamic places of worship in the United States, a "31% increase from the 2010 count." The U.S. states with the highest number of mosques were New York (343), California (304), Texas (224), Florida (157), and New Jersey (141), with New York gaining the highest number of mosques compared to 2011 (86 additional). As part of a sampled survey, the US Mosque Survey reports that 6% of mosques self identified as Shi'ite. Pew Research Center notes that 61% of respondents to the survey "say that women have served on the board at some point in the last five years."

Within the Muslim community in the United States there exist a number of different traditions. As in the rest of the world, the Sunni Muslims are in the majority. Shia Muslims, especially those in the Iranian immigrant community, are also active in community affairs. All four major schools of Islamic jurisprudence (fiqh) are found among the Sunni community.

Muslims in the United States have increasingly made their own culture; there are various Muslim comedy groups, rap groups, Scout troops and magazines, and Muslims have been vocal in other forms of media as well.

Hijab is commonly worn by Muslim women in the United States, and is a very distinctive cultural feature of Muslims in America. According to a Pew Research Center poll from 2011, 36% of Muslim American women reported wearing hijab whenever they were in public, with an additional 24% indicating they wore it most or some of the time, while only 40% indicated that they never wore the headcover. Contrary to popular beliefs about assimilation, the study found that the number of women wearing hijab was in fact higher among native-born Muslim women compared to first-generation Muslim immigrants. In the 1990s, however, hijabs were not commonly seen in the United States, as overt Islamization became more apparent only during the 21ˢᵗ century. Compared to some nations in Western Europe, such as France and the Netherlands, there have been relatively few controversies surrounding the hijab in everyday life, a product of "pro-religious freedom" laws allowing for a wide range of religious accommodations, and also due to greater support for multiculturalism.

Politics

To date, four Muslims have served in the United States Congress, all members of the Democratic Party. The first was Keith Ellison, who took office representing Minnesota in 2007.

Party politics

In the 2000 Presidential election, 78 percent of Muslim Americans supported Republican candidate George W. Bush over Democratic candidate Al Gore. However, due to the invasions of Afghanistan and Iraq which took place under the Bush Administration, as well as what some call an increased anti-Muslim rhetoric from the Republican Party after the September 11 attacks, support for the Republican Party among American Muslims has declined sharply.

Ilhan Omar and Rashida Tlaib are the first Muslim women elected to serve in Congress.

By 2008, Democratic candidate Barack Obama got 67% to 90% of the Muslim vote depending on region. In total, Obama won 89% of the Muslim vote, with his Republican opponent John McCain getting only 2%. Some of his opponents question Obama's religious faith.

By 2012, Barack Obama's support slightly falls to 85%, with 4% voting for his Republican opponent, Mitt Romney.

American Muslim political engagement is increasing, as 75% of American Muslims surveyed by ISPU reported being registered to vote, an increase of 15% from 2016 data. In January 2019, Sadaf Jaffer became the first female Muslim American mayor, first female South Asian mayor, and first female Pakistani-American mayor in the United States, of Montgomery in Somerset County, New

Jersey. In June 2022, Republican candidate Mehmet Oz became the first Muslim to be nominated by a major party for the U.S. Senate.

One of the largest Islamic organizations is the Islamic Society of North America (ISNA) which says that 27% of mosques in U.S. are associated with it. ISNA is an association of immigrant Muslim organizations and individuals that provides a common platform for presenting Islam. It is composed mostly of immigrants. Its membership may have recently exceeded ASM, as many independent mosques throughout the United States are choosing to affiliate with it. ISNA's annual convention is the largest gathering of Muslims in the United States.

The second largest Muslim organization is the community under the leadership of W. Deen Mohammed or the American Society of Muslims with 19% of mosques, mostly African-Americans having an affiliation with it. It was the successor organization to the Nation of Islam, once better-known as the Black Muslims. The association recognizes the leadership of Warith Deen Mohammed. This group evolved from the Black separatist Nation of Islam (1930–1975). The majority of its members are African Americans. This has been a 23-year process of religious reorientation and organizational decentralization, in the course of which the group was known by other names, such as the American Muslim Mission, W.Deen Mohammed guided its members to the practice of mainstream Islam such as salat or fasting, and teaching the basic creed of Islam the shahadah.

The Muslim Students' Association (MSA) is a group dedicated, by its own description, to Islamic societies on college campuses in Canada and the United States for the good of Muslim students. The MSA is involved in providing Muslims on various campuses the opportunity to practice their religion and to ease and facilitate such activities. MSA is also involved in social activities, such as fund raisers for the homeless during Ramadan. The founders of MSA would later establish the Islamic Society of North America and Islamic Circle of North America.

The Islamic Information Center (IIC) is a "grass-roots" organization that has been formed for the purpose of informing the public, mainly through the media, about the real image of Islam and Muslims. The IIC is run by chairman (Hojatul-Islam) Imam Syed Rafiq Naqvi, various committees, and supported by volunteers.

The Shia Muslim Foundation (SMF) works to support civic rights of American Shia Muslims, and to advocate on social and political issues. SMF is noted for working with both Shia community leaders and Shia Islamic scholars and clergy in accomplishing its work.

The Ahmadiyya Muslim Community was established in the U.S. in 1921, before the existence of Nation of Islam, according to its members.

Muslim Congress is another National Muslim Organization. It is primarily a Social Welfare organization and runs many social projects, including Food Distribution to the homeless in their "No More Hunger" project and also provides Scholarship. It is under the leadership of Islamic Scholars.

Political

Muslim political organizations lobby on behalf of various Muslim political interests. Organizations such as the American Muslim

Council are actively engaged in upholding human and civil rights for all Americans.

- The Council on American–Islamic Relations (CAIR) is the United States largest Muslim civil rights and advocacy group, originally established to promote a positive image of Islam and Muslims in America. CAIR presents itself as representing mainstream, moderate Islam, and has condemned acts of terrorism and has been working in collaboration with the White House on "issues of safety and foreign policy." The group has been criticized for alleged links to Islamic terrorism and it has been designated as a terrorist group by the United Arab Emirates.

- The Muslim Public Affairs Council (MPAC) is an American Muslim public service and policy organization headquartered in Los Angeles and with offices in Washington, D.C. MPAC was founded in 1988. The mission of MPAC "encompasses promoting an American Muslim identity, fostering an effective grassroots organization, and training a future generation of men and women to share our vision. MPAC also works to promote an accurate portrayal of Islam and Muslims in mass media and popular culture, educating the American public (both Muslim and non-Muslim) about Islam, building alliances with diverse communities and cultivating relationships with opinion- and decision-makers."

- The American Islamic Congress is a small secular Muslim organization that promotes "religious pluralism". Their official Statement of Principles states that "Muslims have been profoundly influenced by their encounter with America. American Muslims are a minority group, consisting largely of immigrants and children of immigrants, who have prospered in America's climate of religious tolerance and civil rights. The lessons of our unprecedented experience of acceptance and success must be carefully considered by our community." The AIC holds an annual essay writing competition, the Dream Deferred Essay Contest, focusing on civil rights in the Middle East.

- The Free Muslims Coalition states it was created to "eliminate broad base support for Islamic extremism and terrorism" and to strengthen secular democratic institutions in the Middle East and the Muslim World by supporting Islamic reformation efforts.

- Muslims for Bush was an advocacy group aiming to drum up support from Muslims for President George W. Bush. It was co-founded by Muhammad Ali Hasan and his mother Seeme, who were prominent donors to the Republican Party. In 2010, co-founder Muhammad Ali Hasan left the Republican Party. Muslims for Bush has since been reformed into the bipartisan Muslims for America.

- American Muslim Political Action Committee (AMPAC) was created in July 2012 by MD Rabbi Alam, a Bangladeshi-born American politician. This newly created organization is one of America's largest Muslim civil liberties advocacy organizations. It is headquartered in Kansas City, Missouri, with two regional offices in New York City and Madison, Wisconsin. AMPAC a bipartisan political platform for Muslim Americans to participate in political races. AMPAC presents an Islamic perspective on issues of importance to the American public, and seeks to empower the American Muslim community and encourage its social and political activism. On September 11, 2013, AMPAC organized the Million Muslim March which took place at the National Mall in Washington, D.C.

- The Islamic Center of Passaic County, the American Arab Civic Organization, and the American Muslim Union, all based in Paterson, New Jersey, voice Muslims' opposition to terrorism, including the November 2015 Paris attacks.

- In November 2022, Nabeela Syed was elected as the first state legislature. In the Illinois 51st district, she defeated a republican incumbent. She is also one of the very few Muslim women and youngest political figures at the age of 23.

Charitable

Charitable donations within the Muslim American community are impacted by domestic political and social climates. ISPU found in 2017 that, "23% of Muslim Americans increased their giving to organizations associated with their faith community and 18% joined, donated to, or volunteered at a civic organizations for the first time as a result of the 2016 national elections. A 2021 study showed that Muslim Americans donated more to charity than other Americans during 2020. Most of the donations were given to causes supporting poverty relief, COVID-19 relief, civil rights, and religious research.

In addition to the organizations listed above, other Muslim organizations in the United States serve more specific needs. For example, some organizations focus almost exclusively on charity work. As a response to a crackdown on Muslim charity organizations working overseas such as the Holy Land Foundation, more Muslims have begun to focus their charity efforts within the United States.

- Inner-City Muslim Action Network (IMAN) is one of the leading Muslim charity organizations in the United States.

- Islamic Relief USA is the American branch of Islamic Relief Worldwide, an international relief and development organization. Its stated goal is "to alleviate the suffering, hunger, illiteracy and diseases worldwide without regard to color, race or creed."

- Project Downtown is a non profit organization originated in Miami Fl. From what started as two men giving away a few sandwiches eventually turned into an array of chapters all over the United States giving away thousands of packets of food, hygiene bags, clothes, and other necessities of life to those who cannot afford it. The motto of Project Downtown is "We feed you for the sake of God alone, no reward do we seek, nor thanks." (Quran 76:9)

- Compassionate Care Network, Chicago, CCNchicago was formed 14 years ago to offer basic health screening for the uninsured population in the community. It offers health screening for obesity, hypertension, diabetes and health awareness for the indigent people.

- American Muslim Health Professionals is a nonprofit organization, founded in 2004, which aims to unite Muslim health professionals and provide information on health.

Cultural

There are two museums dedicated to the history of Islamic culture in the U.S. and abroad. The International Museum of Muslim Cultures in Jackson, Mississippi opened in early 2001. America's Islamic Heritage Museum, in Washington, D.C., opened on April 30, 2011.

There are also numerous cultural organizations centering the Muslim community in the U.S.

- Muslim Writers Collective (MWC) is one of the leading Muslim arts and culture organizations in the United States, founded in 2014 in New York City, and holding monthly open mics across the country. According to a Vice magazine article published in 2016, "At a time when Islamophobia has reached new virulent and violent heights, MWC provides a space for young Muslims to honor their humanity."

Research and think tanks

The Institute for Social Policy and Understanding, with offices in Dearborn, MI and Washington, DC, is an independent, nonpartisan research organization specializing in addressing the most pressing challenges facing the American Muslim community and in bridging the information gap between the American Muslim community and the wider society.

Views

American populace's views on Islam

A nationwide survey conducted in 2003 by the Pew Research Center and the Pew Forum on Religion and Public Life reported that the percentage of Americans with an unfavorable view of Islam increased by one percentage point between 2002 and 2003 to 34%, and then by another two percentage points in 2005 to 36%. At the same time the percentage responding that Islam was more likely than other religion to encourage violence fell from 44% in July 2003 to 36% in July 2005.

The July 2005 Pew survey also showed that 59% of American adults view Islam as "very different from their religion," down one percentage point from 2003. In the same survey 55% had a favorable opinion of Muslim Americans, up four percentage points from 51% in July 2003. A December 2004 Cornell University survey shows that 47% of Americans believe that the Islamic religion is more likely than others to encourage violence among its believers.

According to a research by the New America foundation and the American Muslim Initiative found in 2018, 56 percent of Americans believed Islam was compatible with American values and 42 percent said it was not. About 60 percent believed US Muslims were as patriotic as others, while 38 percent they were not. The study also found that a big majority of Americans - 74 percent - accepted there was "a lot" of bigotry against Muslims existed. Researchers also found that Republicans were more likely to hold negative perceptions of Muslims with 71 percent.

A 2021 Pew study found that 78% of Americans believe Muslims face discrimination, which was a higher percentage than for other religions.

In a 2007 survey titled Muslim Americans: Middle Class and Mostly Mainstream, the Pew Research Center found Muslim Americans to be "largely integrated, happy with their lives, and moderate with respect to many of the issues that have divided Muslims and Westerners around the world."

47% of respondents said they considered themselves Muslims first and Americans second. However, this was compared to 81% of British Muslims and 69% of German Muslims, when asked the equivalent question. A similar disparity exists in income, the percentage of American Muslims living in poverty is 2% higher than the general population, compared to an 18% disparity for French Muslims and 29% difference for Spanish Muslims.

Politically, American Muslims both supported larger government and are socially conservative. Despite their social conservatism, 71% of American Muslims expressed a preference for the Democratic Party. The Pew Research survey also showed that nearly three quarters of respondents believed that American society rewards them for hard work regardless of their religious background.

The same poll also reported that 40% of U.S. Muslims believe that Arab Muslims carried out the 9/11 attacks. Another 28% do not believe it and 32% said they had no opinion. Among the 28% who doubted that Arab Muslims were behind the conspiracy, one-fourth said the U.S. government or President George W. Bush was responsible. 26% of American Muslims believe the U.S.-led "war on terror" is a sincere effort to root out international terrorism. 5% of those surveyed had a "very favorable" or "somewhat favorable" view of Al-Qaeda. 35% of American Muslims stated that the decision for military action in Afghanistan was the right one and 12% supported the use of military force in Iraq.

Although American Muslims do report feeling discriminated against as a religious minority, they are just as likely as the general public (81%) to say they value their American Identity. In fact, a 2018 study done by the Institute for Social Policy and Understanding asserts that, "a higher religious identity correlates with a higher American identity among all Americans, especially Muslims."

American Muslim life after the September 11 attacks

After the September 11 attacks, America saw an increase in the number of hate crimes committed against people who were perceived to be Muslim, particularly those of Middle Eastern and South Asian descent. More than 20 acts of discrimination and violence were documented in the post 9/11 era by the U.S. Department of Justice. Some of these acts were against Muslims living in America. Other acts were against those accused of being Muslims, such as Sikhs, and people of Arabian and South-Asian backgrounds. A publication in Journal of Applied Social Psychology found evidence that the number of anti-Muslim attacks in America in 2001 increased from 354 to 1,501 following 9/11. The same year, the Arab American Institute reported an increase in anti-Muslim hate crimes ranging from discrimination and destruction of private property to violent threats and assaults, some of which resulted in deaths.

In a 2007 survey, 53% of American Muslims reported that it was more difficult to be a Muslim after the 9/11 attacks. Asked to name the most important problem facing them, the options named by more than ten percent of American Muslims were discrimination (19%), being viewed as a terrorist (15%), public's ignorance about Islam (13%), and stereotyping (12%). 54% believe that the U.S. government's anti-terrorism activities single out Muslims. 76% of surveyed Muslim Americans stated that they are very or somewhat concerned about the rise of Islamic extremism around the world, while 61% express a similar concern about the possibility of Islamic extremism in the United States.

On a small number of occasions Muslim women who wore distinctive hijab were harassed, causing some Muslim women to stay at home, while others temporarily abandoned the practice. In November 2009 Amal Abusumayah, a mother of four young girls, had her hijab pulled following derogatory comments while grocery shopping. In 2006, one California woman was shot dead as she walked her child to school; she was wearing a headscarf and relatives and Muslim leaders believe that the killing was religiously motivated. While 51% of American Muslims express worry that women wearing hijab will be treated poorly, 44% of American Muslim women who always wear hijab express a similar concern.

In 2011, The Learning Channel (TLC) broadcast a television series, All-American Muslim, depicting the lives of different American Muslims in Dearborn, Michigan.

Even 16 years after 9/11, studies show that 42% Muslim Americans report bullying of their children in school because of their faith. One in four bullying incidents involving Muslims is rerouted to have involved a teacher or other school official. Policies regarding immigration and airport security have also impacted Muslim American Lives after 9/11, with Muslims being twice as likely as any other faith group surveyed to be stopped at the border for additional screening. 67% of Muslims who were stopped at a US border also reported that they were easily identifiable as a member of their faith group. The climate of the 2016 presidential election and the policies that followed have also affected the lives and sentiments of Muslims Americans when it comes to their own safety. Muslims and Jews are, "most likely to express fear for their personal safety or that of their family from white supremacist groups as a result of the 2016 elections." Overall, the majority of nonwhite Muslims do report some level of race-based discrimination in the past year. When it comes to religious based discrimination, Muslim Americans as a whole were the most likely faith group to report it.

Terrorism that involved Muslim perpetrators began in the United States with the 1993 shootings at CIA Headquarters in Langley, Virginia, followed by the 1993 World Trade Center bombing in New York City. After the September 11 attacks and the start of the Afghanistan war in 2001, there was concern about the potential radicalization of American Muslims.

Between 2001 and the end of 2009, there were 46 publicly reported incidents of "domestic radicalization and recruitment to jihadist terrorism" that involved at least 125 people between 2001 and the end of 2009. There had been an average of six cases per year since 2001, but that rose to 13 in 2009.

While the seeming increase in cases may be alarming, half "involve single individuals, while the rest represent 'tiny conspiracies,' " according to Congressional testimony. Furthermore, a 2012 study by the University of North Carolina indicated that the yearly number of cases of alleged plots by Muslim-Americans appears to be declining. The total of 20 indictments for terrorism in 2011 is down from 26 in 2010 and 47 in 2009 (the total since 9/11 is 193). The number of Muslim-Americans indicted for support of terrorism also fell, from 27 individuals in 2010 to just eight in 2011 (the total since 9/11 stands at 462). Also in apparent decline is the number of actual attacks: Of the 20 suspects indicted for terrorism, only one was charged with carrying out a terrorist act. This number is down from the six individuals charged with attacks in 2010.

Muslim Americans are significantly represented among those who tip authorities off to alleged plots having given 52 of the 140 documented tips regarding individuals involved in violent terrorist plots since 9/11 up to 2012.

The Boston Marathon bombing in 2013 caused 280 injuries, and 5 civilian and police deaths. Attempted attacks, like the Curtis Culwell Center attack and 2015 Boston beheading plot have attracted substantial media coverage and inflamed community relations. In 2015 the New America Foundation released information about violent extremist groups in the US. While the Boston Marathon bombing had a high injury toll, only four deaths were counted by the group, and the group's count of only deaths from violent extremism showed that since 9/11, 48 people had been killed by anti-government extremists, compared to 28 by Jihadists.

Some Muslim Americans have been criticized because of perceived conflicts between their religious beliefs and mainstream American value systems. Muslim cab drivers in Minneapolis, Minnesota have been criticized for refusing passengers for carrying alcoholic beverages or dogs. The Minneapolis-Saint Paul International Airport authority has threatened to revoke the operating authority of any driver caught discriminating in this manner. There are reported incidents in which Muslim cashiers have refused to sell pork products to their clientele.

Jihadist extremism

At least one American not of recent immigrant background, John Walker Lindh, has been imprisoned, convicted on charges of working with the Taliban and carrying weapons against American soldiers. He had converted to Islam while in the United States, moved to Yemen to study Arabic, and then went to Pakistan, where he was recruited by the Taliban.

Another American that was not of recent immigrant background, José Padilla, of Puerto Rican descent and the first Hispanic-American to be imprisoned and convicted on suspicion of plotting a radiological bomb ("dirty bomb") attack. He was detained as a material witness until June 9, 2002, when President George W. Bush designated him an enemy combatant and, arguing that he was not entitled to trial in civilian courts, had him transferred to a military prison. He had converted to Islam while serving his last jail sentence in prison, and went to Pakistan where he was recruited into Al-Qaeda.

In 2015 four U.S. Marines were killed and three injured in Chattanooga, Tennessee by a twenty four-year-old Kuwaiti man, a naturalized US citizen with an engineering degree.

Islamophobia

According to a 2011 Gallup poll, over the preceding decade, there had been an increase in Islamophobia, which it defined as "an exaggerated fear, hatred, and hostility toward Islam and Muslims that is perpetuated by negative stereotypes resulting in bias, discrimination, and the marginalization and exclusion of Muslims from social, political, and civic life." Another 2011 poll provided by The Washington Post through the Public Religion Research Institute states that 48 percent of Americans are uncomfortable with Muslim women wearing the burqa. A 2014 Pew Research Center survey found that Muslims were the most disliked religious group in the United States with an average "cold" rating of 40 (out of 100), which is lower than the 41 cold ratings received by atheists. According to a poll in November 2015 by the Public Religion Research Institute 56 percent of Americans believe that the values of Islam are at odds with the American values and ways of life.

Public institutions in the U.S. have also drawn fire for accommodating Islam at the expense of taxpayers. The University of Michigan–Dearborn and a public college in Minnesota have been criticized for accommodating Islamic prayer rituals by constructing footbaths for Muslim students using taxpayer money. Critics said this special accommodation, which is made to satisfy the needs of Muslims alone, is a violation of Constitutional provisions separating church and state. Along the same constitutional lines, a San Diego public elementary school is being criticized for making special accommodations, specifically for American Muslims, by adding Arabic to its curriculum and giving breaks for Muslim prayers. Some critics said exceptions have not been made for any religious group in the past, and they see this as an endorsement of Islam.

The first American Muslim Congressman, Keith Ellison, created controversy when he compared President George W. Bush's actions after the September 11, 2001 attacks to Adolf Hitler's actions after the Nazi-sparked Reichstag fire, saying that Bush was exploiting the aftermath of 9/11 for political gain, as Hitler had exploited the Reichstag fire to suspend constitutional liberties. The United States Holocaust Memorial Museum and the Anti-Defamation League condemned Ellison's remarks. The congressman later retracted the statement, saying that it was "inappropriate" for him to have made the comparison.

In April 2018, former President Donald Trump instigated a ban on Muslim immigration to America that still reverberates today. America had already some of the lowest percentages (about 1.1% of the total US population) of Muslims among Western nations, and with the ban in 2018, many African Muslims were also barred from traveling to the U.S. or seeking refuge there. The ban had a dramatic impact, but the measure was immediately rescinded in 2021, when Joe Biden took office. Muslim Americans, rights advocates and immigration experts, however, say the policy continues to have a lingering effect on Muslim citizens, as well as on their family members living abroad, unable to join their loved ones in America.

War on Terrorism

War on terrorism, term used to describe the American-led global counterterrorism campaign launched in response to the terrorist attacks of September 11, 2001. In its scope, expenditure, and impact on international relations, the war on terrorism was comparable to the Cold War; it was intended to represent a new phase in global political relations and has had important consequences for security, human rights, international law, cooperation, and governance.

Pakistan agreed to assist USA to carry out attacks in Afghanistan. Pakistan received huge funds from USA for this purpose. According to USA, these funds were not properly used by Pakistan for the purpose for which they were provided.

It is interesting to read what the Committee in US has to say on Assistance to Pakistan.

Some Excerpts

```
[Senate Hearing 110-564]

[From the U.S. Government Publishing Office]

                                    S. Hrg. 110-564

       U.S. FOREIGN ASSISTANCE TO PAKISTAN

=======================================================

                      HEARING

                    BEFORE THE
```

SUBCOMMITTEE ON INTERNATIONAL DEVELOPMENT AND

FOREIGN ASSISTANCE, ECONOMIC AFFAIRS, AND

INTERNATIONAL ENVIRONMENTAL PROTECTION

OF THE

COMMITTEE ON FOREIGN RELATIONS

UNITED STATES SENATE

ONE HUNDRED TENTH CONGRESS

FIRST SESSION

____

DECEMBER 6, 2007

____

Printed for the use of the Committee on
Foreign Relations

Available via the World Wide Web: http://www.
gpoaccess.gov/congress/

index.html

U.S. GOVERNMENT PRINTING OFFICE

45-127 PDF   WASHINGTON DC: 2008

But most troubling of all, we do not seem to
have accomplished very much with the more than
$10 billion we have provided Pakistan since
2001.

Clearly this assistance has not enabled the Pakistan military to eliminate the safe havens on Pakistani soil enjoyed by al-Qaeda and the Taliban.

It has not prevented militants based in Pakistan from slipping across the border into Afghanistan and attacking American and NATO forces, as well as Afghan civilians loyal to President Karzai.

It does not seem to have assisted in bringing internal stability to Pakistan.

It manifestly has not promoted either democracy or a respect for human rights and the rule of law in Pakistan.

It has not given us a Pakistani leadership prepared to do American bidding--though certainly this is not the intent of U.S. assistance, nor should we ever expect that U.S. aid will produce a compliant recipient government.

While U.S. assistance has played a useful role in addressing the basic human needs of some Pakistanis, Pakistan's deficiencies in this area are so great that American aid has been little more than a drop in the bucket.

And obviously, if the polls about anti-Americanism in Pakistan are to be believed, this $10 billion has not won many friends for the United States.

And indeed, this $10 billion figure that is customarily mentioned represents only part of the story. The size of the classified transfers from Washington to Islamabad can only be guessed at. Some analysts suggest covert payments may have exceeded $10 billion, raising the total U.S. assistance package to Pakistan over the past 6 years to something approaching $20 billion.

Killing of Osama bin Laden

It took nearly a decade following the September 11, 2001 terrorist attacks on New York City and Washington, D.C. for American intelligence authorities to realize that al Qaeda founder Osama bin Laden—mastermind of the 9/11 plot—hadn't been skulking in a cave or a remote tribal area of Pakistan. For about the last five years of his life as a fugitive, his home had been a large compound in Abbottabad, shared with several wives and children and a handful of supporters. The location was scarcely a mile from the Pakistan Military Academy in Kakul.

On May 2, 2011, Osama bin Laden, the founder and first leader of the Islamist militant group al-Qaeda, was shot and killed at his compound in the Pakistani city of Abbottabad by United States Navy SEALs of SEAL Team Six (also known as DEVGRU). The operation, code-named Operation Neptune Spear, was carried out in a CIA-led mission, with the Joint Special Operations Command (JSOC) coordinating the Special Mission Units involved in the raid. In addition to SEAL Team Six, participating units under JSOC included the 160th Special Operations Aviation Regiment (Airborne), also known as the "Night Stalkers," and the CIA's Special Activities Division, which heavily recruits from former JSOC Special Mission Units. The success of the operation ended a nearly decade-long manhunt for bin Laden, who was accused of masterminding the September 11 attacks on the United States.

Chapter 3

India

------ ❈ ------

Islam is India's second-largest religion, with 14.2% of the country's population, or approximately 172.2 million people, identifying as adherents of Islam in a 2011 census. India also has the third-largest number of Muslims in the world. The majority of India's Muslims are Sunni, with Shia making up around 15% of the Muslim population.

Islam spread in Indian communities along the Arab coastal trade routes in Gujarat and along the Malabar Coast shortly after the religion emerged in the Arabian Peninsula. Islam arrived in the inland of Indian subcontinent in the 7th century when the Arabs conquered Sindh and later arrived in Punjab and North India in the 12th century via the Ghaznavids and Ghurids conquest and has since become a part of India's religious and cultural heritage. The Barwada Mosque in Ghogha, Gujarat built before 623 CE, Cheraman Juma Mosque (629 CE) in Methala, Kerala and Palaiya Jumma Palli (or The Old Jumma Masjid, 628–630 CE) in Kilakarai, Tamil Nadu are three of the first mosques in India which were built by seafaring Arab merchants. According to the Legend of Cheraman Perumals, the first Indian mosque was built in 624 CE at Kodungallur in present-day Kerala with the mandate of the last ruler (the Tajudeen Cheraman Perumal) of the Chera dynasty, who converted to Islam during the lifetime of Muhammad (c. 570–632). Similarly, Tamil Muslims on the eastern coasts also claim that they converted to Islam in Muhammad's lifetime. The local mosques date to the early 700s.

History

Origins

The vast majority of the Muslims in India belong to South Asian ethnic groups. However, some Indian Muslims were found with detectable, traceable levels of gene flow from outside, primarily from the Middle East and Central Asia. However, they are found in very low levels. Sources indicate that the castes among Muslims developed as the result of the concept of Kafa'a. Those who are referred to as Ashrafs are presumed to have a superior status derived from their foreign Arab ancestry, while the Ajlafs are assumed to be converts from Hinduism, and have a lower status.

Many of these ulema also believed that it is best to marry within one's own caste. The practice of endogamous marriage in one's caste is strictly observed in India. In two of the three genetic studies referenced here, in which is described that samples were taken from several regions of India's Muslim communities, it was again found that the Muslim population was overwhelmingly similar to the local non-Muslims associated, with some having minor but still detectable levels of gene flow from outside, primarily from Iran and Central Asia, rather than directly from the Arabian peninsula.

Research on the comparison of Y chromosomes of Indian Muslims with other Indian groups was published in 2005. In this study 124 Sunnis and 154 Shias of Uttar Pradesh were randomly selected for their genetic evaluation. Other than Muslims, Hindu higher and middle caste group members were also selected for the genetic analysis. Out of 1021 samples in this study, only 17 samples showed E haplogroup and all of them were Shias. The very minor increased frequency however, does place these Shias, solely with regards to their haplogroups, closer to Iraqis, Turks and Palestinians.

Early history of Islam in India

Trade relations have existed between Arabia and the Indian subcontinent since ancient times. Even in the pre-Islamic era, Arab traders used to visit the Konkan-Gujarat coast and Malabar Coast, which linked them with the ports of Southeast Asia. Newly Islamised Arabs were Islam's first contact with India. Historians Elliot and Dowson say in their book The History of India, as told by Its Own Historians, that the first ship bearing Muslim travellers was seen on the Indian coast as early as 630 CE. H.G. Rawlinson in his book Ancient and Medieval History of India claims that the first Arab Muslims settled on the Indian coast in the last part of the 7th century CE. (Zainuddin Makhdoom II "Tuhafat Ul Mujahideen" is also a reliable work.) This fact is corroborated by J. Sturrock in his Madras District Manuals and by Haridas Bhattacharya in Cultural Heritage of India Vol. IV. With the advent of Islam Arabs became a prominent cultural force in the world. Arab merchants and traders became the carriers of the new religion and they propagated it wherever they went.

According to popular tradition, Islam was brought to Lakshadweep islands, situated just to the west of Malabar Coast, by Ubaidullah in 661 CE. His grave is believed to be located on the island of Andrott. A few Umayyad (661–750 CE) coins were discovered from Kothamangalam in the eastern part of Ernakulam district, Kerala. According to Kerala Muslim tradition, the Masjid

Zeenath Baksh at Mangalore is one of the oldest mosques in the Indian subcontinent. According to the Legend of Cheraman Perumals, the first Indian mosque was built in 624 CE at Kodungallur in present-day Kerala with the mandate of the last the ruler (the Cheraman Perumal) of Chera dynasty, who converted to Islam during the lifetime of the Islamic prophet Muhammad (c. 570–632). According to Qissat Shakarwati Farmad, the Masjids at Kodungallur, Kollam, Madayi, Barkur, Mangalore, Kasaragod, Kannur, Dharmadam, Panthalayini, and Chaliyam, were built during the era of Malik Dinar, and they are among the oldest Masjids in the Indian subcontinent. It is believed that Malik Dinar died at Thalangara in Kasaragod town.

The first Indian mosque, Cheraman Juma Mosque, is thought to have been built in 629 CE by Malik Deenar although some historians say the first mosque was in Gujarat in between 610 and 623 CE. In Malabar, the Mappilas may have been the first community to convert to Islam. Intensive missionary activities were carried out along the coast and many other natives embraced Islam. According to legend, two travellers from India, Moulai Abdullah (formerly known as Baalam Nath) and Maulai Nuruddin (Rupnath), went to the court of Imam Mustansir (427–487 AH)/(1036-1094 CE) and were so impressed that they converted to Islam and came back to preach in India in 467 AH/1073 CE. Moulai Ahmed was their companion. Abadullah was the first Wali-ul-Hind (saint of India). He came across a married couple named Kaka Akela and Kaki Akela who became his first converts in the Taiyabi (Bohra) community.

Arab–Indian interactions

Historical evidence shows that Arabs and Muslims interacted with Indians from the early days of Islam and possibly before the arrival of Islam in Arab regions. Arab traders transmitted the numeral system developed by Indians to the Middle East and Europe.

Many Sanskrit books were translated into Arabic as early as the 8th century. George Saliba in his book "Islamic Science and the Making of the European Renaissance", writes that "some major Sanskrit texts began to be translated during the reign of the second Abbasid caliph al-Mansur (r. 754–775), if not before; some texts on logic even before that, and it has been generally accepted that the Persian and Sanskrit texts, few as they were, were indeed the first to be translated."

Commercial intercourse between Arabia and India had gone on from time immemorial, with for example the sale of dates and aromatic herbs by Arabs traders who came to Indian shores every spring with the advent of the monsoon breeze. People living on the western coast of India were as familiar with the annual coming of Arab traders as they were with the flocks of monsoon birds; they were as ancient a phenomenon as the monsoon itself. However, whereas monsoon birds flew back to Africa after a sojourn of few months, not all traders returned to their homes in the desert; many married Indian women and settled in India.

The advent of Muhammad (569–632 CE) changed the idolatrous and easy-going Arabs into a nation unified by faith and fired with zeal to spread the gospel of Islam. The merchant seamen who brought dates year after year now brought a new faith with them. The new faith was well received by South India. Muslims were allowed to build mosques, intermarry with Indian women, and very soon an Indian-Arabian community came into being. Early in the 9th century, Muslim missionaries gained a notable convert in the person of the King of Malabar.

According to Derryl N. Maclean, a link between Sindh (currently province of Pakistan) and early partisans of Ali or proto-Shi'ites can be traced to Hakim ibn Jabalah al-Abdi, a companion of Muhammad, who traveled across Sind to Makran in the year 649 CE and presented a report on the area to the Caliph. He supported Ali, and died in the Battle of the Camel alongside Sindhi Jats. He was also a poet and few couplets of his poem in praise of Ali ibn Abu Talib have survived, as reported in Chachnama.

During the reign of Ali, many Jats came under the influence of Islam. Harith ibn Murrah Al-abdi and Sayfi ibn Fil' al-Shaybani, both officers of Ali's army, attacked Sindhi bandits and chased them to Al-Qiqan (present-day Quetta) in the year 658. Sayfi was one of the seven partisans of Ali who were beheaded alongside Hujr ibn Adi al-Kindi in 660 CE, near Damascus.

Muhammad bin Qasim (672 CE) at the age of 17 was the first Muslim general to invade the Indian subcontinent, managing to reach Sindh. In the first half of the 8th century CE, a series of battles took place between the Umayyad Caliphate and the Indian kingdoms; resulted in Umayyad campaigns in India checked and contained to Sindh. Around the 10th century, Muslim Central Asian nomadic empire, the Ghaznavids, under Mahmud of Ghazni (971–1030 CE), was the second, much more ferocious invader, using swift-horse cavalry and raising vast armies united by ethnicity and religion, repeatedly overran South Asia's north-western plains. Eventually, under the Ghurids, the Muslim army broke into the North Indian Plains, which lead to the establishment of the Islamic Delhi Sultanate in 1206 by the slaves of the Ghurid dynasty. The sultanate was to control much of North India and to make many forays into South India. However, internal squabbling resulted in the decline of the sultanate, and new Muslim sultanates such as the Bengal Sultanate in the east breaking off, while in the Deccan the Urdu-speaking colonists from Delhi, who carried the Urdu language to the Deccan, founded the Bahmanid Empire. In 1339, Shah Mir became the first Muslim ruler of Kashmir, inaugurating the Salatin-i-Kashmir or Shah Mir dynasty.

Under the Delhi Sultanate, there was a synthesis of Indian civilization with that of Islamic civilization, and the integration of the Indian subcontinent with a growing world system and wider international networks spanning large parts of Afro-Eurasia, which had a significant impact on Indian culture and society. The time period of their rule included the earliest forms of Indo-Islamic architecture, increased growth rates in India's population and economy, and the emergence of the Hindustani language. The Delhi Sultanate was also responsible for repelling the Mongol Empire's potentially devastating invasions of India in the 13th and 14th centuries. The period coincided with a greater use of mechanical technology in the Indian subcontinent. From the 13th century onwards, India began widely adopting mechanical technologies from the Islamic world, including water-raising wheels with gears and pulleys, machines with cams and cranks, papermaking technology, and the spinning wheel.

In the early 16th century, northern India, being then under mainly Muslim rulers, fell again to the superior mobility and firepower of a new generation of Central Asian warriors. The resulting Mughal Empire did not stamp out the local societies it came to rule, but rather balanced and pacified them through new administrative practices and diverse and inclusive ruling elites, leading to more systematic, centralised, and uniform rule. Eschewing tribal bonds and Islamic identity, especially under Akbar, the Mughals united their far-flung realms through loyalty, expressed through a Persianised culture, to an emperor who had near-divine status. The Mughal state's economic policies, deriving most revenues from agriculture and mandating that taxes be paid in the well-regulated silver currency, caused peasants and artisans to enter larger markets. The relative peace maintained by the empire during much of the 17th century was a factor in India's economic expansion, resulting in greater patronage of painting, literary forms, textiles, and architecture. The Mughal Empire was the world's largest economy in the 17th century, larger than Qing China and Western Europe, with Mughal India producing about a quarter of the world's economic and industrial output.

In the 18th century, Mughal power had become severely limited. By the mid-18th century, the Marathas had routed Mughal armies and invaded several Mughal provinces from the Punjab to Bengal. By this time, the dominant economic powers in the Indian subcontinent were Bengal Subah under the Nawabs of Bengal and the South Indian Kingdom of Mysore under Hyder Ali and Tipu Sultan, before the former was devastated by the Maratha invasions of Bengal, leading to the economy of the Kingdom of Mysore overtaking Bengal. The British East India Company conquered Bengal in 1757 and then Mysore in the late 18th century. The last Mughal emperor, Bahadur Shah II, had authority over only the city of Old Delhi (Shahjahanabad), before he was exiled to Burma by the British Raj after the Indian Rebellion of 1857.

Role in the Indian independence movement

The contribution of Muslim revolutionaries, poets and writers is documented in the history of India's struggle for independence. Titumir raised a revolt against the British Raj. Abul Kalam Azad, Hakim Ajmal Khan and Rafi Ahmed Kidwai are other Muslims who engaged in this endeavour. Ashfaqulla Khan of Shahjahanpur conspired to loot the British treasury at Kakori (Lucknow). Khan Abdul Gaffar Khan (popularly known as "Frontier Gandhi") was a noted nationalist who spent 45 of his 95 years of life in jail; Barakatullah of Bhopal was one of the founders of the Ghadar Party, which created a network of anti-British organisations; Syed Rahmat Shah of the Ghadar Party worked as an underground revolutionary in France and was hanged for his part in the unsuccessful Ghadar Mutiny in 1915; Ali Ahmad Siddiqui of Faizabad (UP) planned the Indian Mutiny in Malaya and Burma, along with Syed Mujtaba Hussain of Jaunpur, and was hanged in 1917; Vakkom Abdul Khadir of Kerala participated in the "Quit India" struggle in 1942 and was hanged; Umar Subhani, an industrialist and millionaire from Bombay, provided Mahatma Gandhi with Congress expenses and ultimately died for the cause of independence. Among Muslim women, Hazrat Mahal, Asghari Begum, and Bi Amma contributed in the struggle for independence from the British.

Other famous Muslims who fought for independence against British rule were Abul Kalam Azad, Mahmud al-Hasan of Darul Uloom Deoband, who was implicated in the famous Silk Letter Movement to overthrow the British through an armed struggle, Husain Ahmad Madani, former Shaikhul Hadith of Darul Uloom Deoband, Ubaidullah Sindhi, Hakim Ajmal Khan, Hasrat Mohani, Syed Mahmud, Ahmadullah Shah, Professor Maulavi Barkatullah, Maghfoor Ahmad Ajazi, Zakir Husain, Saifuddin Kitchlew, Vakkom Abdul Khadir, Manzoor Abdul Wahab, Bahadur Shah Zafar, Hakeem Nusrat Husain, Khan Abdul Gaffar Khan, Abdul Samad Khan Achakzai, Colonel Shahnawaz, Mukhtar Ahmed Ansari, Rafi Ahmed Kidwai, Fakhruddin Ali Ahmed, Ansar Harwani, Tak Sherwani, Nawab Viqarul Mulk, Nawab Mohsinul Mulk, Mustsafa

Husain, V. M. Obaidullah, S.R. Rahim, Badruddin Tyabji, Abid Hasan and Moulvi Abdul Hamid.

Until 1920, Muhammad Ali Jinnah, later the founder of Pakistan, was a member of the Indian National Congress and was part of the independence struggle. Muhammad Iqbal, poet and philosopher, was a strong proponent of Hindu–Muslim unity and an undivided India, perhaps until 1930. Huseyn Shaheed Suhrawardy was also active in the Indian National Congress in Bengal, during his early political career. Mohammad Ali Jouhar and Shaukat Ali struggled for the emancipation of the Muslims in the overall Indian context, and struggled for independence alongside Mahatma Gandhi and Abdul Bari of Firangi Mahal. Until the 1930s, the Muslims of India broadly conducted their politics alongside their countrymen, in the overall context of an undivided India.

Partition of India

I find no parallel in history for a body of converts and their descendants claiming to be a nation apart from the parent stock.

—Mahatma Gandhi, opposing the division of India on the basis of religion in 1944.

The partition of India was the partition of British India led to the creation of the dominions of Pakistan (that later split into the Islamic Republic of Pakistan and the People's Republic of Bangladesh) and India (later Republic of India). The Indian Independence Act 1947 had decided 15 August 1947, as the appointed date for the partition. However, Pakistan celebrates its day of creation on 14 August.

The partition of India was set forth in the Act and resulted in the dissolution of the British Indian Empire and the end of the

British Raj. It resulted in a struggle between the newly constituted states of India and Pakistan and displaced up to 12.5 million people with estimates of loss of life varying from several hundred thousand to a million (most estimates of the numbers of people who crossed the boundaries between India and Pakistan in 1947 range between 10 and 12 million). The violent nature of the partition created an atmosphere of mutual hostility and suspicion between India and Pakistan that plagues their relationship to this day.

The partition included the geographical division of the Bengal province into East Bengal, which became part of Pakistan (from 1956, East Pakistan). West Bengal became part of India, and a similar partition of the Punjab province became West Punjab (later the Pakistani Punjab and Islamabad Capital Territory) and East Punjab (later the Indian Punjab, as well as Haryana and Himachal Pradesh). The partition agreement also included the division of Indian government assets, including the Indian Civil Service, the Indian Army, the Royal Indian Navy, the Indian railways and the central treasury, and other administrative services.

The two self-governing countries of India and Pakistan legally came into existence at the stroke of midnight on 14–15 August 1947. The ceremonies for the transfer of power were held a day earlier in Karachi, at the time the capital of the new state of Pakistan, so that the last British Viceroy, Lord Mountbatten of Burma, could attend both the ceremony in Karachi and the ceremony in Delhi. Thus, Pakistan's Independence Day is celebrated on 14 August and India's on 15 August.

After Partition of India in 1947, two-thirds of the Muslims resided in Pakistan (both east and West Pakistan) but a third resided in India. Based on 1951 census of displaced persons, 7,226,000 Muslims went to Pakistan (both West and East) from India while

7,249,000 Hindus and Sikhs moved to India from Pakistan (both West and East). Some critics allege that British haste in the partition process increased the violence that followed. Because independence was declared prior to the actual Partition, it was up to the new governments of India and Pakistan to keep public order. No large population movements were contemplated; the plan called for safeguards for minorities on both sides of the new border. It was a task at which both states failed. There was a complete breakdown of law and order; many died in riots, massacre, or just from the hardships of their flight to safety. What ensued was one of the largest population movements in recorded history. According to Richard Symonds: At the lowest estimate, half a million people perished and twelve million became homeless.

However, many argue that the British were forced to expedite the Partition by events on the ground. Once in office, Mountbatten quickly became aware if Britain were to avoid involvement in a civil war, which seemed increasingly likely, there was no alternative to partition and a hasty exit from India. Law and order had broken down many times before Partition with much bloodshed on both sides. A massive civil war was looming by the time Mountbatten became Viceroy. After the Second World War, Britain had limited resources, perhaps insufficient to the task of keeping order. Another viewpoint is that while Mountbatten may have been too hasty he had no real options left and achieved the best he could under difficult circumstances. The historian Lawrence James concurs that in 1947 Mountbatten was left with no option but to cut and run.

The alternative seemed to be involvement in a potentially bloody civil war from which it would be difficult to get out.

Demographics

With around 204 million Muslims (2019 estimate), India's Muslim population is the world's third-largest and the world's largest Muslim-minority population. India is home to 10.9% of the world's Muslim population. According to Pew Research Center, there can be 213 million Muslims in 2020, India's 15% population. Indian Muslim have a fertility rate of 2.36, the highest in the nation as per as according to year 2019-21 estimation. While Government of India at Lok Sabha have estimated the Muslim population at 19.75 to 20 crore for 2023 year, out of 138.8 to 140.0 crore total population, thus constituting around (14.22%–14.28%) of the nation's population respectively.

Muslim populations (top 5 countries) Est. 2020

Country	Muslim Population	Percentage of Total Muslim Population
Indonesia	231,070,000	12.2%
Pakistan	233,046,950	11.2%
India	**207,000,000**	**10.9%**
Bangladesh	153,700,000	9.20%
Nigeria	110,263,500	5.8%

Muslims represent a majority of the local population in Lakshadweep (96.2%) and Jammu and Kashmir (68.3%). The largest concentration – about 47% of all Muslims in India, live in the three states of Uttar Pradesh, West Bengal, and Bihar. High concentrations of Muslims are also found in the states of Andhra Pradesh, Assam, Delhi, Gujarat, Jharkhand, Karnataka, Kerala, Madhya Pradesh, Maharashtra, Manipur, Rajasthan, Tamil Nadu, Telangana, Tripura, and Uttarakhand.

Population growth rate

Historical Muslim Population Growth in India		
Year	Pop.	±%
1901	29,900,000	—
1911	30,800,000	+3.0%
1921	31,200,000	+1.3%
1931	35,800,000	+14.7%
1941	42,400,000	+18.4%
1951	35,400,000	–16.5%
1961	46,900,000	+32.5%
1971	61,400,000	+30.9%
1981	80,300,000	+30.8%
1991	106,700,000	+32.9%
2001	138,200,000	+29.5%

2011	172,200,000	+24.6%

After India's independence and the creation of Pakistan in 1947, the Muslim population in India declined from 42,400,000 in 1941 to 35,400,000 in the 1951 census, due to the Partition of India. The Pakistan Census, 1951 identified the number of displaced persons in the country at 7,226,600, presumably all Muslims refugees who had entered Pakistan from India. Around 35 million Muslims stayed back after Partition as Jawaharlal Nehru (then the Prime Minister of India) have ensured the confidence that they would be treated fairly in this democratic nation.

In 1941 Census, there were 94.5 million Muslims living in the Undivided India (inc. Pakistan and Bangladesh), comprising 24 percent of the population. Partition, in fact, has eventually drained India of 60% of its Muslim population.

Former Minister of Law and Justice of India, Dr Bhimrao Ramji Ambedkar during partition, have advocated for a full population exchange between the Muslim and Hindu minorities of India and Pakistan for maintenance of law, order and peace in both the newly formed nations by citing- "That the transfer of minorities is the only lasting remedy for communal peace is beyond doubt" in his own written book "Pakistan or partition of India" respectively.

However, a complete population exchange did not occur and was made impossible due to the earlier signing of the Liaquat–Nehru Pact in 1950, which sealed the borders of both nations completely. Ultimately, this led to the cessation of migration of refugees from both sides. As a result of this, a large number of Muslims in India, a significant number of Hindus in East Pakistan (present-day Bangladesh) and a minuscule number of Hindus in the Sindh province of West Pakistan remained. Meanwhile, the East Punjab state of India and the West Punjab province of Pakistan saw a full population exchange between Muslim and Hindu/Sikh minorities during the time of Partition.

Illegal Immigrants

India is the home of some 40,000 illegal Rohingya Muslim refugees, with approximately 18,000 registered with the United Nations High Commissioner for Refugees (UNHCR). But even people with refugee cards are being detained across India due to security concerns. On 17 November 2016, Union Minister of State for Home, Kiren Rijiju, stated in the Rajya Sabha that, according to available inputs, there are around 20 million (2 crore) illegal Bangladeshi migrants staying in India. Illegal immigrants in Assam are estimated to number between 16 lakh and 84 lakh, in a total population of 3.12 crore according to the 2011 Census. A report published by DNA has revealed that the Bangladeshi-origin Muslim population has grown to 5-7% in bordering districts of Assam and Bengal simultaneously. Muminul Aowal, an eminent Assamese Muslim Minority Development Board Chairman, has reported that Assam has about 1.3 crore Muslims of which around 90 lakh are of Bangladeshi origin. According to Chief Minister Himanta Biswa Sarma, among the 19 lakh individuals excluded from the Assam National Register of Citizens, 7 lakh are Muslims. Dr. Kuntal Kanti Chattoraj, HOD of the Department of Geography at P.R.M.S. Mahavidyalaya, Bankura, has revealed that an estimated 6.28 million Bangladeshi Muslims have infiltrated into West Bengal over the decades.

Projections

Muslims in India have a much higher total fertility rate (TFR) compared to that of other religious communities in the country. Because of higher birthrates the percentage of Muslims in India has risen from about 9.8% in 1951 to 14.2% by 2011. However, since 1991, the largest decline in fertility rates among all religious groups in India has occurred among Muslims. The Sachar Committee Report shows that the Muslim Population Growth has slowed down and will be on par with national averages. The Sachar Committee Report estimated that the Muslim proportion will stabilise at between 17% and 21% of the Indian population by 2100. Pew Research Center have projected that India will have 310 million Muslims by 2050, out of total 1.668 billion people, thus constituting 18.4% of the country's population. United Nations have projected India's future population. It will rise to 170.53 crore by 2050, and then it will decline to 165.97 crore by 2100 year respectively. Muslim population will rise to minimum 282.14 million (forming 17% of the country's population) to maximum 348.53 million (forming 21% of the country's population) by 2100.

Religiosity

On 29 June 2021, Pew Research Center reports on Religiosity have been published, where they completed 29,999 face-to-face interviews with non-institutionalized adults ages 18 and older living in 26 states and three union territories across India. They Interviewed 3,336 Muslims and found that 79% of those interviewes believed in the existence of God with absolute certainty, 12% believes in the existence of God with less certainty and 6% of the Indian Muslims have declared themselves as Atheists by citing that they don't believe in any God. However 91% of Muslim interviewed have said religion plays a big part in their lives.

CSDS study reports, have found that Indian Muslims have become 'less religious' since 2016. In that same year, the study found that 97 per cent of Muslim respondents have said that they prayed regularly. However, in 2021, it was found that only 86 per cent of Muslim youth prayed regularly which is an absolute decline of 11 percentage points from the last five years respectively.

According to sociologists Roger and Patricia Jeffery, socio-economic conditions rather than religious determinism is the main reason for higher Muslim birthrates. Indian Muslims are poorer and less educated compared to their Hindu counterparts. Noted Indian sociologist, B.K. Prasad, argues that since India's Muslim population is more urban compared to their Hindu counterparts, infant mortality rates among Muslims is about 12% lower than those among Hindus.

However, other sociologists point out that religious factors can explain high Muslim birthrates. Surveys indicate that Muslims in India have been relatively less willing to adopt family planning measures and that Muslim women have a larger fertility period since they get married at a much younger age compared to Hindu women.

On the other hand, it is also documented that Muslims tend to adopt family planning measures. A study conducted by K.C. Zacharia in Kerala in 1983 revealed that on average, the number of children born to a Muslim woman was 4.1 while a Hindu woman gave birth to only 2.9 children. Religious customs and marriage practices were cited as some of the reasons behind the high Muslim birth rate. According to Paul Kurtz, Muslims in India are much more resistant to modern contraception than are Hindus and, as a consequence, the decline in fertility rate among Hindu women is much higher compared to that of Muslim women.

The National Family and Health survey conducted in 1998–99 highlighted that Indian Muslim couples consider a substantially higher number of children to be ideal for a family as compared to Hindu couples in India. The same survey also pointed out that percentage of couples actively using family planning measures was more than 49% among Hindus against 37% among Muslims. According to a district wise fertility study by Saswata Ghosh, Muslim TFR (total fertility rate) is closer to that of the Hindu community in most southern states. Also TFR tends to be high for both communities in Northern states such as Uttar Pradesh and Bihar. This study was based on the last census of the country from 2011.

Denominations

There are two major denominations amongst Indian Muslims. The majority of Indian Muslims (over 85%) belong to the Sunni branch of Islam, which is being followed by 130 million people, While a substantial minority (over 13%) belong to the Shia branch, which is being followed by 40 million people respectively. There are also tiny minorities of Ahmadiyya and Quranists across the country numbering 1 million each.

Sunni

Indian Sunnis largely follow the Hanafi school of Islamic law.

The majority of Indian Sunnis follow the Barelvi movement which was founded in 1904 by Ahmed Razi Khan of Bareilly in defense of traditional Islam as understood and practised in South Asia and in reaction to the revivalist attempts of the Deobandi movement. In the 19th century the Deobandi, a revivalist movement in Sunni Islam was established in India. It is named after Deoband a small town northeast of Delhi, where the original madrasa or seminary of the movement was founded. From its early days this movement has been influenced by Wahhabism. A minority of Indian Muslims also follow the Ahl-i Hadith movement.

In the coastal Konkan region of Maharashtra, the local Konkani Muslims follow the Shafi'i school of Sunni Islamic jurisprudence.

Shia

Shia Muslims are a large minority among India's Muslims forming about 13% of the total Muslim population. However, there has been no particular census conducted in India regarding sects, but Indian sources like Times of India and Daily News and Analysis reported Indian Shia population in mid 2005–2006 to be up to 25% of the entire Muslim population of India which accounts them in numbers between 40,000,000 to 50,000,000 of 157,000,000 Indian Muslim population. However, as per an estimation of one reputed Shia NGO Alimaan Trust, India's Shia population in early 2000 was around 30 million with Sayyids comprising just a tenth of the Shia population. According to some national and international sources Indian Shia population is the world's second-largest after Iran.

Bohra

Bohra Shia was established in Gujarat in the second half of the 11th century. This community's belief system originates in Yemen, evolved from the Fatimid were persecuted due to their adherence to

Fatimid Shia Islam – leading the shift of Dawoodi Bohra to India. After occultation of their 21st Fatimid Imam Tayyib, they follow Dai as representative of Imam which are continued till date.

Dā'ī Zoeb appointed Maulai Yaqoob (after the death of Maulai Abdullah), who was the second Walī al-Hind of the Fatimid dawat. Moulai Yaqoob was the first person of Indian origin to receive this honour under the Dā'ī. He was the son of Moulai Bharmal, minister of Hindu Solanki King Jayasimha Siddharaja (Anhalwara, Patan). With Minister Moulai Tarmal, they had honoured the Fatimid dawat along with their fellow citizens on the call of Moulai Abdullah. Syedi Fakhruddin, son of Moulai Tarmal, was sent to western Rajasthan, India, and Moulai Nuruddin went to the Deccan (death: Jumadi al-Ula 11 at Don Gaum, Aurangabad, Maharashtra, India).

One Dai succeeded another until the 23rd Dai in Yemen. In India also Wali-ul-Hind were appointed by them one after another until Wali-ul-Hind Moulai Qasim Khan bin Hasan (11th and last Wali-ul-Hind, d. 950 AH, Ahmedabad).

Due to persecution by the local Zaydi Shi'a ruler in Yemen, the 24th Dai, Yusuf Najmuddin ibn Sulaiman (d. 1567 CE), moved the whole administration of the Dawat (mission) to India. The 25th Dai Jalal Shamshuddin (d. 1567 CE) was first dai to die in India. His mausoleum is in Ahmedabad, India. The Dawat subsequently moved from Ahmedabad to Jamnagar, Mandvi, Burhanpur, Surat and finally to Mumbai and continues there to the present day, currently headed by 53rd Dai.

Asaf Ali Asghar Fyzee was a Bohra and 20th century Islamic scholar from India who promoted modernization and liberalization of Islam through his writings. He argued that with changing time modern reforms in Islam are necessary without compromising on basic "spirit of Islam".

Khojas

The Khojas are a group of diverse people who converted to Islam in South Asia. In India, most Khojas live in the states of Gujarat, Maharashtra, Rajasthan and the city of Hyderabad. Many Khojas have also migrated and settled over the centuries in East Africa, Europe and North America. The Khoja were by then adherents of Nizari Ismailism branch of Shi'ism. In the late 19th and early 20th centuries, particularly in the aftermath of the Aga Khan case a significant minority separated and adopted Twelver Shi'ism or Sunni Islam, while the majority remained Nizārī Ismā'īlī.

Sufis

Sufis (Islamic mystics) played an important role in the spread of Islam in India. They were very successful in spreading Islam, as many aspects of Sufi belief systems and practices had their parallels in Indian philosophical literature, in particular nonviolence and monism. The Sufis' orthodox approach towards Islam made it easier for Hindus to practice. Sulthan Syed Ibrahim Shaheed, Hazrat Khawaja Muin-ud-din Chishti, Qutbuddin Bakhtiar Kaki, Nizamuddin Auliya, Shah Jalal, Amir Khusrow, Alauddin Sabir Kaliyari, Shekh Alla-ul-Haq Pandwi, Ashraf Jahangir Semnani, Waris Ali Shah, Ata Hussain Fani Chishti trained Sufis for the propagation of Islam in different parts of India. The Sufi movement also attracted followers from the artisan and untouchable communities; they played a crucial role in bridging the distance between Islam and the indigenous traditions. Ahmad Sirhindi, a prominent member of the Naqshbandi Sufi advocated the peaceful conversion of Hindus to Islam.

Ahmadiyya

The Ahmadiyya movement was founded in 1889 by Mirza Ghulam Ahmad of Qadian. He claimed to be the promised messiah and mahdi awaited by the Muslims and obtained a considerable number of followers initially within the United Provinces, the Punjab and Sindh. Ahmadis claim the Ahmadiyya movement to embody the latter day revival of Islam and the movement has also been seen to have emerged as an Islamic religious response to the Christian and Arya Samaj missionary activity that was widespread in 19th century India. After the death of Ghulam Ahmad, his successors directed the Ahmadiyya Community from Qadian which remained the headquarters of the community until 1947 with the creation of Pakistan. The movement has grown in organisational strength and in its own missionary programme and has expanded to over 200 countries as of 2014 but has received a largely negative response from mainstream Muslims who see it as heretical, due mainly to Ghulam Ahmad's claim to be a prophet within Islam.

Ahmaddiya have been identified as sects of Islam in 2011 Census of India apart from Sunnis, Shias, Bohras and Agakhanis. India has a significant Ahmadiyya population. Most of them live in Rajasthan, Odisha, Haryana, Bihar, Delhi, Uttar Pradesh, and a few in Punjab in the area of Qadian. In India, Ahmadis are considered to be Muslims by the Government of India (unlike in neighbouring Pakistan). This recognition is supported by a court verdict (Shihabuddin Koya vs. Ahammed Koya, A.I.R. 1971 Ker 206). There is no legislation that declares Ahmadis non-Muslims or limits their activities, but they are not allowed to sit on the All India Muslim Personal Law Board, a body of religious leaders India's government recognises as representative of Indian Muslims. Ahmadiyya are estimated to be from 60,000 to 1 million in India.

Quranists

Non-sectarian Muslims who reject the authority of hadith, known as Quranists, Quraniyoon, or Ahle Quran, are also present in India. In South Asia during the 19th century, the Ahle Quran movement formed partially in reaction to the Ahle Hadith movement whom they considered to be placing too much emphasis on hadith. Notable Indian Quranists include Chiragh Ali, Aslam Jairajpuri, Khwaja Kamal-ud-Din, and Abdullah Chakralawi.

Pasmanda Muslim Mahaz

Pasmanda Muslim Mahaz ('Marginalised Muslim Front') is an Indian Muslim activist organization based in Patna, Bihar. Founded in 1998, it represents the concerns of the "Pasmanda" Muslims, a new identity that integrates the Dalit Muslims (Arzals) and backward-caste Muslims (Ajlafs). The organization represents the union of several Dalit and backward-caste Muslim organisations under the leadership of Ali Anwar, who is himself a backward-caste Muslim of the Ansari (weaver) caste.

Islamic traditions in India

Sufism is a mystical dimension of Islam, often complementary with the legalistic path of the sharia had a profound impact on the growth of Islam in India. A Sufi attains a direct vision of oneness with God, often on the edges of orthodox behaviour, and can thus become a Pir (living saint) who may take on disciples (murids) and set up a spiritual lineage that can last for generations. Orders of Sufis became important in India during the thirteenth century following the ministry of Moinuddin Chishti (1142–1236), who settled in Ajmer and attracted large numbers of converts to Islam because of his holiness. His Chishti Order went on to become the most influential Sufi lineage in India, although other orders from Central Asia and Southwest Asia also reached India and played a major role in the spread of Islam. In this way, they created a large literature in regional languages that embedded Islamic culture deeply into older South Asian traditions.

Intra-Muslim relations

Shia–Sunni relations

The Sunnis and Shia are the biggest Muslim groups by denomination. Although the two groups remain cordial, there have been instances of conflict between the two groups, especially in the city of Lucknow.

Society and culture

Religious administration

The religious administration of each state is headed by the Mufti of the State under the supervision of the Grand Mufti of India, the most senior, most influential religious authority and spiritual leader of Muslims in India. The system is executed in India from the Mughal period.

Muslim institutes

There are several well established Muslim institutions in India. Here is a list of reputed institutions established by Muslims in India.

Modern universities and institutes

- Al-Ameen Educational Society
- Aliah University

- Aligarh Muslim University
- Jamia Markazu Saqafathi Sunniyya
- Ma'dinu Ssaquafathil Islamiyya
- B. S. Abdur Rahman University
- Darul Huda Islamic University
- Darul Uloom Deoband
- Darul Uloom Nadwatul Ulama
- Farook College, Kozhikode
- Ibn Sina Academy of Medieval Medicine and Sciences
- Integral University
- Jamal Mohamed College, Tiruchirappalli
- Hamdard University, Delhi
- Jamia Millia Islamia, New Delhi
- M.S.S. Wakf Board College, Madurai (The only college in India run by a State Wakf Board)
- Madeenathul Uloom Arabic College, Pulikkal, Malappuram
- Maulana Azad National Urdu University Hyderabad
- Maulana Mazharul Haque Arabic and Persian University Patna Bihar
- Maulana Azad College of Arts and Science, Aurangabad
- Muslim Educational Association of Southern India
- Muslim Educational Society, Kerala
- National College of Engineering, Tirunelveli
- Osmania University, Hyderabad
- Pocker Sahib Memorial Orphanage College, Tirurangadi
- Thangal Kunju Musaliar College of Engineering, Kollam

- Karim City College, Jamshedpur

Traditional Islamic universities

- Al Jamea tus Saifiyah, Bohra

- Al Jamiatul Ashrafia, Barelvi

- Jamia Darussalam, Oomerabad

- Al-Jame-atul-Islamia, Uttar Pradesh

- Jamia Nizamia, Hyderabad

- Manzar-e-Islam, Bareilly

- Raza Academy

- Sunni Cultural Center, Karanthur, Kerala

Leadership and organisations

- The Ajmer Sharif Dargah and Dargah-e-Ala Hazrat at Bareilly Shareef are prime center of Sufi oriented Sunni Muslims of India.

- Indian Shia Muslims form a substantial minority within the Muslim community of India comprising between 25% and 31% of total Muslim population in an estimation done during mid-2005 to 2006 of the then Indian Muslim population of 157 million. Sources like The Times of India and DNA reported Indian Shia population during that period between 40,000,000 to 50,000,000 of 157,000,000 Indian Muslim population.

- The Deobandi movement, another section of the Sunni Muslim population, originate from the Darul Uloom Deoband, an influential religious seminary in the district of Saharanpur of Uttar Pradesh. The Jamiat Ulema-e-Hind, founded by Deobandi scholars in 1919, became a political mouthpiece for the Darul Uloom.

- The Jamaat-e-Islami Hind, founded in 1941, advocates the establishment of an Islamic government and has been active in promoting education, social service and ecumenical outreach to the community.

Caste system among Indian Muslims

Although Islam does not recognize any castes, the caste system among South Asian Muslims refers to units of social stratification that have developed among Muslims in South Asia.

Stratification

In some parts of South Asia, the Muslims are divided as Ashrafs and Ajlafs. Ashrafs claim to be derived from their foreign ancestry. They, in turn, are divided into a number of occupational castes.

Barrani was specific in his recommendation that the "sons of Mohamed" [i.e. Sayyid] be given a higher social status than the others. His most significant contribution in the fatwa was his analysis of the castes with respect to Islam. His assertion was that castes would be mandated through state laws or "Zawabi" and would carry precedence over Sharia law whenever they were in conflict. Every act which is "contaminated with meanness and based on ignominity, comes elegantly [from the Ajlaf]". He sought appropriate religious sanction to that effect. Barrani also developed an elaborate system of promotion and demotion of imperial officers ("Wazirs") that was primarily on the basis of their caste.

In addition to the ashraf/ajlaf divide, there is also the arzal caste among Muslims, who were regarded by anti-caste activists like Babasaheb Ambedkar as the equivalent of untouchables. The term "Arzal" stands for "degraded" and the Arzal castes are further subdivided into Bhanar, Halalkhor, Hijra, Kasbi, Lalbegi, Maugta,

Mehtar etc. They are relegated to "menial" professions such as scavenging and carrying night soil.

Some South Asian Muslims have been known to stratify their society according to qaums. Studies of Bengali Muslims in India indicate that the concepts of purity and impurity exist among them and are applicable in inter-group relationships, as the notions of hygiene and cleanliness in a person are related to the person's social position and not to his/her economic status. Muslim Rajput is another caste distinction among Indian Muslims.

Some of the upper and middle caste Muslim communities include Syed, Shaikh, Shaikhzada, Khanzada, Pathan, Mughal, and Malik. Genetic data has also supported this stratification. In three genetic studies representing the whole of South Asian Muslims, it was found that the Muslim population was overwhelmingly similar to the local non-Muslims associated with minor but still detectable levels of gene flow from outside, primarily from Iran and Central Asia, rather than directly from the Arabian Peninsula.

The Sachar Committee's report commissioned by the government of India and released in 2006, documents the continued stratification in Muslim society.

Interaction and mobility

Data indicates that the castes among Muslims have never been as rigid as that among Hindus. They have good interactions with the other communities. They participate in marriages and funerals and other religious and social events in other communities. Some of them also had inter-caste marriages since centuries but mostly they preferred to marry in the same caste with a significant number of marriages being consanguineous. In Bihar state of India, cases had been reported in which the higher caste Muslims have opposed the burials of lower caste Muslims in the same graveyard.

Criticism

Some Muslim scholars have tried to reconcile and resolve the "disjunction between Quranic egalitarianism and Indian Muslim social practice" through theorizing it in different ways and interpreting the Quran and Sharia to justify casteism.

While some scholars theorize that Muslim castes are not as acute in their discrimination as that among Hindus, Dr. Babasaheb Ambedkar argued otherwise, arguing the social evils in Muslim society were "worse than those seen in Hindu society". He was critical of Ashraf antipathy towards the Ajlaf and Arzal and attempts to palliate sectarian divisions. He condemned the Indian Muslim community of being unable to reform like Muslims in other countries such as Turkey did during the early decades of the twentieth century.

Segregation

Segregation of Indian Muslims from other communities began in the mid-1970s when the first communal riots occurred. This was heightened after the 1989 Bhagalpur violence in Bihar and became a trend after the demolition of the Babri Masjid in 1992. Soon several major cities developed ghettos, or segregated areas, where the Muslim population moved into. This trend, however, did not help with the anticipated security the anonymity of ghetto was thought to have provided. During the 2002 Gujarat riots, several such ghettos became easy targets for the rioting mobs, as they enabled the profiling of residential colonies. This kind of ghettoisation can be seen in Mumbai, Delhi, Kolkata and many cities of Gujarat where a clear socio-cultural demarcation exists between Hindu-dominated and Muslim-dominated neighbourhoods.

In places like Gujarat, riots and alienation of Muslims have led to large-scale ghettoisation of the community. For example, the Juhapura area of Ahmadabad has swelled from 250,000 to 650,000 residents since 2002 riots. Muslims in Gujarat have no option but to head to a ghetto, irrespective of their economic and professional status.

An increase in ghetto living has also shown a strengthening of stereotyping due to a lack of cross-cultural interaction, and reduction in economic and educational opportunities at large. Secularism in India is being seen by some as a favour to the Muslims, and not an imperative for democracy.

Art and architecture

The Taj Mahal in Agra is one of India's most iconic monuments. (Some Experts believe that Shah Jahan did not build Taj Mahal but forcefully took the possession from a Rajput king)

A rebuilt structure of the old Cheraman Juma Mosque, Kerala, which is often considered as the first Masjid of India

Asafi Imambargah, also known as Bara Imambara at Lucknow

The Humayun's Tomb in Delhi

Gol Gumbaz at Bijapur, Karnataka, has the second largest pre-modern dome in the world after the Byzantine Hagia Sophia.

Bahauddin Makbara, mausoleum of the Wazir of Junagadh, Gujarat

400-year-old Makkah Masjid, Hyderabad. (Photo: 1885)

The Asafi Mosque within the Asafi Imambargah Complex at Lucknow

The Rumi Darwaza at Lucknow

Gole-Gumma, Mousoleum of Nawab Wahab Khan, Kurnool, Andhra Pradesh

Charminar, the most famous of the monuments of Hyderabad

Red Fort, Delhi

Jama Masjid, Delhi, one of the largest mosques in India

Sir Syed Mosque, Aligarh Muslim University, Aligarh

Architecture of India took new shape with the advent of Islamic rule in India towards the end of the 12th century CE. New elements were introduced into the Indian architecture that include: use of shapes (instead of natural forms); inscriptional art using decorative lettering or calligraphy; inlay decoration and use of coloured marble, painted plaster and brightly coloured glazed tiles. Quwwat-ul-Islam Mosque built in 1193 CE was the first mosque to be built in the Indian subcontinent; its adjoining "Tower of Victory", the Qutb Minar also started around 1192 CE, which marked the victory of Muhammad of Ghor and his general Qutb al-Din Aibak, from Ghazni, Afghanistan, over local Rajput kings, is now a UNESCO World Heritage Site in Delhi.

In contrast to the indigenous Indian architecture which was of the trabeate order, i.e. all spaces were spanned by means of horizontal beams, the Islamic architecture was arcuate, i.e. an arch or dome was adopted as a method of bridging a space. The concept of arch or dome was not invented by the Muslims but was, in fact, borrowed and further perfected by them from the architectural styles of the post-Roman period. Muslims used a cementing agent in the form of mortar for the first time in the construction of buildings in India. They further put to use certain scientific and mechanical formulae, which were derived by experience of other civilisations, in their constructions in India. Such use of scientific principles helped not only in obtaining greater strength and stability of the construction materials but also provided greater flexibility to the architects and builders. One fact that must be stressed here is that, the Islamic elements of architecture had already passed through different experimental phases in other countries like Egypt, Iran and Iraq before these were introduced in India. Unlike most Islamic monuments in these countries, which were largely constructed in brick, plaster and rubble, the Indo-Islamic monuments were typical mortar-masonry works formed of dressed stones. It must be emphasized that the development of the Indo-Islamic architecture was greatly facilitated by the knowledge and skill possessed by the Indian craftsmen, who had mastered the art of stonework for centuries and used their experience while constructing Islamic monuments in India.

Islamic architecture in India can be divided into two parts: religious and secular. Mosques and Tombs represent the religious architecture, while palaces and forts are examples of secular Islamic architecture. Forts were essentially functional, complete with a little township within and various fortifications to engage and repel the enemy.

Mosques

There are more than 300,000 active mosques in India, which is higher than any other country, including the Muslim world. The mosque or masjid is a representation of Muslim art in its simplest form. The mosque is basically an open courtyard surrounded by a pillared verandah, crowned off with a dome. A mihrab indicates the direction of the qibla for prayer. Towards the right of the mihrab stands the minbar or pulpit from where the Imam presides over the proceedings. An elevated platform, usually a minaret from where the Faithful are summoned to attend prayers is an invariable part of a mosque. Large mosques where the faithful assemble for the Friday prayers are called the Jama Masjids.

Tombs and Mausoleum

The tomb or maqbara could range from being a simple affair (Aurangazeb's grave) to an awesome structure enveloped in grandeur (Taj Mahal). The tomb usually consists of a solitary compartment or tomb chamber known as the huzrah in whose centre is the cenotaph or zarih. This entire structure is covered with an elaborate dome. In the underground chamber lies the mortuary or the maqbara, in which the corpse is buried in a grave or qabr. Smaller tombs may have a mihrab, although larger mausoleums have a separate mosque located at a distance from the main tomb. Normally the whole tomb complex or rauza is surrounded by an enclosure. The tomb of a Muslim saint is called a dargah. Almost all Islamic monuments were subjected to free use of verses from the Quran and a great amount of time was spent in carving out minute details on walls, ceilings, pillars and domes.

Styles of Islamic architecture in India

Islamic architecture in India can be classified into three sections: Delhi or the imperial style (1191–1557 CE); the provincial style, encompassing the surrounding areas like Ahmedabad, Jaunpur and the Deccan; and the Mughal architecture style (1526–1707 CE).

Law, politics, and government

Certain civil matters of jurisdiction for Muslims such as marriage, inheritance and waqf properties are governed by the Muslim Personal Law, which was developed during British rule and subsequently became part of independent India with some amendments. Indian Muslim personal law is not developed as a Sharia law but as an interpretation of existing Muslim laws as part of common law. The Supreme Court of India has ruled that Sharia or Muslim law holds precedence for Muslims over Indian civil law in such matters.

Muslims in India are governed by "The Muslim Personal Law (Shariat) Application Act, 1937." It directs the application of Muslim Personal Law to Muslims in marriage, mahr (dower), divorce, maintenance, gifts, waqf, wills and inheritance. The courts generally apply the Hanafi Sunni law for Sunnis; Shia Muslims are independent of Sunni law for those areas where Shia law differs substantially from Sunni practice.

The Indian constitution provides equal rights to all citizens irrespective of their religion. Article 44 of the constitution recommends a uniform civil code. However, attempts by successive political leadership in the country to integrate Indian society under a common civil code is strongly resisted and is viewed by Indian Muslims as an attempt to dilute the cultural identity of the minority groups of the country. The All India Muslim Personal Law Board was established for the protection and continued applicability of "Muslim Personal Law", i.e. Shariat Application Act in India. The Sachar Committee was asked to report about the condition of Muslims in India in 2005. Almost all the recommendations of the Sachar Committee have been implemented.

The following laws/acts of Indian legislation are applicable to Muslims in India (except in the state of Goa) regarding matters of marriage, succession, inheritance, child adoption etc.

1. Muslim Personal Law Sharia Application Act, 1937

2. The Dissolution of Muslim Marriages Act, 1939

3. Muslim Women (Protection of Rights on Divorce) Act, 1986

Note: the above laws are not applicable in the state of Goa. The Goa civil code, also called the Goa Family Law, is the set of civil laws that governs the residents of the Indian state of Goa. In India, as a whole, there are religion-specific civil codes that separately govern adherents of different religions. Goa is an exception to that rule, in that a single secular code/law governs all Goans, irrespective of religion, ethnicity or linguistic affiliation. The above laws are also not applicable to Muslims throughout India who had civil marriages under the Special Marriage Act, 1954.

Bharatiya Muslim Mahila Andolan is an Indian Muslim women's organisation in India. It released a draft on 23 June 2014, 'Muslim Marriage and Divorce Act', recommending that polygamy be made illegal in the Muslim Personal Law of India.

Citizenship (Amendment) Act, 2019 was proposed for the changes in the citizenship and immigration norms of the country by relaxing the requirements for Indian citizenship. The applicability of the amendments are debated in news as it is on religious lines (excluding Muslims).

India's Constitution and Parliament have protected the rights of Muslims but, according to some sources, there has been a growth in a 'climate of fear' and 'targeting of dissenters' under the Bharatiya Janata Party and Modi ministry, affecting the feelings of security and tolerance amongst Indian Muslims. However, these allegations are not universally supported.

Active Muslim political parties

- All India Majlis-e-Ittehadul Muslimeen (AIMIM), led by Asaduddin Owaisi active in states of Telangana, Maharashtra, Bihar, Uttarpradesh, Gujarat and Karnataka.

- Indian Union Muslim League (IUML), led by E. Ahamed active in Kerala.

- All India United Democratic Front (AIUDF), led by Badruddin Ajmal active in Assam state.

- Jammu and Kashmir People's Conference (JKPC), founded by Abdul Ghani Lone and Molvi Iftikhar Hussain Ansari. Led by Sajjad Lone. It is active in Jammu and Kashmir.

- National Conference (NC) main party of Jammu and Kashmir.

- Peoples Democratic Party (PDP) main party of Jammu and Kashmir.

- Apni Party (JKAP) a newly formed party of Jammu and Kashmir

- Peace Party of India of Mohamed Ayub

Muslims in government

India has seen three Muslim presidents and many chief ministers of State Governments have been Muslims. Apart from that, there are and have been many Muslim ministers, both at the centre and at the state level. Out of the 12 Presidents of the Republic of India, three were Muslims – Zakir Husain, Fakhruddin Ali Ahmed and A. P. J. Abdul Kalam. Additionally, Mohammad Hidayatullah, Aziz Mushabber Ahmadi, Mirza Hameedullah Beg and Altamas Kabir held the office of the Chief Justice of India on various occasions since independence. Mohammad Hidayatullah also served as the acting President of India on two separate occasions; and holds the distinct honour of being the only person to have served in all three offices of the President of India, the Vice-President of India and the Chief Justice of India.

The former Vice-President of India, Mohammad Hamid Ansari, former Foreign Minister Salman Khurshid and former Director (Head) of the Intelligence Bureau, Syed Asif Ibrahim are Muslims. Ibrahim was the first Muslim to hold this office. From

30 July 2010 to 10 June 2012, Dr. S. Y. Quraishi served as the Chief Election Commissioner of India. He was the first Muslim to serve in this position. Prominent Indian bureaucrats and diplomats include Abid Hussain, Ali Yavar Jung and Asaf Ali. Zafar Saifullah was Cabinet Secretary of the Government of India from 1993 to 1994. Salman Haidar was the Foreign Secretary from 1995 to 1997 and Deputy Permanent Representative of India to the United Nations. Tayyab Husain was the only politician in Indian history to serve as a Cabinet Minister in the government of three different states at different times. (Undivided Punjab, Rajasthan, Haryana). Influential Muslim politicians in India include Sheikh Abdullah, Farooq Abdullah and his son Omar Abdullah (former Chief Minister of Jammu and Kashmir), Mufti Mohammad Sayeed, Mehbooba Mufti, Chaudhary Rahim Khan, Sikander Bakht, A. R. Antulay, Ahmed Patel, C. H. Mohammed Koya, A. B. A. Ghani Khan Choudhury, Mukhtar Abbas Naqvi, Salman Khurshid, Saifuddin Soz, E. Ahamed, Ghulam Nabi Azad, Syed Shahnawaz Hussain, Asaduddin Owaisi, Azam Khan and Badruddin Ajmal, Najma Heptulla.

Haj subsidy

The government of India subsidized the cost of the airfare for Indian Hajj pilgrims until it was totally phased out in 2018. The decision to end the subsidy was in order to comply with a Supreme Court of India decision of 2011. Starting in 2011, the amount of government subsidy per person was decreased year on year and ended completely by 2018. Maulana Mahmood A. Madani, a member of the Rajya Sabha and general secretary of the Jamiat Ulema-e-Hind, declared that the Hajj subsidy is a technical violation of Islamic Sharia, since the Quran declares that Hajj should be performed by Muslims using their own resources. Influential Muslim lobbies in

India have regularly insisted that the Hajj subsidy should be phased out as it is un-Islamic.

Conflict and controversy

Conversion controversy

The Somnath temple was first attacked by Muslim Turkic invader Mahmud of Ghazni and repeatedly rebuilt after being demolished by successive Muslim rulers, including the Mughals under Aurangzeb.

Considerable controversy exists both in scholarly and public opinion about the conversions to Islam typically represented by the following schools of thought:

1. The bulk of Muslims are descendants of migrants from the Iranian Plateau or Arabs.

2. Conversions occurred for non-religious reasons of pragmatism and patronage such as social mobility among the Muslim ruling elite or for relief from taxes

3. Conversion was a result of the actions of Sunni Sufi saints and involved a genuine change of heart.

4. Conversion came from Buddhists and the en masse conversions of lower castes for social liberation and as a rejection of the oppressive Hindu caste strictures.

5. A combination, initially made under duress followed by a genuine change of heart.

6. As a socio-cultural process of diffusion and integration over an extended period of time into the sphere of the dominant Muslim civilisation and global polity at large.

Embedded within this lies the concept of Islam as a foreign imposition and Hinduism being a natural condition of the natives who resisted, resulting in the failure of the project to Islamize the Indian subcontinent and is highly embroiled within the politics of the partition and communalism in India.

Historians such as Will Durant described Islamic invasions of India as "The bloodiest story in history. Jadunath Sarkar contends that several Muslim invaders were waging a systematic jihad against Hindus in India to the effect that "Every device short of massacre in cold blood was resorted to in order to convert heathen subjects". Hindus who converted to Islam were not immune to persecution due to the Muslim Caste System in India established by Ziauddin al-Barani in the Fatawa-i Jahandari, where they were regarded as an "Ajlaf" caste and subjected to discrimination by the "Ashraf" castes. Others argue that, during the Muslim conquests in the Indian subcontinent, Indian-origin religions experienced persecution from various Muslim conquerors who massacred Hindus, Jains and Buddhists, attacked temples and monasteries, and forced conversions on the battlefield.

Disputers of the "conversion by the sword theory" point to the presence of the large Muslim communities found in Southern India, Sri Lanka, Western Burma, Bangladesh, Southern Thailand, Indonesia and Malaysia coupled with the distinctive lack of equivalent Muslim communities around the heartland of historical Muslim empires in the Indian subcontinent as a refutation to the "conversion by the sword theory". The legacy of the Muslim conquest of South Asia is a hotly debated issue and argued even today.

Muslim invaders were not all simply raiders. Later rulers fought on to win kingdoms and stayed to create new ruling dynasties.

The practices of these new rulers and their subsequent heirs (some of whom were born to Hindu wives) varied considerably. While some were uniformly hated, others developed a popular following. According to the memoirs of Ibn Battuta who travelled through Delhi in the 14th century, one of the previous sultans had been especially brutal and was deeply hated by Delhi's population. Batuta's memoirs also indicate that Muslims from the Arab world, Persia and Anatolia were often favoured with important posts at the royal courts, suggesting that locals may have played a somewhat subordinate role in the Delhi administration. The term "Turk" was commonly used to refer to their higher social status. S.A.A. Rizvi (The Wonder That Was India – II) however points to Muhammad bin Tughluq as not only encouraging locals but promoting artisan groups such as cooks, barbers and gardeners to high administrative posts. In his reign, it is likely that conversions to Islam took place as a means of seeking greater social mobility and improved social standing.

Numerous temples were destroyed by Muslim conquerors. Richard M. Eaton lists a total of 80 temples that were desecrated by Muslim conquerors, but notes this was not unusual in medieval India where numerous temples were also desecrated by Hindu and Buddhist kings against rival Indian kingdoms during conflicts between devotees of different Hindu deities, and between Hindus, Buddhists and Jains. He also notes there were many instances of the Delhi Sultanate, which often had Hindu ministers, ordering the protection, maintenance and repairing of temples, according to both Muslim and Hindu sources, and that attacks on temples had significantly declined under the Mughal Empire.

K. S. Lal, in his book Growth of Muslim Population in Medieval India, claimed that between 1000 and 1500 the Indian population decreased by 30 million, but stated his estimates were tentative and did not claim any finality. His work has come under criticism by historians such as Simon Digby (SOAS, University of London) and Irfan Habib for its agenda and lack of accurate data in pre-census times. Different population estimates by economics historians Angus Maddison and Jean-Noël Biraben also indicate that India's population did not decrease between 1000 and 1500, but increased by about 35 million during that time. The Indian population estimates from other economic historians including Colin Clark, John D. Durand and Colin McEvedy also show there was a population increase in India between 1000 and 1500.

Relations with non-Muslim communities

Muslim–Hindu conflict

The conflict between Hindus and Muslims in the Indian subcontinent has a complex history which can be said to have begun with the Umayyad Caliphate's invasion of Sindh in 711. The persecution of Hindus during the Islamic expansion in India during the medieval period was characterised by destruction of temples, often illustrated by historians by the repeated destruction of the Hindu Temple at Somnath and the anti-Hindu practices of the Mughal emperor Aurangzeb. Although there were instances of conflict between the two groups, a number of Hindus worshipped and continue to worship at the tombs of Muslim Sufi Saints.

During the Noakhali riots in 1946, several thousand Hindus were forcibly converted to Islam by Muslim mobs.

From 1947 to 1991

The aftermath of the Partition of India in 1947 saw large scale sectarian strife and bloodshed throughout the nation. Since then, India has witnessed sporadic large-scale violence sparked by underlying tensions between sections of the Hindu and Muslim communities. These include the 1969 Gujarat riots, the 1970 Bhiwandi riots, the 1983 Nellie massacre, and the 1989 Bhagalpur violence. These conflicts stem in part from the ideologies of Hindu nationalism and Islamic extremism. Since independence, India has always maintained a constitutional commitment to secularism.

Since 1992

The sense of communal harmony between Hindus and Muslims in the post-partition period was compromised greatly by the razing of the Babri Mosque in Ayodhya. The demolition took place in 1992 and was perpetrated by the Hindu nationalist Bharatiya Janata Party and organisations like Rashtriya Swayamsevak Sangh, Bajrang Dal, Vishva Hindu Parishad and Shiv Sena. This was followed by tit for tat violence by Muslim and Hindu fundamentalists throughout the country, giving rise to the Bombay riots and the 1993 Bombay bombings.

In the 1998 Prankote massacre, 26 Kashmiri Hindus were beheaded by Islamist militants after their refusal to convert to Islam. The militants struck when the villagers refused demands from the gunmen to convert to Islam and prove their conversion by eating beef.

Kashmir (1990s)

During the eruption of militancy in the 1990s, following persecution and threats by radical Islamists and militants, the native Kashmiri

Hindus were forced into an exodus from Kashmir, a Muslim-majority region in Northern India. Mosques issued warnings, telling them to leave Kashmir, convert to Islam or be killed. Approximately 300,000–350,000 pandits left the valley during the mid-80s and the 90s. Many of them have been living in abject conditions in refugee camps of Jammu.

Gujarat (2002)

One of the most violent events in recent times took place during the Gujarat riots in 2002, where it is estimated one thousand people were killed, most allegedly Muslim. Some sources claim there were approximately 2,000 Muslim deaths. There were also allegations made of state involvement. The riots were in retaliation to the Godhra train burning in which 59 Hindu pilgrims returning from the disputed site of the Babri Masjid, were burnt alive in a train fire at the Godhra railway station. Gujarat police claimed that the incident was a planned act carried out by extremist Muslims in the region against the Hindu pilgrims. The Bannerjee commission appointed to investigate this finding declared that the fire was an accident. In 2006 the High Court decided the constitution of such a committee was illegal as another inquiry headed by Justice Nanavati Shah was still investigating the matter.

The riots, which took place following the Godhra train burning incident, killed more than 790 Muslims and 254 Hindus, including those killed in the Godhra train fire. These figures were reported to the Rajya Sabha by the Union Minister of State for Home Affairs Sriprakash Jaiswal in May 2005.

In 2004, several Indian school textbooks were scrapped by the National Council of Educational Research and Training after they were found to be loaded with anti-Muslim prejudice. The NCERT argued that the books were "written by scholars hand-picked by the previous Hindu nationalist administration". According to The Guardian, the textbooks depicted India's past Muslim rulers "as barbarous invaders and the medieval period as a Dark Age of Islamic colonial rule which snuffed out the glories of the Hindu empire that preceded it". In one textbook, it was purported that the Taj Mahal, the Qutb Minar and the Red Fort – all examples of Islamic architecture – "were designed and commissioned by Hindus".

West Bengal (2010)

In the 2010 Deganga riots, rioting began on 6 September 2010, when an Islamist mob resorted to arson and violence on the Hindu neighborhoods of Deganga, Kartikpur and Beliaghata under the Deganga police station area. The violence began late in the evening and continued throughout the night into the next morning. The district police, Rapid Action Force, Central Reserve Police Force and Border Security Force all failed to stop the mob violence and the Army was finally deployed. The Army staged a flag march on the Taki Road, while Islamist violence continued unabated in the interior villages off the Taki Road, till Wednesday in spite of the Army's presence and promulgation of prohibitory orders under section 144 of the CrPC.

Assam (2012)

At least 77 people died and 400,000 people were displaced in the 2012 Assam violence between indigenous Bodos and East Bengal rooted Muslims.

Delhi (2020)

The 2020 Delhi riots, which left more than 50 dead and hundreds injured, were triggered by protests against a citizenship law seen by many critics as anti-Muslim and part of Prime Minister Narendra Modi's Hindu nationalist agenda.

Haryana (2023)

The 2023 Haryana riots, stemming from communal clashes during the Brajmandal Yatra pilgrimage, resulted in seven fatalities and over 200 injuries. The violence began when the inclusion of Bajrang Dal activist Monu Manesar, a suspect in the murder of two Muslim men, sparked anger within the Muslim community in Mewat. The BJP government was criticized for allowing Manesar's participation, leading to an organized attack on the procession, triggering retaliatory actions. The government responded with a curfew, internet suspension, and additional troops. Critics blame the BJP government for not preventing the escalation and allowing a potentially volatile situation to unfold.

Muslim–Sikh conflict

Sikhism emerged in the Punjab during the Mughal period. Conflict between early Sikhs and the Muslim power center at Delhi reached an early high point in 1606 when Guru Arjan, the fifth guru of the Sikhs, was tortured and killed by Jahangir, the Mughal emperor. After the death of the fifth beloved Guru his son took his spot as Guru Hargobind, who basically made the Sikhs a warrior religion. Guru ji was the first to defeat the Mughal empire in a battle which had taken place in present Sri Hargobindpur in Gurdaspur. Later in the 16th century, Tegh Bahadur became guru in 1665 and led the Sikhs until 1675. Teg Bahadur was executed by the Mughal Emperor Aurangzeb for helping to protect Hindus, after a delegation of Kashmiri Pandits came to him for help when the Emperor condemned them to death for failing to convert to Islam. At this point Aurangzeb had instituted forceful conversions on the basis of charging citizens with crimes then sparing them from punishments (up to death) if they converted. This led to a high increase of violence between the Sikhs and Hindus as well as rebellions in Aurangzeb's empire. This is an early example which illustrates how the Hindu-Muslim conflict and the Muslim-Sikh conflicts are connected. After this Guru Gobind Singh and the Sikhs helped the next successor of the throne of India to rise, who was Bahadur Shah Zafar. For a certain period of time good relations were maintained somewhat like they were in Akbar's time until disputes arose again. The Mughal period saw various invaders coming into India through Punjab with which they would loot and severely plunder. Better relations have been seen by Dulla Bhatti, Mian Mir, Pir Budhu Shah, Pir Bhikham Shah, Bulleh Shah.

In 1699, the Khalsa was founded by Guru Gobind Singh, the last guru. A former ascetic was charged by Gobind Singh with the duty of punishing those who had persecuted the Sikhs. After the guru's death, Baba Banda Singh Bahadur became the leader of the Sikh army and was responsible for several attacks on the Mughal empire. He was executed by the emperor Jahandar Shah after refusing the offer of a pardon if he converted to Islam. The decline of Mughal power during the 17th and 18th centuries, along with the growing strength of the Sikh Empire, resulted in a balance of power which protected the Sikhs from more violence. The Sikh empire was absorbed into the British Indian empire after the Second Anglo-Sikh War of 1849.

Massive population exchanges took place during the Partition of India in 1947, and the British Indian province of Punjab was divided into two parts, where the western parts were assigned to Pakistan, while the eastern parts went to India. 5.3 million Muslims moved from India to West Punjab in Pakistan, as 3.4 million Hindus and

Sikhs moved from Pakistan to East Punjab in India. The newly formed governments were completely unequipped to deal with migrations of such staggering magnitude, and massive violence and slaughter occurred on both sides of the border. Estimates of the number of deaths range around roughly 500,000, with low estimates at 200,000 and high estimates at 1,000,000.

Muslim–Buddhist conflict

In 1989 there was a social boycott by the Buddhists of the Muslims of Leh district. The boycott remained in force till 1992. Relations between the Buddhists and Muslims in Leh improved after the lifting of the boycott, although suspicions remained.

Prominent Muslims in India

India is home to many eminent Muslims who have made their mark in numerous fields and have played a constructive role in India's economic rise and cultural influence across the world. Out of the 12 Presidents of the Republic of India, three were Muslims – Zakir Husain, Fakhruddin Ali Ahmed and A. P. J. Abdul Kalam. Additionally, 4 Muslims: Mohammad Hidayatullah, Aziz Mushabber Ahmadi, Mirza Hameedullah Beg and Altamas Kabir held the office of the Chief Justice of India. Mohammad Hidayatullah also served as the acting President of India on two separate occasions; and holds the distinct honour of being the only person to have served in all three offices of the President of India, the Vice-President of India and the Chief Justice of India. Tayyab Husain serves as a Cabinet Minister in the government of three different states (Punjab, Rajasthan, Haryana) at different times and became the only politician in Indian history to do so.

The former Vice-President of India, Mohammad Hamid Ansari, former Foreign Minister Salman Khurshid are Muslims. Dr. S. Y. Quraishi and Syed Nasim Ahmad Zaidi both served as the Chief Election Commissioner of India. Prominent Indian Muslim bureaucrats and diplomats include Abid Hussain, Ali Yavar Jung and Asaf Ali. Zafar Saifullah was Cabinet Secretary of the Government of India from 1993 to 1994. Salman Haidar was Indian Foreign Secretary from 1995 to 1997 and Deputy Permanent Representative of India to the United Nations. Numerous Muslims have achieved high rank in the Indian Police Service, with several attaining the rank of Director General of Police and serving as commanders of both state and Central Armed Police Forces. In 2013, IPS officer Syed Asif Ibrahim became the first Muslim Director of the Intelligence Bureau, the seniormost appointment in the service. There have been seven Muslim Chief Ministers of Indian states (other than Jammu and Kashmir):

1. Barkatullah Khan (Rajasthan: 1971–73)

2. Abdul Ghafoor (Bihar: 1973–75)

3. C. H. Mohammed Koya (Kerala: 1979)

4. Anwara Taimur (Assam: 1980–81)

5. A. R. Antulay (Maharashtra: 1980–82)

6. Mohammed Alimuddin (Manipur: 1973–74)

7. M. O. H. Farook was a three-time CM of the Union Territory of Pondicherry.

Some of the most popular and influential as well as critically acclaimed actors and actresses of the Indian film industry are Muslims. These include Yusuf Khan (stage name Dilip Kumar),

Shah Rukh Khan, Salman Khan, Aamir Khan, Saif Ali Khan, Madhubala, Nawazuddin Siddiqui, Naseeruddin Shah, Johnny Walker, Shabana Azmi, Waheeda Rehman, Mumtaz, Amjad Khan, Ajit Khan, Kader Khan, Feroz Khan, Sanjay Khan, Meena Kumari, Prem Nazir, Mammootty, Dulquer Salmaan, Asif Ali, Nargis, Irrfan Khan, Farida Jalal, Arshad Warsi, Mehmood, Ali Fazal, Farhan Akhtar, Zeenat Aman, Raza Murad, Farooq Sheikh and Tabu.

Some of the best known film directors of Indian cinema include Mehboob Khan, Khwaja Ahmad Abbas, Nasir Hussain, Kamal Amrohi, K. Asif, Anees Bazmee, Kabir Khan, Ali Abbas Zafar and the Abbas–Mustan duo. Indian Muslims also play pivotal roles in other forms of performing arts in India, particularly in music, modern art and theatre. M. F. Husain is one of India's best known contemporary artists. Academy Awards winners Resul Pookutty and A. R. Rahman, Naushad, Salim–Sulaiman and Nadeem Akhtar of the Nadeem–Shravan duo are some of India's celebrated musicians. Abrar Alvi penned many of the greatest classics of Indian cinema. Prominent poets and lyricists include Shakeel Badayuni, Sahir Ludhianvi and Majrooh Sultanpuri. Popular Indian singers of Muslim faith include Mohammed Rafi, Anu Malik, Lucky Ali, Javed Ali, Armaan Malik, Adnan Sami, Talat Mahmood and Shamshad Begum. Another famous personality is the Padma Vibhushan awardee tabla maestro Zakir Hussian.

Sania Mirza, from Hyderabad, is the highest-ranked Indian woman tennis player. Prominent Muslim names in Indian cricket (the most popular sport of India) include Iftikhar Ali Khan Pataudi, Mansoor Ali Khan Pataudi and Mohammad Azharuddin, who captained the Indian cricket team on various occasions. Other famous Muslim cricketers in India are Mushtaq Ali, Syed Kirmani, Arshad Ayub, Mohammad Kaif, Munaf Patel, Zaheer Khan, Irfan

Pathan, Yusuf Pathan, Mohammed Shami, Mohammed Siraj and Wasim Jaffer.

India is home to several influential Muslim businessmen. Some of India's most prominent firms, such as Wipro, Wockhardt, Himalaya Health Care, Hamdard Laboratories, Cipla and Mirza Tanners were founded by Muslims. The only two South Asian Muslim billionaires named by Forbes magazine, Yusuf Hamied and Azim Premji, are from India.

Though Muslims are under-represented in the Indian Armed Forces, as compared to Hindus and Sikhs, several Indian military Muslim personnel have earned gallantry awards and high ranks for exceptional service to the nation. Air Chief Marshal I. H. Latif was Deputy Chief of the Air Staff (India) during the Indo-Pakistani War of 1971 and later served as Chief of the Air staff of the Indian Air Force from 1973 to 1976. Air Marshal Jaffar Zaheer (1923–2008) commanded IAF Agra and was decorated for his service during the 1971 Indo-Pakistan War, eventually rising to the rank of air marshal and ending his career as Director-General of Civil Aviation from 1979 to 1980. Indian Army's Abdul Hamid was posthumously awarded India's highest military decoration, the Param Vir Chakra, for knocking-out seven Pakistani tanks with a recoilless gun during the Battle of Asal Uttar in 1965. Two other Muslims – Brigadier Mohammed Usman and Mohammed Ismail – were awarded Maha Vir Chakra for their actions during the Indo-Pakistani War of 1947. High ranking Muslims in the Indian Armed Forces include:

- Lieutenant General Jameel Mahmood (former GOC-in-C Eastern Command: 1992–93),

- Lieutenant General Sami Khan (Commandant of the National Defence Academy: 1985–86, GoC-in-C, Central Command: 1988–89)

- Lieutenant General Pattiarimmal Mohamed Hariz (GOC-in-C, Southern Command: 2016–17),

- Air Marshal Syed Shahid Hussein Naqvi (Deputy Chief of Air Staff: 1997–99, Senior Air Staff Officer, Training Command 1999–2001)

- Lieutenant General Syed Ata Hasnain (GOC XV Corps: 2010–2012, Military Secretary: 2012–13)

- Major General Afsir Karim

- Major General SM Hasnain

- Major General Mohammed Amin Naik.

Abdul Kalam, one of India's most respected scientists and the father of the Integrated Guided Missile Development Programme (IGMDP) of India, was honoured through his appointment as the 11th President of India. His extensive contribution to India's defence industry lead him to being nicknamed as the Missile Man of India and during his tenure as the President of India, he was affectionately known as People's President. Syed Zahoor Qasim, former Director of the National Institute of Oceanography, led India's first scientific expedition to Antarctica and played a crucial role in the establishment of Dakshin Gangotri. He was also the former Vice Chancellor of Jamia Millia Islamia, Secretary of the Department of Ocean Development and the founder of Polar Research in India. Other prominent Muslim scientists and engineers include C. M. Habibullah, a stem cell scientist and director of Deccan College of Medical Sciences and Center for Liver Research and Diagnostics, Hyderabad. In the field of Yunani medicine, one can name Hakim Ajmal Khan, Hakim Abdul Hameed and Hakim Syed Zillur Rahman. Salim Ali, was an Indian ornithologist and naturalist, also known as the "birdman of India".

In the list of most influential Muslims list by Georgetown University, there were 21 Indians (in 2017) like Maulana Mahmood Madani, Akhtar Raza Khan, Zakir Abdul Karim Naik, Wahiduddin Khan, Abul Qasim Nomani Syed Muhammad Ameen Mian Qaudri, Aamir Khan and Aboobacker Ahmad Musliyar. Mahmood Madani, leader of Jamiat Ulema-e-Hind and MP was ranked at 36 for initiating a movement against terrorism in South Asia. Syed Ameen Mian has been ranked 44th in the list.

In January 2018, Jamitha reportedly became the first woman to lead a Jumu'ah prayer service in India.

According to Pew Research Center,

Population growth and religious composition in India

India's population has more than tripled in the six decades following Partition, from 361 million (36.1 crore) people in the 1951 census to more than 1.2 billion (120 crore) in 2011. As of 2020, India gains roughly 1 million (10 lakh) inhabitants each month, putting it on course to surpass China as the world's most populous country by 2030, according to the United Nations Population Division.

Though religious groups grew at uneven rates between 1951 and 2011, every major religion in India saw its numbers rise. For example, Hindus increased from 304 million (30.4 crore) to 966 million (96.6 crore), Muslims grew from 35 million (3.5 crore) to 172 million (17.2 crore), and the number of Indians who say they are Christian rose from 8 million (0.8 crore) to 28 million (2.8 crore).

India's population boom in the 20th century coincided with an economic transformation that brought major improvements in life expectancy, living standards and food production. But there is a consensus among experts that India's economic development has been hindered in part by the strains that population growth has put on schools, health care and natural resources. Since the 1950s, Indian governments have worked with international agencies to promote a range of birth control methods, from contraceptives to forced sterilizations. Today, some states and territories discourage large families with penalties, such as barring parents with more than two children from receiving social services or holding political office. In 2017, India's Ministry of Health and Welfare launched a comprehensive family planning program with the goal of bringing fertility down to replacement levels by 2025 by improving health care facilities, access to contraceptives and reproductive health education, particularly in areas with relatively high fertility rates.

India's population growth has slowed, especially since the 1990s

% increase of India's population sizes between census years

	All	Hindus	Muslims	Christians
1951-61	21.6%	20.7%	32.7%	29.0%
1961-71	24.8	23.7	30.9	33.0
1971-81	24.7	24.0	30.7	17.0
1981-91	23.9	22.7	32.9	17.8
1991-2001	21.5	19.9	29.4	22.6
2001-11	17.7	16.7	24.7	15.7

Source: Pew Research Center analysis of Indian census data, 1951-2011.
"Religious Composition of India"

PEW RESEARCH CENTER

India is home to millions of Sikhs, Buddhists and Jains

Counts and shares, by census year

	1951	1961	1971	1981	1991	2001	2011
Counts							
Sikhs	6,820,000	7,850,000	10,380,000	13,090,000	16,430,000	19,220,000	20,830,000
Buddhists	2,670,000	3,260,000	3,910,000	4,760,000	6,480,000	7,960,000	8,440,000
Jains	1,660,000	2,030,000	2,610,000	3,220,000	3,360,000	4,230,000	4,450,000
Others/not specified	1,550,000	1,910,000	2,220,000	2,890,000	3,700,000	7,370,000	10,810,000
Shares							
Sikhs	1.9%	1.8%	1.9%	1.9%	1.9%	1.9%	1.7%
Buddhists	0.7%	0.7%	0.7%	0.7%	0.8%	0.8%	0.7%
Jains	0.5%	0.5%	0.5%	0.5%	0.4%	0.4%	0.4%
Others/not specified	0.4%	0.4%	0.4%	0.4%	0.4%	0.7%	0.9%

Source: Census of India, 1951-2011.
"Religious Composition of India"

PEW RESEARCH CENTER

Looking ahead to 2050

As of the publication of this demographic study, India's 2021 census has been postponed due to the coronavirus pandemic, and results may not be publicly available for years after it is conducted. However, Pew Research Center in 2015 published demographic projections for the world's largest religious groups that extend to 2050. According to that projection, India was home to about 1.4 billion (140 crore) people as of 2020.

Terrorist incidents in India

Year	Number of incidents	Deaths	Injuries
2018	748	350	540
2017	1000	470	702
2016	1025	467	788

Year	Number of incidents	Deaths	Injuries
2015	884	387	649
2014	860	490	776
2013	694	467	771
2012	611	264	651
2011	645	499	730
2010	663	812	660
2009	672	774	854
2008	534	824	1,759
2007	149	626	1,187
2006	167	722	2,138
2005	146	466	1,216
2004	108	334	949
2003	196	472	1,183
2002	184	599	1,186
2001	234	660	1,144
2000	180	671	761
1999	112	469	591

Year	Number of incidents	Deaths	Injuries
1998	61	398	411
1997	193	853	1,416
1996	213	569	952
1995	179	361	616
1994	107	389	405
1993	42	525	1,564
1992	237	1,152	917
1991	339	1,113	1,326
1990	349	907	1,042
1989	324	874	769
1988	358	966	1,033
1987	166	506	429
1986	96	340	163
1985	39	51	79
1984	159	195	364
1983	47	59	217
1982	13	64	102

Year	Number of incidents	Deaths	Injuries
1981	16	24	12
1980	10	17	13
1979	20	31	19

Terrorism in India

Terrorism in India, according to the Home Ministry, poses a significant threat to the people of India. Compared to other countries, India faces a wide range of terror groups. Terrorism found in India includes Islamic terrorism, ultranationalist terrorism, and left-wing terrorism. India is one of the countries most impacted by terrorism.

A common definition of terrorism is the systematic use or threatened use of violence to intimidate a population or government for political, religious, or ideological goals.

In 2022, India ranked 13th on the Global Terrorism Index. India continues to face a number of terror attacks from Islamic groups in Kashmir, Sikh separatists in Punjab, and secessionist groups in Assam. The regions with long term terrorist activities have been Jammu and Kashmir, east-central and south-central India (Naxalism) and the Seven Sister States. In August 2008, National Security Advisor M K Narayanan has said that there are as many as 800 terrorist cells operating in the country. As of 2013, 205 of the country's 608 districts were affected by terrorist activity. Terror attacks caused 231 civilian deaths in 2012 in India, compared to 11,098 terror-caused deaths worldwide, according to the State

Department of the United States; or about 2% of global terror fatalities while it accounts for 17.5% of global population.

Reports have alleged and implicated terrorism in India to be sponsored by Pakistan. In July 2016, the Government of India released data on a string of terror strikes in India since 2005 that claimed 707 lives and left over 3,200 injured.

2001 Attack on Indian parliament

Terrorists on 13 December 2001 attacked the Parliament of India, resulting in a 45-minute gun battle in which 9 policemen and parliament staff were killed. All five terrorists were also killed by the security forces and were identified as Pakistani nationals. The attack took place around 11:40 am (IST), minutes after both Houses of Parliament had adjourned for the day. The suspected terrorists dressed in commando fatigues entered Parliament in a car through the VIP gate of the building. Displaying Parliament and Home Ministry security stickers, the vehicle entered the Parliament premises. The terrorists set off massive blasts and used AK-47 rifles, explosives, and grenades for the attack. Senior Ministers and over 200 members of parliament were inside the Central Hall of Parliament when the attack took place. Security personnel sealed the entire premises, which saved many lives.

Mumbai Terrorist Attacks

From November 26 through November 29, 2008, an ongoing and coordinated terrorist attack took place in Mumbai (formerly Bombay), India. According to news reports, the intended victims of these attacks were ordinary Mumbaikars as well as U.S. citizens, Britons, and Jews. The attacks were executed in the heart of India's financial capital and a top Indian tourist destination.

Mumbai is the commercial and entertainment center of India and one of the top 10 centers of global financial commerce in the world. It is India's largest city and one of the world's most populous metropolitan areas.

Ten armed terrorists using automatic weapons and grenades carried out the attacks. The attackers entered Mumbai from the Arabian Sea by speedboats that were onboard trawlers, coming ashore at two locations in Colaba. At this point, the terrorists split into their attack formations and went in different directions. The first reported attack occurred around 9:30 p.m. on November 26 at the Cafe Leopold, a popular tourist restaurant in Colaba.

The attacks were carried out by 10 gunmen who were believed to be connected to Lashkar-e-Taiba, a Pakistan-based terrorist organization. Armed with automatic weapons and hand grenades, the terrorists targeted civilians at numerous sites in the southern part of Mumbai, including the Chhatrapati Shivaji railway station, the popular Leopold Café, two hospitals, and a theatre. While most of the attacks ended within a few hours after they began at around 9:30 pm on November 26, the terror continued to unfold at three locations where hostages were taken—the Nariman House, where a Jewish outreach centre was located, and the luxury hotels Oberoi Trident and Taj Mahal Palace & Tower.

By the time the standoff ended at the Nariman House on the evening of November 28, six hostages as well as two gunmen had been killed. At the two hotels, dozens of guests and staff were either trapped by gunfire or held hostage. Indian security forces ended the siege at the Oberoi Trident around midday on November 28 and at the Taj Mahal Palace on the morning of the following day. In all, at least 174 people, including 20 security force personnel and 26 foreign nationals, were killed. More than 300 people were injured. Nine of the 10 terrorists were killed, and one was arrested.

The attackers

Amid speculation regarding the identity of the terrorists, an unknown group calling itself Mujahideen Hyderabad Deccan claimed responsibility for the attacks in an e-mail; however, the e-mail was later traced to a computer in Pakistan, and it became obvious that no such group existed. The way the terrorists had reportedly singled out Western foreigners at both of the luxury hotels and at the Nariman House led some to believe that the Islamic militant group al-Qaeda was possibly involved, but this appeared not to be the case after the lone arrested terrorist, Ajmal Amir Kasab, provided substantial information regarding the planning and execution of the attacks. Kasab, a native of Pakistan's Punjab province, told investigators that the 10 terrorists underwent prolonged guerrilla-warfare training in the camps of Lashkar-e-Taiba. He further revealed that the team of terrorists had spent time at the headquarters of a second and related organization, Jamaat-ud-Dawa, in the city of Muridke before traveling from Punjab to the port city of Karachi and setting out for Mumbai by sea.

After first traveling aboard a Pakistani-flagged cargo ship, the gunmen hijacked an Indian fishing boat and killed its crew; then, once they were near the Mumbai coast, they used inflatable dinghies to reach Badhwar Park and the Sassoon Docks, near the city's Gateway of India monument. At that point the terrorists split into small teams and set out for their respective targets. Kasab—who was charged with various crimes, including murder and waging war—later retracted his confession. In April 2009 his trial began, but it experienced several delays, including a stoppage as officials verified that Kasab was older than age 18 and thus could not be tried in a juvenile court. Although he pled guilty in July, the trial continued, and in December he recanted, proclaiming his innocence. In May 2010 Kasab was found guilty and sentenced to death; he was executed two years later. In June 2012 Delhi police arrested Sayed Zabiuddin Ansari (or Syed Zabiuddin), who was suspected of being one of those who trained the terrorists and guided them during the attacks. In addition, David C. Headley, a Pakistani American, pleaded guilty in 2011 to helping the terrorists plan the attacks, and in January 2013 he was sentenced in a U.S. federal court to 35 years in prison.

Connections to Pakistan

With evidence pointing to the attacks' having originated within Pakistan's territory, India on November 28, 2008, requested the presence of Lieut. Gen. Ahmed Shuja Pasha, director general of Pakistan's intelligence agency, as its investigation process got under way. Pakistan at first agreed to this request but subsequently backpedaled, offering to send to India a representative for the director general instead of Pasha himself. The immediate impact of the attacks was felt on the ongoing peace process between the two countries. Alleging inaction by Pakistani authorities on terrorist elements, Pranab Mukherjee, India's external affairs minister, stated, "If they don't act, then it will not be business as usual." India later canceled its cricket team's tour of Pakistan that had been scheduled for January–February 2009.

India's attempt at pressuring Pakistan to crack down on terrorists within its borders was strongly supported by the international community. U.S. Secretary of State Condoleezza Rice and British Prime Minister Gordon Brown toured both India and Pakistan following the attacks in Mumbai. In a flurry of diplomatic activity that was essentially viewed as an exercise in "conflict prevention," U.S. officials and others urged Pakistan's civilian government to take action against those suspected of involvement in the attacks. There were concerns that tensions might escalate between the two nuclear-armed neighbours. India, however, refrained from amassing troops at the Pakistan border as it had following the December 13, 2001, attack on India's parliament, which had also been carried out by Pakistan-based militants. Instead, India focused on building international public support through various diplomatic channels and through the media. India made a plea to the UN Security Council for sanctions against Jamaat-ud-Dawa, contending that the group was a front organization for Lashkar-e-Taiba, which had been banned by Pakistan in 2002. Acceding to India's request, the Security Council imposed sanctions on Jamaat-ud-Dawa on December 11, 2008, and formally declared the group a terrorist organization.

Pakistan claimed to have arrested Zaki-ur-Rehman Lakhvi, a senior leader of Lashkar-e-Taiba and the suspected mastermind of the Mumbai attacks, on December 8, 2008. Pakistani security forces carried out raids on Jamaat-ud-Dawa offices across the country. This crackdown, however, lasted only a few days, after which the security cordons that had been placed around Jamaat-ud-Dawa offices were relaxed. Pakistani Prime Minister Yousaf Raza Gillani stated that the activities of Jamaat-ud-Dawa should not be blocked, since "thousands of people are benefiting" from what he described as the group's "welfare activities." Pakistan further maintained that India did not provide it with sufficient evidence against a number of suspected terrorists and that any action against these suspects was possible only after such evidence had been provided "through diplomatic channels instead of the media." Pakistan refused India's demand that it extradite 20 people for their alleged involvement in several terrorist attacks on Indian territory. During his 2011 trial, however, Headley gave detailed testimony about the involvement of both Lashkar-e-Taiba and the Pakistani intelligence agency in the Mumbai attacks.

Reaction in India

The terrorist attacks in Mumbai exposed loopholes in the security system that India had in place to deal with this "new brand" of terrorism—urban warfare characterized by symbolic attacks, multiple targets, and high casualties. Subsequent reports indicated that several intelligence warnings by Indian as well as U.S. sources had preceded the attacks but that authorities, citing the lack of "actionable intelligence," had ignored them. Moreover, there was an inordinate delay in the deployment of India's elite National Security Guards, whose commandos reached the besieged hotels some 10 hours after the first shootings took place on November 26. The lack of coordination between authorities in the Indian capital of New Delhi and officials in Maharashtra state also weakened the immediate crisis response. India's interior minister, Shivraj Patil, who was widely criticized in the aftermath of the attacks, tendered his resignation on November 30, 2008, declaring that he took "moral responsibility" for the assault.

The November attacks prompted the Indian government to introduce important new institutions as well as legal mechanisms to fight terrorism. On December 17, 2008, the Indian parliament consented to the creation of the National Investigation Agency, a federal counterterrorism group whose functions would be similar to many of those of the U.S. Federal Bureau of Investigation. Parliament also approved amendments to the Unlawful Activities

(Prevention) Act that incorporated stringent mechanisms to contain and investigate terrorism. Although myriad comparisons were made between the September 11, 2001, attacks in the United States and those that occurred in Mumbai, the latter outbreak of terrorism was of a much more-limited scale, in terms of both casualties and financial implications. The Mumbai attacks did, however, evoke a similarly strong national and international outcry against such violence and renewed calls to increase efforts to deal with the menace of terrorism.

Terrorist attacks in Mumbai include:

- 12 March 1993 – 13 bombs killed 257

- 6 December 2002 – Bus bomb in Ghatkopar, killed 2

- 27 January 2003 – Bicycle bomb in Vile Parle, killed 1

- 13 March 2003 – Train bomb in Mulund, killed 10

- 28 July 2003 – Bus bomb in Ghatkopar, killed 4

- 25 August 2003 – Two Bombs near the Gateway of India and Zaveri Bazaar, killed 50

- 11 July 2006 – Seven train bombs killed 209

- 26 November 2008 to 29 November 2008 – Coordinated series of attacks, killed 172.

- 13 July 2011 – Bomb explosions at three locations, killed 26 Pune

- 13 February 2010 – a bomb explosion at the German Bakery in Pune killed fourteen people, and injured at least 60 more

- 1 August 2012 – four bomb explosion at various locations on JM Road, Pune injured 1 person

Chapter 4

China

---✦✦---

Islam has been practiced in China since the 7ᵗʰ century CE. Muslims are a minority group in China, representing around 2 percent of the total population (17–25 million people). Though Hui Muslims are the most numerous group, the greatest concentration of Muslims are in Xinjiang, which contains a significant Uyghur population. Lesser yet significant populations reside in the regions of Ningxia, Gansu and Qinghai. Of China's 55 officially recognized minority peoples, ten of these groups are predominantly Sunni Muslim.

The Silk Road, which was a series of extensive inland trade routes that spread all over the Mediterranean to East Asia, was used since 1000 BCE and continued to be used for millennia. For more than half of this long period of time, most of the traders were Muslim and moved towards the East. Not only did these traders bring their goods, they also carried with them their culture and beliefs to East Asia. Islam was one of the many religions that gradually began to spread across the Silk Road during the "7ᵗʰ to the 10ᵗʰ centuries through war, trade and diplomatic exchanges".

During the Tang and Song dynasties, Muslims in China worshipped various kinds of "spirits" alongside Allah.

Tang dynasty

According to Chinese Muslims' traditional accounts, Islam was first introduced to China in 616–18 by the Companions of Muhammad: Sa'd ibn Abi Waqqas, Wahab ibn Abu Kabcha and another. It is noted in other accounts that Wahab Abu Kabcha reached Canton by sea in 629 CE.

The introduction of Islam mainly happened through two routes: from the southeast following an established path to Guangdong and from the northwest through the Silk Road. Sa'd ibn Abi Waqqas, along with the Companion Suhayla Abu Arja and Hassan ibn Thabit, and the Tabi'un Owais al-Qarani, returned to China from the Arabian Peninsula in 637 by the Yunnan-Manipur-Chittagong route, then reached Arabia by sea. Some sources date the introduction of Islam in China to 650 CE, the third sojourn of Sa'd ibn Abi Waqqas, when he was sent as an official envoy to Tang emperor Gaozong during the reign of the Rashid Caliph Uthman's reign. Emperor Gaozong, the Tang emperor who is said to have received the envoy then ordered the construction of the Huaisheng Mosque in Guangzhou in memory of Muhammad, which was the first mosque in the country.

While modern secular historians tend to say that there is no evidence that Waqqas himself ever came to China, they do believe that Muslim diplomats and merchants came to Tang China within a few decades from the beginning of the Muslim era.

The early Tang dynasty had a cosmopolitan culture, with intensive contacts with Central Asia and significant communities of (originally non-Muslim) Central and Western Asian merchants resident in Chinese cities, which helped the introduction of Islam. The first major Muslim settlements in China consisted of Arab and Persian merchants, with comparatively well-established, even if somewhat segregated, mercantile Muslim communities existing in the port cities of Guangzhou, Quanzhou and Hangzhou on China's southeastern seaboard, as well as in the interior centers such as Chang'an, Kaifeng and Yangzhou during the Tang and especially Song eras. Around 879, Chinese rebels killed about 120,000–200,000 mostly Arab and Persian foreigners in Guanzhou in the Guangzhou massacre. It is believed that the profile of Muslims as traders led to the government ignoring Muslims in the 845 Huichang persecution of Buddhism, even though it virtually extinguished Zoroastrianism and the Church of the East in China.

In 751, the Abbasid Caliphate defeated Tang China at the Battle of Talas, marking the end of Tang westward expansion and resulting in Muslim control of Transoxiana for the next 400 years.

Song dynasty

By the time of the Song dynasty, Muslims had come to play a major role in the import/export industry. The office of Director General of Shipping was consistently held by a Muslim during this period. In 1070, the Song emperor Shenzong invited 5,300 Muslims from Bukhara, to settle in Song China in order to create a buffer zone between the Song and the Liao dynasties in the northeast. Later on, these Muslims settled between the Sung capital of Kaifeng and Yenching (modern day Beijing). They were led by Prince Amir Sayyid "Su-fei-er" (his Chinese name), who was called the "father" of the Muslim community in China. Prior to him, Islam was named by the Tang and Song Chinese as Dashi fa ("law of the Arabs"). He renamed it to Huihui Jiao ("the Religion of the Huihui").

It is reported that "in 1080, another group of more than 10,000 Arab men and women are said to have arrived in China on horsebacks to join Sofeier. These people settled in all provinces". Pu Shougeng, a Muslim foreign trader, stands out in his work to help the Yuan conquer Southern China, the last outpost of Song power. In 1276, Song loyalists launched a resistance against Mongol efforts to take over Fuzhou. The Yuanshih (Yuan dynasty official history) records that Pu Shougeng "abandoned the Song cause and rejected the emperor...by the end of the year, Quanzhou submitted to the Mongols". In abandoning the Song cause, Pu Shougeng mobilized troops from the community of foreign residents, who massacred the Song emperor's relatives and Song loyalists. Pu Shougeng and his troops acted without the help of the Mongol army. Pu Shougeng himself was lavishly rewarded by the Mongols. He was appointed military commissioner for Fujian and Guangdong.

Tombs of Imams

On the foothills of Mount Lingshan are the tombs of two of the four companions that Muhammad sent eastwards to preach Islam. Known as the 'Holy Tombs', they house the companions Sa-Ke-Zu and Wu-Ko-Shun. The other two companions went to Guangzhou and Yangzhou. The Imam Asim, is said to have been one of the first Islamic missionaries in China. He was a man who lived in c. 1000 CE in Hotan. The shrine site includes the reputed tomb of the Imam, a mosque, and several related tombs. There is also a maqam of the Shia Imam Ja'far al-Sadiq.

Yuan dynasty

Bukhara and Samarqand were visited by Qiu Chuji. At the same time the Mongols imported Central Asian Muslims to serve as administrators in China, the Mongols also sent ethnic Han and Khitans from China to serve as administrators over the Muslim population in Bukhara and Samarqand in Central Asia, using foreigners to curtail the power of the local peoples of both lands. The surname of Li was held by one of Yelu Ahai's staff of Han descent. There were various Han craftsmen. Tangut, Khitan and Han peoples took control over gardens and fields from the Muslims. Han people were moved to Central Asian areas like Besh Baliq, Almaliq, and Samarqand by the Mongols where they worked as artisans and farmers.

During the Mongol-founded Yuan dynasty (1271–1368), large numbers of Muslims settled in China. The Mongols, a minority in China, gave foreign immigrants, such as Buddhists, Christians, Muslims and Jews from West Asia an elevated status over locals including Khitan and Jurchens as part of their governing strategy, thus giving Muslims a heavy influence. Mongols recruited and forcibly relocated hundreds of thousands of Muslim immigrants from Western and Central Asia to help them administer their rapidly expanding empire. The Mongols used Arab, Persian and Buddhist Uyghur administrators, generically known as semu [色目] ("various eye color"), to act as officers of taxation and finance. Muslims headed many corporations in China in the early Yuan period. Muslim scholars were brought to work on calendar making and astronomy. The architect Yeheidie'erding (Amir al-Din) learned from Han architecture to help design the construction of the capital of the Yuan Dynasty, Dadu (also known as Khanbaliq or present-day Beijing).

Genghis Khan and his successors forbade Islamic practices like halal butchering, as well as other restrictions. Muslims had to slaughter sheep in secret. Genghis Khan outright called Muslims and Jews "slaves", and demanded that they follow the Mongol method of eating rather than the halal method. Circumcision was also forbidden. Jews were affected by these laws and forbidden by the Mongols to eat Kosher. Towards the end of the Yuan dynasty, corruption and persecution became so severe that Muslim generals joined the Han Chinese in rebelling against the Mongols. The founder of the Ming dynasty, Hongwu Emperor, led Muslim generals like Lan Yu against the Mongols, whom they defeated in combat. Some Muslim communities had a name in Chinese which meant "barracks" or "thanks", which many Hui Muslims claim comes from the gratitude which Chinese people have towards them for their role in defeating the Mongols.

Among all the [subject] alien peoples only the Hui-hui say "we do not eat Mongol food". [Cinggis Qa'an replied:] "By the aid of heaven we have pacified you; you are our slaves. Yet you do not eat our food or drink. How can this be right?" He thereupon made them eat. "If you slaughter sheep, you will be considered guilty of a crime." He issued a regulation to that effect... [In 1279/1280 under Qubilai] all the Muslims say: "if someone else slaughters [the animal] we do not eat". Because the poor people are upset by this, from now on, Musuluman [Muslim] Huihui and Zhuhu [Jewish] Huihui, no matter who kills [the animal] will eat [it] and must cease slaughtering sheep themselves, and cease the rite of circumcision.

Ming dynasty

Middle to late Ming period

During the following Ming dynasty, Muslims continued to be influential around government circles. Six of Ming dynasty founder Hongwu Emperor's most trusted generals are said to have been Muslim, including Lan Yu who, in 1388, led a strong imperial Ming army out of the Great Wall and won a decisive victory over the Mongols in Mongolia, effectively ending the Mongol dream to re-conquer China. During the war fighting the Mongols, among the Ming Emperor Zhu Yuanzhang's armies was the Hui Muslim Feng Sheng. Zhu Yuanzhang also wrote a praise of Islam, The Hundred-word Eulogy. It was recorded that "His Majesty ordered to have mosques built in Xijing and Nanjing [the capital cities], and in southern Yunnan, Fujian and Guangdong. His Majesty also personally wrote baizizan [a eulogy] in praise of the Prophet's virtues." Additionally, the Yongle Emperor hired Zheng He, perhaps the most famous Chinese of Muslim birth although at least in later life not a Muslim himself, to lead seven expeditions to the Indian Ocean from 1405 and 1433. However, during the Ming Dynasty, new immigration to China from Muslim countries was restricted in an increasingly isolationist nation. The Muslims in China who were descended from earlier immigration began to assimilate by speaking Chinese and by adopting Chinese names and culture. Mosque architecture began to follow traditional Chinese architecture. This era, sometimes considered the Golden Age of Islam in China, also saw Nanjing become an important center of Islamic study.

Taoism and Confucianism influenced Islam around and before this time, and because of their influence and the lack of proficiency many imams had with writing in Chinese, many Muslims had vastly different conceptions of God from Muslims in western countries. They also came up with Taoist-influenced names for Allah different from the typical 99 names.

Muslims in Ming dynasty Beijing were given relative freedom by the Chinese, with no restrictions placed on their religious practices or freedom of worship and being normal citizens in Beijing. In contrast to the freedom granted to Muslims, followers of Tibetan

Buddhism and Catholicism suffered from restrictions and censure in Beijing.

The Hongwu Emperor decreed the building of multiple mosques throughout China in many locations. A Nanjing mosque was built by the Xuande Emperor. Weizhou Grand Mosque, considered as one of the most beautiful, was constructed during the Ming dynasty.

When the Qing dynasty invaded the Ming dynasty in 1644, Muslim Ming loyalists led by Muslim leaders Milayin, Ding Guodong and Ma Shouying led a revolt in 1646 against the Qing during the Milayin rebellion in order to drive the Qing out and restore the Ming Prince of Yanchang Zhu Shichuan to the throne as the emperor. The Muslim Ming loyalists were crushed by the Qing with 100,000 of them, including Milayin and Ding Guodong killed.

Qing dynasty

The Manchu-led Qing dynasty (1644–1912) witnessed multiple revolts, with several major revolts headed by Muslim leaders. During the Qing dynasty's conquest of the Ming dynasty from 1644; Muslim Ming loyalists in Gansu led by Muslim leaders Milayin and Ding Guodong led a revolt in 1646 against the Qing during the Milayin rebellion in order to drive the Qing out and restore the Ming Prince Zhu Shichuan to the throne as emperor. The Muslim Ming loyalists were supported by Hami's Sultan Sa'id Baba and his son Prince Turumtay. The Muslim Ming loyalists were joined by Tibetan and Han peoples in the revolt. After fierce fighting, and negotiations, a peace agreement was agreed in 1649, where Milayan and Ding nominally pledged allegiance to the Qing and were given ranks as members of the military. When the other Ming loyalists in southern China resumed hostilities, the Qing were forced to withdraw their forces from Gansu to fight them, Milayan and Ding once again took up arms and rebelled against the Qing. The Muslim Ming loyalists were then crushed by the Qing with 100,000 of them, including Milayin, Ding Guodong, and Turumtay killed in battle.

The Confucian Hui Muslim scholar Ma Zhu (1640–1710) served with the Southern Ming loyalists against the Qing. Zhu Yu'ai (the Ming Prince Gui) was accompanied by Hui refugees when he fled from Huguang to the Burmese border in Yunnan and as a mark of their defiance against the Qing and loyalty to the Ming, they changed their surname to Ming.

In Guangzhou, the national monuments known as "The Muslim's Loyal Trio" are the tombs of Ming loyalist Muslims who were martyred while fighting in battle against the Qing during the Ming–Qing transition period in Guangzhou. The Ming Muslim loyalists were called Jiaomen sanzhong "Three defenders of the faith".

The Muslim revolt in the northwest occurred due to violent and bloody infighting between Muslim groups (Gedimu, Khafiya and Jahriyya). The rebellion in Yunnan occurred because of repression by Qing officials, resulting in bloody Hui rebellions, most notably the Dungan revolt, which occurred mostly in Xinjiang, Shaanxi and Gansu, from 1862 to 1877. The Manchu government ordered the execution of several million rebels in the Dungan revolt. The Hui Muslim population of Beijing was unaffected from the Muslim rebels during the Dungan revolt.

Elisabeth Allès wrote that the relationship between Hui Muslim and Han peoples continued normally in the Henan area, with no ramifications or consequences from the Muslim rebellions of other areas. Allès wrote "the major Muslim revolts in the mid-19th century which involved the Hui in Shaanxi, Gansu and Yunnan, as well as the Uyghurs in Xinjiang, do not seem to have had any direct effect on this region of the central plain."

However, many Muslims like Ma Zhan'ao, Ma Anliang, Dong Fuxiang, Ma Qianling and Ma Julung defected to the Qing dynasty and helped the Qing General Zuo Zongtang exterminate the Muslim rebels. These Muslim generals belonged to the Khafiya sect, and they abetted in the Qing massacre of Jahariyya rebels. Zuo relocated the Han from Hezhou as a reward for the Muslims for helping the Qing to kill other Muslim rebels. In 1895, another Dungan Revolt broke out, and loyalist Muslims such as Dong Fuxiang, Ma Anliang, Ma Guoliang, Ma Fulu and Ma Fuxiang suppressed and massacred the rebel Muslims led by Ma Dahan, Ma Yonglin and Ma Wanfu. The Muslim army, Kansu Braves, led by General Dong Fuxiang fought for the Qing dynasty against the foreigners during the Boxer Rebellion. They included well known generals like Ma Anliang, Ma Fulu and Ma Fuxiang.

In Yunnan, the Qing armies exterminated only the Muslims who had rebelled and spared Muslims who took no part in the uprising.

Uyghurs in Turfan and Hami and their leaders like Emin Khoja allied with the Qing against Uyghurs in Altishahr. The Qing dynasty enfeoffed (granted freehold property in exchange for pledged service) the rulers of Turpan, in eastern present-day Xinjiang and Hami (Kumul) as autonomous princes, while the rest of the Uyghurs in Altishahr (the Tarim Basin) were ruled by Begs. Uyghurs from Turpan and Hami were appointed by China as officials to rule over Uyghurs in the Tarim Basin.

Many Muslims chose to live among Confucians, worshipped Chinese gods and Allah, and perform religious functions, including prayer, in Confucian temples as well as mosques during the late Qing dynasty, and likely before then as well. Some even prostrated before idols and made offerings to them.

Republic of China

In the 1900s decade, it is estimated that there were 20 million Muslims in China proper (that is, China excluding the regions of Mongolia and Xinjiang). Of these, almost half resided in Gansu, over a third in Shaanxi (as defined at that time) and the rest in Yunnan.

The Qing dynasty fell in 1912, and the Republic of China was established by Sun Yat-sen, who immediately proclaimed the equality of the Han, Hui, Manchu, Mongol, and Tibetan peoples. This led to some improvement in relations between these different peoples. The end of dynasty also marked an increase in Sino-foreign interactions. This led to increased contact between Muslim minorities in China and the Islamic states of the Middle East. In 1912, the Chinese Muslim Federation was formed in the capital Nanjing. Similar organization formed in Beijing (1912), Shanghai (1925) and Jinan (1934).

In the 1910s, many Chinese Muslims syncretized their beliefs with Confucianism, and worshipped Chinese gods alongside Allah.

During the rule of the Kuomintang party, Muslim warlords (such as the Ma clique) were appointed as military governors of the provinces of Qinghai, Gansu and Ningxia. Bai Chongxi was a Muslim General and Defence Minister of China during this time.

During the Second Sino-Japanese war, the Japanese destroyed 220 mosques and killed countless Hui by April 1941. The Hui of Dachang was subjected to slaughter by the Japanese. During the Rape of Nanking, the mosques contained dead bodies after the Japanese slaughters. According to Wan Lei, "statistics showed that the Japanese destroyed 220 mosques and killed countless Hui people by April 1941." The Japanese followed a policy of economic oppression which involved the destruction of mosques and Hui communities and made many Hui jobless and homeless. Another policy was one of deliberate humiliation. This included soldiers smearing mosques with pork fat, forcing Hui to butcher pigs to feed the soldiers, and forcing girls to serve as sex slaves. Hui cemeteries were destroyed for military reasons. Many Hui fought in the war against Japan.

In 1937, during the Battle of Beiping–Tianjin, the Chinese government received a telegram from Muslim General Ma Bufang that he was prepared to fight the Japanese. Immediately after the Marco Polo Bridge Incident, Ma Bufang arranged for a cavalry division under the Muslim General Ma Biao to be sent east to battle the Japanese. Ethnic Turkic Salar Muslims made up the majority of the first cavalry division which was sent by Ma Bufang.

By 1939, at least 33 Hui Muslims had studied at Cairo's Al-Azhar University. Before the Sino-Japanese War of 1937, there existed more than a hundred known Muslim periodicals. Thirty journals were published between 1911 and 1937. Although the Linxia region remained a center of religious activities, many Muslim cultural activities had shifted to Beijing. National organizations like the Chinese Muslim Association were established for Muslims. Muslims served extensively in the National Revolutionary Army and reached positions of importance, like General Bai Chongxi, who became Defence Minister of the Republic of China.

In the Kuomintang Islamic insurgency, Muslim Kuomintang National Revolutionary Army forces in Northwest China, in Gansu, Qinghai, Ningxia, Xinjiang, as well as Yunnan, continued an unsuccessful insurgency against the communists from 1950 to 1958, after the general civil war was over. Muslims affiliated with the Kuomintang also moved to Taiwan within this time.

People's Republic of China

When the People's Republic of China was established in 1949, Muslims, along with all other religions in China, suffered repression especially during the Cultural Revolution (1966–1976). Islam, like all religions including traditional Chinese religion, was persecuted by the Red Guards who were encouraged to smash the Four Olds. Numerous places of worship, including mosques, were attacked.

In 1975, in what would be known as the Shadian incident, there was an uprising among Hui Muslims and became the only large scale ethnic rebellion during the Cultural Revolution. In crushing the rebellion, the PLA massacred 1,600 Hui with MIG fighter jets used to fire rockets onto the village. Following the fall of the Gang of Four, apologies and reparations were made. During that time, the government also constantly accused Muslims and other religious groups of holding "superstitious beliefs" and promoting "anti-socialist trends". The government began to relax its policies towards Muslims in 1978.

After the advent of Deng Xiaoping in 1979, Muslims enjoyed a period of liberalisation. New legislation gave all minorities the freedom to use their own spoken and written languages, to develop their own culture and education and to practice their religion. More Chinese Muslims than ever before were allowed to go on pilgrimage to Mecca.

There is an ethnic separatist movement among the Uyghur minority, who are a Turkic people with their own language. Uyghur separatists are intent on establishing their own state, which existed for a few years in the 1930s and as a Soviet Communist puppet state, the Second East Turkestan Republic in 1944–1950. The Soviet Union supported Uyghur separatists against China during the Sino-Soviet split. Following the collapse of the Soviet Union, China feared potential separatist goals of the Muslim majority in Xinjiang.

In the past, celebrating at religious functions and going on Hajj to Mecca was encouraged by the Chinese government for Uyghur members of the Communist party. From 1979 to 1989, 350 mosques were built in Turpan. Whereas 30 years later, the government was building "re-education" camps for interning Muslims without charge in Turpan.

In 1989, China banned a book titled "Xing Fengsu" ("Sexual Customs") which insulted Islam and placed its authors under arrest after protests in Lanzhou and Beijing by the Hui, during which the police provided protection to the Hui protestors and the government organized public burnings of the book. Hui Muslim protestors who violently rioted by vandalizing property during the protests against the book were let off by the Chinese government and went unpunished while Uyghur protestors were imprisoned.

Since the 1980s, Islamic private schools (Sino-Arabic schools (中阿學校)) have been supported and permitted by the Chinese government in Muslim areas, only specifically excluding Xinjiang from allowing these schools because of separatist sentiment there. After secondary education is completed, Hui students are permitted to embark on religious studies under an Imam.

21st century

In 2007, anticipating the coming "Year of the Pig" in the Chinese calendar, depictions of pigs were banned from CCTV "to avoid conflicts with Muslim minorities". This is believed to refer to China's population of 20 million Muslims (to whom pigs are considered "unclean"). Hui Muslims enjoy freedoms such as practising their religion, building mosques at which their children attend, while Uyghurs in Xinjiang experience more strict controls.

There are about 24,400 mosques in Xinjiang, an average of one mosque for every 530 Muslims, which is higher than the number of churches per Christian person in England.

In March 2014, the Chinese media estimated that there were around 300 Chinese Muslims active in ISIS territories. The Chinese government stated in May 2015 that it would not tolerate any form of terrorism and would work to "combat terrorist forces, including ETIM, [to] safeguard global peace, security and stability."

Muslims were reported in 2015 to have been featured as hosts and directors on the Chinese New Year Gala.

In response to the 2015 Charlie Hebdo shooting, Chinese state-run media attacked Charlie Hebdo for publishing the cartoons insulting Muhammad, with the state-run Xinhua advocating limiting freedom of speech, while the Chinese Communist Party-owned tabloid Global Times said the attack was "payback" for what it characterised as Western colonialism and accusing Charlie Hebdo of trying to incite a clash of civilizations.

In the five years to 2017, a 306% rise in criminal arrests was seen in Xinjiang and the arrests there accounted for 21% of the national total, despite the region contributing just 1.5% of the population. The increase was seen as driven by the government's "Strike Hard" campaign. In 2017, driven by a 92% in security spending there that year, an estimated 227,882 criminal arrests were made in Xinjiang.

In August 2018, the authorities were vigorously pursuing the suppression of mosques, including their widespread destruction, over Muslim protests. Also at that time, the growing of long beards and the wearing of veils or Islamic robes for Uyghurs, were banned. All vehicle owners were required to install GPS tracking devices.

NPR reported that from 2018 to 2020 the repression of non-Uyghur Muslims intensified. Imams have been restricted to practicing within the region their household is registered in. Prior to these restrictions China had hundreds of itinerant Imams. During this period the Chinese government forced nearly all mosques in Ningxia and Henan to remove their domes and Arabic script. In 2018 new language restrictions forced hundreds of Arabic schools in Ningxia and Zhengzhou to close.

A 2019 paper from the Gallatin School of Individualized Study interviewed Hui Muslims in Xining, Lanzhou, and Yinchuan and found that none saw the recent policies or government as detrimental to their religious lives. Although some foresaw a future of Islam in China much different than what they were used to, they did not seem to worry if it was good or bad as long as they had access to mosques, halal food and security. Arabic calligraphy was also reported by The Hindu in 2019 to be commonplace at the Linxia Hui Autonomous Prefecture. The National reported in the same year of a female ahong in Xi'an teaching those in her mosque how to pray and read the Quran in Arabic.

Chinese Muslims reportedly celebrated Ramadan on 2021 in the cities of Shanghai and Beijing. The Star reported in the same year that Uyghurs in Xinjiang made prayers for Aidilfitri.

Repression of Uyghurs

By 2013, the repression of Uyghurs extended to the disappearance of dissidents and the imposition of life imprisonment sentences on academics who were convicted of promoting social interactions between Uyghurs. Hui Muslims who are employed by the state are allowed to fast during Ramadan unlike Uyghurs in the same positions, the number of Hui going on Hajj was reported to be expanding in 2014 and Hui women are allowed to wear veils, while Uyghur women are discouraged from wearing them. Uyghurs find it difficult to get passports to go on Hajj. The Xinjiang Muslim Association in China and the Chinese embassy in Malaysia have denied that Uyghurs are banned from fasting, inviting foreigners to come see it for themselves.

In July 2014, Reuters reported that Uyghurs in Shanghai could practise their religion, with some expressing more freedom there than in Xinjiang.

The Associated Press (AP) reported in late November 2018 that Uyghur families were required to allow local government officials to live in their homes as "relatives" in a "Pair Up and Become Family" campaign. While the official was living in a home, the residents were closely watched and not allowed to pray or wear religious clothing. Authorities said that the program was voluntary but Muslims who were interviewed by AP expressed concern that refusal to cooperate would lead to serious repercussions.

Tibetan-Muslim sectarian violence

In Tibet, the majority of Muslims are Hui people. Hatred between Tibetans and Muslims stems from events during the Muslim warlord Ma Bufang's rule in Qinghai such as the Ngolok rebellions (1917–1949) and the Sino-Tibetan War. Violence subsided after 1949 under Communist Party repression but reignited as strictures were relaxed.

Riots broke out in March 2008 between Muslims and Tibetans over incidents such as suspected human bones in and deliberate contamination of soups served in Muslim-owned establishments and overpricing of balloons by Muslim vendors. Tibetans attacked Muslim restaurants. Fires set by Tibetans resulted in Muslim deaths and riots. The Tibetan exile community sought to suppress reports reaching the international community, fearing damage to the cause of Tibetan autonomy and fueling Hui Muslim support of government repression of Tibetans generally. In addition, Chinese-speaking Hui have problems with Tibetan Hui (the Tibetan speaking Kache minority of Muslims). The main mosque in Lhasa was burned down by Tibetans during the unrest.

The majority of Tibetans viewed the wars against Iraq and Afghanistan after 9/11 positively and it had the effect of galvanizing anti-Muslim attitudes among Tibetans and resulted in an anti-Muslim boycott against Muslim owned businesses. Tibetan Buddhists propagate a false libel that Muslims cremate their Imams and use the ashes to convert Tibetans to Islam by making Tibetans inhale the ashes.

Internment camps and restrictions on religious freedom

The Xinjiang re-education camps are officially called "Vocational Education and Training Centers" by the Chinese government. The camps have been operated by the Xinjiang Uyghur Autonomous Regional government since 2014. However, the efforts of the camps strongly intensified after a change of head for the region. Alongside the Uyghurs, other Muslim minorities have also been reported to be held in these re-education camps. As of 2019, 23 nations in the United Nations have signed a letter condemning China for the camps and asking them to close them.

In May 2018, news media outlets reported that hundreds of thousands of Muslims were being detained in massive extrajudicial internment camps in western Xinjiang. These were called as "re-education" camps and later, "vocational training centres" by the government, intended for the "rehabilitation and redemption" to combat terrorism and religious extremism.

In August 2018, the United Nations said that credible reports had led it to estimate that up to a million Uyghurs and other Muslims were being held in "something that resembles a massive internment camp that is shrouded in secrecy". The U.N.'s International Convention on the Elimination of All Forms of Racial Discrimination said that some estimates indicated that up to 2 million Uyghurs and other Muslims were held in "political camps for indoctrination", in a "no-rights zone". By that time, conditions in Xinjiang had deteriorated so far that they were described by political scientists as "Orwellian" and observers drew comparisons with Nazi concentration camps. In response to the UN panel's finding of indefinite detention without due process, the Chinese government delegation officially conceded that it was engaging in widespread "resettlement and re-education" and state media described the controls in Xinjiang as "intense", but not permanent.

On 31 August 2018, the United Nations committee called on the Chinese government to "end the practice of detention without lawful charge, trial and conviction", to release the detained persons, to provide specifics as to the number of interred individuals and the reasons for their detention and to investigate the allegations of "racial, ethnic and ethno-religious profiling". A BBC report quoted an unnamed Chinese official as saying that "Uighurs enjoyed full rights", pointing out that "those deceived by religious extremism... shall be assisted by resettlement and re-education".

In October 2018, BBC News published an investigative exposé claiming based on satellite imagery and testimony that hundreds of thousands of Uyghurs and other Muslim minorities are being held without trial in internment camps in Xinjiang. On the other hand, the United States Department of Defense believes that around 1 million to 3 million people have been detained and placed in the re-education camps. Some sources quoted in the article say "as far as I know, the Chinese government wants to remove Uyghur identity from the world." The New York Times suggests that China has been successful in keeping countries, notably Muslim majority nations, to be quiet about the camps in Xinjiang due to its diplomatic and economic power, but when countries do decide to criticize the country, they do so in groups in hopes of lessening punishments from China.

On 28 April 2020, the U.S. Commission on International Religious Freedom issued the "International Religious Freedom Annual Report 2020". The report states that "individuals have been sent to the camps for wearing long beards, refusing alcohol, or other behaviors authorities deem to be signs of "religious extremism".

Former detainees report that they suffered torture, rape, sterilization, and other abuses. In addition, nearly half a million Muslim children have been separated from their families and placed in boarding schools. During 2019, the camps increasingly transitioned from "reeducation" to forced labor as detainees were forced to work in cotton and textile factories. Outside the camps, the government continued to deploy officials to live with Muslim families and to report on any signs of "extremist" religious behavior. Meanwhile, authorities in Xinjiang and other parts of China have destroyed or damaged thousands of mosques and removed Arabic-language signs from Muslim businesses."

On 17 June 2020, President Donald Trump signed the Uyghur Human Rights Policy Act, which authorizes the imposition of U.S. sanctions against Chinese government officials responsible for re-education camps.

People

Ethnic groups

Muslims live in every region in China. The highest concentrations are found in the northwest provinces of Xinjiang, Gansu and Ningxia, with significant populations also found throughout Yunnan Province in Southwest China and Henan Province in Central China. Of China's 55 officially recognized minority peoples, ten groups are predominantly Muslim. The largest groups in descending order are Hui (9.8 million in year 2000 census or 48% of the officially tabulated number of Muslims), Uyghur (8.4 million, 41%), Kazakh (1.25 million, 6.1%), Dongxiang (514,000, 2.5%), Kyrgyz (144,000), Uzbeks (125,000), Salar (105,000), Tajik (41,000), Bonan (17,000) and Tatar (5,000). However, individual members of traditionally Muslim groups may profess other religions or none at all. Additionally, Tibetan Muslims are officially classified along with the Tibetan people. Muslims live predominantly in the areas that border Central Asia, Tibet and Mongolia, i.e. Xinjiang, Ningxia, Gansu and Qinghai, which is known as the "Quran Belt".

There are several population estimates. Counting up the number of people of traditionally Muslim nationalities who were enumerated in the 2000 census reported a total of 20.3 million members of Muslim nationalities, of which again 96% belonged to just three groups: Hui 9.8 million, Uyghurs 8.4 million, and Kazakhs 1.25 million. A 2009 study done by the Pew Research Center concluded there are 21,667,000 Muslims in China, accounting for 1.6% of the total population. According to the CIA World Factbook, about 1.8% of the total population in China are Muslims, meaning 25 million. Another ref estimated "around 40 million people". According to the textbook, "Religions in the Modern World", it states that the "numbers of followers of any one tradition are difficult to estimate and must in China as everywhere else rely on statistics compiled by the largest institutions, either those of the state – which tend to underestimate – or those of the religious institutions themselves – which tend to overestimate. If we include all the population of those designated 'national' minorities with an Islamic heritage in the territory of China, then we can conclude that there are some 20 million Muslims in the People's Republic of China."

Other nationalities that are traditionally Muslim include Kyrghyz, Tajiks, Uzbeks, Tatars, Salar, Bonan and Dongxiang. According to SARA there are approximately 36,000 Islamic places of worship, more than 45,000 imams, and 10 Islamic schools in the country. Within the next two decades from 2011, Pew projects a slowing down of the Muslim population growth in China compared to previous years, with Muslim women in China having a 1.7 fertility rate. Many Hui Muslims voluntarily limit themselves to one child in China since their Imams preach to them about the benefits of population control, while the number of children Hui in different areas are allowed to have varies between one and three children. Chinese family planning policy allows minorities including Muslims to have up to two children in urban areas and three to four children in rural areas.

An older estimate of the Muslim population of the then Qing Empire belongs to the Christian missionary Marshall Broomhall. In his book, published in 1910, he produced estimates for each province, based on the reports of missionaries working there, who had counted mosques, talked to mullahs, etc. Broomhall admits the inadequacy of the data for Xinjiang, estimating the Muslim population of Xinjiang (i.e., virtually the entire population of the province at the time) in the range from 1,000,000 (based on the total population number of 1,200,000 in the contemporary Statesman's Yearbook) to 2,400,000 (2 million "Turki", 200,000 "Hasak" and 200,000 "Tungan", as per George Hunter). He uses the estimates of 2,000,000 to 3,500,000 for Gansu (which then also included today's Ningxia and parts of Qinghai), 500,000 to 1,000,000 for Zhili (i.e., Beijing, Tianjin and Hebei), 300,000 to 1,000,000 for Yunnan and smaller numbers for other provinces, down to 1,000 in Fujian. For Mongolia (then, part of the Qing Empire) he takes an arbitrary range of 50,000 to 100,000. Summing up, he arrives to the grand total of 4,727,000 to 9,821,000 Muslims throughout the Qing Empire of its last years, i.e. just over 1–2% of the entire country's estimated population of 426,045,305. The 1920 edition of New International Yearbook: A Compendium of the World's

Progress gave the number "between 5,000,000 and 10,000,000" as the total number of Muslims in the Republic of China.

Islamic education

Hui Muslim Generals like Ma Fuxiang, Ma Hongkui, and Ma Bufang funded schools or sponsored students studying abroad. Imam Hu Songshan and Ma Linyi were involved in reforming Islamic education inside China.

Muslim Kuomintang officials in the Republic of China government supported the Chengda Teachers Academy, which helped usher in a new era of Islamic education in China, promoting nationalism and Chinese language among Muslims, and fully incorporating them into the main aspects of Chinese society. The Ministry of Education provided funds to the Chinese Islamic National Salvation Federation for Chinese Muslim's education. The President of the federation was General Bai Chongxi (Pai Chung-hsi) and the vice president was Tang Kesan (Tang Ko-san). 40 Sino-Arabic primary schools were founded in Ningxia by its Governor Ma Hongkui.

Imam Wang Jingzhai studied at Al-Azhar University in Egypt along with several other Chinese Muslim students, the first Chinese students in modern times to study in the Middle East. Wang recalled his experience teaching at madrassas in the provinces of Henan (Yu), Hebei (Ji), and Shandong (Lu) which were outside of the traditional stronghold of Muslim education in northwest China, and where the living conditions were poorer and the students had a much tougher time than the northwestern students. In 1931 China sent five students to study at Al-Azhar in Egypt, among them was Muhammad Ma Jian and they were the first Chinese to study at

Al-Azhar. Na Zhong, a descendant of Nasr al-Din (Yunnan) was another one of the students sent to Al-Azhar in 1931, along with Zhang Ziren, Ma Jian, and Lin Zhongming.

Hui Muslims from the Central Plains (Zhongyuan) differed in their view of women's education than Hui Muslims from the northwestern provinces, with the Hui from the Central Plains provinces like Henan having a history of women's Mosques and religious schooling for women, while Hui women in northwestern provinces were kept in the house. However, in northwestern China reformers started bringing female education in the 1920s. In Linxia, Gansu, a secular school for Hui girls was founded by the Muslim warlord Ma Bufang, the school was named Shuada Suqin Women's Primary School after his wife Ma Suqin who was also involved in its founding. Hui Muslim refugees fled to northwest China from the central plains after the Japanese invasion of China, where they continued to practice women's education and build women's mosque communities, while women's education was not adopted by the local northwestern Hui Muslims and the two different communities continued to differ in this practice.

General Ma Fuxiang donated funds to promote education for Hui Muslims and help build a class of intellectuals among the Hui and promote the Hui role in developing the nation's strength.

Sectarian tensions

Hui-Uyghur tension

Tensions between Hui Muslims and Uyghurs arise because Hui troops and officials often dominated the Uyghurs in the past, and crushed the Uyghurs' revolts. Xinjiang's Hui population increased by over 520 percent between 1940 and 1982, an average annual growth of 4.4 percent, while the Uyghur population only grew at 1.7 percent. This dramatic increase in Hui population led inevitably to significant tensions between the Hui and Uyghur populations. Many Hui Muslim civilians were killed by Uyghur rebellion troops in 1933 known as the Kizil massacre. During the 2009 rioting in Xinjiang that killed around 200 people, "Kill the Han, kill the Hui." is a common cry spread across social media among Uyghur extremists. Some Uyghurs in Kashgar remember that the Hui army at the Battle of Kashgar (1934) massacred 2,000 to 8,000 Uyghurs, which causes tension as more Hui moved into Kashgar from other parts of China. Some Hui criticize Uyghur separatism and generally do not want to get involved in conflict in other countries. Hui and Uyghur live separately, attending different mosques.

The Uyghur militant organization East Turkestan Islamic Movement's magazine Islamic Turkistan has accused the Chinese "Muslim Brotherhood" (the Yihewani) of being responsible for the moderation of Hui Muslims and the lack of Hui joining jihadist groups in addition to blaming other things for the lack of Hui Jihadists, such as the fact that for more than 300 years Hui and Uyghurs have been enemies of each other, no separatist Islamist organizations among the Hui, the fact that the Hui view China as their home, and the fact that the "infidel Chinese" language is the language of the Hui.

Hui sects

There have been many occurrences of violent sectarian fighting between different Hui sects. Sectarian fighting between Hui sects led to the Jahriyya rebellion in the 1780s and the 1895 revolt. After a hiatus after the People's Republic of China came to power, sectarian in fighting resumed in the 1990s in Ningxia between different sects. Several sects refuse to intermarry with each other. One Sufi sect circulated an anti-Salafi pamphlet in Arabic.

Tibetan Muslims

In Tibet, the majority of Muslims are Hui people. Hatred between Tibetans and Muslims stems from events during the Muslim warlord Ma Bufang's rule in Qinghai such as Ngolok rebellions (1917–49) and the Sino-Tibetan War, but in 1949 the Communists put an end to the violence between Tibetans and Muslims, however, new Tibetan-Muslim violence broke out after China engaged in liberalization. Riots broke out between Muslims and Tibetans over incidents such as bones in soups and prices of balloons and Tibetans accused Muslims of being cannibals who cooked humans in their soup and of contaminating food with urine. Tibetans attacked Muslim restaurants. Fires set by Tibetans which burned the apartments and shops of Muslims resulted in Muslim families being killed and wounded in the 2008 mid-March riots. Due to Tibetan violence against Muslims, the traditional Islamic white caps have not been worn by many Muslims. Scarfs were removed and replaced with hairnets by Muslim women in order to hide. Muslims prayed in secret at home when in August 2008 the Tibetans burned the Mosque. The repression of Tibetan separatism by the Chinese government is supported by Hui Muslims. In addition, Chinese-speaking Hui have problems with Tibetan Hui (the Tibetan-speaking Kache minority of Muslims).

The main Mosque in Lhasa was burned down by Tibetans and Chinese Hui Muslims were violently assaulted by Tibetan rioters in the 2008 Tibetan unrest. Tibetan exiles and foreign scholars alike ignore this and do not talk about sectarian violence between Tibetan Buddhists and Muslims. The majority of Tibetans viewed the wars against Iraq and Afghanistan after 9/11 positively and it had the effect of galvanizing anti-Muslim attitudes among Tibetans and resulted in an anti-Muslim boycott against Muslim owned businesses. Tibetan Buddhists propagate a false libel that Muslims cremate their Imams and use the ashes to convert Tibetans to Islam by making Tibetans inhale the ashes, even though the Tibetans seem to be aware that Muslims practice burial and not cremation since they frequently clash against proposed Muslim cemeteries in their area.

Religious practices

Islamic education in China

In the two decades up to 2006, a wide range of Islamic educational opportunities were developed to meet the needs of China's Muslim population. In addition to mosque schools, government Islamic colleges and independent Islamic colleges, more students went overseas to continue their studies at international Islamic universities in Egypt, Saudi Arabia, Syria, Iran, Pakistan and Malaysia. Qīngzhēn (清真) is the Chinese term for certain Islamic institutions. Its literal meaning is "pure truth".

Muslim groups

The vast majority of China's Muslims are Sunni Muslims. A notable feature of some Muslim communities in China is the presence of female imams. Islamic scholar Ma Tong recorded that the 6,781,500 Hui in China predominately followed the Orthodox form of Islam (58.2% were Gedimu, a non-Sufi mainstream tradition that opposed unorthodoxy and religious innovation), mainly adhering to the Hanafi Maturidi Madhhab. However a large minority of Hui are members of Sufi groups. According to Tong, 21% Yihewani, 10.9% Jahriyya, 7.2% Khuffiya, 1.4% Qadariyya and 0.7% Kubrawiyya. Shia Chinese Muslims are mostly Ismailis, including Tajiks of the Tashkurgan and Sarikul areas of Xinjiang.

The predominant religion of Äynu people is Alevism, a tradition identified with Shia Islam, although a few profess Sunni Islam.

Chinese Muslims and the Hajj

It is known that Admiral Zheng He (1371–1435) and his Muslim crews had made the journey to Mecca and performed the Hajj during one of the former's voyages to the western ocean between 1401 and 1433. Other Chinese Muslims may have made the Hajj pilgrimage to Mecca in the following centuries; however, there is little information on this. General Ma Lin made a Hajj to Mecca. General Ma Fuxiang along with Ma Linyi sponsored Imam Wang Jingzhai when he went on hajj to Mecca in 1921. Yihewani Imam Hu Songshan went on Hajj in 1925.

Briefly during the Cultural Revolution, Chinese Muslims were not allowed to attend the Hajj and only did so through Pakistan, but this policy was reversed in 1979. Chinese Muslims now attend the Hajj in large numbers, typically in organized groups of roughly 10,000 each year, with a record 10,700 Chinese Muslim pilgrims from all over the country making the Hajj in 2007. Over 11,000 from Xinjiang reportedly went to the Hajj in 2019.

Representative bodies

Islamic Association of China

Established by the government, the Islamic Association of China claims to represent Chinese Muslims nationwide. At its inaugural meeting on May 11, 1953, in Beijing, representatives from 10 nationalities of the People's Republic of China were in attendance. The association was to be run by 16 Islamic religious leaders charged with making "a correct and authoritative interpretation" of Islamic creed and canon. Its brief is to compile and spread inspirational speeches and help imams "improve" themselves, and vet sermons made by clerics around the country.

Some examples of the religious concessions granted to Muslims are:

- Muslim communities are allowed separate cemeteries

- Muslim couples may have their marriage consecrated by an Imam

- Muslim workers are permitted holidays during major religious festivals

- Chinese Muslims are also allowed to make the Hajj to Mecca, and more than 45,000 Chinese Muslims have done so in recent years.

Culture and heritage

Although contacts and previous conquests have occurred before, the Mongol conquest of the greater part of Eurasia in the 13th century permanently brought the extensive cultural traditions of China, central Asia and western Asia into a single empire, albeit one of separate khanates, for the first time in history. The intimate interaction that resulted is evident in the legacy of both traditions. In China, Islam influenced technology, sciences, philosophy and the arts. For example, the Chinese adopted much Islamic medical knowledge such as wound healing and urinalysis. However, the Chinese were not the only ones to benefit from the cultural exchanges of the Silk Road. Islam showed many influences from Buddhist China in their new techniques in art, especially when humans began to be depicted in paintings which was thought to be forbidden in Islam. In terms of material culture, one finds decorative motifs from central Asian Islamic architecture and calligraphy and the marked halal impact on northern Chinese cuisine.

Taking the Mongol Eurasian Empire as a point of departure, the ethnogenesis of the Hui, or Sinophone Muslims, can also be charted through the emergence of distinctly Chinese Muslim traditions in architecture, food, epigraphy and Islamic written culture. This multifaceted cultural heritage continues to the present day.

Military

Muslims have often filled military positions, and many Muslims have joined the Chinese army. Muslims served extensively in the Chinese military, as both officials and soldiers. It was said that the Muslim Dongxiang and Salar were given to "eating rations", a reference to military service.

Islamic architecture in China

In Chinese, a mosque is called qīngzhēn sì (清真寺) or "pure truth temple". The Huaisheng Mosque and Great Mosque of Xi'an (first established during the Tang era) and the Great Southern Mosque in Jinan, whose current buildings date from the Ming Dynasty, do not replicate many of the features often associated with traditional mosques. Instead, they follow traditional Chinese architecture. Mosques in western China incorporate more of the elements seen in mosques in other parts of the world. Western Chinese mosques were more likely to incorporate minarets and domes while eastern Chinese mosques were more likely to look like pagodas. An important feature in Chinese architecture is its emphasis on symmetry, which connotes a sense of grandeur; this applies to everything from palaces to mosques. One notable exception is in the design of gardens, which tends to be as asymmetrical as possible. Like Chinese scroll paintings, the principle underlying the garden's composition is to create enduring flow; to let the patron wander and enjoy the garden without prescription, as in nature herself. The Qingjing Mosque was built in 1009.

On the foothills of Mount Lingshan are the tombs of two of the four companions that Muhammad sent eastwards to preach Islam. Known as the "Holy Tombs", they house the companions Sa-Ke-Zu and Wu-Ko-Shun—their Chinese names, of course. The other two companions went to Guangzhou and Yangzhou.

As in all regions the Chinese Islamic architecture reflects the local architecture resembling temples in its style. However, in Western China the mosques resemble those of the Middle East, with tall, slender minarets, curvy arches and dome shaped roofs. In northwest China where the Chinese Hui have built their mosques, there is a combination of east and west. The mosques have flared Chinese-style roofs set in walled courtyards entered through archways with miniature domes and minarets. The first mosque was the Great Mosque of Xian or the Xian Mosque, which was created in the Tang Dynasty in the 7th century. In July 2019, Indonesian Islamic scholar Said Aqil Siradj said that Chinese authorities including those in Xinjiang were building and repairing mosques along with creating hundreds of halal restaurants.

Ningxia officials notified on 3 August 2018 that the Weizhou Grand Mosque will be forcibly demolished on Friday because it had not received the proper permits before construction. Officials in the town were saying the mosque had not been given proper building permits, because it is built in a Middle Eastern style and include numerous domes and minarets. The residents of Weizhou alarmed each other by social media and finally stopped the mosque destruction by public demonstrations. According to a September 2020 report by the Australian Strategic Policy Institute, since 2017, Chinese authorities have destroyed or damaged 16,000 mosques in Xinjiang – 65% of the region's total.

Halal food in China

Halal food has a long history in China. The arrival of Arabian and Persian merchants during the Tang and Song dynasties saw the introduction of the Muslim diet. Chinese Muslim cuisine adheres strictly to the Islamic dietary rules with mutton and lamb being the predominant ingredient. The advantage of Muslim cuisine in China is that it has inherited the diverse cooking methods of Chinese cuisine for example, braising, roasting, steaming, stewing and many more. Due to China's multicultural background Muslim cuisine retains its own style and characteristics according to regions. Restaurants serving such cuisine are frequented by both Muslim and Han Chinese customers.

Due to the large Muslim population in Western China, many Chinese restaurants cater to Muslims or the general public but are run by Muslims. In most major cities in China, there are small Islamic restaurants or food stalls typically run by migrants from

Western China (e.g., Uyghurs), which offer inexpensive noodle soup. Lamb and mutton dishes are more commonly available than in other Chinese restaurants, due to the greater prevalence of these meats in the cuisine of western Chinese regions. Commercially prepared food can be certified Halal by approved agencies. In Chinese, halal is called qīngzhēncài (清真菜) or "pure truth food". Beef and lamb slaughtered according to Islamic rituals is also commonly available in public markets, especially in North China. Such meat is sold by Muslim butchers, who operate independent stalls next to non-Muslim butchers.

In October 2018, the government launched an official anti-halal policy, urging officials to suppress the "pan-halal tendency", seen as an encroachment by religion into secular life and a source of religious extremism.

Calligraphy

Sini

Sini is a Chinese Islamic calligraphic form for the Arabic script. It can refer to any type of Chinese Islamic calligraphy, but is commonly used to refer to one with thick and tapered effects, much like Chinese calligraphy. It is used extensively in mosques in Eastern China and to a lesser extent in Gansu, Ningxia and Shaanxi. A famous Sini calligrapher is Hajji Noor Deen Mi Guangjiang.

Martial arts

There is a long history of Muslim development and participation at the highest level of Chinese wushu. The Hui started and adapted many of the styles of wushu such as bajiquan, piguazhang and liuhequan. There were specific areas that were known to be centers of Muslim wushu, such as Cang County in Hebei Province. These traditional Hui martial arts were very distinct from the Turkic styles practiced in Xinjiang.

Literature

The Han Kitab was a collection of Chinese Islamic texts written by Chinese Muslim which synthesized Islam and Confucianism. It was written in the early 18th century during the Qing dynasty. Han is Chinese for Chinese and kitab (ketabu in Chinese) is Arabic for book. Liu Zhi wrote his Han Kitab in Nanjing in the early 18th century. The works of Wu Sunqie, Zhang Zhong and Wang Daiyu were also included in the Han Kitab.

The Han Kitab was widely read and approved of by later Chinese Muslims such as Ma Qixi, Ma Fuxiang and Hu Songshan. They believed that Islam could be understood through Confucianism.

Education

A lot of Chinese students including male and females join International Islamic University, Islamabad to gain Islamic knowledge. For some Muslim groups in China, such as the Hui and Salar minorities, coeducation is frowned upon; for some groups such as Uyghurs, it is not.

Women imams

With the exception of China, the world has very few mosques directed by women. Among the Hui, women are allowed to become imams or ahong, and a number of woman-only mosques have been established. The tradition evolved from earlier Quranic schools for girls, with the oldest, the Wangjia Hutong Women's Mosque in Kaifeng, dating to 1820.

Famous Muslims in China

Explorers

- Zheng He, mariner and explorer
- Fei Xin, Zheng He's translator
- Ma Huan, a companion of Zheng He
- Generals from the Qing era:
- Xu Shiheng
- Ma Rulong
- Ma Xinyi (late Qing dynasty)

Generals in the Republic of China:

- Ma Zhancang
- Ma Fuyuan
- Ma Ju-lung
- Ma Zhanhai
- Bai Chongxi
- Ma Ching-chiang (Lt. General)

Warlords of the Ma clique during the Republic of China era:

- Ma Bufang
- Ma Zhongying
- Ma Fuxiang
- Ma Hongkui

- Ma Dunjing
- Ma Hongbin
- Ma Dunjing (1906-1972)
- Ma Lin
- Ma Qi
- Ma Hu-shan
- Ma Zhan'ao
- Ma Qianling
- Ma Fushou
- Ma Fulu
- Ma Anliang
- Ma Guoliang
- Ma Buqing
- Ma Bukang
- Ma Jiyuan
- Ma Chengxiang
- Ma Haiyan

Generals from the 36ᵗʰ Division (National Revolutionary Army):

- Ma Sheng-kuei
- Su Chin-shou
- Pai Tzu-li
- Du Wenxiu, Ma Hualong and Ma Zhan'ao, leaders of the Panthay Rebellion in Yunnan and the Muslim rebellion in northwestern China

- Ma Shenglin, great-uncle of Ma Shaowu and rebel during the Panthay Rebellion

- Ma Zhanshan, guerilla during the Second Sino-Japanese War

- Zuo Baogui (1837–1894), Qing Muslim general from Shandong who died while defending Pingyang, Korea, from the Japanese

Religious

- Liu Zhi (c. 1660 – c. 1739), Islamic author (Qing dynasty).

- Qi Jingyi (1656–1719), Sufi master who introduced the Qadiriyyah school to China

- Ma Laichi (1681?–1766?), Sufi master who brought the Khufiyya Naqshbandi movement to China

- Ma Mingxin (1719–1781), founder of the Jahriyya Naqshbandi movement

- Ma Wanfu, founder of the Yihewani

- Ma Qixi (1857–1914), founder of the Xidaotang

- Ma Yuanzhang, Jahriyya Sufi leader

- Wang Jingzhai, one of the four famous Imams of the Republican period

- Hu Songshan (1880–1956), Yihewani reformer and Chinese nationalist

Scholars and writers

- Tohti Tunyaz, historian

- Ma Zhu, Islamic scholar and Southern Ming loyalist

- Yusuf Ma Dexin, first translator of the Qur'an into Chinese

- Muhammad Ma Jian, author of the most popular Chinese translation of the Qur'an
- Wang Daiyu, Master Supervisor of the Imperial Observatory (Ming dynasty)
- Zhang Chengzhi, contemporary author
- Pai Hsien-yung, contemporary author, son of Bai Chongxi.
- Yusuf Liu Baojun, contemporary author and historian

Officials

- Ma Xinyi, (馬新貽), official and a military general of the late Qing dynasty in China
- Ma Linyi Gansu Minister of Education
- Tang Kesan, representative of the Kuomintang in XikangBai Shouyi, historian

Martial arts

- Ma Xianda, martial artist
- Wang Zi-Ping, member of the Righteous and Harmonious Fists (the "Boxers") during the Boxer Rebellion
- Chang Dongsheng, martial artist and Shuai jiao teacher

Arts

- Mi Fu, painter, poet and calligrapher during the Song dynasty
- Noor Deen Mi Guangjiang, calligrapher

Islam

The vast majority of Chinese Muslim adults come from 10 ethnic minority groups that traditionally practice Islam, the two largest being the Hui people and the Uyghur people. Most of China's Muslims live in the country's northwestern region, particularly in the areas of Gansu, Qinghai, Ningxia and Xinjiang.

Roughly 9 in 10 Chinese Muslims are either Hui or Uyghur

Government-designated ethnic groups that traditionally practice Islam

	Number of adults	% of all Muslim ethnic groups	% of all Chinese adults
Hui	8,291,749	46%	0.75%
Uyghur	7,717,361	43	0.69
Kazakh	1,094,518	6	0.10
Dongxiang	466,976	3	0.04
Kirgiz	140,601	1	0.01
Salar	101,781	1	0.01
Tajik	35,771	<0.5	<0.01
Baoan	14,703	<0.5	<0.01
Uzbek	8,766	<0.5	<0.01
Tatar	2,646	<0.5	<0.01
All Muslim ethnic groups	17,874,872	100	1.61

Note: "All Muslim ethnic groups" account for 1.61% of China's adult population. In surveys, a small share of people in these ethnic groups do not identify as Muslim and a small share of Han Chinese do identify as Muslim.
Source: Census of China, 2020.
"Measuring Religion in China"

PEW RESEARCH CENTER

Because there is heavy overlap between religion and ethnicity among these minority groups, there is less uncertainty about the size of China's Muslim population than there is about some of its other religious groups, such as Buddhists and Christians.

Chinese authorities and international scholars generally estimate there are 18 million Muslim adults in China. Pew Research Center's estimate is in the same ballpark but slightly lower, at about 17 million, for reasons discussed below.

Notwithstanding the relative consensus around Muslim population numbers, studying Islam in China comes with many challenges. To begin with, the Chinese government has been accused by international organizations of human rights abuses and genocide against Uyghurs and other Muslims. Some Chinese Muslim scholars have reportedly been detained, while some foreigners who study Islam in China have been barred from traveling to the country.

In this climate, Chinese Muslims may hesitate to discuss their religious identity, beliefs or practices with survey researchers, and some may have moved away (or been pushed away) from their traditional religion. Compounding the uncertainty, the Chinese General Social Survey (CGSS), a key source of data, has not been conducted in Xinjiang – home to nearly all Uyghurs in China – since 2013.

History of Islam in China

How many Muslims are there in China?

Most Chinese Uyghurs and Huis identify as Muslim

% of adults in each ethnic group who say Islam is their religious belief (zongjiao xinyang)

Uyghur	94%
Hui	93
Han	<0.5

Note: Han is China's majority ethnicity. Zongjiao xinyang typically refers to belief in organized religion and connotes formal religious affiliation.
Source: Pooled data from the 2017 and 2018 Chinese General Social Survey (CGSS). Uyghur estimates come from aggregated 2010 and 2012 CGSS data. "Measuring Religion in China"

PEW RESEARCH CENTER

Pew Research Center's estimate of the number of Chinese Muslims differs from those typically cited by the Chinese government.

China's 10 traditionally Muslim ethnic groups are among 56 ethnicities measured in the Chinese census. Official estimates of the size of China's Muslim population – including those generated by the Islamic Association of China, the government agency that oversees Islamic affairs – typically add up the total populations of the traditionally Muslim ethnic groups, assuming that every member of those 10 groups, without exception, is Muslim, and that there are absolutely no Muslims among the Han majority.

By this method of estimation, there were roughly 18 million Muslim adults in China in 2020, accounting for 1.6% of China's adult population. The two largest of the sub-groups were Hui (8.3 million adults), followed by Uyghurs (7.7 million adults).

However, there are limitations to using ethnicity as a proxy for Muslim identity.

First, this approach assumes that all members of predominantly Muslim ethnic groups identify as Muslim, which surveys indicate is not the case. For example, 7% of Hui adults do not identify as Muslim, according to data from the 2017 and 2018 CGSS. Likewise, older survey data indicates that about 6% of Uyghurs did not identify as Muslim. (Since then, there has been no survey with a sufficient sample size to analyze Muslim identification among Uyghurs.)

Second, the conventional estimation approach fails to account for Muslim converts of other ethnicities, especially those from the Han majority. Although Han Muslims are rare – only about one in every 1,500 Han adults say their religious belief (zongjiao xinyang 宗教信仰) is Islam, according to surveys – they still could add up to substantial numbers, given that there are 1.02 billion Han adults in China.

To correct for these issues, Pew Research Center demographers estimate that roughly 90% of people in China's 10 Muslim-majority ethnic groups identify as Muslims and that roughly 700,000 Han Chinese identify with Islam, yielding a total estimate of about 17 million Muslims in China, or around 2% of the adult population. By contrast, the Islamic Association of China's method – adding up the entire populations of the 10 Muslim-majority ethnic groups and assuming that no one in the Han majority is Muslim – yields an estimate that is higher by nearly 1 million adults.

Demographic traits

Most Uyghur and Hui people belong to the Sunni branch of Islam, but they differ in other ways.

Culturally, Hui people, who began a period of rapid assimilation into the mainstream Han Chinese culture during 14th century, have a good deal in common with the Han majority, including the Han Chinese language and surnames. By contrast, Uyghurs – who until the last century had limited interactions with the Han Chinese – mainly speak Uyghur, a Turkic language. They also differ in appearance and culture from the Han majority.

In addition, Hui and Uyghur people differ on several sociodemographic measures. Uyghurs, on average, are less likely to live in cities and have fewer years of education than the Hui, who are similar to the Han majority on these measures. About 17% of Uyghur people have an urban household registration, or urban hukou (户口), compared with around 40% of Hui and Han people, according to the 2020 Chinese census. Around 5%

of Uyghur adults (ages 18 and older) have a college degree or more education, while roughly 10% of Hui and Han adults are college educated.

Fertility

In the past decade, predominantly Muslim ethnic groups have grown more quickly than the majority Han population.

Between the 2010 and 2020 censuses, the number of adults in predominantly Muslim ethnic groups grew by 9% to 17.9 million, while the Han majority grew 5% to 1.02 billion.

This disparity may have resulted, at least in part, from the Chinese Government's less stringent controls on family size for minorities under the one-child policy, which was in effect from 1980 to 2016. While Han Chinese were restricted to having one child per family (or two, if they met certain conditions), ethnic minorities were allowed to have as many as three children per family.

The relatively young age structure of the Muslim population also fuels population growth: 27% of people in China's predominantly Muslim ethnic minorities are younger than 15, compared with 17% of the ethnic Han majority, according to the 2020 Chinese census.

Also, according to Chinese censuses, the total fertility rate among Uyghur women was 1.84 children per woman in 2010 and 1.99 in 2000, substantially higher than the rate among both Hui women (1.42 in 2010 and 1.53 in 2000) and Han women (1.15 in 2010 and 1.18 in 2000). Fertility rates by ethnicity from the 2020 census were not available when this report was written.

In recent years, however, there have been reports of forced birth control methods imposed on Uyghurs and other Muslim ethnic groups in Xinjiang, including mandatory pregnancy checks and sterilizations, as well as coercive IUD implantations and abortions. Scholars expect that Uyghur growth rates will slow as a result of such measures, while the rate among Han Chinese may rise after the Chinese government relaxed restrictions on family sizes, first in 2016 and again in 2021.

Beliefs and practices among Hui Muslims

Since Muslims are a small share of China's population and surveys often omit regions with large Muslim populations, data on the beliefs and practices of Chinese Muslims is sparse. For example, the CGSS has a sufficient number of respondents to reliably report on the beliefs and practices only of Hui Muslims.

In this section, we analyze 2018 CGSS figures on self-identified Hui Muslims and compare them with Chinese adults who formally identify with folk religion, Buddhism or Christianity. Because this analysis relies on respondents who chose a zongjiao xinyang in the CGSS survey – or who said a parent or spouse has a zongjiao xinyang – it excludes those who may engage with one of these religions but do not formally affiliate with it.

According to this analysis, Hui Muslims are the most likely of China's major religious groups to grow up with at least one parent who shares their religion.

Among all Hui respondents who claim Islam as their zongjiao xinyang, nearly all (96%) grew up with a Muslim mother, much higher than the rate among adults who identify with Buddhism

(52%) and self-identified Christians (31%), according to the 2018 CGSS.

This high level of religious similarity among Muslims also reflects the fact that Islam in China rarely draws converts from other religions. Likewise, the low level of similarity between Christians and their parent(s)' religion during childhood suggests that most of China's self-identified Christians come from non-Christian backgrounds.

Survey data indicates that Muslims are also the most likely of China's major religious groups to marry within their religion. Most Hui Muslim adults (96%) share the same faith as their spouse or cohabitating partner. The comparable figures are substantially lower among adults who identify with folk religion (78%), Buddhism (45%) and Christianity (38%), according to the 2018 CGSS.

Recent change in religious activity

In each of the five CGSS waves between 2010 and 2017, roughly half or more of Muslim respondents (47% to 62%) said they attend zongjiao activities at least a few times a year. In 2018, only 30% said so. This could reflect a change in the way Chinese Muslims answer survey questions in the face of increasingly restrictive government policies, or a change in actual behavior, or some of both.

For comparison, in 2018, 73% of Chinese Christians said they participated in zongjiao activities at least a few times a year, as did 51% of adherents of folk religions and 36% of Buddhists. None of these groups registered a significant decline in self-reported zongjiao participation between 2010 and 2018.

Geographic distribution of Muslims in China

Nearly all of China's Uyghurs (99%) live in one province, Xinjiang. Hui people are more widely dispersed, with an estimated 10% in Xinjiang and 42% in the other northwestern provinces of Gansu, Ningxia and Qinghai. The remaining half are scattered across the country, with a significant concentration in Henan (8%) and Yunnan (6%).

China's predominantly Muslim groups are heavily concentrated in the northwest

Distribution of Chinese Muslim-majority ethnic groups, by province

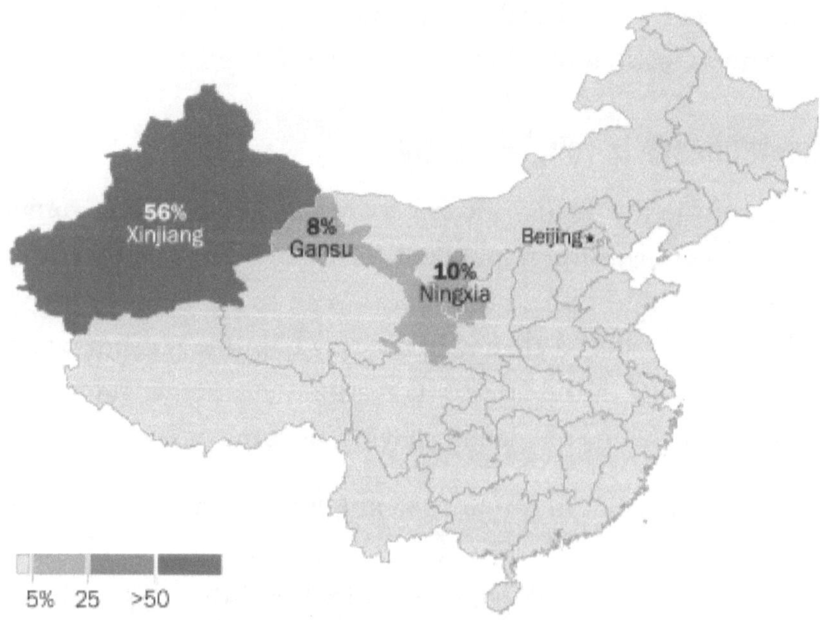

Source: Census of China, 2020. Data is only available for mainland China. "Measuring Religion in China"

PEW RESEARCH CENTER

The remaining eight predominantly Muslim ethnic groups, which make up roughly 10% of China's Muslim-majority groups – Baoan, Dongxiang, Kazakh, Kirgiz, Salar, Tajik, Tatar and Uzbek peoples – mostly reside in the northwestern provinces of Xinjiang, Gansu and Qinghai. There is a particularly heavy concentration of Kazakh, Kirgiz, Tajik, Tatar and Uzbek people in Xinjiang.

As of 2014, Xinjiang was home to 63% of China's mosques – about 24,500 of a nationwide total of 39,000 mosques, according to data from the Islamic Association of China. About one-quarter of China's mosques were in other northwestern provinces – Gansu (12%), Ningxia (11%) and Qinghai (3%) – while the remaining 11% of mosques were in other parts of the country.

Challenges of studying Islam in China

Studying Muslims in China is difficult for several reasons. The vast majority reside in the northwestern provinces of Xinjiang and Ningxia – mountainous, sparsely populated areas that are often excluded in national surveys for practical reasons. And even when Muslims are surveyed, the samples generally are too small to allow separate analysis and reporting of subgroups, such as by age cohort or gender.

Moreover, the CGSS has not been conducted in Xinjiang since 2013, which leaves no way to assess the current religious beliefs and practices of Uyghur adults in Xinjiang – an estimated 43% of all adults in China's Muslim-majority ethnic groups.

The Chinese government's treatment of Muslims adds to the challenges. Muslims who are surveyed may be guarded in their responses, while scholars who study Muslims have faced personal hardship.

For example, Ilham Tohti, a Beijing-based economist and Uyghur who criticized Chinese government policies in Xinjiang, was found guilty of "separatism" in 2014 and is serving a life sentence in prison. Rahile Dawut, a professor of Uyghur traditions at Xinjiang University, disappeared ahead of a trip to Beijing in 2017 and has not been heard from since, according to reports in The New York Times and other media.

U.S. scholars have claimed they were banned from traveling to China in connection with their work on Uyghurs. German anthropologist Adrian Zenz, whose online investigations have uncovered extensive visual evidence of conditions in Xinjiang, was sued in 2021 by Chinese companies for his work, which the Chinese Foreign Ministry described as "malicious smearing acts," The Washington Post reported.

Discussions of Muslims' views and demographic characteristics in this report are based on the CGSS, which is the only nationally representative survey with sufficient sample sizes to allow such an analysis, though the CGSS has not been conducted in Xinjiang since 2013 and CGSS data collected outside of Xinjiang includes few Uyghur respondents.

The number of Hui Muslims in the CGSS is large enough for analysis, but Hui respondents in the CGSS are so geographically concentrated that their survey estimates have large margins of sampling error on some measures. For instance, the share of Hui Muslim adults who attend religious activities once a week or more (11%) in the 2018 CGSS has a margin of error of plus or minus 8 percentage points, compared with 6 points for Christians and 2 points for Buddhists.

Sampling coverage issues in the CGSS also pose challenges to estimating the number of Muslims in China. Overall, predominantly Muslim ethnic minorities, particularly Huis, are oversampled in the CGSS even though some regions with large minority populations have been omitted in recent waves. The CGSS includes a larger share of Muslim ethnic minorities than China's census and the default CGSS weight does not correct for this imbalance. To address this issue, Center researchers adjusted the weight in the CGSS so that the share of adults in predominantly Muslim ethnic groups matches the share of those ethnic groups in the census.

Sidebar: Human rights abuses in China's Xinjiang region

The Chinese government's actions against Uyghur Muslims in the northwestern region of Xinjiang have drawn international attention and censure in recent years.

Human rights groups have accused China of subjecting hundreds of thousands of Muslims to mass internment, surveillance and torture. There have been reports of forced abortions and sterilizations, forced organ harvesting, forced relocation and labor, and forced separation of children. Amnesty International has said that China's "draconian repression of Muslims in Xinjiang amounts to crimes against humanity," and the U.S. State Department has described China's treatment of Uyghurs as genocide. In 2022, the UN High Commissioner of Human Rights issued a report saying that "serious human rights violations have been committed" in Xinjiang and that "the extent of arbitrary and discriminatory detention of members of Uyghur and other predominantly Muslim groups … may constitute international crimes, in particular crimes against humanity."

The Chinese government has denied these allegations. In July 2022, China reportedly tried to stop the release of a UN report detailing abuses against Muslims. Chinese officials have said camps in Xinjiang are for vocational education and training and are meant to counter religious extremism and poverty in the region.

Accusations of repression of Uyghurs and other Muslims by the Chinese government date back many years. In 2005, Human Rights Watch described the "systematic repression of religion … in Xinjiang as a matter of considered state policy," at a "level of punitive control seemingly designed to entirely refashion Uyghur religious identity to the state's purposes."

However, human rights groups say the crackdown intensified after the 2009 riots in Urumqi, the capital of the Xinjiang Uyghur Autonomous Region, which left nearly 200 people dead. The Chinese government labeled the riots as terrorism arising from Islamic extremism and expanded regulation and surveillance in the name of de-extremization.

Many religious practices among Uyghurs and other Muslim-majority ethnic groups in Xinjiang that previously were respected as ethnic customs now face tight regulation. For instance, the government has banned face coverings in public; made it illegal for parents to let children attend religious activities or religious schools; cracked down on "underground" Muslim schools and study groups; and increased penalties on Muslims who follow traditional Islamic marriage and divorce laws. The Chinese government also has intensified the enforcement of restrictions on the number of children allowed for Uyghur Muslims and severely punished those who exceed the limit.

For decades in the 1970s, '80s, '90s and 2000s, the government imposed a "one-child policy" that limited births among Han Chinese, a policy that was often realized with forced contraceptives, sterilization and abortions. During this period, urban Uyghur couples were allowed to have two children and rural Uyghur couples could have three children. In 2016, the Chinese government relaxed the one-child cap for most of the population while enforcing birth controls for minorities. In 2021, the policy was again adjusted to allow up to three children per couple, but with no exceptions for ethnic minorities.

Xinjiang's birthrate has fallen significantly in recent years: In 2019, the region's crude birth rate – the number of births per 1,000 people – hovered below the national average (10.5) for the first time, at 8.1, nearly half the rate three years earlier, according to the National Bureau of Statistics of China.

The decline in the birth rate is particularly pronounced in southern Xinjiang, which has a heavier concentration of ethnic minorities. For instance, between 2016 and 2018, the crude birth rate in Kashgar, a 92% Uyghur prefecture, dropped in half from 18.2 births to 7.9 per 1,000 people. These large changes in fertility patterns coincide with government interventions, which may have been designed to reduce growth in ethnically Muslim populations in Xinjiang.

Moreover, the strict prohibition on providing formal religious education to children may disrupt the intergenerational transmission of religious beliefs and practices among Muslim-majority ethnic minorities in Xinjiang and other parts of China.

Who are the Uyghurs and why is China being accused of genocide?

(Ref: BBC News)

China has been accused of committing crimes against humanity and possibly genocide against the Uyghur population and other mostly-Muslim ethnic groups in the north-western region of Xinjiang.

The Uyghurs are the largest minority ethnic group in China's north-western province of Xinjiang.

Human rights groups believe China has detained more than one million Uyghurs against their will over the past few years in a large network of what the state calls "re-education camps", and sentenced hundreds of thousands to prison terms.

A series of police files obtained by the BBC in 2022 has revealed details of China's use of these camps and described the routine use of armed officers and the existence of a shoot-to-kill policy for those trying to escape.

The US is among several countries to have previously accused China of committing genocide in Xinjiang. The leading human rights groups Amnesty and Human Rights Watch have published reports accusing China of crimes against humanity.

China denies all allegations of human rights abuses in Xinjiang. The Chinese government - speaking after details of the Xinjiang Police Files were published - said the peace and prosperity brought to Xinjiang as a result of its anti-terrorism measures were the best response to "all sorts of lies".

Who are the Uyghurs?

There are about 12 million Uyghurs, mostly Muslim, living in Xinjiang, which is officially known as the Xinjiang Uyghur Autonomous Region (XUAR).

The Uyghurs speak their own language, which is similar to Turkish, and see themselves as culturally and ethnically close to Central Asian nations. They make up less than half of the Xinjiang population.

Recent decades have seen a mass migration of Han Chinese (China's ethnic majority) into Xinjiang, allegedly orchestrated by the state to dilute the minority population there.

China has also been accused of targeting Muslim religious figures and banning religious practices in the region, as well as destroying mosques and tombs.

Uyghur activists say they fear that the group's culture is under threat of erasure.

Xinjiang is a mostly desert region and produces about a fifth of the world's cotton. Human rights groups have voiced concerns that much of that cotton export is picked by forced labour, and in 2021 some Western brands removed Xinjiang cotton from their supply chains, leading to a backlash against the brands from Chinese celebrities and netizens.

In December 2020, research seen by the BBC showed that up to half a million people were being forced to pick cotton in Xinjiang. There is evidence that new factories have been built within the grounds of the re-education camps.

The region is also rich in oil and natural gas and because of its proximity to Central Asia and Europe is seen by Beijing as an important trade link.

In the early 20th Century, the Uyghurs briefly declared independence for the region but it was brought under the complete control of China's new Communist government in 1949.

What are the allegations against China?

Several countries, including the US, UK, Canada and the Netherlands, have accused China of committing genocide - defined by international convention as the "intent to destroy, in whole or in part, a national, ethnical, racial or religious group".

The declarations follow reports that, as well as interning Uyghurs in camps, China has been forcibly mass sterilising Uyghur women to suppress the population, separating children from their families, and attempting to break the cultural traditions of the group.

The US Secretary of State, Antony Blinken, has said China is committing "genocide and crimes against humanity".

The UK parliament declared in April 2021 that China was committing a genocide in Xinjiang.

A UN human rights committee in 2018 said it had credible reports that China was holding up to a million people in "counter-extremism centres" in Xinjiang.

The Australian Strategic Policy Institute found evidence in 2020 of more than 380 of these "re-education camps" in Xinjiang, an increase of 40% on previous estimates.

Analysis of data contained in the latest police documents, called the Xinjiang Police Files, showed that almost 23,000 residents - or more than 12% of the adult population of one county - were in a camp or prison in the years 2017 and 2018. If applied to Xinjiang as a whole, the figures would mean the detention of more than 1.2 million Uyghur and other Turkic minority adults.

The UK Foreign Secretary Liz Truss said the files contained "shocking details of China's human rights violations".

Media caption,

In 2018, the BBC found all reporting was tightly controlled

Earlier, leaked documents known as the China Cables made clear that the camps were intended to be run as high security prisons, with strict discipline and punishments.

People who have managed to escape the camps have reported physical, mental and sexual torture. Women have spoken of mass rape and sexual abuse.

What was the build-up to the crackdown?

Anti-Han and separatist sentiment rose in Xinjiang from the 1990s, sometimes flaring into violence. In 2009 about 200 people died in clashes in Xinjiang, which the Chinese blamed on Uyghurs who wanted their own state. But in recent years a massive security crackdown has crushed dissent.

Xinjiang is now covered by a pervasive network of surveillance, including police, checkpoints, and cameras that scan everything from number plates to individual faces. According to Human Rights Watch, police are also using a mobile app to monitor people's behaviour, such as how much electricity they are using and how often they use their front door.

Since 2017, when President Xi Jinping issued an order saying all religions in China should be Chinese in orientation, there have been further crackdowns. Campaigners say China is trying to eradicate Uyghur culture.

The Xinjiang Police Files, which all date from before 2019, shed further light on Uyghurs being punished for alleged crimes that took place years ago. Many appear to have been targeted for their mobile phone use, for listening to "illegal lectures" or not using their phones enough, which is regarded as a sign the user is trying to evade digital surveillance.

Media caption,

China's ambassador: "There is no such concentration camp in Xinjiang"

What does China say?

China denies all allegations of human rights abuses in Xinjiang. In response to the Xinjiang Police Files, China's foreign ministry spokesman told the BBC that the documents were "the latest example of anti-China voices trying to smear China". He said Xinjiang enjoyed stability and prosperity and residents were living happy, fulfilled lives.

China says the crackdown in Xinjiang is necessary to prevent terrorism and root out Islamist extremism and the camps are an effective tool for re-educating inmates in its fight against terrorism.

It insists that Uyghur militants are waging a violent campaign for an independent state by plotting bombings, sabotage and civic unrest, but it is accused of exaggerating the threat in order to justify repression of the Uyghurs.

China has dismissed claims it is trying to reduce the Uyghur population through mass sterilisations as "baseless", and says allegations of forced labour are "completely fabricated".

Observer Research Foundation

Five years of sinification of Islam in China

Author: Ayjaz Wani

Expert Speak Raisina Debates

Published on Oct 18, 2023

In 2019, the Chinease Islamic Association (CIA) and Communist Party of China (CPC) officials met in Beijing to implement the "Five-Year Planning Outline for Persisting in the Sinification of Islam" to make Islam compatible with socialism by 2022. The conference was necessary to fulfil the objectives set forth by the 19th National Party Congress and General Secretary Xi Jinping. Xi stressed sinicisation in 2015, and by 2018, the Communist Party of China (CPC) had drawn up national plans for reconciling Islam and socialist society—implemented over the next five years. The law ensured that Islam in China reflects the nation's values and contributes to the "Core Socialist Values". According to the 32-point plan for Islam, religious extremist ideology has permeated certain areas, causing Muslims to participate in violent terrorist activities. The emergence of these problems poses a severe threat to the social stability and national security of China. Under the Law, Beijing attempted to reorient Muslims of China towards core socialist values and linked religion to a "mental illness" that needs to be cured.

The emergence of these problems poses a severe threat to the social stability and national security of China.

Muslims of China and the new law

There are approximately 25 million Muslims in China today, including Hui, Uyghurs, Kazakhs, Tatars, and others. However, the sinicisation and degree of acculturation with Hans and Chinese society vary between these groups geographically, economically, ethnically and linguistically. Islam reached China around the 7th century via trade routes, and Muslim traders settled in coastal trading hubs. They built mosques and shrines and had a brief period of social prominence during the Yuan dynasty (1279-1368). During the Ming Dynasty, the Han Chinese rulers banned outsiders and Muslims from exhibiting their culture, including hairstyles, clothing, language, and surnames. In response, the Muslims assimilated themselves with the dominant Han culture, spoke Chinese, and adopted Chinese names—were forebears of the Hui Muslims. These Hui Muslims were scattered throughout China and complied with Confucian values after Chinese rulers introduced new books from the 18th century. In 1952, the CPC translated the holy book of Muslims into Chinese to draw parallels between Islam and communism and described that both ideologies were not averse to each other.

The Muslims assimilated themselves with the dominant Han culture, spoke Chinese, and adopted Chinese names—were forebears of the Hui Muslims.

Similarly, Communist China incorporated 12 million Muslims, primarily from Uyghurs, Kazaks, and Uzbeks of the northwestern province of Xinjiang in 1949. With a contested history and centrifugal tendencies, the Xinjiang region remained under Chinese imperial control for only 425 years until 1949. Subsequently, Uyghur Muslims living in restive Xinjiang were targeted for greater sinicisation and much-needed social cohesion with Han culture. When the Cultural Revolution started from 1966 to 1976, the Uyghur customs, culture, and ideas were particularly attacked and were considered, "foreign invaders and aliens" by Mao Zedong's wife, Jiang Qing. The CPC attempted to reorient Uyghur Muslims of Xinjiang 'inwards' under mainland China's cultural influence. However, the unique geographical template of the region resulted in outside cultural influences penetrating the region, ultimately keeping it oriented outwards. Since 2017, under Xi's guidance, Uyghur Muslims have been sent to detention centres to decrease external cultural impact for offences such as violating the government's family planning policy, growing a long beard, and wearing a veil or skull cap. To suppress the population growth of the Uyghur Muslims, their women were subjected to forced sterilisation, abortions and forced implantation of intrauterine devices. These policies severely suppressed the population growth among the Uyghur Muslims of the region and the 2020 Statistical Yearbook on Xinjiang lacks birth rates and ethnic population breakthroughs for the first time.

Uyghur Muslims living in restive Xinjiang were targeted for greater sinicisation and much-needed social cohesion with Han culture.

Beijing systematically demonised Muslims all over China and viewed Islam as a threat to CPC primacy. Under the pretext of social stability, the CPC unleashed a string of human rights violations and curbed the religious freedom of Muslims. After 2019, the Hui Muslims who acclimatised to the Chinese culture in the 14th century were imprisoned, and Hui students who travelled abroad were also detained and sent to re-education camps. This constant stigma of alienation and branding of foreigners eventually led to protests. In May 2023, Hui Muslims of Yunnan province protested and clashed with hundreds of Chinese security forces against the partial demolition of the Najiaying Mosque.

China deflects global condemnation

The cultural aggression towards the Muslim minorities of China, especially in Xinjiang has been repeatedly criticised by Western democracies. CPC's treatment of Muslims in Xinjiang has been deemed as "genocide" by Canada, the United States (US), and other countries. Sanctions were imposed on the CPC officials and the US also prohibited the export of goods that could potentially be used by the CPC to further oppress the Uyghur population. The CPC and Beijing defended the suppression of Uyghur Muslims and their Islamic culture on the flimsy pretext of separatism, occasional violent extremism, and terrorism.

Sanctions were imposed on the CPC officials and the US also prohibited the export of goods that could potentially be used by the CPC to further oppress the Uyghur population.

The CIA plays a key role in promoting China's interests worldwide, especially in the Muslim world. To this end, it oversees religious outreach with Muslim countries and arranges official exchanges with Muslim leaders and institutions. The CIA's guided tours and wide-ranging religious engagement have proven to be effective tools for China in deflecting criticism from major Muslim nations concerning its internal prosecution of Muslims. By promoting an Islamic soft power and building relations with Muslim nations through the CIA, China has been able to deflect criticism and present a more positive image of its policies towards Muslim minorities.

XI uses sinicisation to consolidate power

President Xi has strengthened his grip on power through a comprehensive campaign to eliminate officials who are deemed disloyal, corrupt, or ineffective. He has filled the National Congress of CPC with his allies, and loyalists, thereby, solidifying his power base within the Politburo and the Politburo Standing Committee. On the other side, to retain his grip over Chinese society, Xi frequently expressed concerns about Islam and its traditions. Subsequently, the sinicisation law among Muslim minorities was used by the CPC to consolidate political power and elevate Xi's status as an autocratic populist in China. For this hardened approach against Muslim minorities, Xi has received public commendation throughout China.

The sinicisation law among Muslim minorities was used by the CPC to consolidate political power and elevate Xi's status as an autocratic populist in China.

While the CPC uses the Islamic threat for parochial gains, however, the sinification has created a paradox where the Hui

Muslim minorities continue to be stigmatised due to their perceived foreign origin despite centuries of cultural assimilation. Despite the Chinese anti-Muslim campaign has ultimately led to cultural genocide, Xi still stresses on deepening control over "illegal religious activities" to preserve the "hard-won social stability".

*****

Ayjaz Wani *is a Fellow with the Strategic Studies Programme at the Observer Research Foundation.*

Xinjiang: New frontier

Most Uighurs in China live in the region called Xinjiang, a Chinese term to mean "new frontier" or "borderland".

Because of its location along the ancient Silk Road, Xinjiang has a long history of cross-migration by different minority groups.

In China, it has been officially referred to as the Xinjiang Uighur Autonomous Region (XUAR) since 1955. Other ethnic groups including Han Chinese, Kazakhs, Kyrgyz, Mongols, Tajiks, Uzbeks and Tatars also live in the area.

Located in China's far northwest, Xinjiang covers more than 1.6 million sq km (617,763 sq miles) comparable to Iran in terms of land area. It is the largest region of China and makes up about a sixth of the country's entire land area. It is rich in oil and natural gas and boasts a natural beauty that has attracted international filmmakers.

In 1933, an independent East Turkestan was briefly declared by the then-majority Uighurs, but its borders were unsettled and its army was soon defeated by nationalist Chinese led by Chiang Kai-shek.

A second East Turkestan republic was declared in 1944 with Soviet backing. But in 1949, China's new Communist rulers who had defeated Chiang in the civil war annexed the region with the nod of Joseph Stalin, the then Soviet leader, ending the Uighurs' dream of an independent homeland.

Beijing insists it has an ancient claim to Xinjiang – dating back to 206BC – and considers it an "inseparable part of the Chinese nation".

Uighurs disagree, saying that borders in the region have been drawn and redrawn for centuries, depending on the dominant power, including the Mongols and the Turkic Karakhanid. Overseas Uighurs also say that their religion, language and cultural practices clearly distinguish Xinjiang from the rest of China.

'History written by winners'

Indiana University Professor Bovingdon Gardner, author of the book The Uyghurs: Stranger in Their Own Land, says that when it comes to the issue of sovereignty "there isn't any universal agreement on what constitutes sovereign claim of a territory" for the Uighurs.

"So there's no lever with which to sort of pry [prise] apart the claims" of China and the Uighurs.

Dru Gladney, a professor and expert on Uighur studies who is now affiliated with Pomona College in California, adds that "history is always written by the conquerors".

But he notes that even in the Chinese language, Beijing refers to Xinjiang as a "new frontier".

"So the very name suggests that it's new to China, and its own history shows that the region was rarely completely under Chinese control," he said.

Since 1949, when Mao Zedong's communist army took control of Xinjiang, out-migration has increased substantially, with Uighurs leaving the region to escape political and religious repression, leading to a gradual decline of their once majority population.

Other waves of migration occurred during the great famines of the 1950s and 60s, followed by Mao's bloody Cultural Revolution, which saw many intellectuals purged or summarily executed.

Hundreds of thousands, if not millions, of Uighurs and other Muslim minority groups eventually escaped to neighbouring Central Asian countries, including Kazakhstan, Kyrgyzstan, Tajikistan and Uzbekistan. Others fled to Afghanistan and Turkey.

Following renewed political tensions in recent years, thousands of refugees escaped to Europe, while more than 1,000 eventually made it across the Atlantic to the United States. The Uighur population in the US have since increased to at least 9,000 in 2015.

Meanwhile, millions of Han Chinese started resettling in Xinjiang with Beijing's encouragement, and they now make up the second-largest ethnic group in the region, diluting the dominance of the Uighur population in their own homeland and creating new sources of tension.

At the same time, human rights observers have also accused Beijing of rolling out birth-control policies targeting Uighurs and other minority groups, aiming to cut 2.6-4.5 million births within 20 years.

'Bogeyman of anti-terror fight'

In early 2017, shortly before the mass arrests and re-education programmes were rolled out by Beijing, Zhu Hailun, then head of the Xinjiang Communist Party Political and Legal Affairs Commission, was quoted as saying that with the "powerful fist" of the Chinese government, "all separatist activities and all terrorists shall be smashed to pieces" in Xinjiang.

Months later, the unprecedented crackdown on the Uighurs began. Chinese President Xi Jinping had also said in 2017 that all religions in the country should have a Chinese orientation in line with his policy of "Sinification".

At the crux of the strained relations, scholars say, is the Uighurs' desire for a homeland and to express their identity and China's determination to impose total control – from the way people worship to how many children they should have and what they should eat – anxious of the potential risk not only to the country's territorial integrity but also the dominance of the Communist Party.

The authorities also closely control the Catholic Church in China, and put pressure on regions such as Tibet, where the Dalai Lama was forced into exile after the territory was annexed in 1950. Beijing has also insisted that it will choose the next Dalai Lama.

In a 2009 Democracy Now interview, Nury Turkel, former president of the Uyghur American Association, called the Uighurs "the other Tibetans you never heard of".

The tensions have been building over time, sometimes erupting into violence.

In the 1990s, there were attacks linked to the East Turkestan Islamic Movement (ETIM), a group advocating for violence to create an independent state of East Turkestan to replace Xinjiang.

In February 1997, hundreds of peaceful protesters were allegedly shot to death by Chinese soldiers in what Uighurs now call the Gulja massacre, referring to the city near the border with Kazakhstan.

The 9/11 attacks on New York and the so-called US "war against terror" that stretched from Iraq to Afghanistan and Pakistan, which partly borders Xinjiang, eventually led Beijing to launch its own campaign against "extremism" targeting Uighurs, calling any protests in the region an act of "separatism".

In the regional capital, Urumqi, many Uighurs were reported killed in 2009 in clashes that Beijing blamed on Uighurs. Then in July 2011 clashes between Uighurs and Han Chinese in the ancient city of Kashgar killed 14 people and injured 40 others.

The crackdown gradually became more intense with Uighur activists and even scholars denounced as Muslim "terrorists" and thrown in jail or hastily sentenced to death. Uighurs, who had travelled abroad and later returned to China, were suspected of promoting "extreme" views and interrogated.

What is life like in Xinjiang?

In a report in June, Amnesty International described life in Xinjiang as a "dystopian hellscape", with former detainees revealing torture and other rights abuses committed "in an effort to forcibly instill a secular, homogeneous Chinese nation" according to the ideals of the country's Communist Party.

Surveillance in Xinjiang is also pervasive with countless camera monitors installed in big cities, such as the capital, Urumqi, making it impossible for journalists to speak to Uighurs, without them risking possible arrest.

A 2019 report by Human Rights Watch (HRW) said the government was using a mobile application to store data of Uighurs and other Turkic Muslims, in order to monitor their movement through facial recognition.

The goal is apparently "to identify patterns of, and predict, the everyday life and resistance" of Xinjiang's population, "and ultimately, to engineer and control reality". Using technology, residents are also being flagged for their relationships, their communications, their travel histories, or for being related to someone the authorities consider as suspicious, HRW said.

There have also been reports of the government banning Muslims from fasting during Ramadan, or women wearing veils and men growing their beards long. Muslims were also reportedly forced to eat pork, which is prohibited in Islam.

In 2020, an investigation conducted by the Australian Strategic Policy Institute (ASPI), using satellite imagery and ground reporting, also revealed "thousands of mosques" in the region have either been damaged or destroyed in just three years.

In response, China said the governments at various levels in Xinjiang "have consistently improved the public services of mosques", but did not address the specific allegations of ASPI.

What does China say?

China has vehemently denied the accusations of genocide and other abuses, insisting that the policy of Xi Jinping towards Uighurs is aimed at "tackling extremism", while giving minorities the skills to become more employable and contribute to the economy.

In a previous interview with Al Jazeera, Einar Tangen, a political analyst who advises the Chinese government, told Al Jazeera that Beijing considers re-education and training a necessary measure to address poverty.

"This is not something that they are doing because they are trying to be mean to the Uighurs. They actually think that this is helping. They [Beijing] cannot afford to have people who have no future. It is not just about terrorism. They are really anti-poverty."

In another interview with Al Jazeera, Tangen said the economic situation in Xinjiang had "improved dramatically over the years" and people there were better off.

"People live longer. They have better opportunities," he said.

In a recent article published by Xinhua, the government said its programme against "extremism" in Xinjiang was in compliance "with the principles and spirit of a series of international counter-terrorism resolutions, including the UN Global Counter-Terrorism Strategy".

It says that because of its counterterrorism and "deradicalisation measures", there have been "no violent terrorist cases for over four consecutive years in the region".

Beijing added that since 2018, 151,000 people in "poverty-stricken families in southern Xinjiang" have secured jobs away from their homes, most of them working in other parts of the region, while almost 15,000 are working in other parts of China.

The government said many now earn an annual income of 45,000 yuan ($7,000), several times higher than what they would have earned from farming or working in their hometowns.

"Xinjiang-related issues are not about human rights, ethnicity or religion at all, but about combating violent terrorism and separatism."

Source: Al Jazeera

Chapter 5

Russia

Islam is a major religious minority in the Russian Federation, which has the largest Muslim population in Europe. According to the US Department of State in 2017, Muslims in Russia numbered 14 million or roughly 10% of the total population. One of the Grand Muftis of Russia, sheikh Rawil Gaynetdin, estimated the Muslim population of Russia at 25 million in 2018.

Recognized under the law and by Russian political leaders as one of Russia's traditional religions, Islam is a part of Russian historical heritage, and is subsidized by the Russian government. The position of Islam as a major Russian religion, alongside Orthodox Christianity, dates from the time of Catherine the Great, who sponsored Islamic clerics and scholarship through the Orenburg Assembly.

The history of Islam and Russia encompasses periods of conflict between the Muslim minority and the Orthodox majority, as well as periods of collaboration and mutual support. Robert Crews's study of Muslims living under the Tsar indicates that "the mass of Muslims" was loyal to that regime after Catherine, and sided with it over the Ottoman Empire. After the Russian Empire fell, the Soviet Union introduced a policy of state atheism, which impeded the practice of Islam and other religions and led to the execution and suppression of various Muslim leaders. Following the collapse of the Soviet Union, Islam regained a legally recognized space in Russian politics. Despite having made Islamophobic comments during the Second Chechen War, President Vladimir Putin has since subsidized mosques and Islamic education, which he called an "integral part of Russia's cultural code", and encouraged immigration from Muslim-majority former Soviet states.

Muslims form a majority of the population of the republics of Tatarstan and Bashkortostan in the Volga Federal District and predominate among the nationalities in the North Caucasian Federal District located between the Black Sea and the Caspian Sea: the Circassians, Balkars, Chechens, Ingush, Kabardin, Karachay, and numerous Dagestani peoples. Also, in the middle of the Volga Region reside populations of Tatars and Bashkirs, the vast majority of whom are Muslims. Other areas with notable Muslim minorities include Moscow, Saint Petersburg, the republics of Adygea, North Ossetia-Alania and Astrakhan, Moscow, Orenburg and Ulyanovsk Oblasts. There are over 5,000 registered religious Muslim organizations, equivalent to over one sixth of the number of registered Russian Orthodox religious organizations of about 29,268 as of December 2006.

History

In the mid-7th century AD, as part of the Muslim conquest of Persia, Islam was introduced to the Caucasus region, parts of which were later permanently incorporated by Russia. The first people to become Muslims within current Russian territory, the Dagestani people (region of Derbent), converted after the Arab conquest of the region in the 8th century. The first Muslim state in the future Russian lands was Volga Bulgaria (922). The Tatars of the Khanate of Kazan inherited the population of believers from that state. Later most of the European and Caucasian Turkic peoples also became followers of Islam. The Mongol rulers of the Golden Horde were Muslims from 1313. By the 1330s, three of the four major khanates of the Mongol Empire had become Muslim.

The Tatars of the Crimean Khanate, the last remaining successor to the Golden Horde, continued to raid Southern Russia and burnt down parts of Moscow in 1571. Until the late 18th century, the Crimean Tatars maintained a massive slave-trade with the Ottoman Empire and the Middle East, exporting about 2 million slaves from Russia and Ukraine over the period 1500–1700.

From the early 16th century up to and including the 19th century, all of Transcaucasia and southern Dagestan was ruled by various successive Iranian empires (the Safavids, Afsharids, and the Qajars), and their geopolitical and ideological neighboring arch-rivals, on the other hand, the Ottoman Turks. In the respective areas they ruled, in both the North Caucasus and South Caucasus, Shia Islam and Sunni Islam spread, resulting in a fast and steady conversion of many more ethnic Caucasian peoples in adjacent territories.

The period from the Russian conquest of Kazan in 1552 by Ivan the Terrible to the ascension of Catherine the Great in 1762 featured systematic Russian repression of Muslims through policies of exclusion and discrimination - as well as the destruction of Muslim culture by the elimination of outward manifestations of Islam such as mosques. The Russians initially demonstrated a willingness in allowing Islam to flourish as Muslim clerics were invited into the various regions to preach to the Muslims, particularly the Kazakhs, whom the Russians viewed with contempt. However, Russian policy shifted toward weakening Islam by introducing pre-Islamic elements of collective consciousness. Such attempts included methods of eulogizing pre-Islamic historical figures and imposing a sense of inferiority by sending Kazakhs to highly élite Russian military institutions. In response, Kazakh religious leaders attempted to bring religious fervor by espousing pan-Turkism, though many were persecuted as a result. The government of Russia paid Islamic scholars from the Ural-Volga area working among the Kazakhs.

Islamic slavery did not have racial restrictions. Russian girls were legally allowed to be sold in Russian-controlled Novgorod to Tatars from Kazan in the 1600s by Russian law. Germans, Poles, and Lithuanians were allowed to be sold to Crimean Tatars in Moscow. In 1665, Tatars were allowed to buy Polish and Lithuanian slaves from the Russians. Before 1649, Russians could be sold to Muslims under Russian law in Moscow. This contrasted with other places in Europe outside Russia where Muslims were not allowed to own Christians.

The Cossack Hetmanate recruited and incorporated Muslim Mishar Tatars. Cossack rank was awarded to Bashkirs. Muslim Turkics and Buddhist Kalmyks served as Cossacks. The Cossack Ural, Terek, Astrakhan, and Don Cossack hosts had Kalmyks in their ranks. Mishar Muslims, Teptiar Muslims, service Tatar Muslims, and Bashkir Muslims joined the Orenburg Cossack Host. Cossack non-Muslims shared the same status with Siberian Cossack Muslims. Muslim Cossacks in Siberia requested an Imam. Cossacks in Siberia included Tatar Muslims like in Bashkiria.

Bashkirs and Kalmyks in the Imperial Russian Army fought against Napoleon's Grande Armée during the French invasion of Russia. They were judged suitable for inundating opponents but not intense fighting. They were in a non-standard capacity in the military. Arrows, bows, and melee combat weapons were wielded by the Muslim Bashkirs. Bashkir women fought among the regiments. Denis Davidov mentioned the arrows and bows wielded by the Bashkirs. Napoleon's forces faced off against Kalmyks on horseback. Napoleon faced light mounted Bashkir forces. Mounted Kalmyks and Bashkirs numbering 100 were available to Russian commandants during the war against Napoleon. Kalmyks and Bashkirs served in the Russian army in France. A nachalnik was present in every one of the 11 cantons of the Bashkir host which was created by Russia after the Pugachev Rebellion. Bashkirs had the military statute of 1874 applied to them. Muslims were exempt from military conscription during World War I.

While total expulsion (as practiced in other Christian nations such as Spain, Portugal and Sicily) was not feasible to achieve a homogeneous Russian-Orthodox population, other policies such as land grants and the promotion of migration by other Russian and non-Muslim populations into Muslim lands displaced many Muslims, making them minorities in places such as some parts of the South Ural region and encouraging emigration to other parts such as the Ottoman Empire and neighboring Persia, and almost annihilating the Circassians, Crimean Tatars, and various Muslims of the Caucasus. The Russian army rounded up people, driving Muslims from their villages to ports on the Black Sea, where they awaited ships provided by the neighboring Ottoman Empire. The explicit Russian goal involved expelling the groups in question from their lands. They were given a choice as to where to be resettled: in the Ottoman Empire, in Persia, or Russia far from their old lands. The Russo-Circassian War ended with the signing of loyalty oaths by Circassian leaders on 2 June 1864. Afterward, the Ottoman Empire offered to harbor the Circassians who did not wish to accept the rule of a Christian monarch, and many emigrated to Anatolia (the heart of the Ottoman Empire) and ended up in modern Turkey, Syria, Jordan, Palestine, Iraq, and Kosovo. Many other Caucasian Muslims ended up in neighboring Iran - sizeable numbers of Shia Lezgins, Azerbaijanis, Muslim Georgians, Kabardins, and Laks. Various Russian, Caucasus, and Western historians agree on the figure of c. 500,000 inhabitants of the highland Caucasus being deported by Russia in the 1860s. A large proportion of them died in transit from disease. Those that remained loyal to Russia were settled into the lowlands, on the left bank of the Kuban' River. The trend of Russification has continued at different paces in the rest of Tsarist and Soviet periods, so that as of 2014 more Tatars lived outside the Republic of Tatarstan than inside it.

A policy of deliberately enforcing anti-modern, traditional, ancient conservative Islamic education in schools and Islamic ideology was enforced by the Russians in order to deliberately hamper and destroy opposition to their rule by keeping them in a state of torpor to and prevent foreign ideologies from penetrating in.

Communist rule oppressed and suppressed Islam, like other religions in the Soviet Union. Many mosques (for some estimates, more than 83% in Tatarstan) were closed. For example, the Märcani Mosque was the only acting mosque in Kazan at that time.

Islam in the post-Soviet period

There was much evidence of official conciliation toward Islam in Russia in the 1990s. The number of Muslims allowed to make pilgrimages to Mecca increased sharply after the embargo of the Soviet era ended in 1991. In 1995, the newly established Union of Muslims of Russia, led by Imam Khatyb Mukaddas of Tatarstan, began organizing a movement aimed at improving inter-ethnic understanding and ending lingering misconceptions of Islam among non-Muslim Russians. The Union of Muslims of Russia is the direct successor to the pre-World War I Union of Muslims, which had its own faction in the Russian Duma. The post-Communist union formed a political party, the Nur All-Russia Muslim Public Movement, which acts in close coordination with Muslim imams to defend the political, economic, and cultural rights of Muslims. The Islamic Cultural Center of Russia, which includes a madrassa (religious school), opened in Moscow in 1991. In the 1990s, the number of Islamic publications has increased. Among them are few magazines in Russian, namely: "И с л а м" (transliteration: Islam), "Э х о   К а в к а з а" (Ekho Kavkaza) and "И с л а м с к и й   в е с т н и к" (Islamsky Vestnik), and the Russian-language newspaper "А с с а л а м" (Assalam), and "Н у р у л ь   И с л а м" (Nurul Islam), which are published in Makhachkala, Dagestan.

Kazan has a large Muslim population (probably the second after Moscow urban group of the Muslims and the biggest indigenous group in Russia) and is home to the Russian Islamic University in Kazan, Tatarstan. Education is in Russian and Tatar. In Dagestan there are number of Islamic universities and madrassas, notable among them are: Dagestan Islamic University, Institute of Theology and International Relations, whose rector Maksud Sadikov was assassinated on 8 June 2011.

Talgat Tadzhuddin was the Chief Mufti of Russia. Since Soviet times, the Russian government has divided Russia into a number of Muslim Spiritual Directorates. In 1980, Tazhuddin was made Mufti of the European USSR and Siberia Division. Since 1992, he has headed the central or combined Muslim Spiritual Directorate of all of Russia.

In 2005, Russia was granted the status of an observer state in the Organisation of Islamic Cooperation.

Russian president Vladimir Putin has said that Orthodox Christianity is much closer to Islam than Catholicism is.

A chain e-mail spread a hoax speech attributed to Putin which called for tough assimilation policies on immigrants, no evidence of any such speech can be found in Russian media or Duma archives.

Russian Muslim soldiers killed in the Russo-Ukrainian War in 2022. The ethnically non-Russian republics of the Russian Federation suffered heavy losses in the war in Ukraine. Islam has been expanding under Putin's rule. Tatar Muslims are engaging in a revival under Putin.

According to The Washington Post, "Russian Muslims are split regarding the [Russian] intervention in Syria, but more are pro- than anti-war." The Grand Mufti of Russia, Talgat Tadzhuddin and other Russia's Muslim leaders supported the Russian invasion of Ukraine. Chechnya's Kadyrovite forces have fought alongside the Russian forces in Ukraine.

After a Quran burning incident that happened in Sweden during Eid al-Adha, Russian president Vladimir Putin defended the Quran by stating that It's a crime in Russia to disrespect the Quran and other holy books.

Islam in the North Caucasus

In the late 1980s and early 1990s, the Northern Caucasus experienced an Islamic (as well as a national) renaissance. Also radical and extremist streams of Islam started taking root, initially in western (upland) Dagestan.

In 1991, Chechnya declared independence as the Chechen Republic of Ichkeria. Russian Army forces were commanded into Grozny in 1994, but, after two years of intense fighting, the Russian troops eventually withdrew from Chechnya under the Khasavyurt Accord. Chechnya preserved its de facto independence until 1999. However, the Chechen government's grip on Chechnya was weak, especially outside the ruined capital Grozny. The areas controlled by separatist groups grew larger and the country became increasingly lawless. Aslan Maskhadov's government was unable to rebuild the region or to prevent a number of warlords from taking effective control. The relationship between the government and radicals deteriorated. In March 1999, Maskhadov closed down the Chechen parliament and introduced aspects of Sharia. Despite this concession, extremists such as Shamil Basayev and the Saudi-born Islamist Ibn Al-Khattab continued to undermine the Maskhadov government. In April 1998, the group publicly declared that its long-term aim was the creation of a union of Chechnya and Dagestan under Islamic rule and the expulsion of Russians from the entire Caucasian Region. This eventually led to the invasion of militants in Dagestan and the start of the Second Chechen War in 1999. The Chechen separatists were internally divided between the Islamic extremists, the more moderate pro-independent Muslim Chechens and the traditional Islamic authorities with various positions towards Chechen independence. An interim Russian-controlled administration was imposed in Chechnya in 2000, headed by the ex-Mufti and, therefore, religious leader of Sufism, Akhmad Kadyrov. Encouraged by the Russian strategy of using the traditional Islamic structures and leaders against the Islamic extremists, there was a process of religious radicalisation in Chechnya and other Northern Caucasus regions.

At the end of the Second Chechen War, in 2005, Chechen rebel leader, Abdul-Halim Sadulayev, decreed the formation of a Caucasus Front against Russia, among Islamic believers in the North Caucasus, in an attempt to widen Chechnya's conflict with Russia. After his death, his successor, Dokka Umarov, declared continuing jihad to establish an Islamic fundamentalist Caucasus Emirate in the North Caucasus and beyond. Insurgency in the North Caucasus continued until 2017. The police and the FSB carried out mass arrests and used harsh interrogation techniques. Some of those who closely followed the teachings of Islam have lost their jobs; mosques have also been closed.

Russian president Vladimir Putin has allowed the de facto implementation of Sharia law in Chechnya by Ramzan Kadyrov, including polygamy and enforced veiling.

There was large anger from mostly Muslims from the Caucasus against the Charlie Hebdo cartoons in France. Putin is believed to have backed protests by Muslims in Russia against Charlie Hebdo cartoons and the West.

Demographics and Branches

More than 90% of Muslims in Russia adhere to Sunni Islam of the Hanafi and Shafi'i schools. In a few areas, notably Dagestan, Chechnya and Ingushetia, there is a tradition of Sunni Sufism, which is represented by Qadiriyya, Naqshbandi and Shadhili orders. Naqshbandi–Shadhili spiritual master Said Afandi al-Chirkawi received hundreds of visitors daily.

Baku Mosque in Astrakhan, former Sunni, presently belonging to the Twelver Shia community.

About 10%, or more than two million, are Shia Muslims, mostly of Twelver Shi'ism branch. At first, they are the Azeris, who historically and still currently been nominally followers of Shi'a Islam, as their republic split off from the Soviet Union, significant number of Azeris immigrated to Russia in search of work. In addition to them, some of the indigenous peoples of Dagestan, such as the Lezgins (a minority) and the Tats (a majority), are Shias too. Nizari Isma'ili Muslims—another Shia branch—are represented only by the Pamiris, migrants from Tajikistan.

There is also an active presence of Ahmadis.

In 2021, Putin announced that some 20% of Russian aviation industry employees are Muslims.

Conversions

Most Muslims in Russia belong to ethnic minorities but in the recent years there have been conversions among the Russian majority as well, one of the country's main Islamic institutions, the Moscow-based Spiritual Administration of Muslims of the Russian Federation (DUM RF) estimating the ethnic Russian converts to number into the "tens of thousands" while some converts themselves give numbers between 50,000 and 70,000.

Hajj

A record 18,000 Russian Muslim pilgrims from all over the country attended the Hajj in Mecca, Saudi Arabia in 2006. In 2010, at least 20,000 Russian Muslim pilgrims attended the Hajj, as Russian Muslim leaders sent letters to the King of Saudi Arabia requesting that the Saudi visa quota be raised to at least 25,000–28,000 visas for Muslims. Due to overwhelming demand from Russian Muslims, on 5 July 2011, Muftis requested President Dmitry Medvedev's assistance in increasing the allocated by Saudi Arabia pilgrimage quota in Vladikavkaz. The III International Conference on Hajj Management attended by some 170 delegates from 12 counties was held in Kazan from 7 – 9 July 2011.

Language controversies

For centuries, the Tatars constituted the only Muslim ethnic group in European Russia, with Tatar language being the only language used in their mosques, a situation which saw rapid change over the course of the 20th century as a large number of Caucasian and Central Asian Muslims migrated to central Russian cities and began attending Tatar-speaking mosques, generating pressure on the imams of such mosques to begin using Russian. This problem is evident even within Tatarstan itself, where Tatars constitute a majority.

Public perception of Muslims

A survey published in 2019 by the Pew Research Center found that 76% of Russians had a favourable view of Muslims in their country, whereas 19% had an unfavourable view.

Islam in Moscow

According to the 2010 Russian census, Moscow has less than 300,000 permanent residents of Muslim background, while some estimates suggest that Moscow has around 1 million Muslim residents and up to 1.5 million more Muslim migrant workers. The city has permitted the existence of four mosques. The mayor of Moscow claims that four mosques are sufficient for the population. The city's economy "could not manage without them," he said. There are currently four mosques in Moscow, and 8,000 in the whole of Russia. Muslim migrants from Central Asia have had an impact on the culture with Samsa becoming one of the most popular take away foods in the city.

List of Russian muftiates

All-Russia boards			
Grand Muftiates	**Grand Muftis**	**Term of office**	**Head-quarters**
The Central Spiritual Administration of the Muslims of Russia	Sheikh-ul-Islam Talgat Tadzhuddin	1992–present	Ufa
The Spiritual Administration of the Muslims of Russian Federation	Sheikh Rawil Ğaynetdin	2014–present	Moscow
Muftiate	**Mufti**	**Term of office**	**Head-quarters**
The Spiritual Assembly of the Muslims of Russia	Albir Krganov	2016–present	Moscow

Interregional boards

Muftiates	Muftis	Term of office	Headquarters
The Coordinating Center of North Caucasus Muslims	Ismail Berdiyev	2003–present	Moscow and Buynaksk
The Spiritual Administration of the Muslims of the Asian Part of Russia	Nafigulla Ashirov	1997–present	Moscow and Tobolsk

Notable regional muftiates

Muftiates	Muftis	Term of office	Headquarters
The Muftiate of the Republic of Dagestan	Sheikh Ahmad Afandi Abdulaev	1998–present	Makhach-kala
The Spiritual Administration of the Muslims of the Republic of Adygea and Krasnodar Krai	Askarbiy Kardanov	2012–present	Maykop

Notable regional muftiates

Muftiates	Muftis	Term of office	Headquarters
The Spiritual Administration of the Muslims of the Republic of Bashkortostan	Ainur Birgalin	2019–present	Ufa
The Spiritual Administration of the Muslims of the Chechen Republic	Salah Mezhiev	2014–present	Grozny
The Spiritual Administration of the Muslims of the Republic of Ingushetia	Sheikh Muhammed Al-boghatchiev		Magas
The Spiritual Administration of the Muslims of the Kabardino-Balkarian Republic	Hazrataliy Dzasejev	2010–present	Nalchik

Notable regional muftiates

Muftiates	Muftis	Term of office	Headquarters
The Spiritual Administration of the Muslims of the Karachay-Cherkess Republic	Ismail Berdiyev	1991–present	Cherkessk
The Spiritual Administration of the Muslims of the Republic of North Ossetia–Alania	Khajimurat Gatsalov	2011–present	Vladika-vkaz
The Spiritual Administration of the Muslims of the Republic of Tatarstan	Kamil Samigullin	2013–present	Kazan

Notable Russian Muslims

- Khabib Nurmagomedov is a former professional mixed martial artist.

- Islam Makhachev is a professional mixed martial artist and current UFC undisputed lightweight champion.

- Usman Nurmagomedov is a professional mixed martial artist.

- Umar Nurmagomedov is a professional mixed martial artist.

- Rudolf Nureyev was considered the greatest male ballet dancer of his generation.

- Marat Safin a former world No. 1 tennis player.

- Vyacheslav Polosin was a former Russian Orthodox Church priest who was at the forefront of a campaign to make Orthodox Christmas a public holiday in Russia and converted to Islam in 1999.

- Alina Zagitova is a figure skater.

- Shamil Musaev is a freestyle wrestler.

- Movlid Khaybulaev is a professional mixed martial artist.

- Movsar Evloev is a mixed martial artist, who is currently competing in the featherweight division of the UFC. A professional since 2014, he has also competed at 1 Global, where he is the former bantamweight.

- Imam Shamil was a political leader and Imam of Dagestan, who resisted against Russian expansion of the Caucasus.

- Ramazan Ramazanov is a kickboxer.

Chapter 6

Japan

The history of Islam in Japan is relatively brief in relation to the religion's longstanding presence in other nearby countries, and forms a minority of its historical and current population. Islam is one of the smallest minority faiths in Japan, representing around 0.18% of the total population as of 2019. Despite a small initial population base, immigration from Muslim majority countries has made Islam one of the fastest growing religions in the country in terms of percentage increase, with its followers growing by approximately 110%, from 110,000 in 2010 to 230,000 at the end of 2019, out of the total population of Japan of around 126 million.

While there were isolated occasions of Muslim presence in Japan before the 19th century, today, approximately 90% of Muslims in Japan are of foreign origin, with the rest being native Japanese converts.

History

Early history

There are isolated records of contact between Islam and Japan before the opening of the country in 1853, possibly as early as the 1700s; some Muslims did arrive in earlier centuries, although these were isolated incidents. Some elements of Islamic philosophy were also distilled as far as back as the Heian period through Chinese and Southeast Asian sources.

The earliest Muslim records of Japan can be found in the works of the Persian cartographer Ibn Khordadbeh, who has been understood by Michael Jan de Goeje to mention Japan as the "lands of Waqwaq" twice: "East of China are the lands of Waqwaq, which are so rich in gold that the inhabitants make the chains for their dogs and the collars for their monkeys of this metal. They manufacture tunics woven with gold. Excellent ebony wood is found there." And: "Gold and ebony are exported from Waqwaq." Mahmud Kashgari's 11th century atlas indicates the land routes of the Silk Road and Japan in the map's easternmost extent.

The first recorded Muslim in history to go to Japan was Sadr ud-Din, sent by Yuan China in 1275 as a diplomatic delegation ordering the Japanese to submit to the Yuan emperor between the two Mongol invasions of Japan. He was beheaded by the Japanese. A Buddhist monk criticised the executions of the envoys.

The Persian historian Rashid al-Din Hamadani mentioned Japan twice in his historical work Jami' al-tawarikh as Jimingu and described it having many cities and mines.

During that period there was contact between the Hui, general Lan Yu of the Ming dynasty and the swordsmiths of Japan. According to Chinese sources, Lan Yu owned 10,000 Katana, Hongwu Emperor was displeased with the general's links with Kyoto and more than 15,000 people were implicated for alleged treason and executed. Lan Yu's ethnicity is disputed with some Hui claiming he was Hui but his biography in official Ming records do not mention him being Hui.

In the 13th century, a manuscript written by Persians from Quanzhou in China for the Japanese monk Keisei was brought back to Japan.

Early European accounts of Muslims and their contacts with Japan were maintained by Portuguese sailors who mention a passenger aboard their ship, an Arab who had preached Islam to the people of Japan. He had sailed to the islands in Malacca in 1555.

In the 17th century, Iranian merchants from Thailand arrived to Nagasaki during the Edo period. The Iranian Shaykh Ahmad fought and defeated Japanese merchants who attempted a coup against the Thai king in 1611. In the 17th century text Safine-ye Solaymani, Shia writer Mohammad Ibrahim described Japan and its culture, economy, recent political upheavals and their relationship with foreign merchants.

Modern records

In the late 1870s, the biography of Muhammad was translated into Japanese. This helped Islam spread and reach the Japanese people, but only as a part of the history of cultures.

Another important contact was made in 1890 when Sultan and Caliph Abdul Hamid II of the Ottoman Empire dispatched a naval vessel to Japan for the purpose of saluting the visit of Japanese Prince Komatsu Akihito to the capital of Constantinople several years earlier. This frigate was called the Ertugrul, and was destroyed in a storm on the way back along the coast of Wakayama Prefecture on September 16, 1890. The Kushimoto Turkish Memorial and Museum are dedicated in honor of the drowned diplomats and sailors.

In 1891, an Ottoman crew who were shipwrecked on the Japanese coast the previous year were assisted in their return to Constantinople by the Imperial Japanese navy. Shotaro Noda, a journalist who accompanied them, became the earliest known Japanese convert during his stay in the Ottoman capital.

Early 20th century

In the wake of the October Revolution, several hundred Tatar Muslim refugees from Central Asia and Russia were given asylum in Japan, settling in several main cities and formed small communities. Some Japanese converted to Islam through contact with these Muslims. Historian Caeser E. Farah documented that in 1909 the Russian-born Ayaz İshaki and writer Abdurreshid Ibrahim (1857–1944), were the first Muslims who successfully converted the first ethnic Japanese, when Kotaro Yamaoka converted in 1909 in Bombay after contacting Ibrahim and took the name Omar Yamaoka. Yamaoka became the first Japanese to go on the Hajj. Yamaoka and Ibrahim were traveling with the support of nationalistic Japanese groups like Black Dragon Society (Kokuryūkai). Yamaoka in fact had been with the intelligence service in Manchuria since the Russo-Japanese war. His official reason for traveling was to seek the Ottoman Sultan and Caliph's approval for building a mosque in Tokyo. This approval was granted in 1910. The Tokyo Mosque, was finally completed on 12 May 1938, with generous financial support from the zaibatsu. Its first imams were Abdul-Rashid Ibrahim and Abdülhay Kurban Ali (Muhammed-Gabdulkhay Kurbangaliev) (1889–1972). However, Japan's first mosque, the Kobe Mosque was built in 1935, with the support of the Turko-Tatar community of traders there. On 12 May 1938, a mosque was dedicated in Tokyo. Another early Japanese convert was Bunpachiro Ariga, who about the same time as Yamaoka went to India for trading purposes and converted to Islam under the influence of local Muslims there, and subsequently took the name Ahmed Ariga. Yamada Toajiro was for almost 20 years from 1892 the only resident Japanese trader in Constantinople. During this time he served unofficially as consul. He converted to Islam, and took the name Abdul Khalil, and made a pilgrimage to Mecca on his way home.

Japanese nationalists and Islam

In the late Meiji period, close relations were forged between Japanese military elites with an Asianist agenda and Muslims to find a common cause with those suffering under the yoke of Western hegemony. In 1906, widespread propaganda campaigns were aimed at Muslim nations with journals reporting that a Congress of religions was to be held in Japan where the Japanese would seriously consider adopting Islam as the national religion and that the Emperor was at the point of becoming a Muslim.

Nationalistic organizations like the Ajia Gikai were instrumental in petitioning the Japanese government on matters such as officially recognizing Islam, along with Shintoism, Christianity and Buddhism as a religion in Japan, and in providing funding and training to Muslim resistance movements in Southeast Asia, such as the Hizbullah, a resistance group funded by Japan in the Dutch Indies. The Greater Japan Muslim League (大日本回教協会, Dai Nihon Kaikyō Kyōkai) founded in 1930, was the first official Islamic organisation in Japan. It had the support of imperialistic circles during World War II, and caused an "Islamic Studies Book". During this period, over 100 books and journals on Islam were published in Japan. While these organizations had their primary aim in intellectually equipping Japan's forces and intellectuals with better knowledge and understanding of the Islamic world, dismissing them as mere attempts to further Japan's aims for a "Greater Asia" does not reflect the nature of depth of these studies. Japanese and Muslim academia in their common aims of defeating Western colonialism had been forging ties since the early twentieth century, and with the destruction of the last remaining Muslim power, the Ottoman Empire, the advent of hostilities in World War II and the possibility of the same fate awaiting Japan, these academic and political exchanges and the alliances created reached a head. Therefore, they were extremely active in forging links with academia and Muslim leaders and revolutionaries, many of whom were invited to Japan.

Shūmei Ōkawa, by far the highest-placed and most prominent figure in both Japanese government and academia in the matter of Japanese-Islamic exchange and studies, managed to complete his translation of the Qur'an in prison, while being prosecuted as an alleged class-A war criminal by the victorious Allied forces for being an 'organ of propaganda'. Charges were dropped due to the results of psychiatric tests.

Post–World War II

The Japanese invasion of China and South East Asian regions during the Second World War brought the Japanese in contact with Muslims. Those who converted to Islam through them returned to Japan and established in 1953 the first Japanese Muslim organisation, the "Japan Muslim Association", which was officially granted recognition as a religious organization by the Japanese government in June 1968. The second president of the association was Ryoichi Mita also known as Umar Mita, who was typical of the old generation, learning Islam in the territories occupied by the Japanese Empire. He was working for the South Manchuria

Railway, which virtually controlled the Japanese territory in the northeastern province of China at that time. Through his contacts with Chinese Muslims, he formally became a Muslim in 1941 at Beijing and changed his name to Umar Mita. Then in 1945 he returned to Japan after the war. He made the Hajj in 1958, the first Japanese in the post-war period to do so. He also made a Japanese translation of the Qur'an from a Muslim perspective for the first time. Al Jazeera also made a documentary regarding Islam and Japan called "Road to Hajj – Japan".

The economic boom in the country in the 1980s saw an influx of immigrants to Japan, including from majority Muslim nations. These immigrants and their descendants form the majority of Muslims in the country. Today, there are Muslim student associations at some Japanese universities. In 2016, Japan accepted 0.3% of refugee applicants, many of whom are Muslims.

Demographics

In 1941, one of the chief sponsors of the Tokyo Mosque asserted that the number of Muslims in Japan numbered 600, with just three or four being native Japanese. Some sources state that in 1982 the Muslims numbered 30,000 (half were natives). Of the ethnically Japanese Muslims, the majority are thought to be ethnic Japanese women who married immigrant Muslims who arrived during the economic boom of the 1980s, but there are also a small number of intellectuals, including university professors, who have converted. Most estimates of the Muslim population in the 2000s give a range around 100,000 total. Islam remains a minority religion in Japan. Conversion is more prominent among young ethnic Japanese married women, as claimed by The Modern Religion as early as the 1990s.

The true size of the current Muslim population in Japan remains a matter of speculation. Japanese scholars such as Hiroshi Kojima of the National Institute of Population and Social Security Research and Keiko Sakurai of Waseda University suggest a Muslim population of around 70,000 in 2007, of which perhaps 90% are resident foreigners and about 10% native Japanese. Of the immigrant communities, in order of population size, are Indonesians, Indians, Pakistanis and Bangladeshis. The Pew Research Center estimated that there were 185,000 Muslims in Japan in 2010. For 2019 it was estimated that the numbers rose to 230,000, due to the more friendly policies towards immigration, the Japanese converts being estimated at 50,000, and Japan now has more than 110 mosques compared to 24 in 2001. As of 2020, nearly half of the Muslims in Japan were Indonesians, Filipinos, and Malaysians. Another 2019 estimate places the total number at 200,000, with a ratio of 90:10 for those of foreign origin to native Japanese converts.

Japan's first mosque was the Kobe Muslim Mosque, established in 1935. According to japanfocus.org, as of 2009 there were 30 to 40 single-story mosques in Japan, The largest of which is the Tokyo Mosque, plus another 100 or more apartment rooms set aside for prayers in the absence of more suitable facilities. 90% of these mosques use the 2nd floor for religious activities and the first floor as a halal shop (imported food; mainly from Indonesia and Malaysia), due to financial problems, as membership is too low to cover the expenses. Most of these mosques have only a capacity of 30 to 50 people. In 2016, the first ever mosque tailored for native Japanese worshipers (as opposed to services in foreign languages) was opened. As of 2023, there is one Ahmadi mosque in Japan, The Japan Mosque. It was established in 2015 by Mirza Masroor Ahmad, the mosque has a capacity of 500 worshippers, the largest of any mosque in Japan.

Notable Muslims

- Antonio Inoki
- Dewi Sukarno
- Kōhan Kawauchi
- Masatoşi Gündüz İkeda
- Mitsutarō Yamaoka
- Ryoichi Mita
- Shotaro Noda
- Sultan Nour
- Tani Yutaka

Chapter 7

Canada

Islam in Canada is a minority religion practised by approximately 5% of the population. A majority of Muslims are of immigrant backgrounds consisting a diverse range of ethnic groups. Muslims have lived in Canada since 1871 and the first mosque was established in 1938. Most Canadian Muslims are Sunni, while a significant minority are Shia.

There are a number of Islamic organizations and seminaries (madrasas). Opinion polls show most Muslims feel "very proud" to be Canadians, and majority are religious and attend mosque at least once a week. More than half of Canadian Muslims live in Ontario, with significant populations also living in Quebec, Alberta, and British Columbia.

The percentage of Muslims in Canada is 4.9% as of the 2021 census. In the Greater Toronto Area, 10% of the population is Muslim, and in Greater Montreal, 8.7% of the population is Muslim.

Historical population		
Year	**Pop.**	**±%**
1854	3	—
1871	13	+333.3%
1901	47	+261.5%
1911	797	+1595.7%
1921	478	−40.0%
1931	645	+34.9%
1971	33,430	+5082.9%
1981	98,160	+193.6%
1991	253,260	+158.0%
2001	579,645	+128.9%
2011	1,053,945	+81.8%
2021	1,775,715	+68.5%

Four years after Canada's founding in 1867, the 1871 Canadian Census found 13 European Muslims among the population. The first Muslim organization in Canada was registered by immigrants from greater Syria living in Regina, Saskatchewan in 1934. The first Canadian mosque was constructed in Edmonton in 1938 when there were approximately 700 European Muslims in the country. The building is now part of the museum at Fort Edmonton Park. The years after World War II saw a small increase in the Muslim population. However, Muslims were still a distinct minority. It was only after the removal of European immigration preferences in the late 1960s and early 1970s that Muslims began to arrive in significant numbers.

Bosniaks and Albanian Muslims were the founders of Jami Mosque, the first mosque in Toronto in 1968, whose readjustment into masjid (originally an old Catholic school building) occurred on June 23, 1973. The mosque was readjusted for the Bosniaks, with the support of the local Christians. Later, with the action of University of Toronto professor Qadeer Baig, it was purchased by Asian Muslims, while Albanians and Bosniaks later founded the Albanian Muslim Society and Bosanska džamija (Bosnian Mosque) respectively. The oldest mosque in Toronto, with the oldest minaret in Ontario built in Osmanic style is in Etobicoke, part of the Bosnian Islamic Centre.

The first Madrasa (Islamic seminary) in North America, Al-Rashid Islamic Institute was established in Cornwall, Ontario in 1983 to teach Hafiz and Ulama and focuses on the traditional Hanafi school of thought. The Seminary was established by Mazhar Alam, originally from Bihar, India, under the direction of his teacher the leading Indian Tablighi scholar Muhammad Zakariya Kandhlawi. Due to its proximity to the US border city of Massena the school has historically had a high percentage of American students. Their most prominent graduate, Muhammad Alshareef completed his Hifz in the early 1990s then went on to form the AlMaghrib Institute.

As with immigrants in general, Muslim immigrants have come to Canada for a variety of reasons. These include higher education, security, employment, and family reunification. Others have come for religious and political freedom, and safety and security, leaving behind civil wars, persecution, and other forms of civil and ethnic strife. In the 1980s, Canada became an important place of refuge for those fleeing the Lebanese Civil War. The 1990s saw Somali Muslims arrive in the wake of the Somali Civil War as well as Bosniaks fleeing the breakup of the former Yugoslavia. However Canada has yet to receive any significant numbers of Iraqis fleeing the Iraqi War. But in general almost every Muslim country in the world has sent immigrants to Canada – from Pakistan, Bosnia and Herzegovina and Albania to Yemen and Bangladesh.

According to the Canadian Census of 1971 there were 33,000 Muslims in Canada. In the 1970s large-scale non-European immigration to Canada began. This was reflected in the growth of the Muslim community in Canada. In 1981, the Census listed 98,000 Muslims. The 1991 Census indicated 253,265 Muslims.

By 2001, the Islamic community in Canada had grown to more than 579,000. In the same year, the fertility rate for Muslims in Canada was higher than the rate for other Canadians (an average of 2.4 children per woman for Muslims in 2001, compared with 1.6 children per woman for other populations in Canada).

Population estimates for the Census 2006 pointed to a figure of 800,000. As of May 2013, Muslims account for 3.2% of the total population, with a total of over a million. In January 2017, six Muslims were killed in a shooting attack at a Quebec city mosque.

In the contemporary era, there are halal restaurants across Canada, including over 1000 in the Greater Toronto Area.

One of the first Islamic internet radio stations, Canadian Islamic Broadcasting Network, was started in 2019.

National and ethnic origins

According to the 2011 National Household Survey, there were 424,925 Muslims living in the Greater Toronto Area equalling 7.7% of the total metropolitan population, of which the Muslim community consists of persons of Pakistani, Bangladeshi, Indian, Iranian, African, Arab, Caucasian, Southeast Asian, and Latin descent. Greater Montreal's Muslim community was 221,040 in 2011 or nearly 6% of the total metropolitan population which includes a highly diverse Muslim population from Western/Southern Europe, Caribbean, North Africa, the Middle East, and the Indian subcontinent. Canada's national capital Ottawa hosts many Lebanese, South Asian and Somali Muslims, where the Muslim community numbered approximately 65,880 or 5.5% in 2011. In addition to Toronto, Ottawa and Montreal, nearly every major Canadian metropolitan area has a Muslim community, including Vancouver (73,215), where more than a third are of Iranian descent, Calgary (58,310), Edmonton (46,125), Windsor (15,575), Winnipeg (11,265), and Halifax (7,540). In recent years, there has been rapid population growth in Calgary and Edmonton because of the booming economy.

Branches or denominations

Major Canadian cities have local Muslim organizations that deal mainly with issues pertaining to their home city, but that support national associations. Most Muslim organizations on the national level are umbrella groups and coordination bodies. Student-led initiatives are generally well supported and successful, including annual events such as MuslimFest and the Reviving the Islamic Spirit conference, the largest Islamic event in Canada.

Sunni Muslims

The majority of Canadian Muslims follow Sunni Islam.

Few are Shia Muslims

Ahmadiyya Muslims

The Ahmadiyya Muslim Community has about 50 Local Chapters scattered across Canada, mainly in southern Ontario. The community has 25 places of worship in Canada. Baitun Nur is the largest mosque in Canada.

Progressive Muslims

In May 2009, the Toronto Unity Mosque / el-Tawhid Juma Circle was founded by Laury Silvers, a University of Toronto religious studies scholar, alongside Muslim gay-rights activists El-Farouk Khaki and Troy Jackson. Unity Mosque/ETJC is a gender-equal, LGBT+ affirming, mosque.

As the Canadian Charter of Rights and Freedoms guarantees freedom of religious expression, Canadian Muslims face no official religious discrimination but have been victims of many hate crimes which have been increasingly going up.

Under Section 2(a) of the Charter, the wearing of a hijab is permitted in schools and places of work, although Quebec has ruled that medical faculties are not required to accommodate Muslim women who wish to be served by female employees. Religious holidays and dietary restrictions are also respected, but outside major urban areas it may be difficult to find halal food. It is also often difficult to observe Islamic rules against usury. Some Muslims in some parts of Canada have asked to have family dispute courts to oversee small family cases but were faced with rigorous opposition from both within the Muslim community (both conservative and liberal), and by non-Muslim groups.

In 2011, the Harper government attempted to ban the niqab during citizenship ceremonies. In 2015, the Federal Court of Appeal ruled against the ban, and the Supreme Court turned down the government's appeal.

Canadian Muslim Social Organizations

There are several organizations working to support the Canadian Muslim community by representing their causes and voices, and channeling the efforts of Muslims for the greater good of Canadians as well as people struggling in other parts of the world. Some are listed below:

1. Muslim Association of Canada (MAC) is a charitable organization and a grassroots movement to establish an Islamic presence in Canada that is balanced, constructive, and integrated in the social fabric and culture of Canada.

2. National Council of Canadian Muslims (NCCM) is an independent, non-partisan and non-profit organization that protects Canadian human rights and civil liberties, challenges discrimination and Islamophobia.

3. Islamic Relief Canada helps Canadian Muslims channel charitable contributions to not only Canadians but people in need across the globe. Their platform helps strengthen the relationship between donors and beneficiaries by providing a high level of transparency.

4. Canadian Council of Muslim Women (CCMW) is an organization dedicated to the empowerment, equality and equity of all Muslim women in Canada. It has chapters all over Canada and has launched several projects through community engagement, public policy, stakeholder engagement and amplified awareness of the social injustices that Muslim women and girls endure in Canada.

5. Muslim Welfare Canada works to fight hunger through its food banks and meals on wheels programs for senior citizens. They also run homes/shelters for women and children as well as refugees.

6. Canadian Islamic Broadcasting Network - An online radio station that was setup in 2019 with the intention of broadcasting Islamic information across Canada via internet radio. The main focus of the station is to provide Islamic Talk programming.

7. Muslim Federal Employee Network is national level network for Muslims in the Federal Public Service. It plays a key leadership role in supporting the Government of Canada to become a model of inclusion of Muslim public servants. The Muslim Federal Employees Network provides an open and safe forum for Muslim and non-Muslim employees to connect and discuss issues related to the promotion of a healthy and inclusive work environment for Muslim employees in the federal public service.

In a 2016 Environics poll, 83% of Muslims were "very proud" to be Canadian, compared with 73% of non-Muslim Canadians who said the same thing. Canadian Muslims reported "Canada's freedom and democracy" as the greatest source of pride, and "multiculturalism and diversity" as the second greatest. 94% of Canadian Muslims reported a "strong" or "very strong" sense of belonging to Canada. 78% of Canadian Muslims attend mosque at least once a week. 73% of women wear some sort of head-covering in public (58% wear the hijab, 13% wear the chador and 2% wear the niqab). Both pride in being Canadian and having a strong sense of belonging had increased in Canadian Muslims as compared to a 2006 survey. Mosque attendance and wearing a head covering in public had also increased since the 2006 survey.

A 2016 survey found that 36% of Canadian Muslims (47% of those aged 18–34) agreed that homosexuality should be generally accepted by society, while 43% disagreed. Older Muslims (55%) and those with the lowest incomes (56%) were more likely to disagree. The acceptance of homosexuality was higher among the Muslims born in Canada (52%) and South Africa (42%) than Muslims born in Pakistan (0%), Middle East (0%) and North Africa (0%).

Opinion on Muslims

According to the surveys conducted by the Angus Reid Institute (ARI), 24% of the Canadians had a favorable opinion of Islam in 2013 which increased to 34% in the 2016 survey and in Quebec, it increased from 16% in 2013 to 32% in 2016.

The Liberal Party (45%) voters and New Democratic Party voters (42%) have more favourable opinion on Muslims, than compared to Conservative Party voters (24%).

A majority (75%) of the Canadians strongly support allowing Muslim women to wear hijab in public. However, the wearing of full face and body covering niqab and burka is strongly opposed. Only three-in-ten Canadians are supportive of it.

Chapter 8

France

Islam in France is a minority faith. Muslims are estimated to represent around 4% of the nation's population as per Statista and Le Monde, although Insee claims that in metropolitan France this percentage can reach 10%. After conquering much of the Iberian peninsula, the Umayyad Muslim forces invaded modern day southern France, but were defeated by the Frankish Christian army led by Charles Martel at the Battle of Tours in 732 AD, thus preventing the possible Islamisation of Western Europe. During a later incursion, Muslims established the fortress Fraxinetum. France's Muslim population grew starting in the second half of the 20th century, following immigration from former French colonies and protectorates in Africa and the Middle East.

The majority of Muslims in France belong to the Sunni denomination and are of foreign origins. Sizeable minorities of Shia, Ahmadiyya and non-denominational Muslims also exist. The French overseas region of Mayotte has a majority Muslim population.

According to a survey in which 536 people of Muslim origin participated, 39% of Muslims in France surveyed by the polling group IFOP said they observed Islam's five prayers daily in 2008, a steady rise from 31% in 1994, according to the study published in the Catholic daily La Croix. Mosque attendance for Friday prayers has risen to 23% in 2008, up from 16% in 1994, while Ramadan observance has reached 70% in 2008 compared to 60% in 1994. Alcohol consumption also declined from 39% to 34%.

History

Early history

After their conquest of Hispania and invasion of Gaul, the Arab Umayyads were defeated at the Battle of Tours in 732. Septimania however remained under Arab control until 759.

In 838, the Annales Bertiniani record that Muslims raided Marseille in southern France, plundered its religious houses and took captive both men and women, clerical and lay, as slaves. In 842, the Annales report a raid in the vicinity of Arles. In 869, raiders returned to Arles and captured the archbishop, Roland. They accepted a ransom in return for the archbishop, but when they handed him over he was already dead. The construction of a castle in the Camargue following these raids up the Rhône may have induced raiders to try points further east, culminating in the establishment of a permanent base of operations at Fraxinetum. In 887, Muslim forces from Al-Andalus conquered several bases in France and established the emirate of Fraxinet. They were eventually defeated and expelled in 975.

During the winter of 1543–1544, after the siege of Nice, Toulon was used as an Ottoman naval base under admiral Hayreddin Barbarossa. The Christian population was temporarily evacuated, and Toulon Cathedral was briefly converted into a mosque until the Ottomans' departure.

After the expulsion of the Moriscos from Spain in 1609–1614, about 50,000 Moriscos entered France, according to the research of Henri Lapeyre.

1960-1970s labor immigration

Muslim immigration, mostly male, was high in the late 1960s and 1970s. These immigrants mostly hailed from Algeria and other former French colonies in North Africa; however, Islam has had an older history in France, since the Great Mosque of Paris was built in 1922, as a sign of recognition from the French Republic to the fallen Muslim tirailleurs mainly coming from Algeria, in particular at the battle of Verdun and the takeover of the Douaumont fort.

French Council of the Muslim Faith

Though the French State is secular, in recent years the government has tried to organize a representation of French Muslims. In 2002, the then Interior Minister Nicolas Sarkozy initiated the creation of a "French Council of the Muslim Faith" (Conseil Français du Culte Musulman – CFCM), though wide criticism claimed this would only encourage communitarianism. Though the CFCM is informally recognized by the national government, it is a private nonprofit association with no special legal status. As of 2004, it is headed by the rector of the Paris Mosque, Dalil Boubakeur – who harshly criticized the controversial Union of Islamic Organizations of France (UOIF) for involving itself in political matters during the 2005 riots. Sarkozy's views on laïcité have been widely criticized by left- and right-wing members of parliament; more specifically, he was accused, during the creation of the CFCM, of favoring the more extreme sectors of Muslim representation in the Council, in particular the UOIF.

Second generation immigrants

The first generation of Muslim immigrants, who are today mostly retired from the workforce, kept strong ties with their countries, where their families lived. In 1976, the government passed a law allowing families of these immigrants to settle in France. Thus, the spouses, children, and other family members of these immigrants also came to France. Most immigrants, realizing that they could not or did not want to return to their homeland, asked for French nationality before quietly retiring. However, many live alone in housing projects, having now lost their ties with their families and friends back from their home countries.

Olivier Roy indicates that for first-generation immigrants, the fact that they are Muslims is only one element among others. Their identification with their country of origin is much stronger: they see themselves first through their descent (Algerians, Moroccans, Tunisians, etc.).

The false claim that a third of newborns in France have Muslim parents, is brought up in sensationalist American immigration discourse.

Maghrebis

According to Michèle Tribalat, a researcher at INED, people of Maghrebi origin in France represent 82% of the Muslim population (43.2% from Algeria, 27.5% from Morocco, and 11.4% from Tunisia). Others are from sub-Saharan Africa (9.3%) and Turkey (8.6%). She estimated that there were 3.5 million people of Maghrebi origin (with at least one grandparent from Algeria, Morocco, or Tunisia) living in France in 2005 corresponding to 5.8% of the total French metropolitan population (60.7 million in 2005). Maghrebis have settled mainly in the industrial regions in France, especially in the Paris region. Many famous French people like Edith Piaf, Isabelle Adjani, Arnaud Montebourg, Alain Bashung, Dany Boon, and many others have varying degrees of Maghrebi ancestry.

In 2005, the percentage of young people under 18 of Maghrebi origin (at least one immigrant parent) was about 7% in Metropolitan France, 12% in Greater Paris and above 20% in French département of Seine-Saint-Denis.

In 2008, the French national institute of statistics, INSEE, estimated that 11.8 million foreign-born immigrants and their direct descendants (born in France) lived in France representing 19% of the country's population. About 4 million of them are of Maghrebi origin.

According to some non-scientific sources between 5 and 6 million people of Maghrebin origin live in France corresponding to about 7–9% of the total French metropolitan population.

Religious practices

The great majority of Muslims practice their religion in the French framework of laïcité, as a religious code of conduct must not infringe the public area. A study in 2008 found that 39% pray (salat) five times a day, 23% attend mosque on Fridays, 70% observe the fast of Ramadan, and 66% abstain from alcohol. Rachel Brown shows that some Muslims in France alter some of these religious practices, particularly food practices, as a means of showing "integration" into French culture. According to expert Franck Fregosi: "Although fasting during Ramadan is the most popular practice, it ranks more as a sign of Muslim identity than piety, and it is more a sign of belonging to a culture and a community", and he added that not drinking alcohol "seems to be more a cultural behavior".

Some Muslims (the UOIF for example) request the recognition of an Islamic community in France (which remains to be built) with an official status.

Two main organizations are recognized by the French Council of Muslim Faith (CFCM): the "Federation of the French Muslims" (Fédération des musulmans de France) with a majority of Moroccan leaders, and the controversial "Union of Islamic Organisations of France" (Union des organizations islamiques de France) (UOIF). In 2008, there were about 2,125 Muslim places of worship in France.

Education

Since publicly funded state schools in France must be secular, owing to the 1905 separation of Church and State, Muslim parents who wish their children to be educated at a religious school often choose private (and therefore fee-paying, though heavily subsidized) Catholic schools, of which there are many. Few specifically Muslim schools have been created. There is a Muslim school in La Réunion (a French island to the east of Madagascar), and the first Muslim collège (a school for students aged eleven to fifteen) opened its doors in 2001 in Aubervilliers (a suburb northeast of Paris), with eleven students. Unlike most private schools in the United States and the UK, these religious schools are affordable for most parents since they may be heavily subsidized by the government (teachers' wages in particular are covered by the state).

Radicalization

In November 2015 in the aftermath of the Paris attacks, French authorities for the first time closed three mosques with extremist activities and radicalization being given as the reason. The mosques were located in Lagny-sur-Marne, Lyon, and Gennevilliers. Muslim community leaders widely condemned the Paris attacks in public statements and expressed their support for the French government's attempts to oppose Islamist extremism.

Due to the deadly attacks in 2015, France changed the character of Islamist radicalization from a security threat to constitute a societal problem. President François Hollande and Prime Minister Manuel Valls saw the fundamental values of the French republic being challenged and called them attacks against fundamental secular, enlightenment, and democratic values along with "what makes us who we are".

In 2016, French authorities reported that 120 of the 2,500 Islamic prayer halls were disseminating Salafist ideas and 20 mosques were closed due to findings of hate speech. In 2016, French authorities stated that 15000 of the 20000 individuals on the list of security threats belong to Islamist movements.

In 2018, EU anti-terror coordinator Gilles de Kerchove estimated there to be 17,000 radicalized Muslims and jihadists living in France.

In 2018, French intelligence services monitored around 11,000 individuals with suspected ties to radical Islamism. France has sentenced a large number of individuals for terrorist-related offenses which have increased the prison population. This in turn has created an issue with radicalization in French prisons.

In February 2019, authorities in Grenoble closed the Al-Kawthar Mosque for six months due to it propagating a "radical Islamist ideology". The Al-Kawthar Mosque had about 400 regular visitors. In several of the sermons, the imam legitimized armed jihad, violence, and hatred towards followers of other religions' anti-republican values and promoted Sharia law.

In November 2019, French authorities closed cafés, schools, and mosques in about 15 neighborhoods due to them disseminating political Islam and communitarian ideas.

In October 2020, President Emmanuel Macron announced a crackdown on "Islamist separatism" in Muslim communities in France, saying a bill with this objective would be sent to parliament in "early 2021." Among the measures, would be a ban on foreign imams, restrictions on homeschooling, and the creation of an "Institute of Islamology" to tackle Islamic fundamentalism. His government introduced a bill that would punish with jail terms and fine any doctor who provides virginity certificates for traditional, religious marriages. ANCIC stated it supported the government's stand against "virginity tests" but warned that in some cases women were in "real danger" and "a ban would simply deny the existence of such community practices, without making them disappear". The association suggested that the issue be "tackled quite differently so that women and men free themselves and reject the weight of [such] traditions." On 16 February 2021, the law passed the lower house 347—151 with 65 abstentions.

Terrorist attacks in France

France had its first occurrences with religious extremism in the 1980s due to French involvement in the Lebanese Civil War. In the 1990s, a series of attacks on French soil were executed by the Armed Islamic Group of Algeria (GIA).

In the 1990–2010 time span, France experienced repeated attacks linked to international jihadist movements. Le Monde reported on 26 July 2016 that "Islamist Terrorism" had caused 236 dead in France in the preceding 18-month period.

In the 2015–2018 timespan in France, 249 people were killed and 928 wounded in a total of 22 terrorist attacks.

The deadly attacks in 2015 in France changed the issue of Islamist radicalization from a security threat to also constitute a social problem. President François Hollande and Prime Minister Manuel Valls saw the fundamental values of the French republic being challenged and called them attacks against secular, enlightenment and democratic values along with "what makes us who we are".

Although jihadists in the 2015-onward timeframe legitimized their attacks with a narrative of reprisal for France's participation in the international coalition fighting the Islamic State, Islamic terrorism in France has other, deeper and older causes. The main reasons France suffers frequent attacks are, in no particular order:

- France's secular domestic policies (Laïcité) which jihadists perceive to be hostile towards Islam. Also, France's status as an officially secular nation and jihadists label France as "the flagship of disbelief".

- France has a strong cultural tradition in comics, which in the context of Muhammad cartoons is a question of freedom of expression.

- France has a large Muslim minority

- France's foreign policy towards Muslim countries and jihadist fronts. France is seen as the spearhead directed against jihadist groups in Africa, just as the United States is seen as the main force opposing jihadist groups elsewhere. France's former foreign policies such as that as its colonization of Muslim countries is also brought up in jihadist propaganda, for example, that the influence of French education, culture and political institutions had served to erase the Muslim identity of those colonies and their inhabitants.

- Jihadists consider France as a strong proponent of disbelief. For instance, Marianne, the national emblem of France, is considered as "a false idol" by jihadists and the French to be "idol worshippers". France also has no law against blasphemy and an anticlerical satirical press which is less respectful towards religion than that of the US or the United Kingdom. The French nation state is also perceived as an obstacle towards establishing a caliphate.

In 2020 two Islamic terrorist attacks were foiled by authorities, bringing the total to 33 since 2017 according to Laurent Nuñez, the director of CNRLT, who declared that Sunni Islamist terrorism was a prioritised threat. Nuñez drew parallels between the three attacks of 2020 which all were attacks on "blasphemy and the will to avenge their prophet".

Law against Islamist extremism

After the murder of Paty, a bill was put forward to fight Islamist extremism and separatism to fight the roots of jihadist violence. It was approved by the National Assembly in February 2021.

A new bill was introduced, which makes it unlawful to threaten a public servant in order to gain an exception or special treatment which carries a penalty of up to five years in prison. The legislation expands the powers of authorities to close places of worship and religious organisations when they promote "hate or violence". The law requires religious funds from abroad exceeding €10,000 to be declared and the relevant accounts to be certified, so as to regulate the donations from countries such as Turkey, Qatar and Saudi Arabia. Millions of euros in funding had previously reached France from countries such as Turkey, Morocco and Saudi Arabia.

It provides stricter rules for allowing home-schooling in order to prevent parents taking children out of school in order to let them pursue their education in underground Islamist institutions. Doctors performing virginity tests would be subject to fines or prison sentences. These changes were prompted by a number of cases of Muslim men trying to have their marriages annulled by accusing their spouse of having had sex before marriage. Authorities will have to refuse residency documents to applicants who practise polygamy. Forced marriage, which The French ministry of the interior states affects 200,000 women in France, was likewise required to be combated with greater scrutiny from registrars.

Integration

Accepted French citizens

Notwithsanding the islamist extremists' terrorist attacks in France, including the Charlie Hebdo and Nice terror attacks, some studies have concluded that France is the European country where Muslims integrate the best and feel the most for their country and that French Muslims have the most positive opinions about their fellow citizens of different faiths. A 2006 study from the Pew Research Center on Integration is one such study. In Paris and the surrounding Île-de-

France region where French Muslims tend to be more educated and religious, the vast majority rejects violence and say they are loyal to France according to studies by Euro-Islam, a comparative research network on Islam and Muslims in the West sponsored by GSRL Paris/CNRS France and Harvard University. On the other hand, a 2013 IPSOS survey published by the French daily Le Monde, indicated that only 26% of French respondents believed that Islam was compatible with French society (compared to 89% identifying Catholicism as compatible and 75% identifying Judaism as compatible). A 2014 survey by the Pew Research Center showed that out of all Europeans, the French view Muslim minorities most favorably with 72% having a favorable opinion. Other research has shown how these positive attitudes are not always reflected in popular opinion and the subject of Muslim integration in France is much more nuanced and complex.

In April 2018 an Algerian Muslim woman refused to shake hands with an official for religious reasons at a citizenship ceremony. As an applicant must demonstrate being integrated into society as well as respect for French values, officials considered her not integrated and denied her citizenship application.

Religiosity

According to a poll by Institut français d'opinion publique in 2020, 46% of Muslims gave the view that their religious beliefs were more important than the values and laws of the French Republic, more than twice the fraction of the French public (17%). Among Muslims under 25 years of age a large majority (74%) considered their religion more important than French laws and values.

LGBT acceptance

The 2009 Gallup poll showed that 35% of the French Muslims believed that homosexuality is morally acceptable.

Unemployment

In October 2020, the unemployment among Muslims was far higher at 14% than the population at large (8%).

Education

According to a poll by Institut Montaigne in 2016, 15% of Muslims in France had no academic qualification at all and 25% had less than secondary education (Baccalauréat). 12% had more than 2 years higher education, a further 20% had more than 2 years. It been estimated that Muslim students form more than 10% of the students in the French Catholic schools.

Discrimination

In 2010, a study entitled Are French Muslims Discriminated Against in Their Own Country? found that "Muslims sending out resumes in hopes of a job interview had 2.5 times less chance than Christians" with similar credentials "of a positive response to their applications".

Another example is the 2004 French hijab ban, which forced young females out of public schools and led to a 10-year increase in unemployment (this discrimination is both religious and socioeconomic in nature).

Other examples of discrimination against Muslims include the desecration of 148 French Muslim graves near Arras. A pig's head was hung from a headstone and profanities insulting Islam and

Muslims were daubed on some graves. Destruction and vandalism of Muslim graves in France were seen as Islamophobic by a report of the European Monitoring Centre on Racism and Xenophobia. Several of Mosques have also been vandalized in France over the years. On 14 January 2015, it was reported that 26 mosques in France had been subject to attack since the Charlie Hebdo shooting in Paris.

On 29 June 2017, a man who had schizophrenia attempted to ram his vehicle into a crowd of worshipers exiting a mosque in Créteil, a suburb of Paris, though no one was injured. Le Parisien claims the suspect, of Armenian origin, wanted to "avenge the Bataclan and Champs-Elysées" attacks.

In 2019, The French Institute for Public Research (IFOP) conducted the study from August 29 to September 18, based on a sample of 1007 Muslims aged 15 and above. According to the study, 40% of Muslims in France felt that they were discriminated against. More than a third of these instances were recorded in the past five years, suggesting an increase in the overall mistreatment of Muslims in France over recent years. The survey found that 60% of women wearing a headscarf were subject to discrimination. 37% of Muslims in France have been a victim of verbal harassment or defamatory insults. The study, however, revealed that 44% of Muslim women who do not wear headscarves found themselves being a victim of verbal harassment or defamatory insults. The survey found that 13% of incidents of religious discrimination happened at police control points and 17% happened at job interviews. 14% of incidents occurred while the victims were looking to rent or buy accommodation. The IFOP stated that 24% of Muslims were exposed to verbal aggression during their lifetime, compared to 9% among non-Muslims. In addition, 7% of Muslims were physically attacked, compared to 3% of non-Muslims.

In 2019, according to the French Ministry of Interior, 154 anti-religious acts targeted Muslims, while those targeting Jews stood at 687, and those against Christians was 1,052. Most of these acts consisted of vandalism of "property of a religious nature."

Public opinion

A February 2017 poll of 10 000 people in 10 European countries by Chatham House found on average a majority (55%) were opposed to further Muslim immigration, with opposition especially pronounced in Austria, Poland, Hungary, France and Belgium. Except for Poland, all of those had recently suffered jihadist terror attacks or been at the center of a refugee crisis. A survey published in 2019 by the Pew Research Center found that 72% of French respondents had a favorable view of Muslims in their country, whereas 22% had an unfavourable view.

Repercussions

The 2005 French riots have been controversially interpreted as an illustration of the difficulty of integrating Muslims in France, and smaller-scale riots have been occurring throughout the 1980s and 1990s, first in Vaulx-en-Velin in 1979, and in Vénissieux in 1981, 1983, 1990 and 1999.

Furthermore, although Interior Minister Nicolas Sarkozy claimed that most rioters were immigrants and already known to the police, the majority were, in fact, previously unknown to the police.

In 2014, an analysis by The Washington Post showed that between 60 and 70% of the prison population in France are Muslim or come from Muslim backgrounds while Muslims constitute 12% of the population of France. The claims in this article have been refuted: the headline figure was based on research in 4 Paris and north regions prisons out of a total 188 by Professor Farhad Khosrovkhavar later said his best estimate was 40–50%, but that data is not recorded by French authorities. Statistics on ethnicity and religion are banned in France. In 2013, 18,300 (27%) of the 67,700 French prison population registered for Ramadan, an indication of their religious affiliation.

Hijab

The wearing of hijab in France has been a very controversial issue since 1989. The debate essentially concerns whether Muslim girls who choose to wear hijab may do so in state schools. A secondary issue is how to protect the free choice and other rights of young Muslim women who do not want the veil, but who may face strong pressure from families or some traditionalists. Similar issues exist for civil servants and the acceptance of male Muslim medics in medical services.

In 1994, the French Ministry for Education sent out recommendations to teachers and headmasters to ban the veil in educational institutions. According to a 2019 study by the Institute of Labor Economics, more girls with a Muslim background born after 1980 graduated from high school after the 1994 restrictions were introduced. While secularism is often criticized for restricting freedom of religion, the study suggested that "public schools ended up promoting the educational empowerment of some of the most disadvantaged groups of female students".

Leila Babes in her book "The Veil Demystified", believe that wearing the veil does not derive from a Muslim religious imperative.

The French government and a large majority of public opinion are opposed to the wearing of a "conspicuous" sign of religious expression (dress or symbol), whatever the religion, as this is incompatible with the French system of laïcité. In December 2003, President Jacques Chirac said that it breaches the separation of church and state and would increase tensions in France's multicultural society, whose Muslim and Jewish populations are both the biggest of their kind in Western Europe.

The issue of Muslim hijabs has sparked controversy after several girls refused to uncover their heads in class, as early as 1989. In October 1989, three Muslim schoolgirls wearing the Islamic headscarf were expelled from the collège Gabriel-Havez in Creil (north of Paris). In November, the First Conseil d'État ruling affirmed that the wearing of the Islamic headscarf, as a symbol of freedom of religious expression, in public schools was not incompatible with the French school system and the system of laïcité. In December, a first ministerial circular (circulaire Jospin) was published, stating teachers had to decide on a case-by-case basis whether to ban the wearing of Islamic headscarves.

In January 1990, three schoolgirls were expelled from the collège Pasteur in Noyon, north of Paris. The parents of one expelled schoolgirl filed a defamation action against the principal of the collège Gabriel-Havez in Creil. As a result, the teachers of a collège in Nantua (eastern part of France, just to the west of Geneva, Switzerland) went on strike to protest the wearing of the Islamic headscarf in school. A second ministerial circular was published in October, to restate the need to respect the principle of laïcité in public schools.

In September 1994, a third ministerial circular (circulaire Bayrou) was published, making a distinction between "discreet" symbols to be tolerated in public schools, and "ostentatious" symbols, including the Islamic headscarf, to be banned from public schools. In October, some students demonstrated at the lycée Saint Exupéry in Mantes-la-Jolie (northwest of Paris) to support the freedom to wear Islamic headscarves in school. In November, approximately twenty-four veiled schoolgirls were expelled from the lycée Saint Exupéry in Mantes-la-Jolie and the lycée Faidherbe in Lille.

In December 2003, President Chirac decided that the law should prohibit the wearing of visible religious signs in schools, according to laïcité requirements. The law was approved by parliament in March 2004. Items prohibited by this law include hijabs, Jewish yarmulkes, or large Christian crosses. It is still permissible to wear discreet symbols of faith such as small crosses, Stars of David, or Fatima's hands.

Two French journalists working in Iraq, Christian Chesnot and Georges Malbrunot were taken hostage by the "Islamic Army in Iraq" (an Iraqi resistance militant movement) under accusations of spying. Threats to kill the two journalists if the law on headscarves was not revoked were published on the Internet by groups claiming to be the "Islamic Army in Iraq". The two journalists were later released unharmed.

The arguments resurfaced when, on 22 June 2009, at the Congrès de Versailles, President Nicolas Sarkozy declared that the Islamic burqa is not welcome in France, claiming that the full-length, body-covering gown was a symbol of subservience that suppresses women's identities and turns them into "prisoners behind a screen." A parliamentary commission of thirty-two deputies led by André Gerin (PCF), was also formed to study the possibility of banning the public wearing of the burqa or niqab. There is suspicion, however, that Sarkozy is "playing politics in a time of economic unhappiness and social anxiety."

A Muslim group spokesman expressed serious concern over the proposed legislation, noting that "even if they ban the burqa, it will not stop there," adding that "there is a permanent demand for legislating against Muslims. This could go really bad, and I'm scared of it. I feel like they're turning the screws on us."

On 25 January 2010 it was announced that the parliamentary committee, having concluded its study, would recommend that a ban on veils covering the face in public locations such as hospitals and schools be enacted, but not in private buildings or on the street.

In February 2019, Decathlon, Europe's largest sports retailer, announced plans to begin selling a sports hijab in their stores in France. Decathlon had begun selling the product in Morocco the previous week, but the plan was criticized on social media, with several politicians expressing discomfort with the product being sold. Decathlon originally stood firm, arguing it was focused on "democratizing" sports. The company released a statement saying its goal was to "offer them a suitable sports product, without judging." While Nike had already sold hijabs in France, Decathlon was met with much more scrutiny. Multiple salespeople were threatened physically in stores. The company also received hundreds of calls and emails in regard to the product. Decathlon was forced to backtrack and has since halted its plans to sell the sports hijab. Many throughout France were left disappointed with one Muslim entrepreneur, who didn't consider selling sport hijabs, stating, "it's a shame that Decathlon didn't stand firm."

Politics

Formal as well as informal Muslim organizations help the new French citizens to integrate. Several political parties like Parti égalité et Justice have now appeared. Their most frequent activities are homework help and language classes in Arabic, ping pong, Muslim discussion groups etc. are also common. However, most important associations active in assisting with the immigration process are either secular (GISTI, for example) or ecumenist (such as the protestant-founded Cimade).

The most important national institution is the CFCM (Conseil Français du Culte Musulman) this institution was designed on the model of the "Consistoire Juif de France" and of the "Fédération protestante de France" both Napoleonic creations. The aim of the CFCM (like its Jewish and protestant counterparts) is to discuss religious problem with the state, participate in certain public institutions, and organize the religious life of French Muslims. The CFCM is elected by the French Muslims through local election. It is the only official instance of the French Muslims.

There were four organizations represented in the CFCM elected in 2003, GMP (Grande mosquée de Paris), UOIF (Union des organizations islamiques de France), FNMF (Fédération nationale des musulmans de France) CCMTF (Comité de coordination des musulmans Turcs de France). In 2008 a new council was elected. The winner was RMF (Rassemblement des musulmans de France) with a large majority of the votes, followed by the UOIF and the CCMTF. It is a very broad and young organization and there is a beginning of consensus on major issues. Other elections took place since then, the latest was due in 2019 but is still pending.

Other organizations exist, such as PCM (Muslim Participation and Spirituality), which combine political mobilization (against racism, sexism etc.) and spiritual meetings, and put emphasis on the need to get involved in French society – by joining organizations, registering to vote, working with your children's schools etc. They do not have clear-cut political positions as such but push for active citizenship. They are vaguely on the left in practice.

The government has yet to formulate an official policy towards making integration easier. As mentioned above, it is difficult to determine in France who may be called a Muslim. Some Muslims in France describe themselves as "non-practicing". Most simply observe Ramadan and other basic rules but are otherwise secular.

Statistics

Due to a law dating from 1872, the French Republic prohibits performing census by making distinction between its citizens regarding their race or their beliefs. However, that law does not concern surveys and polls, which are free to ask those questions if they wish. The law also allows for an exception for public institutions such as INED or INSEE whose job it is to collect data on demographics, social trends and other related subjects, on condition that the collection of such data has been authorized by the CNIL and the National Council of Statistical Information (CNIS [fr]).

Estimations based on declaration

Surveys from INED and the INSEE in October 2010 concluded that France has 2.1 million "declared Muslims".

In 2023, Muslims made up 10% of the French population, according to INSEE.

Estimations based on people's geographic origin

According to the French Government, which does not have the right to ask direct questions about religion and uses a criterion of people's geographic origin as a basis for calculation, there were between 3 and 3.2 million Muslims in metropolitan France in 2010. Thirteen years later, the proportion of Muslims in France rose to 10%, according to INSEE.

The government counted all those people in France who migrated from countries with a dominant Muslim population, or whose parents did.

The United States Department of State placed it at roughly 10%, [while two 2007 polls estimated it at about 3% of the total population. The CIA World Factbook places it at 7–9%.

A Pew Forum study, published in January 2011, estimated 4.7 million Muslims in France in 2010 (and forecasted 6.9 million in 2030).

The French polling company IFOP estimated in 2016 that French Muslims number between 3 and 4 million and criticized suggestions of a significant demographic religious slide. IFOP claims that they make up 5.6% of those older than 15, and 10% of those younger than 25. According to an IFOP survey for the newspaper La Croix in 2011, based on a combination of previous surveys, 75% of people from families "of Muslim origin" said they were believers. This is more than the previous study in 2007 (71%) but less than the one before 2001 (78%). This variation, caused by the declarative aspect of the survey, illustrates the difficulty of establishing precisely the number of believers. According to the same survey 155 of those surveyed who had at-least one Muslim parent 84.8% identified as Muslims, 3.4% identified as Christians,

10.0% identified as not religious and 1.3% belonged to other religions.

In 2008, thirty-nine percent of Muslims surveyed by the polling group IFOP said they observed Islam's five prayers daily, a steady rise from 31 percent in 1994, according to the study published in the Catholic daily La Croix.

Mosque attendance for Friday prayers has risen to 23 percent, in 2008 up from 16 percent in 1994, while in 2008 Ramadan observance has reached 70 percent compared to 60 percent in 1994, it said. Drinking alcohol, which Islam forbids, has also declined to 34 percent from 39 percent in 1994, according to the survey of 537 people of Muslim origin.

A 2015 study found that up to 12,000 French Muslims converted to Christianity, but cited that this number may be underestimated, and it may include only Protestant converts.

According to Michèle Tribalat [fr], a researcher at INED, an acceptance of 5 to 6 million Muslims in France in 1999 was overestimated. Her work has shown that there were 3.7 million people of "possible Muslim faith" in France in 1999 (6.3% of the total population of Metropolitan France). In 2009, she estimated that the number of people of the Muslim faith in France was about 4.5 million.

According to Jean-Paul Gourévitch, there were 8.5 million of Muslim origin (about 1/8 of the population), in metropolitan France in 2017.

In 2017, François Héran, former Head of the Population Surveys Branch at INSEE and Director of INED (French National Institute for Demographic Research) between 1999 and 2009, stated that about one eighth of the French population was of Muslim origin in 2017 (8.4 million).

According to the latest Special Eurobarometer 493 (2019) the Muslim population in France is estimated to be 5% or 3.35 million.

Pew Research Center predicts the Muslim population would rise to 8.6 million or 12.7 percent of the country in 2050 if immigration would be high.

Antisemitism

A survey by the Pew Research Center in 2006 in Germany, France, Great Britain and Spain showed that 71% of French Muslims had a positive view of their fellow Jewish citizens, the highest percentage of positive sentiment, the only majority expressed positively among all the European Muslims polled in Europe and a French exception. A majority of Muslims in France also did not support the Hamas (46% negative vs. 44% positive answers to the question: "Is Hamas' victory good for Palestinians?") and 71% of respondents did not approve of Iran acquiring nuclear weapons. This Muslim-Jewish solidarity in France can be partially explained by the fact that a high percentage of both populations share origins in the Maghreb and the effects of French laïcité on vivre-ensemble (i.e "living-together") in shared civil institutional spaces remaining religiously and politically neutral for all.

French Muslims

Athletes

- Zinedine Zidane, prominent football player
- Franck Ribery, Football player
- Nicolas Anelka, football player, convert
- Hatem Ben Arfa, football player
- Karim Benzema, football player
- Wissam Ben Yedder, football player
- N'Golo Kante, football player
- Houssem Aouar, football player
- Nabil Fekir, football player
- Mohamed Haouas, international rugby player
- Samir Nasri, football player
- Paul Pogba, football player, convert
- Adil Rami, football player
- Franck Ribéry, football player, convert
- Mamadou Sakho, football player
- Moussa Sissoko, football player
- Rabah Slimani, rugby player (both loose head and tight head prop) for Stade Français and in the French national rugby union team, highest paid French player
- Ousmane Dembele, football player
- Benjamin Mendy, football player
- Bacary Sagna, football player

- Djibril Sidibe, football player
- Cédric Doumbé MMA fighter, convert

Arts

- Nasreddine Dinet, painter

Actors

- Leïla Bekhti, award-winning film and television actress, L'Oréal ambassador
- Assaad Bouab, French-Moroccan actor of Call My Agent! fame
- Sami Bouajila, award-winning actor, recipient of two César Awards
- Rachida Brakni, award-winning actress, Comédie française member, wife of Éric Cantona
- Jamel Debbouze, award-winning actor and stand-up comedian, producer, philanthropist, husband of TV journalist and producer Mélissa Theuriau
- Kheiron, Iranian-born French comedian, actor and film director
- Sabrina Ouazani, actress of The Hook Up Plan and Games of Love and Chance fame
- Tahar Rahim, multiple César Award-winning actor, Oscars, BAFTA and Golden Globe nominee
- Omar Sy, award-winning actor, first ever Black winner of the César Award for Best Actor in 2012
- Roschdy Zem, award-winning actor and director

Singers

- Kery James, Guadeloupe-born hip hop artist, convert
- Soprano
- Médine
- Kaaris, convert
- Sadek, convert

Politicians

- Fadela Amara, social worker and feminist activist, former government minister
- Kader Arif, politician, former government minister and current member of the European Parliament
- Azouz Begag, Légion d'Honneur recipient, researcher in economics and sociology, former government minister
- Rachida Dati, lawyer, former Minister of Justice, current Minister of Culture
- Mounir Mahjoubi, technologist, businessman, current Secretary of State for Digital Affairs (came out as gay in 2018).
- Rama Yade, politician, former government minister, married to Jewish high civil servant Joseph Zimet

Academics and writers

- Ghaleb Bencheikh, scientist
- Jean-Louis Michon, writer and translator
- Louis du Couret, explorer, military officer, and writer
- Frantz Fanon, philosopher, psychiatrist, writer

- René Guénon, author and intellectual
- Roger Garaudy, author and philosopher

Business people

- Mohed Altrad, businessman, rugby chairman and writer.
- Mourad Boudjellal, businessman, founder of Soleil Productions comic publishing and sport manager.
- Rafik Smati, businessman, founder and leader of center-right political party Objectif France.

Religious figures

- Dalil Boubakeur, physician, rector of Great Mosque of Paris
- Si Kaddour Benghabrit, founder of the Great Mosque of Paris, WW2 resistant, interfaith helper and candidate to official title of Righteous among the Nations.

Television

- Rachid Arhab, journalist, member of Conseil supérieur de l'audiovisuel
- Mouloud Achour, journalist and talk-show tv presenter
- Ali Baddou, former Philosophy teacher, journalist
- Nagui, long-standing French tv and radio personality, numerous "France's #1 preferred TV host" surveys topper

Chapter 9

Germany

Islam's significance in Germany has largely increased after the labour migration in the 1960s and several waves of political refugees since the 1970s.

According to a representative survey, it is estimated that in 2019, there were 5.3–5.6 million Muslims with a migrant background in Germany (6.4–6.7% of the population), in addition to an unknown number of Muslims without a migrant background. A similar survey in 2016 estimated a number of 4.4–4.7 million Muslims with a migrant background (5.4–5.7% of the population) at that time. An older survey in 2009 estimated a total number of up to 4.3 million Muslims in Germany at that time. There are also higher estimates: according to the German Islam Conference, Muslims represented 7% of the population in Germany in 2012.

In a 2014 academic publication it was estimated that some 20,000-100,000 Germans converted to Islam, numbers which are comparable to that in France and in the United Kingdom.

Demographics

Islam is the largest minority religion in the country, with the Protestant and Roman Catholic confessions being the majority religions. Most Muslims in Germany have roots in Turkey, followed by Arab countries, former Yugoslavia (mostly of Kosovo-Albanian or Bosnian origin), Afghanistan and Iran. There are also a significant minority originated from Sub-Saharan Africa (mostly East Africa) and South Asia (mostly Pakistan). The large majority of Muslims live in former West Germany, including West Berlin. However, unlike in most other European countries, sizeable Muslim communities exist in some rural regions of Germany, especially Baden-Württemberg, Hesse and parts of Bavaria and North Rhine-Westphalia. Owing to the lack of labour immigration before 1989, there are only very few Muslims in the former East Germany. Among the German districts with the highest share of Muslim migrants are Groß-Gerau (district) and Offenbach (district) according to migrants data from the census 2011. The majority of Muslims in Germany are Sunnis, at 75%. There are Shia Muslims (7%) and mostly from Iran.

From the mid-2000s to 2016 there has been a surge migrants to Germany from outside Europe. Of the 680,000 regular migrants, 270,000 were Muslim. Additionally, of the 1,210,000 asylum seekers, 900,000 were Muslim (around 74%). Of the asylum seekers, 580,000 applicants were approved and 320,000 were denied or expected to be denied. According to the Pew Research Center, similar patterns of Muslim migration to Germany should be expected in the future and the Muslim population share is expected to grow.

Prison population

According to the Huffington Post in February 2018 which quired each of the 15 state justice ministries, 12,300 Muslims are in prison and constitute about 20% of the total 65,000 prison population in Germany which constitutes an over-representation. The highest shares are in city states of Bremen (29%), Hamburg (28%) but the share is high also in large states such as Hessen (26%) Baden-Württemberg (26%). The share is lower in the former East Germany.

History

Early history

Muslims first moved to Germany as part of the diplomatic, military and economic relations between Germany and the Ottoman Empire in the eighteenth century. Twenty Muslim soldiers served under Frederick William I of Prussia, at the beginning of the eighteenth century. In 1745, Frederick II of Prussia established a unit of Muslims in the Prussian army called the "Muslim Riders" and consisting mainly of Bosniaks, Albanians and Tatars. In 1760 a Bosnian Muslim corps was established with about 1,000 men. In 1798 a Muslim cemetery was established in Berlin. The cemetery, which moved in 1866, still exists today. A number of German philosophers expressed sympathy for Islam, including Johann Wolfgang von Goethe (who particularly admired the Sufi poetry of Hafez) and later Friedrich Nietzsche (in The Antichrist, he claimed that the Germanic spirit was closer to the Moors of Al-Andalus than that of Greece, Rome and Christianity).

The German Empire had over two million Muslim subjects, mostly Sunnis, in overseas colonies. The Majority lived in German East Africa. Several Muslim revolts against German colonial rule occurred, including the Adamawa Campaign, Maji Maji Rebellion and Abushiri revolt.

1920s to the 1940s

The Islamic Institut Ma'ahad-ul-Islam was founded in 1927 and is now known under the name "Zentralinstitut Islam-Archiv-Deutschland" (Central Islamic Archive Institute) and is the oldest such institution in Germany. Shortly after its founding the Nazi Party came to power the archive was forced to suspend all further work, until after the war. During World War II Grand Mufti of Jerusalem Haj Amin al-Husseini energetically recruited Muslims from occupied territories into several divisions of the Waffen SS (primarily the 13th Waffen Mountain Division of the SS Handschar (1st Croatian) and 21st Waffen Mountain Division of the SS Skanderbeg) and some other units.

In September 1943 Hitler specifically decreed that Muslim Germans could be members of the party as well as people of Christian denominations.

Post-war Germany

After the West German Government invited foreign workers ("Gastarbeiter") in 1961, the figure sharply rose to currently 4.3 million (most of them Turkish from the rural region of Anatolia in southeast Turkey). They are sometimes called a parallel society within ethnic Germans.

According to the German statistical office 9.1% of all newborns in Germany had Muslim parents in 2005.

In 2017, Muslims and Islamic institutions were targeted by attacks 950 times, where houses are painted with Nazi symbols, hijab-wearing women are harassed, threatening letters are sent and 33 people were injured. In nearly all cases, the perpetrators were right-wing extremists.

In May 2018 a court in Berlin upheld the right to the state's neutrality principle by barring a primary school teacher from wearing a headscarf during classes, where the court spokesman stated that children should be free of the influence that can be exerted by religious symbols.

According to a study in 2018 by Leipzig University, 56% of Germans sometimes thought that many Muslims made them feel like strangers in their own country, up from 43% in 2014. In 2018, 44% thought immigration by Muslims should be banned, up from 37% in 2014.

In December 2018, the government of Germany strengthened the control of Saudi, Kuwaiti and Qatari funding for radical mosque congregations. The measure was recommended by an anti-terrorist agency in Berlin (German: Terrorismus-Abwehrzentrum) which since 2015 had started to monitor Safalist proselytizing funding in the wake of the European migrant crisis to prevent refugees from becoming radicalized. Henceforth Gulf authorities are required to report payments and funding to the German Federal Foreign Office (German: Auswärtiges Amt).

Between 2010 and 2016, the number of Muslims living in Germany increased from 3.3 million (4.1% of the population) to nearly 5 million (6.1%). The most important factor in the growth of Germany's Muslim population is immigration.

In December 2018, there were no official statistics on how much funding mosques in Germany received from abroad.

In July 2020, federal state Baden-Württemberg banned face-covering veils for school pupils as an extension of the ban which was already in force for staff.

Denominations

Muslims in Germany belong to several different branches of Islam (approximate data):

- Sunnis 2,640,000

- Alevis 500,000

- Twelvers Shi'as 225,500

- Alawites 70,000

- Ahmadiyya 35,000-45,000

- Salafis 10,300

- Sufis 10,000

- Ismailis 1,900

- Zaydis 800

- Ibadis 270

Islamic organisations

Only a minority of the Muslims residing in Germany are members of religious associations.

Sunni

- Diyanet İşleri Türk İslam Birliği (DİTİB): German branch of the Turkish Presidency for Religious Affairs, Cologne. As of 2016, the Turkish government funds and provides staff for 900 of Germany's roughly 3000 mosques run by DİTİB.

- Islamische Gemeinschaft Milli Görüş: close to the Islamist Saadet Partisi in Turkey, Kerpen near Cologne

- Islamische Gemeinschaft Jamaat un-Nur (de): German branch of the Risale-i Nur Society (Said Nursi)

- Islamische Gemeinschaft in Deutschland organization of Arab Muslims close to the Muslim Brotherhood, Frankfurt

In addition there are numerous local associations without affiliation to any of these organisations. Two organisations have been banned in 2002 because their programme was judged as contrary to the constitution: The "Hizb ut-Tahrir" and the so-called "Caliphate State" founded by Cemalettin Kaplan and later led by his son Metin Kaplan.

Shia

- Islamische Gemeinschaft der schiitischen Gemeinden Deutschlands (IGS): Head organization that unite all Shiite mosques and associations in Germany, with being the Islamic Centre Hamburg the most important Shia mosque in Germany.

- Al-Mustafa Institut Berlin: A branch of the Al-Mustafa International University in Qum, Iran to Islamic theology to students in Germany and Europe.

Ahmadiyya

- Ahmadiyya Muslim Jamaat Deutschland K.d.ö.R.: German branch of the worldwide Ahmadiyya Community. There is no ethnicity or race associated with this community although most of the members of the community residing in Germany are of Pakistani origin. The Ahmadiyya Community was established in Germany in 1923 in Berlin and is one of the largest in Europe. Communities exist in Baden-Württemberg, Lower Saxony, North Rhine-Westphalia, Hesse and Bremen.

- Lahore Ahmadiyya Movement: German branch of the worldwide Lahore Ahmadiyya Movement.

Liberal Islam

- Ibn Ruschd-Goethe mosque in Berlin was founded by Seyran Ateş. The liberal mosque has been condemned by the Turkish religious authority and the Egyptian Fatwa Council at the Al-Azhar University.

- Ibn Rushd Prize for Freedom of Thought

Wahhabism

- King Fahd Academy, sponsored by Saudi Arabia. The school was closed at the end of the 2016/2017 school year, after long-running criticism that it was attracting Islamists to Germany.

- According to the FFGI at Goethe University Frankfurt, wahhabist ideology is spread in Germany as in other European country mostly by an array of informal, personal and organisational networks, where organisations closely associated with the government of Saudi Arabia such as the Muslim World League (WML) and the World Association of Muslim Youth are actively participating.

Others

- Verband der islamischen Kulturzentren: German branch of the conservative Süleymancı sect in Turkey, Cologne

- Verband der Islamischen Gemeinden der Bosniaken: Bosnian Muslims, Kamp-Lintfort near Duisburg

- Zentralinstitut Islam-Archiv-Deutschland e.V.: Documentary of Islamic Foundation-writings since 1739. The Islamic

Institute was founded in 1942 (Sooner called Ma'ahad-ul-Islam Institut).

Umbrella organisations

Furthermore, there are the following umbrella organisations:

- Central Council of Muslims in Germany (Zentralrat der Muslime in Deutschland)

- Islamic Council in Germany (Islamrat in Deutschland)

Education

- The A-Nur-Kita preschool was closed in February 2019 due to its parent organisation, the mosque association Arab Nil Rhein in Mainz propagated material from the Muslim Brotherhood and salafist ideology. Therefore, the parent association was incompatible with the constitution of Germany. This was the first time authorities closed any preschool in Rhineland-Palatinate (German: Rheinland-Pfalz). A-Nur-Kita was the first and only Muslim preschool in Rhineland-Palatinate.

Controversies

As elsewhere in Western Europe, the rapid growth of the Muslim community in Germany has led to social tensions and political controversy, partly connected to Islamic extremism, and more generally due to the perceived difficulties of multiculturalism and fears of Überfremdung.

Antisemitism

Perpetrators of antisemitistic verbal harassment and physical assault as reported by Jewish victims. An attacker may belong to more than 1 group.

A 2012 poll showed that 18% of the Turks in Germany think of Jews as inferior human beings. A 2017 study on Jewish perspectives on antisemitism in Germany by Bielefeld University found that individuals and groups belonging to the extreme right and extreme left were equally represented as perpetrators of antisemitic harassment and assault, while the largest part of the attacks were committed by Muslim assailants. The study also found that 70% of the participants feared a rise in antisemitism due to immigration citing the antisemitic views of the refugees. Many of this started in 2015 when a large quantity of Islamic refugees entered Germany.

According to the Federal Office for the Protection of the Constitution, the majority of Islamist organizations in Germany cultivate antisemitic propaganda and distribute it in various ways.

Islamophobia

Islamophobia in Germany refers to the set of discourses, behaviors and structures which express feelings of anxiety, fear, hostility and rejection towards Islam and/or Muslims in Germany. Islamophobia can manifest itself through discrimination in the workforce, negative coverage in the media, and violence against Muslims. Various Islamic groups in Germany have expressed concerns over the attacks targeting mosques.

In the education system

One issue concerns the wearing of the head-scarf by teachers in schools and universities. The right to practice one's religion, stated by the teachers in question, contradicts in the view of many the neutral stance of the state towards religion. As of 2006, many of the German federal states have introduced legislation banning head-scarves for teachers. However, such a ban in North-Rhein

Westphalia was declared as unconstitutional in 2015 by the Federal Constitutional Court.

In the German federal states with the exception of Bremen, Berlin and Brandenburg, lessons of religious education overseen by the respective religious communities are taught as an elective subject in state schools. It is being discussed whether apart from the Catholic and Protestant (and in a few schools, Jewish) religious education that currently exists, a comparable subject of Islamic religious education should be introduced as a regular part of the curricula. In several states, trials for Islamic religious education are being conducted, while in the states of Hessen, Lower-Saxony and Northrhine-Westphalia, Islamic religious education already is integrated as a regular class. The problem that the cooperation with Islamic organisations is hampered by the fact that none of them can be considered as representative of the whole Muslim community.

The discussion of religious (Islamic) education in German schools started in the 1970s, and also symmetrically with issues of Qur'anic classes as well as its deterrent effects on the integration of Turkish students into the country.

Construction of mosques and other projects

The construction of mosques is occasionally resisted by anti Muslim reactions in the neighborhoods concerned. For example, in 2007 an attempt by Muslims to build a large mosque in Cologne sparked a controversy.

There are now 18 official mosques in the country that have been established as mosques since time immemorial. Muslim places of worship (such as mosques and other places of worship) are estimated at between 1,000 and 1,200. Most of these mosques are temporarily built and are mostly located in rented places, factories or warehouses. According to the archives of the Central Institute of Islam, the most important mosques in Germany are located in cities such as Hamburg, Berlin, Mannheim, Marl, Dortmund, Cologne, Frankfurt, Wesling, Bonn, Zingen, Fortsheim, as well as mosques in the cities of Aachen and Munich are important mosques in Germany. These mosques are far from the city center and are often located in industrial areas.

Islamic Theological Studies

In 2010, the German Ministry of Education and Research established Islamic Theological Studies as an academic discipline at public universities in order to train teachers for Islamic religious education and Muslim theologians. Since then, Islamic theological departments have been established at several universities, conducting research and teaching on Islam from a theological perspective.

Islamic fundamentalism

Concerns of Islamic fundamentalism came to the fore after 11 September 2001, especially with respect to Islamic fundamentalism among second- and third-generation Muslims in Germany - the Hamburg cell, which included Mohamed Atta, was prominent in the planning and execution of 11 September attacks. Also the various confrontations between Islamic religious law (Sharia) and the norms of German Grundgesetz and culture are the subject of intense debate. German critics include both liberals and Christian groups. The former claim that Islamic fundamentalism violates basic fundamental rights whereas the latter maintain that Germany is a state and society grounded in the Christian tradition.

According to a 2007 Federal Ministry of the Interior report almost half of all young Muslims in Germany support fundamentalist views. About 12% of Muslims in Germany identified with moral-religious criticism against Western societal values in combination with corporal punishment up to and including the death penalty.

According to a 2012 poll, 72% of the Turks in Germany believe that Islam is the only true religion and 46% wish that one day more Muslims live in Germany than Christians. According to a 10-year survey by the University of Bielefeld, which dealt with different aspects of attitudes to Islam, "distrust" of Islam is widespread in Germany with only 19 per cent of Germans believing that Islam is compatible with German culture.

According to 2013 study by Social Science Research Center Berlin, two thirds of the Muslims interviewed say that religious rules are more important to them than the laws of the country in which they live, almost 60 per cent of the Muslim respondents reject homosexuals as friends; 45 per cent think that Jews cannot be trusted; and an equally large group believes that the West is out to destroy Islam (Christian respondents' answers for comparison: As many as 9 per cent are openly anti-Semitic; 13 per cent do not want to have homosexuals as friends; and 23 per cent think that Muslims aim to destroy Western culture).

According to a 2012 poll, 25% of the Turks in Germany believe atheists are inferior human beings.

Salafism

Salafism is a part of the Sunni branch of Islam which is a revival of original Islamic ideals. Salafists strive to live exclusively according to the Quran and Sunnah. According to German authorities, Salafism is incompatible with the principles codified in the Constitution of Germany, in particular democracy, the rule of law and a political order based on human rights. According to the German security service, the Salafist movement attracts rising numbers. In 2011 there were an estimated 3800 Salafists in Germany, which rose to 10300 in September 2017. According to head of security office Hans-Georg Maaßen, the Salafist scene in Germany is not dominated by any one single individual, but instead a great many persons have to be monitored.

According to German Federal Agency for Civic Education, the Salafist movement in Germany is centered in the Frankfurt Rhine-Main metropolitan area, North Rhine-Westphalia and Berlin. In these areas, mosques and charismatic imams are the driving factors behind recruitment to the Salafist movement.

In 2016, the interior ministry of North Rhine-Westphalia reported that the number of mosques with a Salafist influence had risen from 30 to 55, which indicated both an actual increase and improved reporting.

In February 2017, the German Salafist mosque organisation Berliner Fussilet-Moscheeverein was banned by authorities. Anis Amri, the perpetrator of the 2016 Berlin truck attack, was said to be among its visitors. In March 2017, the German Muslim community organisation Deutschsprachige Islamkreis Hildesheim was also banned after investigators found that its members were preparing to travel to the conflict zone in Syria to fight for the Islamic State. According to the Federal Agency for Civic Education, these examples show that Salafist mosques not only concern themselves with religious matters, but also prepare serious crimes and terrorist activities.

Islamist scene in Germany

Turkish and Kurdish Islamist groups are also active in Germany, and Turkish and Kurdish Islamists have co-operated in Germany as in the case of the Sauerland terror cell. Political scientist Guido Steinberg stated that many top leaders of Islamist organizations in Turkey fled to Germany in the 2000s, and that the Turkish (Kurdish) Hizbullah has also "left an imprint on Turkish Kurds in Germany. Also many Kurds from Iraq (there are about 50,000 to 80,000 Iraqi Kurds in Germany) financially supported Kurdish-Islamist groups like Ansar al Islam. Many Islamists in Germany are ethnic Kurds (Iraqi and Turkish Kurds) or Turks. Before 2006, the German Islamist scene was dominated by Iraqi Kurds and Palestinians, but since 2006 Kurds and Turks from Turkey are dominant.

In 2016, the German security service estimated that about 24 000 Muslims were part of Islamists movements in Germany, of which 10 000 belonged to the Salafist scene. In 2016, 90 mosques were monitored by the Federal Office for the Protection of the Constitution for their Islamist ideology. These were mostly Arabic-language "backyard mosques" where self-appointed imams exhorted their followers to wage jihad. Since the start of 2017 until April 2018, 80 Islamist extremists without German citizenship were deported to their home countries. In March 2018, there were 760 Islamists in Germany classified as dangerous by police authorities, of which more than half were on German territory and 153 of the latter were in prison. In recent years, Mosques in Germany have been receiving larger quantities of hate mail as well as threats.

Sharia police trial

A group of men were walking the streets of Wuppertal carrying vests labelled "Sharia Police". The men claimed they wanted to talk to young Muslims and discourage them from visiting betting halls, brothels and stop them from drinking alcohol. They were charged with breaching the regulation against carrying political uniforms but were acquitted by the district court in Wuppertal. The prosecutor appealed the decision to the German Federal Court of Justice, which annulled the acquittal in January 2018. In the retrial, the men were convicted and sentenced to pay fines as their garments suggested militancy due to the violent nature of similarly named organisations in the Middle East.

Banning of IHH Germany

In July 2010, Germany outlawed the Internationale Humanitäre Hilfsorganisation e.V. (IHH Germany), saying it had used donations to support Hamas, which is considered by the European Union and Germany to be a terrorist organization, while presenting their activities to donors as humanitarian help. German Interior Minister Thomas de Maiziere said, "Donations to so-called social welfare groups belonging to Hamas, such as the millions given by IHH, actually support the terror organization Hamas as a whole." IHH e.V. was believed by the German Authorities to have collected money in mosques and to have sent $8.3 million to organizations related to Hamas.

Religiosity of young Muslims

Studies show that while not all Muslims are religious, Muslim youths are markedly more religious than non-Muslim youths. A study comparing Turkish Muslim youths living in Germany and

German youth found that the former were more likely to attend religious services regularly (35% versus 14%).

41% of young Turkish Muslim boys and 52% of the girls said they prayed "sometimes or regularly"; 64% of boys and 74% of girls said they wanted to teach their children religion.

Notable Germans immigrants

- Vaneeza Ahmad, Pakistani-German model
- Laith Al-Deen, German singer
- Mehmed Ali Pasha (marshal) was a German-born Ottoman soldier
- Nadiem Amiri, German professional footballer
- Azet, German rapper
- Kristiane Backer, German television presenter, television journalist and author
- Danny Blum, German Soccer player
- Bushido, German rapper
- Denis Cuspert, German militant Islamist and former rapper
- Mahmoud Dahoud, football player
- Ibrahim El-Zayat, European Muslim activist in Germany and has been a functionary in many important Islamic organizations in Germany, Europe, and Saudi Arabia.
- Cemile Giousouf, German politician and a member of the German parliament Bundestag
- Fritz Grobba was a German diplomat during the interwar period and World War II

- Karim Guédé, football player

- Kollegah, German rapper

- Murad Wilfried Hofmann, prominent German diplomat and author

- Hadayatullah Hübsch, German writer and journalist

- Lamya Kaddor, German writer and known for introducing Islamic education in German in public schools in Germany

- Jawed Karim, German-American Internet entrepreneur

- Elsa Kazi was a German writer of one-act plays, short stories, novels and history, and a poet

- Hasnain Kazim, author and journalist, correspondent of the German news magazine Der Spiegel and Spiegel Online

- Rani Khedira, football player

- Sami Khedira, German Soccer player

- Sead Kolašinac, Bosnian professional footballer

- Mojib Latif, Professor, meteorologist and oceanographer

- Johann von Leers was a member of the Waffen SS in Nazi Germany, where he was also a professor known for his anti-Jewish polemics

- Jamal Malik, Professor of Islamic Studies and chair of Religious Studies, University of Erfurt, Germany

- Shkodran Mustafi, German professional footballer

- Nash, German rapper

- Adam Neuser was a popular pastor and theologian

- Morsal Obeidi, murder victim, of Afghan origin

- Nura Habib Omer, German rapper

- Susanne Osthoff, German archaeologist

- Leroy Sané, German football player

- Annemarie Schimmel

- Adel Tawil, German singer

- Bassam Tibi, political scientist and Professor of International Relations

- Pierre Vogel (born 1978), also known as Abu Hamza (Arabic: أبو حمزة), German Salafi Islamist preacher and former professional boxer

- Linda Wenzel, German schoolgirl who went missing in 2016 after converting to Islam and joining Islamic State of Iraq and the Levant

Chapter 10

Poland, Norway, Sweden

A continuous presence of Islam in Poland began in the 14th century. From this time it was primarily associated with the Lipka Tatars, many of whom settled in the Polish–Lithuanian Commonwealth while continuing their traditions and religious beliefs. The first significant non-Tatar groups of Muslims arrived in Poland in the 1970s, though they are a very small minority.

Today, less than 0.1% of the population in Poland is Muslim. The majority of Muslims in Poland are Sunni.

Beginnings

The first Tatar (Lipka) settlers arrived in the 14th century. Although Muslims were involved in earlier Mongol invasions of Poland in the 13th century, these had a purely military character and there are no traces of settlement or conversion of any parts of the Polish population.

On the other hand, Arab merchants including Muslims arrived in Polish lands during the time of Mieszko I, as can be seen by a large number of Arab coins found in numerous archaeological sites throughout modern Poland.

The Tatar tribes arriving in the 14th century settled in the lands of the Grand Duchy of Lithuania. Skilled warriors and great mercenaries, their settlement was promoted by the Grand Dukes of Lithuania, among them Gediminas, Algirdas and Kęstutis. The Tatars who settled in Lithuania, Ruthenia and modern-day eastern Poland were allowed to preserve their Islam religion in exchange for military service. The initial settlements were mostly temporary and most of the Tatars returned to their native lands after their service expired. However, in the late 14th century Grand Duke Vytautas (named by the Tatars Wattad, that is defender of Muslims) and his brother King Władysław Jagiełło started to settle Tatars in the Polish–Lithuanian–Teutonic borderlands. The Lipka Tatars, as they are known, migrated from the lands of the Golden Horde and in large part served in the Polish–Lithuanian military. The largest of such groups to arrive to the area was a tribe of Tokhtamysh, who in 1397 rebelled against his former protector Tamerlane and sought asylum in the Grand Duchy. The Tatars under his command were all granted szlachta (nobility) status, a tradition that was preserved until the end of the Commonwealth in the late 18th century. Light Tatar cavalry, used both as skirmishers and reconnaissance troops took part in many of the battles against the foreign armies in the 15th century and afterwards, including the battle of Grunwald in which the Tatars fought commanded by their leader, Jalal ad-Din khan.

16th–18th century

In the 16th and 17th centuries, additional Tatars found refuge in the lands of the Polish–Lithuanian Commonwealth, mostly of Nogay and Crimean origin. After then until the 1980s, the Muslim faith in Poland was associated primarily with the Tatars. It is estimated that in the 17th century there were approximately 15,000 Tatars in the

Commonwealth of a total population of 8 million. Numerous royal privileges, as well as internal autonomy granted by the monarchs of the Polish-Lithuanian Commonwealth, allowed the Tatars to preserve their religion, traditions and culture throughout the ages. The most notable military clans were granted with Coats of Arms and szlachta status, while many other families melted into the rural and burgher society. The first Tatar settlements were founded near the major towns of the Commonwealth in order to allow for fast mobilization of troops. Apart from religious freedom, the Tatars were allowed to marry Polish and Ruthenian women of Catholic or Orthodox faith, uncommon in Europe of that time. Finally, the May Constitution granted the Tatars with a representation in the Polish Sejm.

Perhaps the only moment in history when the Lipka Tatars fought against the Commonwealth was during the so-called Lipka Rebellion of 1672. The "Deluge" and the ensuing period of constant wars made the szlachta of central Poland associate the Muslim Lipkas with the invading forces of the Ottoman Empire. This, combined with the Counter-Reformation promoted by the Vasa dynasty led the Sejm to gradually limit the privileges of the Polish Muslims; among the measures taken were banning the repair of old Mosques and preventing new ones from being constructed, banning serfdom of Christians under Muslims, banning marriage of Christian females to Muslims, putting limitations on property ownership among Tatars. The Polish–Ottoman Wars fed into the discriminatory atmosphere against them and led to anti-Islamic writings and attacks.

Although King John Casimir of Poland tried to limit the restrictions on their religious freedoms and the erosion of their ancient rights and privileges, the gentry opposed. Finally, in 1672, during the war with the Ottomans, the Lipka Tatar regiments (numbering up to 3,000 men) stationed in the Podolia region of south-east Poland abandoned the Commonwealth at the start of the Polish-Turkish wars that were to last to end of the 17th century with the Peace of Karłowice in 1699. Although the Lipkas initially fought for the victorious Turks, soon their camp was divided onto the supporters of the Turks and a large part of Tatars dissatisfied with the Ottoman rule. Although after the treaty of Buczacz the Tatars were granted lands around the fortresses of Bar and Kamieniec Podolski, the liberties enjoyed by their community within the Ottoman Empire were much less than those within the Commonwealth. Finally, in 1674, after the Polish victory at Chocim, the Lipka Tatars who held the Podolia for Turkey from the stronghold of Bar were besieged by the armies of Jan Sobieski, and a deal was struck that the Lipkas would return to the Polish side subject to their ancient rights and privileges being restored. All the Tatars were pardoned by Sobieski and most of them took part in his campaign against Turkey resulting in the brilliant victory in the battle of Vienna. The Lipka Rebellion forms the background to the novel Fire in the Steppe (Pan Wołodyjowski), the final volume of the Nobel Prize-winning historical Trylogia of Henryk Sienkiewicz. The 1969 film adaptation Colonel Wolodyjowski, directed by Jerzy Hoffman and starring Daniel Olbrychski as Azja Tuhaj-bejowicz, was one of the largest box-office success in the history of Polish cinema.

Although by the 18th century most of the Tatars serving in the military had become polonized, while the lower classes of the Muslim community gradually adopted the Ruthenian language (the predecessor of the modern Belarusian language), traditions were preserved. This led to formation of a distinctive Muslim culture of Central Europe, in which elements of Muslim orthodoxy mixed with religious tolerance and a relatively liberal society. For instance, the women in Lipka Tatar society traditionally had the same rights as men, were granted equal status and could attend common non-segregated schools.

20th century

By the beginning of the 20th century, Lipka Tatars had become so integrated into Polish society that they joined their Roman Catholic brethren in the mass migrations for the United States that gave rise to American Polonia, even founding their own mosque in Brooklyn, New York, which is still in use today. In 1919, at the outbreak of the Polish–Soviet War, two of the Tatar officers serving with the Polish Army Col. Maciej Bajraszewski and Capt. Dawid Janowicz-Czaiński started forming a Tatar cavalry regiment fighting alongside the Polish Army. This unit transformed into a squadron after the war, continued the traditions of Tatar military formations of the Polish-Lithuanian Commonwealth and became one of the most notable achievements of the Polish Tatar community in the 20th century. With the restoration of Polish independence, the Tatar community of Poland numbered around 6,000 people (according to the 1931 national census), mostly inhabiting the regions of Wilno, Nowogródek and Białystok Voivodeships. A large community of the Lipka Tatars remained outside of Polish borders, mostly in Lithuania and Belarus (especially in Minsk, the capital of the Belarusian SSR). Although small, the Tatar community formed one of the most vibrant national minorities of Poland. The Muslim Religious Association (est. 1917) focused on preserving the Muslim faith and religious beliefs. At the same time the Cultural and Educational Association of Polish Tatars worked on the preservation and strengthening of Tatar culture and traditions. In 1929 a Tatar National Museum was created in Wilno and in 1931 a

Tatar National Archive was formed. All the Muslim people drafted into the army were sent to the Tatar Cavalry Squadron of the 13th Cavalry Regiment, which was allowed to use its own uniforms and banners. The Army Oath for Muslim soldiers was different from the one taken from soldiers of other denominations and was sworn in presence of Ali Ismail Woronowicz, the Chief Imam of the Polish Army.

During and after World War II, the Tatar communities of Poland suffered the fate of all the civilian populations of the new German-Soviet and later Polish-Soviet borderlands. The Tatar intelligentsia was in large part murdered by the German occupiers in the AB Action, while much of the civilian population was targeted by post-war expulsions. After the war the majority of Tatar settlements were annexed by the Soviet Union and only three remained in Poland (Bohoniki, Kruszyniany and Sokółka). However, a considerable number of Tatars moved across to the Polish side of the border and settled in several locations in eastern Poland (esp. in Białystok and nearby towns) as well as in western and northern Poland (esp. in Gdańsk and Gorzów Wielkopolski). Nowadays no more than 400–4,000 Muslims of Tatar origin live in Poland and a much larger and active Tatar community lives in Belarus and also in Lithuania. In 1971 the Muslim Religious Association was reactivated and since 1991 the Society of Muslims in Poland is also active. The following year also the Association of Polish Tatars was restored.

The 2002 census showed only 447 people declaring Tatar nationality. According to the 2011 census, there are 1,916 Tatars in Poland (including 1,251 people who declared composite national-ethnic identity, e.g. identify as both Polish and Tatar). In recent years, increasing oppressions from Alexander Lukashenko's authoritarian Government in Belarus and economic hardships prompts a larger number of Lipka Tatars to come to Poland.

In November 2010, a monument to Poland's Islamic leader Dariusz Jagiełło was unveiled in the port city of Gdańsk at a ceremony attended by President Bronislaw Komorowski, as well as Tatar representatives from across Poland and abroad. The monument is a symbol of the important role of Tatars in Polish history. The monument is the first of its kind to be erected in Europe.

Tatars shed their blood in all national independence uprisings. Their blood seeped into the foundations of the reborn Polish Republic

—President of Poland Bronisław Komorowski at the unveiling of the monument in Gdańsk.

Recent years

Apart from the traditional Tatar communities, since the 1960's Poland has also been home to a small, immigrant Muslim community.

In the 1960's and 1970's Poland attracted a number of immigrants from many socialist-friendly Arabic-speaking Muslim states of the Middle East and North Africa. Some of them decided to stay in Poland. In the late 1980s this community became more active and better organized. They have built mosques and praying houses in Warsaw, Białystok, Gdańsk (built by the Tatar community), Wrocław, Lublin and Poznań. There are also praying rooms in Bydgoszcz, Kraków, Łódź, Olsztyn, Katowice and Opole.

Since the overthrow of the Polish communist regime in 1989, other Muslim immigrants have come to Poland. Relatively prominent groups are Turks and fellow ethnic-Slavic Muslims from the former Yugoslavia. There are also smaller groups of immigrants from Bangladesh, Afghanistan, and from other countries, as well as a refugee community coming from Chechnya.

The Polish Shia minority includes foreign students, migrants, and embassy staff, mainly from countries such as Iraq, Iran, Bahrain, Lebanon, along with native converts to Islam. Currently, Shi'ites in the country do not have their own freestanding mosque, but they do meet for weekly Friday prayer and major Islamic holidays.

The exact number of Muslims living in Poland remains unknown as the last all-national census held by the Central Statistical Office in 2011 did not ask for religion.

Tatar–Salafi relations

There's an ongoing conflict between Polish native Sunni Muslim Lipka Tatars, who have a unique approach towards Islam and have been living in Poland for 600 years, and an increasingly vocal group of mainly foreign-born and foreign-sponsored, but also native-born convert, group of Sunni Muslims who adhere to the Salafi movement. The conflict divides country's Sunni Muslims and causes bureaucratic confusion, as both sides lay claim to representation of country's Sunni Muslims. The "native born" Sunni Muslims (Lipka Tatars), run Muzułmański Związek Religijny w Rzeczypospolitej Polskiej (Muslim Religious Union in the Polish Republic), and "foreign born" Sunni Muslims run Liga Muzułmańska w Rzeczypospolitej Polskiej (Muslim League in the Polish Republic). The latter is mainly based upon foreigners living in the country, such as Arabs, Bengalis, Chechens etc. Liga Muzułmańska is also a branch of a worldwide Muslim Brotherhood organization.

Islamophobia

Despite the fact that Muslims in Poland constitute less than 0.1% of the total population, stereotypes, verbal, violent, and physical displays of anti-Islam are widespread and, mostly, socially acceptable. Vandalism and attacks on the very few existing mosques are reported, and women (especially converts) who cover themselves are seen as "traitors" to their own culture.

From January 1, 2013, Poland's Muslims and Jews were both affected by a European Union ban on ritual slaughter after lawmakers deemed halal and kosher practices incompatible with animal rights legislation, specifically the Animal Protection Law of 1997. In December 2014, the Constitutional Tribunal ruled the ban unconstitutional on the grounds that it violated freedom of religion guaranteed by the Polish laws and constitution. Both ways of slaughtering animals were illegal in the country between January 1, 2013 and December, 2014, almost two years, and still is a controversial topic because of the concern of animal cruelty by those practices.

In May, 2016, shortly before the World Youth Day 2016, police in Kraków asked foreigners, mainly among the Muslim community, in the city if they "knew any terrorists". The Polish Ombudsman's office released statement that such actions are offensive and unacceptable.

Notable Muslims

- Tomasz Miśkiewicz, mufti of the Polish Muslim Religious Union
- Selim Chazbijewicz, political scientist and writer
- Osman Achmatowicz, academic and chemist

- Aleksander Jeljaszewicz, unit commander in the Polish army
- Jakub Szynkiewicz, religious scholar and writer
- Veli Bek Jedigar, commander in the Polish army
- Jahangir bey Kazimbeyli, Polish army officer
- Israfil Israfilov, Polish army officer
- Mamed Khalidov, Russian-born Polish mixed martial artist

NORWAY

History

Icelandic annals date the arrival of representatives from the Muslim sultan of Tunis in Norway in the 1260s, after King Håkon Håkonsson had sent embassies to the Sultan with rich gifts. However, the number of Muslims in the country was not significant until the latter half of the 20th century. By 1958, Ahmadiyya missionaries had attracted a small number of converts and established a small community in Oslo. Immigration from Muslim countries to Norway began late compared to other western European countries and did not gather pace until the late 1960s. However, due to the oil boom, labor migration lasted longer than in other countries. The first Pakistani immigrant laborers arrived in 1967. In 1975, labor immigration to Norway was halted, but rules for family reunification were relatively relaxed for several more years. As a result, while most immigrants until the 1970s were laborers, immigration in the 1980s and 1990s was dominated by those seeking asylum.

The number of Muslims in Norway was first registered in official statistics in 1980 when it was given as 1006. These statistics were based on membership of a registered congregation. The actual number is likely to be higher given that few Muslims were then members of a mosque. Historian of religion Kari Vogt estimates that 10% of Norwegian Muslims were members of a mosque in 1980, a proportion which had increased to 70% by 1998. Being a member of a mosque was an alien concept to many immigrants from Muslim countries. The number of registered members of mosques increased to 80,838 in 2004, but then dropped to 72,023 in 2006.

Part of the reason for the drop could be a new methodology in the compilation of statistics.

At the end of the 1990s, Islam passed the Roman Catholic Church and Pentecostalism to become the largest minority religion in Norway, provided Islam is seen as one group. However, as of 2013, the Roman Catholic Church regained its position as the largest minority religion in Norway due to increasing immigration from European countries and less immigration from Muslim-majority countries. In 2009, the total number of registered Muslim congregations was 126. More than 40 prayer locations exist in the city of Oslo.

In 2010 a Muslim from Örebro in Sweden wanted to build a mosque in Tromsø with money from Saudi Arabia but the Norwegian government declined to give permission on the grounds that Saudi Arabia has no freedom of religion and potential Norwegian money to churches in the opposite direction would be stopped as churches are illegal there.

In June 2018, the parliament of Norway passed a bill banning clothing covering the face at educational institutions as well as daycare centres, which included face-covering Islamic veils. The prohibition applies to pupils and staff alike.

Religiosity

Studies conducted for a TV channel in 2006 found that 18% of Norwegian Muslims reported visiting the mosque once a week. A similar study in 2007 reported that 36% of Muslim youth visit the mosque less than once a month.

According to a 2007/2008 survey of students at upper secondary schools in Oslo, 25% of Muslims pray regularly while 12% attend religious services weekly.

Opinion

According to a survey in 2016, about 98% of Norwegian Muslims believed that Human rights are important, about 94% believed Democracy is important, and 95% believed that Muslims should live in peace with Non-Muslims. In the same poll a minority of 47% said that it is not important to follow Sharia law.

According to a 2017 poll, 3 out of 10 Muslims agree it's important to follow Sharia law.

According to a survey of 4,000 Muslims in 2017, only two percent agreed to statements such as "Islam allows the use of violence" and that the September 11 attacks on America in 2001 can be justified.

Radicalizations

About 70 people have left Norway to become foreign fighters in Syria or Iraq, while around 20 have returned.

In May 2019 it was announced that those who had joined the Islamic State who only had residence permits in Norway would have their permits annulled to prevent them from returning to Norway. And in September 2019, 15 foreigners in Norway had their residence permits revoked.

Conversion

In 2004, it was estimated that 500–1,000 Norwegians have converted to Islam. Many Norwegians, both men and women, have converted in order to marry Muslims.

Muslims in Norway are a very fragmented group, coming from many different backgrounds. Kari Vogt estimated in 2000 that there were about 500 Norwegian converts to Islam. The rest are mostly first or second-generation immigrants from a number of countries. The largest immigrant communities from Muslim countries in Norway are from Pakistan, Iraq and Somalia:

Country of origin	Number (2008)
Pakistan	30,134
Somalia	27,881
Iraq	21,795
Bosnia and Herzegovina	15,649
Iran	15,134
Turkey	15,003
Converts	1,000-3,000

An unknown, but presumably high, proportion of these immigrant populations is Muslim. In other words, the largest group of Norwegian Muslims originate in Pakistan, but no single nationality constitute as much as a quarter of the total population.

The Turkish, Pakistani and Iranian communities are quite established in Norway. 55% of Iranians have lived in Norway for more than 10 years. The Iraqis are a more recent group, with 80% of the Iraqi community having arrived in the past 10 years.

In the 1990s there was a wave of asylum seekers from the Balkans, mostly Bosniaks. In recent years most immigrants arrive as part of family reunification.

According to the Verdens Gang newspaper, during the 1990s around 500 people converted to Islam in Norway and this number increased to around 3,000 in 2019.

Organizations

Mosques have been important, not just as places of prayer, but also as a meeting place for members of minority groupings. Several mosques also do different forms of social work, e.g. organising the transport of deceased members back to their countries of origin for burial. The mosques are mostly situated in regular city blocks, and are not easily visible features of the cities.

Some of the earliest attempts to organize Islamic worship in Norway was done by labor organizations as early Muslims were labor migrants. The first mosque was established in 1972 by Pakistani immigrants. Another mosque, the Islamic Cultural Centre (ICC) opened in Oslo in 1974. The initiative for the mosque came from Pakistanis who were helped by the Islamic Cultural Centre which had already opened in Copenhagen in Denmark. The new mosque adhered to the deobandi branch of Sunni Islam. Adherents of the Sufi inspired Barelwi movement, who constituted the majority of Pakistanis in Norway, soon felt the need for a mosque of their own, and opened the Central Jamaat-e Ahl-e Sunnat in 1976. Today this is the second largest mosque in Norway, with over 6,000 members. The first Shia mosque, Anjuman-e hussaini, was founded in 1975, and until 1994 was the only Shia congregation. The Tablighi Jamaat came to Norway in 1977. An Albanian mosque was established in 1989, and a Bosnian mosque in the 1990s. Until the 1990s, mosques and Islamic organizations in Norway were established along ethnic lines. Such establishments were by immigrants from Pakistan, Turkey, Morocco, Arab world, Somalia, The Gambia and Bosnia.

Starting c. 1990, Muslims of different ethnicities and sects came together to form umbrella organizations. The Muslim Defence Committee was established in 1989 to give an Islamic response to the Salman Rushdie affair. The Islamic Women's Group of Norway and Urtehagen Foundation were established in 1991, and in 1993 the Islamic Council of Norway was established to conduct dialogue with the Church of Norway. Another major change in the 1990s was that mosques became more inclusive to women. For example, in 1999 the ICC began offering Arabic and Qur'an classes to women and including women in Eid prayers.

Also in the 1990s, Muslim youth and student associations were established. In 1995, the Muslim Student Society (MSS) was founded at the University of Oslo, driven by a need to find prayer space for Islamic prayer. The MSS soon expanded its activities to include conducting interfaith dialogue, courses on dawah, iftar during Ramadan, and other community projects. In 1996, the Muslim Youth of Norway (NMU) was founded. In 1999, NMU began publishing Explore (later called Ung Muslim) a magazine geared towards Norwegian Muslim youth.

By 2005, only one purpose-built mosque existed in Norway, built by the Sufi-inspired Sunni Muslim World Islamic Mission in Oslo in 1995. Minhaj-ul-Quran International established its mosque and centre in 1987. In 2000, this was the first Norwegian mosque to start performing the adhan - the call to prayer. Initially, the mosque received permission from Gamle Oslo borough to perform the adhan once a week. This was appealed to county authorities by the Progress Party. The ruling of the fylkesmann (county governor) of Oslo and Akershus stated that no permission was required for performing the adhan, leaving the mosque free to perform it at their own discretion. The mosque decided to limit themselves to performing the adhan once a week.

While less than 10% of Muslims were members of an Islamic organization in 1980, this figure rose to 50% in 1990, and increased to 55% by 2007.

Umbrella organisations

The main umbrella organization in Norway is the Islamic Council Norway, which was set up in 1993. As of 2008, it comprises 40 member organisations totalling 60,000 members. One researcher estimates it represents 50-75% of all Norwegian Muslims. Since 1997, the Islamic Council has also had Shia representation. The Islamic Council is regularly consulted by the government in matters of religion. The council is also involved with interfaith dialogue, particularly with the Church of Norway. In 2009, the Islamic Council publicly denounced harassment of homosexuals. Minhaj-ul-Quran has a branch in Norway and community centre was established in Oslo in 1987. In 1991, the Islamic Women's Group Norway (Islamsk Kvinnegruppe Norge) was founded, after an initiative by the Norwegian convert Nina Torgersen. In 1995, a Muslim Students' Society (Muslimsk Studentsamfunn) was established at the University of Oslo, with some of its officers, such as Mohammad Usman Rana, becoming important voices in the Norwegian public sphere. The Islamic foundation Urtehagen was established in 1991 by the Norwegian convert Trond Ali Linstad, at first running a kindergarten and youth club. In 1993, Linstad applied for the first time to establish a Muslim private school. The Labour Party government of Gro Harlem Brundtland rejected the application in 1995, stating that it would be "detrimental to the integration of the children". After the Labour government was replaced by the government of Kjell Magne Bondevik of the Christian People's Party in 1997, Linstad applied again, and his application was approved in 1999. In August 2001, Urtehagen School (Urtehagen friskole) opened with 75 pupils. However, internal conflicts at the school led to its closure in the spring of 2004. Plans to open a similar school in Drammen in 2006 were blocked after the new center-left government stopped all new private schools after coming to power in 2005.

Ahmadiyya

Various Ahmadi mosques include Noor Mosque, opened in Oslo August 1, 1980, and Baitun Nasr Mosque in Furuset, Oslo. There are about 1,700 Ahmadi Muslims in Norway. The majority of the Ahmadi Muslims in Norway are from Pakistan.

Salafi

Profetens Ummah is a Salafist organisation notorious for its statements and vocal demonstrations praising Islamic terrorism. Many Norwegian jihadi fighters for ISIL have links with the organizations, and some Norwegians who joined ISIL were also members of the radical organization Islam Net, founded in 2008.

Non-Denominational Islam

In June 2017, Thee Yezen al-Obaide revealed plans to create a mosque in Oslo named Masjid al-Nisa (The Women's Mosque). In an interview, al-Obaide described the mosque as "a feminist mosque where women have as much space as men. Both men and women should be able to lead prayers, and all genders should be able to pray in the same room." The mosque will also be open to LGBT people and has been compared to the Ibn Ruschd-Goethe mosque in Germany and the Mariam Mosque in Denmark.

Culture

Since 2007, the Islamic Cultural Centre stages an Eid Mela annually that attracts around 5,000 visitors. The event involves food, concerts, and other activities.

Islamic dress

In 2007, a debate arose over banning face veils in higher education but institutions advised against such a bill. Similar debates occurred in 2010 but again did not result in a ban. In 2012, a student at the University of Tromsø was expelled from class by a professor but no general ban was adopted. However, the Oslo City Council and County Board of Østfold banned niqabs in teaching situations at their high schools. Norwegian law does not make reference to the right for people to wear religious headgear, but the issue is part of by the Working Environment Act and the Gender Equality Act. The Norwegian Labour Inspectorate considers refusal to accommodate religious headgear as discrimination. Hijabs have been incorporated into uniforms in the army, healthcare, etc.

In a 2014 poll conducted by the Norwegian Directorate of Integration and Diversity, a majority of Norwegians held negative views over the wearing of the hijab outside the home. Stronger disagreement (75%) was expressed towards the hijab being part of the police uniform in Norway. Concerning the full-cover niqab, 86% expressed a negative or very negative opinion.

In June 2017, the Norwegian government proposed rules banning female students from wearing full-face veils. Education Minister Torbjørn Røe Isaksen said that in their perspective, full-face veils like the hijab have no place in educational settings since they hinder good communication. The administration is subsequently examining the likelihood of controlling the utilization of such pieces of clothing in childcare focuses, schools and colleges.

The Prime Minister of Norway Erna Solberg stated in an interview that in Norwegian work environments it is essential to see each other's faces and therefore anyone who insists on wearing a niqab is in practice unemployable. Solberg also views the wearing of the niqab as a challenge to social boundaries in the Norwegian society, a challenge that would be countered by Norway setting boundaries of its own. Solberg also stated that anyone may wear what they wish in their spare time and that her comments applied to professional life but that any immigrant has the obligation to adapt to Norwegian work life and culture.

In June 2018, the parliament of Norway passed a bill banning clothing covering the face at educational institutions as well as daycare centres, which included face-covering Islamic veils. The prohibition applies to pupils and staff alike.

In April 2019, telecom company Telia received bomb threats after featuring a Muslim woman taking off her hijab in a commercial.

Although the police considered unlikely that the threat would be carried out, delivering such threats is still a crime in Norway.

Interfaith relations

Following the 2015 Copenhagen shootings, Norwegian Muslims were among those taking part in a vigil on February 21, 2015, evening, in which they joined hands with Norwegian Jews and others to form a symbolic protective ring around the Norwegian capital's main synagogue.

In 2010, the Norwegian Broadcasting Corporation after one year of research, revealed that antisemitism was common among Norwegian Muslims. Such antisemitism was condemned by Muslim organizations in Norway.

A 2017 study by the Norwegian Center for Studies of the Holocaust and Religious Minorities found that negative attitudes towards Muslims and Jews were prevalent. 34% of Norwegians had negative attitudes towards Muslims. Among Muslim immigrants who have lived in Norway for at least 5 years, 28.9% had negative attitudes towards Jews (compared to 8.3% for the population). The survey also found that majorities of Norwegian Jews and Norwegian Muslims believed in cooperating with one another to fight discrimination.

Discrimination

Islamophobia refers to the set of discourses, behaviours and structures which express feelings fear, towards Islam and Muslims in Norway. Islamophobia can manifest itself through discrimination in the workforce, negative coverage in the media, and violence against Muslims. In 2004 the slogan, "Ikke mobb kameraten min (Don't touch my hijab)," was adopted by a Norwegian protest movement focused around the case of Ambreen Pervez and a proposed hijab ban. Pervez was told by her employer that she was not to wear her hijab to work. The slogan was an adaption of the French slogans, "Ne touche pas a mon pote (Don't touch my buddy)," and, "Touche pas à mon foulard (Don't touch my hijab.)" A number of employment discrimination cases in Norway arose over the wearing of the hijab.

Public opinion

A 2005 study analyzed the portrayal of Muslims in the 8 largest newspapers of Norway. It found that Muslims were generally portrayed negatively, even more negatively than other immigrants, and only 3% of the articles portrayed Muslims positively.

In a 2014 poll conducted by the Norwegian Directorate of Integration and Diversity, 5 of 10 Norwegians considered Islamic values to be either completely or partially incompatible with Norwegian society.

According to a 2017 poll study by the Norwegian Center for Studies of the Holocaust and Religious Minorities, 34.1% of the population showed strong prejudice against Muslims: 27.8% feels "disgusted" by Muslims; 19.6% would not want Muslims as neighbors; 42% thought that Muslims did not want to integrate into Norway; 39% saw Muslims as a "threat" to Norwegian culture; 31% thought that Muslims wanted to take over Europe. These figures were slightly lower than those from a similar study made in 2011. Nevertheless 75% of Norwegians condemned acts of anti-Muslim violence.

According to a 2020 poll conducted by the Norwegian Directorate of Integration and Diversity, a slight majority of people of Norway (52%) consider Islam incompatible with fundamental values of the Norwegian society. This result had been similar for the last 15 years. By comparison, only a minority (22%) considered Buddhism incompatible with Norwegian values.

SWEDEN

Contacts with the Muslim world dates back to the 7th–10th centuries, when the Vikings traded with Muslims during the Islamic Golden Age. Since the late 1960s and more recently, immigration from predominantly Muslim countries has impacted the demographics of religion in Sweden, and has been the main driver of the spread of Islam in the country.

The Muslim community in Sweden hails from numerous countries, making it a complex and heterogeneous population. According to a 2019 report from the Swedish Agency for Support to Faith Communities, there were 200,445 Muslims in Sweden who practiced their religion regularly; this count came from those registered with Islamic congregations. Population increases between 2004 and 2012 have been attributed to immigrants from Iraq, Somalia, Kosovo and Afghanistan. The US Department of State's Sweden 2014 International Religious Freedom Report set the 2014 figure of Muslims in Sweden at around 600,000 people, 6% of the total Swedish population. A 2017 Pew Research report documents Sweden's Muslim population at 810,000 people, 8.1% of Sweden's total population of 10 million people.

History

Pre-Islamic Arabic coins originating from the Middle East have been found at Iron Age burial sites. Archaeological findings have also shown Viking contact with Islam dating back to the 7th–10th centuries, when the Vikings seem to have been trading with the medieval Islamic world, among others.

The Swedish census in 1930 listed 15 people as belonging to the group "Muslims and other Asian faiths". Although the number of Muslims themselves are not known, one estimate suggests a maximum of 11 but could have been as low as 2.

In modern Sweden, the first registered Muslim groups were Finnish Tatars who emigrated from Finland and Estonia in the 1940s. Islam began to have a noticeable presence in Sweden with immigration from the Middle East beginning in the 1970s. Further waves of immigrants came to Sweden from the former Yugoslav republics, and more recently from Somalia.

Sweden has a number of mosques providing the Muslim communities in Sweden places of worship. The first mosque in Sweden was the Nasir Mosque, built in 1976 in Gothenburg by the Ahmadiyya. It was followed by the Malmö Mosque, 1984, and later, the Uppsala Mosque in 1995. More mosques were built during the 2000s, including the Stockholm Mosque (2000) and the Fittja Mosque (completed 2007), among others. The governments of Saudi Arabia and Libya have financially supported the constructions of some of the largest Mosques in Sweden.

The first meeting between Muslim youth organizations across Europe first took place in Sweden in 1995, in which the Foreign Ministry of Sweden worked with Sveriges Unga Muslimer to hold an international conference titled "Islam in Europe." This led to the creation of the Forum of European Muslim Youth and Student Organizations (FEMYSO).

As of the year 2000, an estimated around 300,000 to 350,000 people of Muslim background lived in Sweden, or 3.5% of total population; thereby included is anyone who fits the broad definition of someone who "belongs to a Muslim people by birth, has Muslim origin, has a name that belongs in the Muslim tradition, etc." regardless of personal religious convictions, of whom about 100,000 were second-generation immigrants (born in Sweden or immigrated as children). In Sweden registration by personal belief is not common and is normally against the law, thus only figures of practising Muslims belonging to an Islamic community can be reported. In 2009, the Muslim Council of Sweden reported 106,327 registered members.

In December 2008, riots broke out in Malmö in the Herrgården section of Rosengård, when the landlord did not renew the contract for the premises of a local mosque. Angry youths occupied the premises for three weeks, at the end of which police coming to evict the occupiers were confronted by about 30 occupiers, including radical Muslims and activists affiliated with the radical leftist Antifaschistische Aktion. The occupiers attacked police with pipe bombs and rocks and the incident rapidly escalated, with protestors arriving from other cities and officials calling in riot police. Rioters set fire to cars, wagons, kiosks, building sheds, recycling stations, and bicycle sheds. After two nights of rioting, 200 adult Malmö residents organized by the Islamiska kulturföreningen ("Islamic Cultural Forum") moved into the streets to mediate, causing the youthful rioters to desist.

In September 2018, the mosque in Alby, Botkyrka via its Green Party member Ali Khalil delivered an offer to the Moderate Party where the 3000 votes of the worshippers would be given to the Moderate Party in exchange for planning permission to build a new mosque. The Green Party forced Khalil to leave the party after the finding was made public by Swedish Television.

In September 2018, the Social Democratic Party in Karlshamn revoked the membership of a Muslim politician after translations from Arabic showed that the politician had campaigned for the supremacy of Islam over Swedish customs, against vulnerable children being taken care of by social services and that women with Arabic heritage should wear the Islamic veil. The statements were verified with interpreters.

In April and May 2019, five senior members of the Swedish Muslim community were detained by the Swedish Migration Agency by orders of the Säpo security police.

In December 2019, the municipality of Skurup banned Islamic veils in educational institutions. Earlier, the municipality of Staffanstorp approved a similar ban.

In 2018, preschools in Biskopsgården district were reprimanded by the Municipality of Gothenburg after Göteborgs-Posten newspaper had found out that 4 out of 5 kindergartens stated they were willing to force girls in their care to wear the Islamic hijab if the parents requested it. The newspaper found a willingness by preschools to force at 27 of the 40 investigated institutions in Malmö, Gothenburg and Stockholm.

Although there are no official statistics of Muslims in Sweden, estimates count 200,000—250,000 people of Muslim background in 2000 (i.e. anyone who fits the broad definition of someone who "belongs to a Muslim people by birth, has Muslim origin, has a name that belongs in the Muslim tradition, etc."), roughly estimated close to 100,000 of which are second-generation. In 2009 a US report stated that there are 450,000 to 500,000 Muslims in Sweden, around 5% of the total population, and that the Muslim Council of Sweden reported 106,327 officially registered members. Swedish estimates are rather 350,000, including nominal Muslims and people from a Muslim background.

Such numbers do not imply religious beliefs or participation; Åke Sander [sv] claimed in 1992 that at most 40–50% of the people of Muslim background in Sweden "could reasonably be considered to be religious", and in 2004, based on discussions and interviews with Muslim leaders, concerning second-generation Muslims born and raised in Sweden that "it does not seem that the percentage they consider to be religious Muslims in a more qualified sense exceeds fifteen percent, or perhaps even less". Sander re-stated in 2004 that "we do not think it unreasonable to put the figure of religious Muslims in Sweden at the time of writing at close to 150,000". Professor Mohammad Fazlhashemi at Umeå University estimates "a good 100,000". About 25,000 are regarded as devout Muslims, visiting Friday prayers and practising daily prayers.

Muslims in Sweden most often originate from Iraq, Iran, Bosnia-Herzegovina, Sandžak and Kosovo, the Iraqis being by far the largest group in 2015. Most Iranians and Iraqis fled as refugees to Sweden during the Iran–Iraq War from 1980 to 1988. The second-largest Muslim group consists of immigrants or refugees from Eastern Europe, particularly from former Yugoslavian countries, most of them being Bosniaks, who number 12,000. There is also a sizeable community of Somalis, who numbered 40,165 in 2011. They are followed by Muslim refugees from Syria and Somalia, two very rapidly growing groups. Two other groups, residing in Sweden for a decade longer, are people from Turkey and Lebanon.

Pew Research Center estimate differs from most other sources and lists the number of self-identified Muslims in Sweden at 810,000 (or 8.1% of the total population) for the year 2016. About a third of these are believed to practice their religion. In order to predict the number of Muslims in Sweden in the year 2050, they looked at three scenarios: zero migration, medium migration (with no new refugees, but same levels of other immigration as recently), and high migration (same total level as 2015-2016). In the year 2050 the number of Muslims in Sweden would be 1,130,000 (or 11.1% of the population) under the zero migration scenario, 2,470,000 (or 20.5% of the population) under the medium migration scenario, and 4,450,000 (or 30.6% of the population) under the high migration scenario. Michael Lipka, editor at Pew, considers the zero and high migration scenarios unlikely. The prediction has been criticized by researchers for not considering that birth rates among immigrants is expected to decrease, and that many immigrants later migrate to other countries or return to their birth countries. On the other hand, the prediction has not considered current asylum seekers waiting for decision, undocumented immigrants and people in a state of impediment to expulsion.

In 2017 Swedish Security Police reported that the number of jihadists in Sweden had risen to thousands from about 200 in 2010. Based on social media analysis, an increase was noted in 2013. BBC reported in 2016 that more than 300 people in Sweden have gone to fight in Iraq and Syria, which makes Sweden a high exporter of jihadists per capita.

Conversion

There are no official statistics on the exact number of Swedish converts to Islam, but Anne Sofie Roald [it], a historian of religions at Malmö University College, estimates the number of converts from the Church of Sweden to Islam to be 3,500 people since the 1960s. Roald further states that conversions are also occurring from Islam to the Church of Sweden, most noticeably by Iranians, but also by Arabs and Pakistanis.

The first known convert to Islam was the famous painter Ivan Aguéli who was initiated into the Shadhiliyya order in Egypt in 1909. It was Aguéli who introduced the French metaphysician René Guénon to Sufism. Aguéli is more known among Sufis by his Muslim name Abdul-Hadi al-Maghribi. Other well-known Swedish converts to Islam are Tage Lindbom, Kurt Almqvist, Mohammed Knut Bernström and Tord Olsson. Lindbom, Almqvist and Olsson are also initiates into various Sufi orders. Bernström translated the Quran into Swedish in 1998.

Places of worship

Several mosques have been built in Sweden since the 1980s, with notable ones in Malmö (1984) and Stockholm (2000). The Bellevue Mosque and the Brandbergen Mosque in the 2000s came to public attention as recruitment and propaganda centers for Islamist terrorism.

In recent years, Islamic places of worship have increasingly been subject to vandalism. Swedish historian Mattias Gardell from Uppsala University sent a survey to 173 mosques, with 106 responding. 59% reported being subject to some sort of physical attack.

Community organisations, funding, and practices

The beginning of nationwide Islamic (Sunni) institutions in Sweden dates back to the creation of FIFS (Förenade Islamiska Församlingar i Sverige) in 1973–1974. In 1982 and 1984 two splits, due to internal rivalries, cultural differences, personal conflicts and funding, brought to the creation of SMF (Svenska Muslimska Förbundet) and ICUS, today IKUS (Islamska Kulturcenterunionen i Sverige).

Other national institutions are BHIRF (Bosnien-Hercegovinas Islamiska riksförbund), founded in 1995 by Bosnian refugees, IRFS (Islamiska Riksförbundet), also since 1995, and SIA (Svenska Islamiska Akademin), founded in 2000 by the former ambassador Mohammed Knut Bernström, with the task of establishing in the future an Islamic university in Sweden, charged with imam education. SIA also publishes since February 2001 the periodical Minaret in Swedish.

There exist also the women association IKF (Islamiska Kvinnoförbund i Sverige), the youth association IUF (Islamiska Ungdomförbundet i Sverige) and the imam association SIR (Sveriges Imamråd). IIF (Islamiska Informationföreningen) is a member association of FIFS aiming at providing information about Islam in Sweden; 1986–2000 it published Salaam, whose editorial board has always been dominated by women, mainly Swedish converts.

National and target organization have also created umbrella organizations in order to simplify their relationships to the state. FIFS and SMF have created in 1990 SMR (Sveriges Muslimska Råd), of which SUM is also member. The IKUS umbrella organization is named IRIS (Islamiska Rådet i Sverige) and includes also IKF, IUF and SIR. Above all, IS (Islamiska samarbetsrådet) deals with financial issues with the commission for state grants to religious communities (SST); it includes FIFS, SMF, IKUS, ISS and SIF.

Islamic Association in Sweden

The Islamic Association in Sweden, (Arabic: الرابطة الأسلامية في السويد) (Swedish: Islamiska förbundet i Sverige, IFiS) was formed according to the records of the Swedish Tax Agency, the protocol of the constituent meeting of The Islamic Association in Sweden (IFiS) on January 27–28, 1995 in the presence of Ahmed Ghanem,

Mostafa Kharraki, Mahmoud Aldebe, Zoheir Berrahmoune, Mahmoud Kalim and Sami al-Sarif. The initiator is the Stockholm organisation Islamiska Förbundet i Stockholm, which runs Stockholm mosque and was found in 1987. IFiS headquarters are located at Stockholm Mosque. According to the IFiS charter, it is a founding member in the Muslim Brotherhood-associated umbrella organisation Federation of Islamic Organisations in Europe whose guidelines it follows. It has started the following organisations, either alone or together with others:

Omar Mustafa is chairman of IFiS since 2011. On 7 April 2013 he was elected to the party committee of the Swedish Social Democratic Party, which was noted by anti-racist magazine Expo as Mustafa, as chairman of IFiS, had invited Salah Sultan and Ragheb Al-Serjany both of whom had spread antisemitic views in al Jazeera interviews and that he also "likes" Egyptian imam Yousef Al-Qaradawi on Facebook. During the Easter of 2013, IFiS invited Yvonne Ridley and Azzam Tamimi to a seminar to a conference it organised together with Ibn Rushd and Sveriges Unga Muslimer. As a result of the discoveries, Mustafa left the Social Democratic Party committee and party.

Muslim Council of Sweden

The Muslim Council of Sweden (Swedish: Sveriges muslimska råd, SMR) is an umbrella organisation of Islamic organisations in Sweden. It was founded in 1990 by representatives of the Förenade islamiska församlingar i Sverige [sv] (FIFS), and the Muslim Association of Sweden (Swedish: Sveriges Muslimska Förbund, SMuF). The former chairwoman of the organisation is Helena Hummasten, who succeeded Mostafa Kharraki.

According to islamologist Sameh Egyptson at Lund University, several people in leadership positions of the council are Islamists and support the Muslim Brotherhood. The council organised a demonstration to protest when Mohamed Morsi was removed from office in Egypt.

In 1999, Mahmoud Aldebe was chairman of the council.

In 1999, the organisation was part of an alliance with the Religious Social Democrats (Swedish: Tro och Solidaritet) faction of the Social Democratic Party, where the council was to gain influence in Swedish politics via quotas for the number of Muslim politicians on election lists for council, region and Riksdag elections. Tro och Solidaritet was to further Islamic interests such as legislation and contracts concerning Muslim holidays, instituting a tax-financed training for imams via the National Agency for Higher Education and rules in working places for the Jumu'ah (Friday prayer). According to Religious Social Democrats chairman Peter Weiderud in 2014, the Religious Social Democrats were still in contact with SMR.

Muslim Youth of Sweden (Sveriges Unga Muslimer)

The organisation Muslim Youth of Sweden (Swedish: Sveriges Unga Muslimer, SUM) with its headquarters at Stockholm Mosque received state aid from the Swedish Agency for Youth and Civil Society (Swedish acronym: MUCF) in the years 2011–2015. SUM had to pay back the government funds for 2016 and 2017 due to the organisation failing to respect the ideals of democracy. A report outlined how sympathisers and activists for extremist movements had leading positions of local chapters of SUM.

A number of Swedish academics member of Antirasistiska Akademin (ArA), among them Edda Manga and Maimuna Abdullahi (also of MMRK) criticized the decision of MUCF to withhold further state aid to the organization.

SUM has a branch in Malmö, named Malmö Unga Muslimer.

In 2019, the administrative court of appeal upheld the decision to deny state aid to the organisation on the grounds that its representatives on occasion had made remarks incompatible with democracy and was ordered to repay 1.4 million SEK.

Islamic Relief

Islamic Relief in Sweden was founded in 1992 and is part of the international Muslim aid charity Islamic Relief which was founded in the UK.

IR in Sweden receives and channels tax funding primarily from government agencies Swedish International Development Cooperation Agency (SIDA) and ForumCiv [sv]. In 2019 IR Sweden received 167 million SEK and 139 million SEK in tax funding.

Muslim Association of Sweden

The Muslim Association of Sweden (Swedish: Sveriges muslimska förbund, SMF) is Sweden's largest Muslim organisation, which represents around 70,000 Muslims in Sweden, which receives state aid from Swedish Agency for Support to Faith Communities. The organization claims to be separate from the Muslim Brotherhood, but does claim to be inspired by its values. For example, one of the representatives of the organization, Mahmoud Aldebe, sent a letter in April 2006 to different Swedish political parties asking to exempt Muslims from Swedish divorce law.

MMRK

Muslimska Mänskliga Rättighetskommittén (MMRK) (loosely translated: "Muslim human rights committee") an organization modeled after the UK-based organisation Cageprisoner. MMRK consider the criminalisation of travelling to commit terror abroad to be a form of racial laws directed towards Muslims. MMRK also claim that returning Foreign Terrorist Fighters do not constitute a security threat. Spokesperson Maimuna Abdullahi also criticized suggestions that travelling to conflict zones should be criminalized in a letter published by Swedish Television.

In May 2010, Munir Awad was invited to speak at a seminar criticizing the anti-terrorism laws of Sweden organized by MMRK. Awad was arrested in December 2010 for the 2010 Copenhagen terror plot for which he was later convicted and sentenced to jail.

MMRK invited the Cageprisoners founders Moazzam Begg and Asim Qureshi to a seminar.

Diyanet

According to Dagens Nyheter in 2017, nine mosques in Sweden have imams sent and paid for by the Turkish Directorate of Religious Affairs (Diyanet). Along with their religious duties, the imams are also tasked with reporting on critics of the Turkish government. According to Dagens Nyheter, propaganda for president Erdogan is openly presented in the mosques.

The Diyanet director of the Swedish branch is Fatih Mehmet Karaca. In November 2016 Karaca forced the finance officer

(Swedish: kassör) of Muslimska församlingen i Malmö mosque (listed above) to resign as the finance officer had expressed views critical of the AKP party which is intolerable according to Diyanet ideology.

Swedish Muslims for Peace and Justice

The Swedish Muslims for Peace and Justice is a self-described peace organization. It was founded in 2008 by a group including the Swedish Parliamentarian Mehmet Kaplan. Kaplan was forced to resign from the Swedish Cabinet due to his association with advocates of violent attacks on Armenians and connections to Islamist militants in Turkey. In 2018 it was headed by former Green Party politician Yasri Khan. Khan was forced to leave the Green Party after he was nominated to the party committee while refusing to shake hands with women on religious grounds.

Hizb ut-Tahrir

In 2012, investigating magazine Expo wrote that the anti-democratic and antisemitic Islamist group Hizb ut-Tahrir had started to establish itself in Sweden. In October 2012 Hizb ut-Tahrir situated its annual "calpiphate conference" in Stockholm. The group at the time had a section for all of Scandinavia which was primarily active in Denmark. The group does not recognize the caliphate as established by ISIL.

In the 2014 and 2018 Swedish general elections, the group campaigned in the Stockholm area for Muslims not to vote.

According to Sayed Jalabi in 2018, the organisation aims to organise a not necessarily violent coup d'état to overthrow the Government of Sweden and instead create a caliphate.

According to a Hizb ut-Tahrir spokesperson for Scandinavia, the organization does not strive to change the political system in Western countries. The Quilliam Foundation, composed of defectors from extremist organizations, Hizb ut-Tahrir does not believe in democratic and open societies and that they hide their intention to abolish democracy in the West.

Educational organizations, their funding, and practices

Ibn rushd studieförbund

Ibn rushd is an educational organization (Swedish: studieförbund) financed by state subsidies from Folkbildningsrådet, a government agency. Principal of the organization (Swedish: förbundsrektor) is Omar Mustafa. The organization gives courses in Dawah (Islamic missionary work). Together with Muslim Youth of Sweden, Ibn Rushd organizes the annual event Muslimska Familjedagarna (MFD) where proponents of sharia law have been invited to seminars.

In 2015, Anas Altikriti was invited to hold a speech at the MFD event.

In 2017, Ibn rushd received 27 million Swedish crowns in state aid for its activities and a further 4.7 million for education of asylum seekers.

Al-Salamskolan

Al-Salamskolan is a charter school in Örebro. It receives about 150-200 thousand Swedish crowns every month from a Saudi foundation connected to the al-Haramain Foundation. The school is run by a foundation controlled by Saudi nationals. Music is banned at the school. Boys and girls are segregated into groups along gender lines for several subjects due to religious reasons. Beyond the national curriculum, the pupils receive ten hours of tuition in Islam and Arabic, which according to the former headmaster at the school was mandatory. In 2017, the school received a 500 000 SEK fine from the Swedish Schools Inspectorate due to deficiencies in its teaching practises. In 2017 the school wanted to fire the chairman of Al-Risalah Scandinavian Foundation, the foundation that funds the school, due to him not being able to be present for meetings.

El Dagve charter school

El Dagve was a Muslim charter school in Jönköping. Headmaster Hassan Meri immatriculated children to the school and received funding from the Jönköping Municipality but sent the pupils to school in their home countries instead, keeping the difference. In 2004 the school was closed by Swedish Work Environment Authority (Swedish: Yrkesinspektionen).

Islamic banking

Al-Azharskolan (Al-Azhar school) is a foundation which runs charter schools with a Muslim profile. In 2019, four of members of the board of directors were convicted of aggravated fraud for having funneled school funds towards a banking project, which would have become the first Islamic bank (which would not have charged interest) in Sweden. Starting a bank would have required around 100-150 million SEK, but existing Swedish banks did not want to facilitate the transfer of funds from investors in the Middle East to Sweden. The Al-Azhar school also caused controversy in 2016 when its school in Vällingby had gender segregated gym classes for children. The Swedish Schools Inspectorate also criticized the school for holding prayers during lesson hours, which violates educational law in Sweden. Of the seven accused, two were acquitted. The verdict was upheld in the appeals court.

As several of the accused also were involved in collecting funds for the construction of a mosque in Rinkeby, the construction company NCC withdrew from the project.

Swedish attitudes towards Islam

As religion a few decades earlier was viewed as receding phenomenon, during the decade leading up to 2016 religion was again in the mainstream discourse due to international conflicts being interpreted in religious terms. In the last SOM survey in 2016 by Gothenburg University, the perception of Islam among the public had become more negative.

In 2006, a survey by the SOM Institute showed that half the Swedish population was negative towards Islam, where 7% expressed a positive attitude, 40% were undecided and 53% were negative. The poll showed that 48% were positive towards Christianity, the most positively rated religion.

In 2007, a study by the Integrationsverket government agency showed that 55% of respondents among the population of Sweden expressed reservations about moving to districts where many Muslims live. This was the same as for 2005.

In 2014, a poll by Gävle University College found that when asked about their attitudes towards veils, in the case of the niqab and the burqa, 84% responded that the niqab was unacceptable and 81% saw the burqa in the same light, a compact resistance to these. The chador was deemed unacceptable by 37% and a "clear majority" found the hijab and the shayla acceptable, 65.0 and 65.2

percent respectively. The report stated that "The question seems to arouse strong feelings against oppression versus the right to wear the clothes you want." The poll showed a slight increase in acceptance for the public wearing of veils. It also stated that "a clear majority (64.4%) of the Swedish population consider Muslim women to be more oppressed than other women in Sweden.". Of the respondents, 26% expressed resistance to all kinds of Islamic veils. In 2017, the Swedish National Board of Student Aid (CSN) eased its longtime grants and loans to students going to Islamic University of Madinah in Saudi Arabia, a religious school for missionaries proselytising the wahhabist variant of Islam. An investigation by Dagens Nyheter found that 71 students had travelled from Sweden with CSN funding since year 2000. The ban of grants was due to that neither women nor non-Muslims in general are allowed to study at Madinah and the ban encompassed all studies at all institutions being hostile to democracy.

According to a 2018 poll by Sifo, 60% of the 1000 participants wanted to ban the Islamic call to prayer using loudspeakers, while 21% responded they should be allowed and 19% were undecided.

Salafism

The Swedish Security Service estimated that there may be about 2,000 Swedish adherents of the puritanical Salafist movement within Sunni Islam. The Salafi movement is split between inward-looking purists and passivists, versus those who are militant. This last group is further divided into those who advocate militant defensive jihad in defense of Muslims, and those who advocate an offensive jihad along the lines of Al-Qaeda or ISIS. The majority of Salafists are passive and inward-oriented, while a small minority are oriented towards offensive jihadism - as opposed a so-called defensive jihad against outside aggression. Unlike in other parts of Europe, there are no Salafi organizations which openly preach jihad in Sweden - Salafi thought is instead spread by informal networks.

In Salafist circles, while topics in the main are uncontroversial, derogatory views towards women, homosexuals, non-believers, and Western governments are frequently expressed. Also it is stressed that Muslims should not integrate into wider Swedish society. The Swedish Defence University concluded in its 2018 report on Salafism in Sweden that since according to Salafi doctrine only following the religious laws is allowed, Salafism is an anti-democratic movement. In contrast to non-Salafis, Salafist preach in Swedish.

In the Stockholm area, non-militant Salafists are predominant in the Tensta and Rinkeby areas among Salafists, while a militant and al-Qaeda supporting movement was predominant in Skärholmen, Alby and Norsborg.

Violent Islamic extremism

According to the Swedish Defence University, since the 1970s, a number of residents of Sweden have been implicated in providing logistical and financial support to or joining various foreign-based transnational Islamic militant groups. Among these organizations are Hezbollah, Hamas, the GIA, Al-Qaeda, the Islamic State, Al-Shabaab, Ansar al-Sunna and Ansar al-Islam.

In the 2000s, according to Europol, Islamists in Sweden were not primarily seeking to commit attacks in Sweden, but were rather using Sweden as a base of operations against other countries and for providing logistical support for groups abroad.

In 2010, the Swedish Security Service estimated that a total of 200 individuals were involved in the Swedish violent Islamist extremist milieu. According to the Swedish Defence University, most of these militants were affiliated with the Islamic State, with around 300 people traveling to Syria and Iraq to join the group and Al-Qaeda associated outfits like Jabhat al-Nusra in the 2012-2017 period.

In the Stockholm area, all networks involving jihadists are also involved in ordinary crime such as theft, burglary, and blackmail whereby they acquire income. Income received from illegal narcotics trading are also used to finance jihadist activity as sympathizers with an ideology which uses violence to reach a higher goal will automatically be drawn into crime. In the Stockholm area, individuals who have joined jihadists in Syria and Iraq have predominantly been male, whereas in Gothenburg they have been both male and female.

In 2017, Swedish Security Service director Anders Thornberg stated that the number of violent Islamic extremists residing in Sweden to number was estimated to be "thousands". The Danish Security and Intelligence Service judged the number of jihadis in Sweden to be a threat against Denmark since two terrorists arriving from Sweden had already been sentenced in the 2010 Copenhagen terror plot.

In March 2018, Kurdish authorities reported they had captured 41 IS supporters with either Swedish citizenship or residence permit in Sweden, of which 5 had key positions in the organization and one was the head of the ISIL propaganda efforts.

According to interviews with authorities in November 2018, about half of those who joined the Islamic State and other groups in the Syrian Civil War had returned to Sweden. Some of the returnees are still radicalized and constitute a security threat.

Under the alias "Abu Bakr al Janabi", an individual located in Sweden translated Islamic State material. As such, he was interviewed by Vice News and The Guardian. In December 2017, 30-year-old Alftaf Yasin Tarid, a KTH Royal Institute of Technology alumn who was born in Iraq, travelled on a flight from Stockholm to Schiphol and he was later arrested when travelling in a car in Rotterdam after meeting other individuals. US authorities had tipped off their Dutch colleagues that Altaf had spread Islamic State propaganda from Sweden under the alias "Abu Bakr Al-Janabi". In December 2018, the trial began which went unreported in Swedish media. In January 2019 he was sentenced to three years in jail for disseminating IS propaganda.

In June 2019, two imams, Abo Raad active at Gävle mosque and another active in Umeå were deported due to them promoting violent extremism. The son of Raad was also to be deported along with other individuals involved in the Islamist scene in Sweden bringing the total to five.

Terrorist attacks and plots

- 2010 Stockholm bombings

- 20-year-old A. Sevigin was detained in February 2016 for attempting to construct a splinter bomb. He was sentenced to five years in prison by Attunda district court for breaching the terrorist laws. The psychiatric evaluation concluded that he was acting from his religious conviction. Previously he had travelled to Turkey in an attempt to join the Islamic State.

- 2017 Stockholm truck attack

- On 31 April 2018, 46-year-old man who had arrived as a refugee from Uzbekistan was arrested when police searched and found explosives on his property. In March 2019 he was sentenced to 7 years in prison for planning a terrorist attack in Sweden in the name of the Islamic State and financing serious crime. He was also given a deportation order and a ban from returning to Sweden again. Four other men were sentenced for falsifying documents or financing serious crime and received prison sentences ranging from 1 to 6 months in prison.

Hate crimes against Muslims

Some Muslims have been victims of violence because of their religion. In October 1991, Shahram Khosravi, a 25-year-old student of Iranian origin, was shot in the face outside the Stockholm University by John Ausonius. In 1993, two young Somali immigrants were stabbed and a local mosque in the city was burned down. The perpetrators of the stabbing were said by police to have been motivated by racial hatred.

The Imam Ali Islamic Centre in Järfälla, the largest Shia mosque in Sweden, was burned down in May 2017 in what police suspect was arson.

2003 and 2005 arson attacks on the Malmö Mosque

An arson attack on the Malmö Mosque took place in 2003, which damaged the mosque and totally destroyed other buildings at the Islamic Center. Another attack took place in October 2005.

2014 mosque arson attacks in Sweden

A series of arson attacks took place during one week at the end of 2014 on three mosques in Sweden. In addition to being struck by Molotov cocktails, some mosques were vandalized with racist graffiti.

Controversies

Antisemitism

A government study in 2006 estimated that 5% of the total adult population and 39% of adult Muslims "harbour systematic antisemitic views". The former Prime Minister Göran Persson described these results as "surprising and terrifying". However, the rabbi of Stockholm's Orthodox Jewish community, Meir Horden, said, "It's not true to say that the Swedes are antisemitic. Some of them are hostile to Israel because they support the weak side, which they perceive the Palestinians to be."

Morality police

Investigating journalists at TV4 reported that self-appointed morality police in migrant areas such as Rinkeby, Tensta, Husby and Hjulsta harass women for wearing skirts, owning dogs or going out alone without the company of a male. The phenomenon has also been reported in the Brandkärr district of Nyköping according to a report by the municipality.

Muslim Council of Sweden

Swedish social anthropologist Aje Carlbom [sv] and parliamentarian Abderisak Aden, who has founded the Islamic Democratic Institute (Islamiska demokratiska institutet), have both stated that they believe that at least part of the leading members of SMR support Islamist ideologies and are influenced by the Egyptian Muslim Brotherhood.

The Muslim Council of Sweden (SMR), an umbrella organization for Swedish Muslim organizations, has been involved in several controversies. In 2006 Mahmoud Aldebe, one of the Board members of SMR, sent letters to each of the major political parties in Sweden demanding special legislation for Muslims in Sweden, including the right to specific Islamic holidays, special public financing for the building of Mosques, that all divorces between Muslim couples be approved by an Imam, and that Imams should be allowed to teach Islam to Muslim children in public schools. The request was condemned by all political parties and the government and the Swedish Liberal Party requested that an investigation be started by the Office of the Exchequer into the use of public funding of SMR. The Chairman of the Board of SMR subsequently stated that it supported the demands made by Aldebe but that it did not think that the letter had been a good idea to communicate them in a list of demands.

Although the Board of SMR did not condemn Aldebe the letter has caused conflict within the organization. SMR has also been accused of being closely allied to the Swedish Social Democratic Party, which has been criticised both inside and outside the party.

Brandbergen Mosque

The Brandbergen Mosque has been described by the FBI terrorism consultant Evan Kohlmann as a propaganda central for the Armed Islamic Group (GIA). According to Kohlmann, people connected to the mosque also participated in the financing of GIA's bombing campaign in France in 1995.

In 2004 an Arabic-language manual, which carried the logo and address of the Brandbergen Mosque, was spread on the internet. The manual described the construction of simple chemical weapons, including how to build a chemical munition from an ordinary artillery round. On December 7, 2006, the Swedish citizen Mohamed Moumou, who is described by the United States Department of the Treasury as an "uncontested leader of an extremist group centered around the Brandbergen Mosque in Stockholm", was put on the United Nations Security Council Committee 1267 list of foreign terrorists.

Investigative journalism uncovers discrimination against women

In 2012, the SVT program Uppdrag granskning visited 10 mosques once with a hidden camera and once with a visible camera. When the representatives were aware of being filmed, they stated that they supported values such as gender equality; however, when two undercover journalists posed as Muslim women with difficulties in their marriage, the answers from the majority of the visited imams were different. The imams told the women that they were expected to sleep with their husbands even if they did not want to and that they were to accept being beaten, and strongly discouraged them from going to the police. Since about half of the visited mosques receive state or local funding, they are expected to promote basic values of Swedish society, such as equal rights between genders and to counteract discrimination and violence.

Radical preachers invited to Sweden

In March 2014 Malmö Municipality withdrew financial support to a local association because they invited a Syrian lecturer who says that homosexuality should be punished by death to a charity event. The organisers said that the lecturer would not attend and hold no speeches, but after a video recording showed him holding a lecture, the sum of money was recalled.

In January 2015, Sigtuna council stopped radical Islamic preacher Haitham al-Haddad from holding a lecture at their premises. He had been invited by Märsta Unga Muslimer (tr: Muslim Youth of Märsta) but when the council was informed of the preacher's homophobic and antisemitic views, the council cancelled the rental contract.

According to criticism by British think-tank Quilliam in May 2015, Sweden is more likely than other countries to allow preachers with radical views to enter the country and spread their views.

In May 2015, radical preacher Said Rageahs was invited to the mosque in Gävle where he promoted the views that whoever insults Mohammed should be killed along with apostates and advocated segregation between Muslims and non-Muslims. The local imams at Gävle mosque ran the webpage muslim.se which espoused similar views (with the death penalty for homosexuality added) and according to islamologist Jan Hjärpe at Lund University their views are typical of the Wahhabi.

Chapter 11

Italy, Greece

ITALY

Islam is a minority religion in Italy. Muslim presence in Italy dates back to the 9th century, when Sicily came under control of the Aghlabid Dynasty. There was a large Muslim presence in Italy from 827 (the first occupation of Mazara) until the 12th century. The Norman conquest of Sicily led to a gradual decline of Islam, due to the conversions and emigration of Muslims toward Northern Africa. A small Muslim community however survived at least until 1300 (the destruction of the Muslim settlement of Lucera).

During the 20th century, the first Somali immigrants from Italian Somaliland began to arrive. In more recent years, there has been migration from Pakistan, the Balkans, Bangladesh, India, Morocco, Egypt, and Tunisia. There are also some converts to Islam in Italy (most notably on the island of Sicily).

Legal status

Islam is not formally recognised by the Italian state. The official recognition of a religion different from Catholicism on behalf of the Italian Government is in fact to be approved by the President of the Republic under request of the Italian Minister of the Interior, following a signed agreement between the proposing religious community and the government. Such recognition does not merely depend on the number of followers of a given religion, and it requires congruence between the proposing religion principles and the Constitution. Official recognition gives an organised religion a chance to benefit from a national "religion tax", known as the Eight per thousand. Other religions, including Judaism and smaller groups, such as the Assemblies of God, The Church of Jesus Christ of Latter-day Saints and the Seventh-day Adventists, already enjoy the official recognition in the form of signed agreements with the Italian government. In late 2004, Italian minister, Giuseppe Pisanu set out in an attempt to create a unified leadership amongst the Muslim community. In 2005, the Consulta per l'Islam Italiano was created. This council is composed of 16 members of the Muslim population that are elected by the Ministry of Interiors. The goal of this council was for the Muslim community to have frequent and harmonious dialogues with the Italian government. The Consulta does not have any real power to make binding decisions. It exists as a platform for the Muslim community. Strong disagreement between Council members slows its work.

History

Saracens

The Italian island of Pantelleria (which lies between the western tip of Sicily and North Africa) was conquered by the Umayyads in 700. The Arabs had earlier raided Roman Sicily in 652, 667 and 720 A.D.; Syracuse in the eastern end of the island was occupied for the first time temporarily in 708, but a planned invasion in 740 failed due to a rebellion of the Berbers of the Maghreb that lasted until 771 and civil wars in Ifriqiya lasting until 799.

Arab attacks on the island of Sardinia were less significant than those on Sicily and eventually failed to achieve the island's conquest, although they induced its separation from the Roman Empire, giving birth to a long period of Sardinian independence, the era of the Judicates.

Conquest of Sicily

According to some sources, the conquest was spurred by Euphemius, a Byzantine commander who feared punishment by Emperor Michael II for a sexual indiscretion. After a short-lived conquest of Syracuse, he was proclaimed emperor but was compelled by loyal forces to flee to the court of Ziyadat Allah in Ifriqiya. The latter agreed to conquer Sicily, with the promise to leave it to Euphemius in exchange for a yearly tribute. To end the constant mutinies of his army, the Aghlabid magistrate of Ifriqiya sent Arabian, Berber, and Andalusian rebels to conquer Sicily in 827, 830 and 875, led by, amongst others, Asad ibn al-Furat. Palermo fell to them in 831, followed by Messina in 843, Syracuse in 878. In 902, the Ifriqiyan magistrate himself led an army against the island, seizing Taormina in 902. Reggio Calabria on the mainland fell in 918, and in 964 Rometta, the last remaining Byzantine toehold on Sicily.

Under the Muslims, agriculture in Sicily prospered and became export oriented. Arts and crafts flourished in the cities. Palermo, the Muslim capital of the island, had 300,000 inhabitants at that time, more than all the cities of Germany combined. The local population conquered by the Muslims were Romanized Catholic Sicilians in Western Sicily and partially Greek speaking Christians, mainly in the eastern half of the island, but there were also a significant number of Jews. These conquered people were afforded freedom of religion under the Muslims as dhimmis. The dhimmi were also required to pay the jizya, or poll tax, and the kharaj or land tax, but were exempt from the tax that Muslims had to pay (Zakaat). The payment of the Jizya is payment for state services and protection against foreign and internal aggression as non Muslims did not pay the Zakaat tax. The conquered population could instead pay the Zakaat tax by converting to Islam. Large numbers of native Sicilians converted to Islam. However, even after 100 years of Islamic rule, numerous Greek-speaking Christian communities prospered, especially in north-eastern Sicily, as dhimmis. This was largely a result of the Jizya system which allowed co-existence. This co-existence with the conquered population fell apart after the reconquest of Sicily, particularly following the death of King William II of Sicily in 1189. By the mid-11th century, Muslims made up the majority of the population of Sicily.

Emirates in Apulia

From Sicily, the Muslims launched raids on the mainland and devastated Calabria. In 835 and again in 837, the Duke of Naples was fighting against the Duke of Benevento and appealed to the Sicilian Muslims for help. In 840 Taranto and Bari fell to the Muslims, and in 841 Brindisi. Muslim attacks on Rome failed in 843, 846 and 849. In 847 Taranto, Bari and Brindisi declared themselves emirates independent from the Aghlabids. For decades the Muslims ruled the Mediterranean and attacked the Italian coastal towns. Muslims occupied Ragusa in Sicily between 868 and 870.

Only after the fall of Malta in 870 did the occidental Christians succeed in setting up an army capable of fighting the Muslims. Over the next two decades, most of the territory held by Muslims on the mainland was liberated from Muslim rule. The Franco-Roman emperor Louis II reconquered Brindisi in 869, Bari in 871 and beat the Arabs at Salerno in 872. The Byzantines retook Taranto in 880. In 882 the Muslims had founded at the mouth of Garigliano between Naples and Rome a new base further in the north, which was in league with Gaeta, and had attacked Campania as well as Sabinia in Lazio. In 915, Pope John X organised a vast alliance of southern powers, including Gaeta and Naples, the Lombard princes and the Byzantines. The subsequent Battle of the Garigliano was successful, and all Saracens were captured and executed, ending any presence of Arabs in Lazio or Campania permanently. A hundred years later, the Byzantines called the Sicilian Muslims to ask for support against a campaign of German emperor Otto II. They beat Otto at the battle of Stilo in 982 and for the next 40 years largely succeeded in preventing his successors from entering southern Italy.

In 1002 a Venetian fleet defeated Muslims besieging Bari. After the Aghlabids were defeated in Ifriqiya as well, Sicily fell in the 10th century to their Fatimid successors, but claimed independence after fights between Sunni and Shia Muslims under the Kalbids.

Raids in Piedmont

After they had conquered the Visigoth Kingdom in Spain (729–765), the Arabs and Berbers from Septimania and Narbonne carried out raids into northern Italy, and in 793 again launched an offensive into northwestern Italy (Nicaea 813, 859 and 880). In 888, Andalusian Muslims set up a new base in Fraxinet near Fréjus in French Provence, from where they started raids along the coast and in inner France.

In 915, after the Battle of Garigliano, the Muslims lost their base in southern Lazio. In 926 King Hugh of Italy called the Muslims to fight against his northern Italian rivals. In 934 and 935 Genoa and La Spezia were attacked, followed by Nicaea in 942. In Piedmont the Muslims got as far as Asti and Novi, and also moved northwards along the Rhône valley and the western flank of the Alps. After defeating Burgundian troops, in 942–964 they conquered Savoy and occupied a part of Switzerland (952–960). To fight the Arabs, Emperor Berengar I, Hugh's rival, called the Hungarians, who in their turn devastated northern Italy. As a result of the Muslim defeat at the Battle of Tourtour, Fraxinet was lost and razed by the Christians in 972. Thirty years later, in 1002, Genoa was invaded, and in 1004 Pisa.

Pisa and Genoa joined forces to end Muslim rule over Corsica (Islamic 810/850-930/1020) and Sardinia. In Sardinia in 1015 the fleet of the Andalusian lord of Dénia come from Spain, settled a temporary military camp as a logistic base to control the Tyrrhenian Sea and Italian peninsula, but in 1016 the fleet was forced to leave its base due to the military intervention of maritime republics of Genoa and Pisa.

The cultural and economical bloom in Sicily that had started under the Kalbids was interrupted by internecine fights, followed by invasions by the Tunisian Zirids (1027), Pisa (1030–1035), and the Romans (1027 onwards). Eastern Sicily (Messina, Syracuse and Taormina) was captured by the Byzantines in 1038–1042. In 1059 Normans from southern Italy, led by Roger I, invaded the island. The Normans conquered Reggio in 1060 (conquered by the Romanin 1027). Messina fell to the Normans in 1061; an invasion by the Algerian Hammadids to preserve Islamic rule was thwarted in 1063 by the fleets of Genoa and Pisa. The loss of Palermo in

1072 and of Syracuse in 1088 could not be prevented. Noto and the last Muslim strongholds on Sicily fell in 1091. In 1090–91, the Normans also conquered Malta; Pantelleria fell in 1123.

A small Muslim population remained on Sicily under the Normans. Roger II hosted at his court, among others, the famous geographer Muhammad al-Idrisi and the poet Muhammad ibn Zafar. At first, Muslims were tolerated by the Normans, but soon pressure from the Popes led to their increasing discrimination; most mosques were destroyed or made into churches. The first Sicilian Normans did not take part in the Crusades, but they undertook a number of invasions and raids in Ifriqiya, before they were defeated thereafter in 1157 by the Almohads.

This peaceful coexistence in Sicily finally ended with the death of King William II in 1189. The Muslim elite emigrated at that time. Their medical knowledge was preserved in the Schola Medica Salernitana; an Arabian-Roman-Norman synthesis in art and architecture survived as Sicilian Romanesque. The remaining Muslims fled, for example to Caltagirone on Sicily, or hid out in the mountains and continued to resist against the Hohenstaufen dynasty, who ruled the island from 1194 on. In the heartland of the island, the Muslims declared Ibn Abbad the last Emir of Sicily.

To end this upheaval, emperor Frederick II, himself a Crusader, instigated a policy to rid Sicily of the few remaining Muslims. This cleansing was done in small part under Papal influence but mostly in order to create a loyal force of troops which could not be influenced by non-Christian infiltrators. In 1224–1239 he deported every single Muslim from Sicily to an autonomous colony under strict military control (so that they could not infiltrate non-Muslim areas) in Lucera in Apulia. Muslims were recruited however by Frederick in the army and constituted his faithful personal bodyguard, since they had no connection to his political rivals. In 1249, he ejected the Muslims from Malta as well. Lucera was returned to the Christians in 1300 at the instigation of the pope by King Charles II of Naples. Muslims were forcefully converted, killed or expelled from Europe. However a Muslim community was still recorded in Apulia in 1336 and very recently in 2009, a genetic study revealed a small genetic Northwest African contribution among today's inhabitants near the region of Lucera.

During Spanish rule of Sicily

During Spanish rule of Sicily, and to escape the Spanish inquisition of the Moriscos (Muslims who had converted to Christianity) in the Iberian peninsula, a few Moriscos migrated to Sicily. During this time there were several attempts to rid Sicily of its extensive formerly Muslim 'Moor' population. The attacks were also directed against crypto-Muslim slaves and Sicilian renegades who refused to deny Islam during the 16th and the 17th centuries. However, it is doubtful that the order was carried out in practice. The main reason that some former Muslims were able to remain in Sicily was that they were openly supported by The Duke of Osuna, now officially installed as viceroy in Palermo, advocated to the Spanish monarch in Madrid for allowing the Moriscos to stay in Sicily.

15th century: Ottomans in Otranto

During this century, the Ottoman Empire was expanding mightily in southeastern Europe. It completed the absorption of the Byzantine Empire in 1453 under Sultan Mehmet II by conquering Constantinople and Galata. It seized Genoa's last bastions in the Black Sea in 1475 and Venice's Greek colony of Euboea in 1479. Turkish troops invaded the Friuli region in northeastern Italy in 1479 and again in 1499–1503. The Apulian harbor town of

Otranto, located about 100 kilometers southeast of Brindisi, was seized in 1480 (Ottoman invasion of Otranto), but the Turks were routed there in 1481 by an alliance of several Italian city-states, Hungary and France led by the prince Alphonso II of Naples, when Mehmet died and a war for his succession broke out. Cem Sultan, pretender to the Ottoman throne, was defeated despite being supported by the pope; he fled with his family to the Kingdom of Naples, where his male descendants were bestowed with the title of Principe de Sayd by the Pope in 1492. They lived in Naples until the 17th century and in Sicily until 1668 before relocating to Malta.

Attacks in the 16th century

It is a subject of debate whether Otranto was meant to be the base for further conquests. In any case, the Ottoman sultans had not given up their ambition to take over the Italian Peninsula and to finally install Islamic sovereignty after the conquest of Constantinople. After the conquests of Ragusa (Dubrovnik) and Hungary in 1526 and the defeat of the Turkish army at Vienna in 1529, Turkish fleets again attacked southern Italy. Reggio was sacked in 1512 by the famous Turkish corsair Khayr al-Din, better known by the nickname of Barbarossa; in 1526 the Turks attacked Reggio again, but this time suffered a setback and were forced to turn their sights elsewhere. In 1538 they defeated the Venetian fleet. In 1539 Nice was raided by the Barbary pirates (Siege of Nice), but an attempted Turkish landing on Sicily failed, as did the attempted conquest of Pantelleria in 1553 and the siege of Malta in 1565.

Next to Spain, the biggest contribution to the victory of the Christian "Holy League" in the battle of Lepanto in 1571 was made by the Republic of Venice, which between 1423 and 1718 fought eight costly wars against the Ottoman Empire. In 1594, the city of Reggio was again sacked by Cığalazade Yusuf Sinan Pasha, a renegade who converted to Islam.

Muslim population in Italy by the year:

Year	Pop.	±%
1999	520,000	—
2009	1,200,000	+130.8%
2016	1,400,000	+16.7%
2022	1,500,000	+7.1%

1999 and 2009 estimates

2016 census

2022 census

According to a 2016 Pew Research Center projection and Brookings, there are 1,400,000 Muslims in Italy (2.3% of the Italian population), almost one third of Italy's foreign population (250.000 have acquired Italian citizenship). The majority of Muslims in Italy are Sunni, with a Shi'ite minority. There are also a few Ahmadi Muslims in the country. This diversity has induced a lack of organization throughout the Italian Muslim community. As a result, the community also lacks cohesive leadership.

Despite undocumented immigrants representing a minority of the Muslims in Italy, considering that undocumented migrants and refugees predominantly come from Muslim countries, the issue of Islam in contemporary Italy has been linked by some political parties (particularly the Lega Nord) with immigration, and more specifically illegal immigration. Immigration has become a prominent political issue, as reports of boatloads of illegal immigrants (or clandestini) dominate news programmes, especially in the summertime. Police forces have not had great success in intercepting many of the thousands of clandestini who land on Italian beaches, mainly because of a political unwillingness, partly fostered by the EU, to address the issue. However, the vast majority of the clandestini landing in Italy are only using the country as a gateway to other EU states, due to the fact that Italy offers fewer economic opportunities and social welfare services for them than Germany, France, or the United Kingdom.

While in medieval times, the Muslim population was almost totally concentrated in Insular Sicily and in the city of Lucera, in Apulia, it is today more evenly distributed, with almost 60% of Muslims living in the North of Italy, 25% in the centre, and only 15% in the South. Muslims form a lower proportion of immigrants than in previous years, as the latest statistical reports by the Italian Ministry of Interior and Caritas indicate that the share of Muslims among new immigrants has declined from over 50% at the beginning of the 1990s (mainly Albanians and Moroccans) to less than 25% in the following decade, due to the massive arrivals from eastern Europe.

Recent points of contention between ethnic Italians and the Muslim immigrant population include the strong presence of crucifixes in public buildings, including school classrooms, government offices, and hospital wards. Adel Smith has attracted considerable media attention by demanding that crucifixes in public facilities be removed. The Italian Council of State, in the Sentence No. 556, 13 February 2006, confirmed the display of the crucifix in government sponsored spaces. Smith was subsequently charged with defaming the Catholic religion in 2006.

In November 2016, Minister of the Interior Angelino Alfano reported that Italy had deported nine imams for inciting racial violence.

In January 2017, community groups representing around 70% of the Muslim community in Italy signed a pact with the government to "reject all forms of violence and terrorism" and to hold prayers in mosques in the Italian language or at least to have them translated.

Muslim prison population in Italy

As of 2013, of the total 64,760 detainees in Italy, approximately 13,500 (20.8%) came from countries with Islamic majorities, mostly Morocco and Tunisia.

Mosques

There are a total of eight mosques in Italy. While Italy is home to the fourth largest Muslim population in Europe, the number of mosques is minute in comparison to France (which is home to over 2,200 mosques) and the United Kingdom (which is home to over 1,500 mosques). The scarcity of mosques in Italy is caused predominantly by the fact that Italy does not officially recognize Islam as a religion. Official state recognition would guarantee and protect places of worship, recognize religious holidays and allow access to public funding.

There have been a number of cases of extraordinary rendition of Muslim activists, as well as attempts by a past government to close mosques. Many mosque constructions are blocked by opposition of local residents. In September 2008 the Lega Nord political party was reported to have introduced a new bill which would have blocked the construction of new mosques in much of the country, arguing that Muslims can pray anywhere, and do not need a mosque. The construction of mosques had already been blocked in Milan. The bill was not approved.

Extremism

In 2007, the Moroccan imam at the mosque in Ponte Felcino in Perugia was deported by the Italian government for extremist views.

Deportation (expulsion) of foreign suspects have been the cornerstone of Italy's preventive counter-terrorism fight against suspected radicals. Every deportee is prohibited from re-entering Italy and therefore the entire Schengen Area, for a period of five years. Italy is able to use this method as many radicalized Muslims are first-generation immigrants and therefore have not yet acquired Italian citizenship. In Italy as elsewhere in Europe, prison inmates show signs of radicalization while incarcerated and in 2018, 41 individuals were deported upon release from prison. Of the 147 deported by the Italian government in the 2015–2017 all were related to jihadism and 12 were imams. From January 2015 to April 2018, 300 individuals were expulsed from Italian soil. The vast majority of the deportees come from North Africa and a smaller group come from the Balkans.

In the mid to late 2010s, a "homegrown" Islamist movement started to emerge in Italy with Islamists writing online content in Italian. While radicalized individuals may get in contact with fellow extremists at mosques, indoctrination and planning of violence take place elsewhere.

From 1 August 2016 to 31 July 2017, a total of eight imams were deported. The following twelve-month period, two were deported.

In July 2016, the Moroccan imam at the Asonna center in Noventa Vicentina was deported for reportedly expressing extremist views and for posing a security threat. While most extremists are banned for 5 to 10 years, Muhammed Madad was banned from returning for 15 years.

In March 2018, police carried out an anti-terrorist operation in Foggia against the Al Dawa unauthorized prayer hall located near the railway station. Egyptian Abdel Rahman Mohy preached to children using Islamic State propaganda.

According to prison authorities in Italy, in October 2018 there were 66 Muslim detainees who either had been sentenced or were awaiting trial for terrorism offences.

Islamophobia

Although Muslim population in Italy is very small compared to its counterparts in France, Germany, Britain and Spain, anti-Islamic feeling in Italy runs high, which became clear following the September 11 attacks and 7 July 2005 London bombings. Survey published in 2019 by the Pew Research Center found that 55% of Italians had an unfavourable view of Muslims. Much of the local Italian media correlates Islam to terrorism as a whole. This contributes to these unfavorable opinions.

Acts of violence against Islamic places of worship

In recent years there have been some acts of violence against Islamic places of worship in Italy:

- On April 24, 1994, a Molotov cocktail caused a fire at the small mosque in albenga's old

- Anti-Islamic attacks following the September 2001 bombings in Sicily and Southern Italy

- On January 24, 2004, a rock thrown from a car broke through the window of the entrance to the Mosque of Segrate,

- In April 2004, the Mosque of Mercy in Savona was the subject of discriminatory spray writing on the door, including a swastika.

- On the night of 3–4 August 2010, an arson attack was carried out in the offices of the Luce mosque in Bologna by unknown persons who entered it by cutting through the fences with a shear. The act has been condemned by the Jewish community in Bologna and by various political forces.

Organizations

A minority of Italian Muslims belong to religious associations, the best known of which are:

- UCOII Unione delle Comunità Islamiche d'Italia (Union of the Islamic Communities and Organizations of Italy)

- Since its founding, the union has been active in the political scene, recently attempting to become the primary Islamic liaison.

- CICI, Centro Islamico Culturale d'Italia, which has its seat in the Mosque of Rome, which is reputed to be the largest mosque in Europe

- COREIS, Comunità Religiosa Islamica Italiana, which has its seat in Milan, but also a branch in Rome.

- USMI, Union of Muslim Students in Italy

- Founded in the 1970s in Perugia and composed mostly of Jordanian, Syrian and Palestine students, the group's ideology is quite similar to the Muslim Brotherhood, the transnational Islamic movement in Egypt in the 1920s.

Notable Muslims

- Edoardo Agnelli, businessman

- Gabriele Torsello, freelance journalist

- Ahmad Gianpiero Vincenzo, founder and president of the organization Intelletuali Musulmani Italiani (Italian Muslim Intellectuals)

- Torquato Cardilli, diplomat

- Vinnie Paz, lyricist and singer

- Leda Rafanelli, poet and publisher

- Adel Smith, activist

- Stephan El Shaarawy, footballer

- Abd al Wahid Pallavicini, Sufi figure and founder of the Italian Islamic religious community (COREIS) and the Interreligious Studies Academy (Accademia ISA)

- Khaby Lame, TikToker

- Ghali, rapper

GREECE

Islam in Greece is represented by two distinct communities; Muslims that have lived in Greece since the times of the Ottoman Empire (primarily in East Macedonia and Thrace) and Muslim immigrants that began arriving in the last quarter of the 20th century, mainly in Athens and Thessaloniki. Muslims in Greece are mainly immigrants from The Middle East (Lebanon, Syria, Iraq, Iran), other Balkan regions (Montenegro, Turkey, Albania, Bosnia & Herzegovina) & North Africa (Morocco, Algeria, Tunisia, Egypt).

Muslims in Greece

The Muslim population in Greece is not homogeneous, since it consists of different ethnic, linguistic and social backgrounds which often overlap. The Muslim faith is the creed of several ethnic groups living in the present territory of Greece, namely the Pomaks, ethnic Turks, certain Romani groups, and Greek Muslims particularly of Crete, Epirus, and western Greek Macedonia who converted mainly in the 17th and 18th centuries. The country's Muslim population decreased significantly as a result of the 1923 population exchange agreement between Greece and the new Turkish Republic, which also uprooted approximately 1.5 million Greeks from Asia Minor. Many of the Muslims of Northern Greece were actually ethnic Greek Muslims from Epirus and Greek Macedonia, whereas the Muslims of Pomak and ethnic Turkish origin (the Western Thrace Turks) from Western Thrace were exempt from the terms of the population exchange. Successive Greek governments and officials consider the Turkish-speaking Muslims of Western Thrace as part of the Greek Muslim minority and not as a separate Turkish minority. This policy is aimed to give the impression that the Muslims of the region are the descendants of Ottoman-era ethnic Greek converts to Islam like the Vallahades of pre-1923 Greek Macedonia and so thereby avoid a possible future situation in which Western Thrace is ceded to Turkey on the basis of the ethnic origin of its Muslim inhabitants.

The term Muslim minority (Μουσουλμανική μειονότητα Musulmanikí mionótita) refers to an Islamic religious, linguistic and ethnic minority in western Thrace, which is part of the Greek administrative region of East Macedonia and Thrace. In 1923, under the terms of the Treaty of Lausanne, the Greek Muslims of Epirus, Greek Macedonia, and elsewhere in mainly Northern Greece were required to immigrate to Turkey; whereas, the Christians living in Turkey were required to immigrate to Greece in an "Exchange of Populations". The Muslims of western Thrace and the Christians of Istanbul and the islands of Gökçeada and Bozcaada (Imvros and Tenedos) were the only populations not exchanged.

There is also a small Muslim community in some of the Dodecanese islands (Turks of the Dodecanese) which, as part of the Italian Dodecanese of the Kingdom of Italy between 1911 and 1947, were not subjected to the exchange of the population between Turkey and Greece in 1923. They number about 3,000, some of whom espouse a Turkish identity and speak Turkish, while others are the Greek-speaking descendants of Cretan Muslims. The community is strongest in the city of Rhodes and on the island of Kos (in particular the village of Platanos).

The Pomaks are mainly located in compact villages in Western Thrace's Rhodope Mountains. While the Greek Roma community is predominantly Greek Orthodox, the Roma in Thrace are mainly Muslim.

Estimates of the recognized Muslim minority, which is mostly located in Thrace, range from 98,000 to 140,000 (between 0.9% and 1.2%), while the illegal immigrant Muslim community numbers between 200,000 and 500,000 predominantly in the area of Asea Albanian immigrants to Greece are usually associated with the Muslim faith, although most are secular in orientation.

Immigrant Muslims in Greece

The first immigrants of Islamic faith, mostly Egyptians, arrived in the early 1950s from Egypt, and are concentrated in the country's two main urban centres, Athens and Thessaloniki. Since 1990, there has been a large increase in the numbers of immigrant Muslims from various countries of the Middle East, North Africa, as well as from Afghanistan, Pakistan, India, Bangladesh, Somalia and Muslim Southeast Asia. However, the bulk of the immigrant Muslim community has come from the Balkan states, specifically from Albania, Albanian communities in North Macedonia, and other former Yugoslav republics. Since the collapse of the Warsaw Pact in Eastern Europe in the early 1990s, Albanian workers started immigrating to Greece, taking low wage jobs in search of economic opportunity, and bringing over their families to settle in cities like Athens and Thessaloniki.

The majority of the immigrant Muslim community resides in Athens. In recognition of their religious rights, the Greek government approved the building of a mosque in July 2006. In addition, the Greek Orthodox Church has donated 300,000 square feet (28,000 m2), worth an estimated $20 million, in west Athens for the purpose of a Muslim cemetery. Greece's government gave the green light to begin construction in 2016, but both commitments continued to remain dead letters by 2017. However, Kostas Gavroglou – Greece's education and religious minister from 2016 to July 2019 – said that the country's first state-sponsored mosque was likely to begin operations in September 2019. Still, the country faces strong opposition from some of its citizens, who consider mosques to be a means of spreading Islam in Europe. Though the construction and operation of this Athenian mosque was within legal regulations, the strong ideological spread of the Greeks will likely perpetuate the controversy. If the mosque is built, it will end an almost two-century wait.

For prayers that are required to be performed in congregation, the Thessaloniki Muslim community meets inside apartments, basements, and garages for worship. In addition, there are very few Muslim cemeteries – forcing some to travel hundreds of kilometres to bury their dead.

In 2010, an unofficial mosque on the island of Crete was targeted in the night without any casualties, likely as a result of anti-Muslim sentiments in the Greek far-right, but no suspects had been identified. There has been anti-Muslim rhetoric from certain right-wing circles, including the Golden Dawn party. A survey published in 2019 by the Pew Research Center found that 37% of Greeks had a favorable view of Muslims, whereas 57% had an unfavourable view.

Conversion to Christianity

There are two groups who have converted in large numbers from Islam to Christianity. The first group are the Turks of the Dodecanese. Being seen as a remnant of the former Ottoman Empire and culturally similar to an alien country (Turkey), many

Turks do not show interest in the Islamic faith in order not to face discrimination by the Greek state.

The second case are the Albanian immigrants who have shown a preference for rapid assimilation into Greek culture. They form the largest migrant group in Greece, and the majority do not want to be identified as Albanian. Many Albanian newcomers change their Albanian name to Greek ones and their religion from Islam to Orthodoxy: Even before emigration, many Muslim people in southern Albania presented themselves as Greeks and adopted Greek names instead of Albanian Muslim ones in order to avoid discrimination before immigrating. As such, they seek to increase their chances to get a Greek visa and work in Greece. After migrating to Greece, they get baptized and change their Muslim or Albanian names in their passports to Greek ones.

Application of Islamic law in Greece

In Greece, Islamic law can be applied in two different situations. One of the two, like in many other countries, is used in the case of private international law when the utilization of a foreign law controlling family relations that may be religious is used due to conflict rules. The second case refers to Greece only, as the only country in the European Union with Islamic religious courts. There have been many international conventions between Greece and Turkey starting in 1881, which have dealt with the Greek minority in Turkey and the Turkish minority in Greece. Consequently, the Mufti, as a religious leader of all the Muslims in Greece, was given power by law to make decisions regarding the personal status of the Muslim minority. This was still the case in Western Thrace, in the northeast of Greece, until 2018, when the laws were largely limited. Even though this law is restricted to only about 120,000 Greek citizens, which represent this minority, the law can be viewed as a certain section of the national Greek legal system.

The Sharia law used to be mandatory among the Muslim citizens of Greece, a situation that stems from the Ottoman era and predates its reinforcement by the 1923 Lausanne Treaty. The mandatory applicability of Sharia law came into international spotlight when a woman from Komotini named Chatize Molla Sali lodged a complaint to the European Court of Human Rights (ECHR) and that is when the law came into the spotlight. She went against Greece due to a dispute over inheritance rights with the sisters of the deceased husband. After her appeal was accepted by the secular justice system of Greece, her win was overruled by the Supreme Court, stating that no one other than a Mufti has the competency to decide on the issues related to inheritance in the Muslim community. The ECHR found unanimously that the mandatory application of Sharia law on the Muslim minority was a violation of the European Convention on Human Rights, particularly Article 14 (prohibition of discrimination), by Greece. In 2018, the applicability of Sharia law in Greece was restricted to cases where all the parties accept its jurisprudence, therefore it can no longer be forced upon people against their will.

History

Greece and Turkey signed the Convention of Istanbul in 1881, which was the first groundwork for the Islamic religious courts. As the Ottoman Empire was slowly losing its European territories, it lost most of Thessaly, which is central Greece today, due to this convention. On the other hand, this convention provided the remaining Muslim population with a set of rights, which allowed them freedom of religion and the survival of Muslim religious courts, which were to keep their legitimacy and make decisions on issues related to religion. Those issues often refer to family and succession law, which fall under the personal status. At the end of the first Balkan war in 1913, Greece and Turkey signed the Athens Treaty of Peace. Greece has conquered new areas, primarily Macedonia and Epirus, and pushed Turkey further away, which left many Turks and other Muslims in Greece's new territories. This new convention protected them and it gave power to the Mufti over laws regarding family and succession among the Muslim population. Some of the laws that were passed in order to enforce these Conventions were later repealed; others have stayed in force, but the laws that were introduced after the most important convention have been limited only recently in 2018. The Convention of Lausanne in 1923, applied to entire Greece except for the Dodecanese islands. Greece and Turkey signed the convention, agreeing that all of the issues related to the personal status of minorities should be dealt with according to religious law and not the civil one. Religious courts were not addressed in this convention, but it left room for the possibility of future different regulations of these questions. This was deemed possible only in case a special commission is formed in order to represent the minority and make decisions. In 1926 this happened in Turkey as it repealed the role of the religious law. Minorities agreed to annul their previous special status and be subject to the new The Turkish Civil Code. Greek authorities, on the other hand, have waited for a long time to consider changing laws that address Muslim family matter until 2018, fearful that Turkey would call for amendments to the Lausanne Treaty.

Sharia in Western Thrace

Muftis make decisions on various questions in accordance with Sharia law as the Islamic legal system primarily based on the Qur'an and Islamic tradition. How Sharia law is interpreted and applied depends on Islamic legal schools of thought and they are often very different from one another. The Muslims of Western Thrace are far from homogenous and vary both ethnically and religiously. Half of these Muslims are of Turkish origin followed by Pomaks and Roma, and the vast majority professes Sunni Islam, while around 10% are from the Sufi Bektashi order. Despite these differences among this Muslim minority of Greece, they all seem to mostly agree on the important aspects of Islamic law regarding their personal status, which is namely considered to be Hanafi law as it was in the Ottoman Empire. There are, on the other hand, areas of conflict between the basis of Sharia family law and both Greek and international legal systems. One of the two areas is the principle of equality of the sexes; Islamic laws that deal with divorce and polygamy prove the unequal treatment of the sexes. The other is the concern for the best interest of the child; there are rules in Islamic law that clash with the rights of the child as guaranteed by the UN Convention that addressed the marriage of minors and child custody.

There were two schools of thought regarding the employment of Islamic law on Muslim communities in Greece. The first and the widespread one states that Sharia law should be applied only to the Muslim community in the Western Thrace region and that other Muslims across Greece (including those on Dodecanese islands) should be under the jurisdiction of the Greek Civil Code, which took effect in 1946. According to the second one, Islamic law should be applied to all Muslims in Greece, regardless of the region in which they live, which is what the Supreme Court held in 1980. It asserted that Mufti being a judge is legally consistent with a concept of a "natural judge". In one case after a divorce, when the woman applied for alimony for her child and herself, the jurisdiction was given to the Mufti from Xanthi in Western Thrace because the ex-spouses were Muslims, despite the fact they were both from Athens. In another more recent case of 2007, the Supreme Court proclaimed that Muftis had many issues involving Muslims within their purview, given that Sharia law covers them. Some of them were marriage, divorce, alimony, inheritance, different issues regarding minors, and others.

The applicability of Sharia law was restricted in 2018, when a law was passed eliminating the mandatory enforcement of the Sharia Law, and limiting its powers, making it optional, and restricted to cases when all parties accept its jurisprudence.

Molla Sali v. Greece

The aforementioned Greek citizen called Chatitze (or Hatijah) Molla Sali lived in Komotini, a city located in North-Eastern Greece in the region of 'East Macedonia and Thrace'. Her deceased husband was also a Greek citizen and he was associated with the Muslim minority of Thrace. After the husband's death, Molla Sali was entitled to the entirety of his property, including estates in Istanbul and Komotini. The deceased husband had written a testament according to the Greek Civil Law, in which he leaves everything to his wife. However, based on their brother being a member of the Muslim community, the late husband's sisters decided to litigate. They argued that issues related to the inheritance of property were subject to Islamic and not civil law and that the Mufti was the one who would look into the matter. This would have given the opportunity to other members of the family to claim parts of the deceased's property. At first, the court disapproved of sister's claims and in 2011 after an appeal, the court stood by its decision on the grounds that the deceased had written a will, which should be respected as his statutory right as a Greek citizen. Then on 7 October 2013, the judgment was annulled by the Court of Cassation, stating that these kinds of issues related to inheritance should be dealt with within the community and by the Mufti according to Islamic law. Even though the case was remitted afterward, nothing has changed and Molla Sali's appeal got rejected. Because of this outcome, Molla Sali was set to lose three-quarters of the property bestowed to her by her late husband. Finally, she appealed to the ECHR complaining about the application of Islamic law to her case, emphasizing that her husband's testament was written in accordance with the Greek Civil Code, which drew a lot of attention outside of Greece. The ECHR in its 2018 ruling, found unanimously that the mandatory application of Sharia law on the Muslim minority to be a violation of the European Convention on Human Rights, particularly Article 14 (prohibition of discrimination), by Greece.

The Molla Sali v. Greece case raised many questions regarding basic human rights. Even though the case narrowly connected to inheritance rights, many other general issues were raised because of it. The focus was put both on an individual and his or her right, and also on the position of Sharia law within the countries with a Muslim minority and within a broader European legal network and the ECHR. According to McGoldrick, some of the specific issues raised were: "(i) the relationship between religious and secular law; (ii) the compatibility of Sharia with contemporary-modern human rights standards...; (iii) the relationship between the individual rights in the ECHR and another human rights treaty which, at least arguably, had as one of its objectives, protecting the minority rights of a group as such; (iv) the nature of minority rights in terms of whether they are mandatory or optional...; (v) the relationship between individual and group rights...; (vi) the relationship between religious autonomy and individual equality, and within the latter, gender equality; (vii) the application and interpretation of ECHR non-discrimination obligations in a religious minority protection context."

Chapter 12

Spain, Portugal

SPAIN

Spain is a Christian majority country, with Islam being a minority religion, practised mostly by immigrants from Muslim majority countries.

Islam was a major religion on the Iberian Peninsula, beginning with the Umayyad conquest of Hispania and ending (at least overtly) with its prohibition by the modern Spanish state in the mid-16th century and the expulsion of the Moriscos in the early 17th century, an ethnic and religious minority of around 500,000 people. Although a significant proportion of the Moriscos returned to Spain, or avoided expulsion, the practice of Islam had faded into obscurity by the 19th century after many years of crypto-Muslims practicing their faith in secret.

While the 2022 official estimation of Centro de Investigaciones Sociológicas (CIS) indicates that 2.8% of the population of Spain has a religion other than Catholicism, according to an unofficial estimation of 2020 by the Union of Islamic Communities of Spain (UCIDE) the Muslim population in Spain represents the 4.45% of the total Spanish population as of 2019, of whom 42% were

Spanish citizens (most of them with foreign family origins), 38% Moroccans, and 20% of other nationalities. In 2024 according to the Islamic Commission of Spain, there are 2.5 million Muslims in Spain, which is about 5.32 percent of the population of 47 million Spaniards. The number of converts, as per the commission, has increased to an estimated 10 times in the past three decades.

History

Conquest

Hispania was the Latin name which was given to the whole Iberian Peninsula, and after the fall of the Western Roman Empire (476) the Germanic tribe of Visigoths, who adopted Christianity, ended up ruling the whole peninsula until the Islamic conquest (during that time they pushed another Germanic tribe out—the Vandals – and conquered another one—the Suevi). It is frequently stated in historical sources that Spain was one of the former Roman provinces where the Latin language and culture grew deep roots. After the fall of the Empire, the Visigoths continued the tradition by becoming what was probably the most Romanized Teutonic tribe. Under Visigothic rule Spain was filled with extreme instability due to lack of communication between the native Spaniards and the new rulers, who followed the Germanic notion of kingship. Visigothic kings were considered the first among equals (the nobility), and they could easily be overthrown if they did not keep the different factions happy.

News of the political unrest which existed from the late 6th century through the early 8th century was eventually received by the rulers of the growing Islamic empire which existed along the North African coast. Several historical sources state that the Islamic caliphate had not actually targeted the Visigothic Kingdom for conquest, but political divisions within it created an opportunity which was successfully exploited by an army which was led by the Muslim general Tariq ibn-Ziyad. The last Visigoth king, Roderick, was not considered a legitimate ruler by all of the inhabitants of the Spanish Kingdom, and some Visigothic nobles aided the Islamic conquest of Spain. One name frequently mentioned is Count Julian of Ceuta who invited Tariq ibn-Ziyad to invade southern Spain because his daughter had been raped by King Roderick.

On April 30, 711, Muslim General Tariq ibn-Ziyad landed at Gibraltar and by the end of the campaign most of the Iberian Peninsula (except for small areas in the north-west such as Asturias and the Basque territory) were brought under Islamic rule. This campaign's turning point was the battle of Guadalete, where the last Visigothic king, Roderick, was defeated by general Tariq ibn-Ziyad. Roderick ceases the throne in the year 711, and is later executed by Tariq ibn-Ziyad. After the defeat of Roderick, the Visigoth dominion over the Iberian Peninsula folded and fell apart from the Northern coast of the Iberian Peninsula, and the province of Septimania (an area of France going from the Pyrenees to Provence), all areas previously under the rule of the Visigoths were now under Islamic rule. Muslim forces attempted to move north-east across the Pyrenees Mountains toward France, but were defeated by the Frankish Christian Charles Martel at the Battle of Tours in 732.

Islamic rule of the Iberian peninsula lasted for varying periods of time, which ranged from only 28 years in the extreme northwest (Galicia) to 781 years in the area which surrounded the city of Granada in the southeast. This Empire added contributions to society such as libraries, schools, public bathrooms, literature, poetry, and architecture. This work was mainly developed through the unification of people of all faiths. While the three major monotheistic religious traditions certainly did borrow from one another in Al-Andalus, benefiting especially by the blooming of philosophy and the medieval sciences in the Muslim Middle East, recent scholarship has brought into question the notion that the peaceful coexistence of Muslims, Jews, and Christians — known as the convivencia — could be defined as "pluralistic." People of other religions could contribute to society and the culture developed in this time. One of the reasons for such great success under this empire was the legal terms offered to the public, which differed from the conditions which were implemented by the Visigoth kingdom which preceded it.

Moreover, the appearance of Sufism on the Iberian Peninsula is especially important because Sufism's "greatest shaykh," Ibn 'Arabi, was himself from Murcia. Nakshbandi Sufi order is the widely followed Sufi order in Spain.

The topic of Convivencia remains a very hotly debated topic among scholars, with some of them believing that Spain was pluralistic under Muslim rule while others believe it was a very difficult place for non-Muslims to live in. Those who believe that Muslim ruled Spain was pluralistic point to the audio narration in the Museum of The Three Cultures in Cordoba, Spain, where the audio narration says that "when the East was not separated from the West, Muslims were not separated from Jews or Christians". Another scholar argues that "It became possible to be a pious Jew who could recite a pre-Islamic ode or a homoerotic poem or take the peripatetic tradition seriously, in great measure because pious Muslims did it". The Muslim ruler Abd-al-Rahman III "worked directly with the Mozarabs, a controversial term which is generally used to refer to Christians who lived under Muslim rule, and placed them in positions of power. Furthermore, the Jews and Christians could practice their religions without fear of harassment or persecution." The Muslim rulers of Spain "relied on the Jews for diplomacy and public administration who were inaugurated into posts of commerce and played important roles in cities such as Toledo and Cordoba".

On the other side of the debate, many scholars believe that Muslim rule of Spain was far from a utopian society where all religions treated each other with respect. In fact, "Uprisings in Cordoba in 805 and 818 were answered with mass executions and the destruction of one of the city's suburbs". In addition, in regard to Jews and Christians in Andalusia, "one 11th-century legal text called them members of "the devil's party" and they "were subject to special taxes and, often, dress codes". Many scholars believe that this more benign view of convivencia "masks the very presence of institutional fundamentalism in medieval Spain – both its Jewish and Muslim manifestations in the nature of forced conversions, exile, lower standards of citizenship, higher taxation and violence". It seems that class distinctions also played a role in convivencia. In fact, "many of the lower echelons of Jewish and Christian society remained segregated or in conflict with their Abrahamic counterparts". Other scholars believe that Christians and Jews were treated as second class citizens where "Under Muslim rule, especially following the arrival of the Almoravids and the Almohades, both Christianity and Judaism were scarcely tolerated and regarded as decidedly "inferior" religions".

In time Islamic migrants from places as diverse as North Africa to Yemen and Syria and Iran invaded territories in the Iberian

Peninsula. The Islamic rulers called the Iberian Peninsula "Al-Andalus".

For a time, Al-Andalus was one of the great Muslim civilizations, reaching its summit with the Umayyad Caliphate in the 10th century. Al-Andalus had the following chronological phases:

- The Al-Andalus province of the Umayyad Caliphate in Damascus (711–756)
- The Independent Umayyad Emirate of Cordoba (756–929)
- The Umayyad Caliphate of Córdoba (929–1031)
- The first Taifas (1031–c. 1091)
- The Almoravid rule (c. 1091–c. 1145)
- The second Taifas (c. 1145–c. 1151)
- The Almohad rule (c. 1151–1212)
- The third Taifas (1212–1238)
- The Kingdom of Granada (1238–1492)
- The late Alpujarras revolt (1568–1571), with two monarchs appointed successively by the Morisco rebels

(Note: the dates when the different taifa kingdoms were annexed by Almoravids and Almohads vary)

The Madrasah of Granada was founded by the Nasrid dynasty monarch Yusuf I, Sultan of Granada in 1349 and housed many of the greatest prominent scholars of the period.

Reconquista

After the disintegration of the Caliphate, Islamic control was gradually eroded by the Christian Reconquista. The Reconquista (Reconquest) was the process by which the Catholic Kingdoms of northern Spain eventually managed to succeed in defeating and conquering the Muslim states of the Iberian Peninsula. The first major city to fall to Catholic powers was Toledo in 1085, which prompted the intervention of Almoravids. After the battle of Las Navas de Tolosa in 1212, most of Al-Andalus fell under control of the Catholic kingdoms, the only exception being the Nasrid dynasty Emirate of Granada. The Granada War (Guerra de Granada) of the Reconquista began in 1482 against the Emirate of Granada. It was not until 1492 that the Emirate of Granada with city of Granada and the Alhambra and Generalife Palaces, the last remaining Muslim territory in al-Andalus, fell in the Battle of Granada to forces of the Catholic Monarchs (los Reyes Catolicos), Queen Isabella I of Castile and her husband King Ferdinand II of Aragon.

After the Reconquista

The conquest was accompanied by the Treaty of Granada signed by Emir Muhammad XII of Granada, allowing the Spanish crown's new Muslim subjects a large measure of religious toleration. They were also allowed the continuing use of their own language, schools, laws and customs. But the interpretation of the royal edict was largely left to the local Catholic authorities. Hernando de Talavera, the first Archbishop of Granada after its Catholic conquest, took a fairly tolerant view.

However 1492 started the monarchy's reversal of freedoms beginning with the Alhambra Decree. This continued when Archbishop Talavera was replaced by the intolerant Cardinal Cisneros, who immediately organised a drive for mass forced conversions and burned publicly thousands of Arabic books (manuscripts). Outraged by this breach of faith, in 1499 the

Mudéjars rose in the First Rebellion of the Alpujarras, which was unsuccessful and only had the effect of giving Ferdinand and Isabella a pretext to revoke the promise of toleration. That same year, the Muslim leaders of Granada were ordered to hand over almost all of the remaining books in Arabic, most of which were burned. (Only medical manuscripts were spared; those manuscripts are in the Escorial library.) Beginning in Valencia in 1502, Muslims were offered the choice of baptism or exile. The option of exile was often not feasible in practice because of the difficulty in uprooting one's family and making the journey to Muslim lands in North Africa, the inability to pay the fee required by the authorities for safe passage, and the general tendency by the authorities to discourage and hinder such exodus.

The majority therefore are forced to accept conversion, becoming known as "New Christians". Many of the New Christians (also called "Moriscos"), though outwardly Catholic, continued to adhere to their old beliefs in private as crypto-Muslims. Responding to a plea from his co-religionists in Spain, in 1504 Ahmad ibn Abi Jum'ah, an Islamic scholar in North Africa, issued a fatwa, commonly named the "Oran fatwa", saying that Muslims may outwardly practice Christianity, as well as drink wine, eat pork and other forbidden things, if they were under "compulsion" to conform or "persecution".

The clandestine practice of Islam continued well into the 16th century. In 1567, King Philip II finally made the use of the Arabic language illegal, and forbade the Islamic religion, dress, and customs, a step which led to the Second Rebellion of Alpujarras, involving acts of brutality from the Muslim rebels, against Christian locals. The Moriscos of Granada were as a result dispersed across Spain. 'Edicts of Expulsion' for the expulsion of the Moriscos were finally issued by Philip III in 1609 against the remaining Muslims in Spain. The expulsion was particularly efficient in the Eastern region of Valencia where they made up 33% of the population and ethnic tensions between Muslim and non-Muslim populations were high, as locals came under harassment by Muslim brigands. The corresponding expulsion of Muslims from the Kingdom of Castille and Andalusia was officially completed in 1614. Unlike the Kingdom of Aragon and Valencia, Moriscos were highly integrated in the rest of Spain significant number of them avoided expulsion or returned en masse, with the protection of non-morisco neighbours and local authorities.

The last mass prosecution against Moriscos for crypto-Islamic practices occurred in Granada in 1727, with most of those convicted receiving relatively light sentences. Some of the Morisco community including these final convicts were said to have kept their identity alive at least through the late eighteenth century.

Nevertheless, communities of Moorish freed slaves known as "moros cortados" continued to be present throughout various parts of Spain, many of which had been freed as a result of a reciprocal deal with Morocco in 1767. Such former slaves, although baptised continued to discreetly practice their religion. As a result of a second Treaty with Morocco in 1799, the King of Spain formally guaranteed the right of Moroccans in Spain to practice their religion in exchange for Spanish Catholics being granted the same rights in Morocco.

Demography and ethnic background

The Spanish Constitution of 1978 declares in Art. 16 that "No one may be compelled to make statements regarding his religion, beliefs or ideologies" which means that all data on religious beliefs is approximated. The evolution of the Muslim population has been linked to the increase of immigration in the last two decades, which began with the entry of Spain in the European Economic Community (1986), following the economic growth and the closure of European borders to third countries. Official estimations by the Centro de Investigaciones sociológicas (CIS) say there are 2.9% believers in other religions, of whom around 2% would be Muslims.

The Autonomous Communities with the highest Muslim population, in absolute terms, are Catalonia, Andalusia, the Community of Madrid, and the Region of Murcia. However, in relation to the overall population within the Autonomous Communities, the cities of Ceuta and Melilla stand out with the highest percentages of Muslims, following the Region of Murcia, Catalonia, and La Rioja. Moreover, it is worth mentioning that the Muslim population in the cities of Ceuta and Melilla, which has close ties to the Moroccan population, has been active in the creation of associations and pioneer in the implementation of Islam related measures in different political fields. Unofficial sources for the subsequent tables and graphics:

Muslim Population		
Year	**Pop.**	**±%**
2003	525,000	—
2004	801,284	+52.6%
2005	1,064,904	+32.9%
2006	1,080,478	+1.5%

2007	1,145,424	+6.0%
2008	1,310,148	+14.4%
2009	1,446,939	+10.4%
2010	1,498,707	+3.6%
2011	1,595,221	+6.4%
2012	1,671,629	+4.8%
2013	1,732,191	+3.6%
2014	1,858,409	+7.3%
2015	1,887,906	+1.6%
2016	1,919,141	+1.7%
2017	1,946,300	+1.4%
2018	1,993,675	+2.4%
2019	2,091,656	+4.9%
2020	2,216,513	+6.0%
2021	2,250,486	+1.5%
2022	2,349,288	+4.4%

Source: The information regarding Muslim population will be found on the first page of each Annual Report (e.g., *Informe 2003*). For this purpose, the Annual Reports must be downloaded.

Islamic organisations

The creation of Islamic communities as legal entities has been an instrument for Muslims to organize themselves in order to communicate with public institutions and achieve the rights established in the legal arrangements. Since the signature of the Cooperation Agreement between the State and the Islamic Commission of Spain in 1992 and the increase of migratory flows, there has been a significant growth of organisations in form of religious communities, associations, and federations. The local communities and associations can incorporate themselves directly within the Islamic Commission or through an already integrated federation. In 2019, there were 49 Islamic federations, 1,704 communities, and 21 associations registered in the Religious Entities Office of the Ministry of Justice (RER). A total of 365 religious entities remained outside the Islamic Commission.

Relations between Islam and the State

In Spain, Islam is considered a minority though "deep-rooted" religion together with Judaism, the Evangelic Church, the Church of Jesus Christ of Latter-day Saints, the Jehovah's Witnesses, Buddhism and the Eastern Orthodox Church. In this sense, the Spanish state established a legal framework for the accommodation of those remarkable religions within the legal framework of cooperative church-state relations. Until now, just the Jewish, the Evangelic and the Muslim communities have signed a formal Agreement with the state.

Muslims and the state in the 20th century

The colonialist policy conducted by the Spanish state during the 19th and the 20th century mostly in North-Africa shaped also the politics toward the Islamic religion in the metropole. After the Spanish Civil War (1936–1939) the dictator Francisco Franco rewarded the engagement of Moroccan troops in his army with the construction of the first modern mosque in the Iberian Peninsula since the Muslim presence in Al-Ándalus during the Middle Ages, namely the Al-Morabito Mosque in Córdoba. Furthermore, at the beginning of the civil war, it was assigned a place within the San Fernando Cemetery in Sevilla (Cementerio de San Fernando) to bury Muslim soldiers, which was closed after the conflict. However, the Spanish State during Franco's dictatorship was defined as a Catholic confessional state and did not recognise any public expression of other religions until the Law of Religious Liberty in 1967, which means that from 1939 to 1967 Muslims could only exercise their religion in the private sphere. From then on, the Muslim community began to organise itself in associations. In 1971, Riay Tatary Bakr, the later president of the Islamic Commission of Spain, helped to create the Association of Muslims in Spain (AME) based in Madrid, which constructed the Madrid Central Mosque or Abu Bakr Mosque with private funds mostly from Saudi Arabia.

The legal framework of religious diversity

In the Spanish case, the legal framework for the governance of religious diversity has its foundations in the historical church-state model. In political science, the theory explaining how historical patterns can influence new policy outcomes is called path dependency. Similarly, there have been many studies linking the governance of Islam in European countries to pre-existing church-state models. During Franco's dictatorship, the Spanish state signed the Concordat of 1953 with the Vatican, which granted the Catholic Church with some privileges such as state funding and the exemption from government taxation. In the Spanish transition to democracy, the government replicated the same model by signing new agreements in 1976 and 1979, which gave the concordat the status of an international treaty.

The Constitution of 1978 stipulated in Article 16 that all beliefs within the Spanish society will be taken into account and the state will maintain cooperative relations with the Catholic Church as well as with other religious denominations. Furthermore, The Organic Law of Religious Liberty (LOLR) of 1980 specified in Article 7 that the state should establish Cooperation Agreements with those "Churches, Confessions and Communities" that had achieved 'deep-rootedness' (Notorio arraigo) in Spanish society, due to their scope and the number of believers. The criteria were the following ones:

- A sufficient number of members, referred to the federation or organism gathering the different churches or denominations of the requesting confession.

- An appropriate and binding juridical organisation for all entities gathered within the organisation.

- Historical roots in Spain, both legal and clandestinely, since a certain time that is deemed appropriate.

- Importance of the social, care and cultural activities conducted by the requesting confession.

- Confession's scope assessed by his territorial extension, the number of local churches, worship places, etc.

- Institutionalisation of the ministers of religion, i.e., proportionality in relation to the members of the confession, study certificate, stability...

This law allowed the state to sign Cooperation Agreements with the Jewish, the Evangelic and the Muslim communities, which were previously recognised as "deep-rooted" religions. The definition of the requirements and procedure for obtaining "deep-rootedness" was reformulated in the Royal Decree 593/2015. In 1984, the Advisory Commission of Religious Liberty (CARL), an administrative organ within the Ministry of Justice, recognised both the Evangelic and the Jewish confessions, and in 1989 the Islamic religion achieved his recognition as well.

Cooperation Agreement between the Spanish State and the Islamic Commission of Spain

Following the church-state model, the agreement would be signed by two parties: on the one side, the Ministry of Justice representing the Spanish State, and on the other side, one representative body for each religious denomination. This obligated the different religious communities to organise themselves in a centralised and hierarchal way within a short period of time. Moreover, this model did not take into account the heterogeneous nature of the communities, especially for the Islamic religion. In 1989, after the recognition of the Islam as "deep-rooted" religion, the Spanish Federation of Islamic Religious Entities (FEERI) was created with 15 federated associations in order to serve as the single interlocutor with the state. However, in 1991 a group of communities left the Federation to form a new one under the name Union of Islamic Communities of Spain (UCIDE). So far, there were two competing Islamic federations, which wanted to monopolise the communication with the state. The request for a Cooperation Agreement should be carried out by the religious confession and then reviewed by the public administration. Both federations started to draft an agreement in parallel. Finally, the solution was found in the creation of the Islamic Commission of Spain, founded by the FEERI and the UCIDE and established on 18 February 1992. Its raison d'être was the "negotiation, signature and follow- up on the Cooperation Agreement with the state" as it is written in the first article of his statutes.

1992 was chosen as the year for the signature of the Cooperation Agreements, due to the 500th anniversary regarding the conquest of the Nasrid Kingdom of Granada and the Expulsion of Jews from Spain. Because of that, many scholars have seen the Agreements as a symbolic act rather than as an instrument for the management of religious diversity. Nevertheless, the agreements aimed to equate the one signed with the Catholic Church and so to accommodate the religions mentioned within public institutions and the school system, to guarantee the exemption from taxation and the involvement of the religious communities in the preservation of their related cultural heritage. The Cooperation Agreement between the State and the Islamic Commission of Spain includes 14 articles and three additional provisions that can be summarised in 9 topics: legal affairs, worship places, imams, marriage and festivities, religious assistance, religious education, fiscal benefits, cultural heritage, and halal products. In the following sections, a summary with relevant facts is provided:

1. Legal affairs: the Islamic Commission of Spain shall validate the incorporation of communities and federations within its body. The communities must be also registered in the Religious Entities Office of the Ministry of Justice. The certification of religious purposes for the creation of religious entities can be issued by their belonging federation in accordance with the Islamic Commission of Spain or directly by the commission.

2. Worship places: mosques or places of worship will be certified by the respective community in conformity with the CIE.

Those worship places enjoy inviolability according to the terms established by law. Moreover, this topic comprises the right of those Islamic communities, which are integrated within the CIE, to the granting of plots in public cemeteries or the ownership of private ones.

3. Imams: on the one side, the Islamic Commission of Spain is the organ that can certify imams and Islamic religious leaders. On the other side, the Ministry of Justice must first recognise those centres for religious instruction. Furthermore, those persons who meet the requirements will be covered by the General Social Security Plan.

4. Marriage and festivities: the marriage celebrated under Islamic Law will be effective if the applicants meet the criteria demanded by the Civil Code. Moreover, the members of the Islamic communities belonging to the Islamic Commission of Spain can apply for the interruption of their work every Friday, the day of collective compulsory prayer, from 1:30 pm till 4 pm, and the cessation of the working day one hour before sunset during the month of Ramadan.

5. Religious assistance: the religious assistance is recognised as a right for Muslims within the Armed Forces and in public centres such as hospitals, penitentiary centres and Alien Internment Centres (CIES). Those public centres are responsible for covering the costs of religious assistance.

6. Religious education: the Spanish school system integrates already the possibility to course catholic religion as an optative subject. Article 10 opens thus the possibility for Muslims to request Islamic religious teaching in the levels of preschool, primary and secondary education. The

communities belonging to the Islamic Commission of Spain will appoint the teachers in conformity with their own federation.

7. Fiscal benefits: the Islamic Commission of Spain as well as the communities, among other fiscal benefits, will be exempt from property taxes and other special contributions, from corporate income taxes and taxes on asset transfers and legal documents.

8. Cultural heritage: both the state and the Islamic Commission of Spain commit themselves to cooperate in order to conserve and promote the historical, cultural, artistic, Islamic heritage, which will continue to serve society for its contemplation and study.

9. Halal products: the Islamic Commission of Spain will elaborate a specific label for halal products in order to guarantee that those have been produced in accordance with Islamic Law. Nevertheless, the animal sacrifice should meet the health regulations in force. On the matter of food supplies in public centres and military units, it will be sought to adapt food and schedule to Islamic precepts.

Implementation of the Cooperation Agreement

The implementation of the Cooperation Agreement has been a long process that has not been yet completed. When the Agreement was signed in 1992, no other regulations regarding the concrete implementation nor financial means were determined directly afterwards. Moreover, since Spain is a semi-federal state, the competencies over the agreed measures correspond to different administrative levels: the Central Government, the Autonomous

Communities, and the Municipal councils. The Agreement did not include, however, any references regarding the jurisdiction of the measures.

Worship places

The Cooperation Agreement identifies mosques and cemeteries as Islamic worship places. In Spain, there are 13 big mosques in the cities of Madrid (2), Valencia (1), Córdoba (2), Granada (1), Ceuta (2), Melilla (2), Fuengirola (1), Marbella (1) and Málaga (1). However, in practice, most common places of worship are small oratories established in commercial premises, garages, and private apartments. The religious communities are mostly renting these establishments, just a minority are private property. A study from 2009 about the religious situation in Castile-La Mancha identified 46 religious communities of which only 4 had a private property. At the autonomic level, the Community of Madrid signed an agreement with the UCIDE in 1998, which referred in the third clause to the promotion of transfer of land to construct mosques and worship places in Madrid. In Catalonia, on the other side, a law was adopted in 2009 to deal with the granting of licenses by municipal councils. Especially in Catalonia, there have been many cases of social opposition to mosques. In a study conducted by Avi Stor 41 cases were reported in Catalonia between 1990 and 2013, the total cases in Spain was 74 from 1985 to 2013.

Religious assistance

The competence over religious assistance varies across the institutions involved. For instance, the central government is responsible for the religious assistance in penitentiary centres except in Catalonia. For the religious assistance in Alien Internment Centres (CIES) has also the Spanish government, under the Directorate-General of the

Police (DGP), the jurisdiction. On the other side, the Autonomous Communities have the competencies in the area of healthcare, thus they have to manage the religious assistance in hospitals and other healthcare centres. In 2006, a decree was adopted to regulate the religious assistance in penitentiary centres, and in 2007 an economic agreement was signed for its financing. Furthermore, the Generalitat de Catalunya signed in 2008 a collaboration agreement with the Islamic and Cultural Council of Catalonia (Consell Islàmic i Cultural de Catalunya) to guarantee the religious assistance in Catalan penitentiary centres through the Directorate General of Religious Affairs (DGAR). This collaboration agreement was updated in 2015 and in 2019, this time with the involvement of the Federation Islamic Council of Catalonia. Until 2019, there were 20 imams for the religious assistance in penitentiary centres in Spain, 8 of them engaged in Catalan prisons. Regarding the religious assistance in CIES, 7 imams were reported in 2019. Moreover, there is no available data for the employment of imams in health care centres. Finally, the religious assistance in the Armed forces, under the jurisdiction of the Ministry of Defence, has not been implemented yet.

Religious education

Education is a complex matter since there is no exact distribution of competencies between the state and the Autonomous Communities. The state establishes some basic rules for applying Article 27 of the Constitution, while the communities have to develop the legislative framework and execute the educational programmes. While the education competencies have been transferred to most of the Autonomous Communities, the Education Ministry remains responsible for the competencies in Andalusia, Aragon, the Canary Islands, Cantabria, Ceuta, and Melilla.

Regarding the regulatory framework, the Spanish government signed an agreement about the designation and economic regime of the Islamic religion teachers that went into effect for the 1996–1997 school year. This agreement referred just to public schools in primary and secondary education, although the Cooperation Agreement explicitly mentioned the semi-private schools, which are co-funded by the Public Administration. In 2000, 20 teachers were designated for the cities of Ceuta and Melilla and in 2005 another 20 teachers would cover the Islamic religious teaching in the communities whose competencies remained by the Spanish State. Since then, the Islamic Commission of Spain has signed different agreements with the remaining Autonomous Communities for the implementation of Islamic religious teaching. However, there was not always the need for an agreement at the autonomic level, since some communities introduced Islamic religious teaching in their school systems on the basis of the Cooperation Agreement of 1992 as in the case of Islamic religious teaching in the primary school for Andalusia. In 2019, a total of 80 Islamic religious teachers were reported. While Navarre, Galicia, and Asturias opened the opportunity to take the subject if the requirements are fulfilled, the Region of Murcia has not yet answered the petitions of the Islamic Commission of Spain. Catalonia began a pilot program for the school year 2020–2021.

Support for Integration Programmes

The Cooperation Agreement established fiscal benefits and tax exemptions for the Islamic religious communities but did not stipulate a financial mechanism similar to the one for the Catholic Church. However, in the aftermath of the Madrid bombings of 2004, the Spanish government saw the need for integrating Muslims in Spanish society besides of formulating policies to ensure national security. In December 2004, the Foundation for Pluralism and Coexistence (FPC) was created to support programmes related to cultural, educative, and social integration for those religions with "deep-rootedness", i.e. the Evangelic Church, Judaism, and Islam. Catalonia's regional government had already in 2000 created the Directorate General of Religious Affairs (DGAR) and in 2004, this public agency launched a programme to provide access to public funding for activities regarding the integration of minority religions, which was developed before the creation of the FPC at the national level.

Halal products

The Agreement stipulated that the Islamic Commission of Spain would be the organization responsible for obtaining the Halal guarantee mark from the Industrial Property Registry. In practice, it was the Islamic Committee of Spain (Junta Islámica de España), one of the communities integrated within the FEERI, that created a Halal Institute in 2003 to regulate and certify food and products in line with the requirements of Islamic rituals under the trademark "Halal Guarantee Distinction of the Islamic Committee" (Marca de Garantía Halal de Junta Islámica). Their claim to be the only official Institution in Spain that guarantees the halal production, however, has not been accomplished since it can be found so far 45 national trademarks in the Spanish Patent and Trademark Office website which refer to the same product categories, without counting the European and international products commercialised in Spain. Furthermore, one of these trademarks was registered by the Islamic Commission of Spain in 2018, claiming its official mandate established in the Cooperation Agreement.

Radicalization and terrorism

Jihadists entered in Spain from 1994, when an al-Qaeda cell was established. In 1996, the Armed Islamic Group of Algeria (GIA), an organisation affiliated with al-Qaeda, founded a cell in the province of Valencia. In the 1995–2003 period, slightly over 100 people were arrested for offences related to militant salafism, an average of 12 per year.

In 2004, Madrid commuters suffered the 2004 Madrid train bombings, which were perpetrated by remnants of the first al-Qaeda cell, members of the Moroccan Islamic Combatant Group (GICM) plus a gang of criminals turned into jihadists.

In the period 2004–2012, there were 470 arrests, an average of 52 per year and four times the pre-Madrid bombings average which indicated that the jihadist threat persisted after the Madrid attack. In the years after the Madrid attack, 90% of all jihadists convicted in Spain were foreigners, mainly from Morocco, Pakistan and Algeria, while 7 out of 10 resided in the metropolitan areas of Madrid or Barcelona. The vast majority were involved in cells linked to organisations such as al-Qaeda, the GICM, the Algerian Salafist group Group for Preaching and Combat which had replaced the GIA, and Tehrik-i-Taliban Pakistan.

In the period 2013, jihadism in Spain transformed to be less overwhelmingly associated with foreigners. Arrests 2013–2017 show that 4 out of 10 arrested were Spanish nationals and 3 out of 10 were born in Spain. Most others had Morocco as a country of nationality or birth with its main focus among Moroccan descendants residing in the North African cities of Ceuta and Melilla. The most prominent jihadist presence was the province of

Barcelona. In 2013 and 2014 there were cells associated with Al-Nusra Front, the Islamic State of Iraq and the Levant.

Attitudes towards Muslims

Survey published in 2019 by the Pew Research Center found that 54% of Spaniards had a favourable view of Muslims, whereas 42% had an unfavourable view.

Portugal

Portugal is an overwhelmingly Christian majority country, with adherents of Islam being a small minority. According to the 2021 census, Muslims represent around 0.4% of the total population of the country. However, many centuries back Islam was a major religion in the territory of modern-day Portugal, beginning with the Muslim conquest of Spain. Today, due to secular nature of the Constitution of Portugal, Muslims are free to convert, practice their religion, and build mosques.

According to the 1991 census recorded by Instituto Nacional de Estatística (the National Statistical Institute of Portugal), there were 9,134 Muslims in Portugal, about 0.09% of the total population. The Muslim population in 2019 was approximately 65,000 people. The majority of Muslims in the country are Sunni, followed by approximately 20,000 to 22,000 Shia Muslims, 65% of them are Ismaili. Most of the Muslim population in the 1990s originated from the former Portuguese overseas provinces of Portuguese Guinea and Portuguese Mozambique with most of the latter having their origin in former Portuguese Goa and Damao (India). Most of the Muslims currently living in Portugal are from the Middle East (including Syria), the Maghreb, Mozambique and Bangladesh.

From 711 to 722, all the territory of what is now Portugal and then the Visigothic Kingdom was invaded and colonised by the Arabic Umayyad Caliphate and subsequent Moorish Sultanates of Arabic, Arabised and Berber people. By the year 1000, Islamic rule was still prevalent in much of what is now Portugal, namely south of the Mondego river, and later, for many more decades, across the Alentejo and Algarve regions of what is modern Portugal. During the period of Muslim conquest, western Iberia was called Gharb

Al-Andalus (the west of Al-Andalus), over the course of Portuguese Reconquista. The Christian military forces retook almost all of former Lusitania and the Muslim Arab and Berber military forces retreated to Algarve in the 1200s and were defeated during the course of the 13th century. However, their presence in Andalusia, a neighboring Spanish region, would stay strong for another 250 years. This presence has left some cultural heritage in Portugal, such as Islamic art and Arabic-inspired toponyms and words. The town of Mértola, in the Alentejo, possesses the only partial remains in the country of an early medieval mosque, changed and converted into a Catholic church (Church of Nossa Senhora da Anunciação) after the Reconquista.

The Islamic Community of Lisbon was formed in March 1968 by a group of Muslim university students who, at the time, were studying in the Portuguese capital. But even before the constitution of the community, in 1966, a committee composed of ten elements (five Muslims and five Christians) asked the Lisbon City Council for a plot of land to build a mosque. The Community, in its beginning, was mostly made up of families from the ex-colonies that went to Portugal after the Carnation Revolution on 25 April 1974, namely Mozambique and Guinea-Bissau, as well as some people from North Africa (Morocco and Algeria), Pakistan, Bangladesh and members of the several embassies of Arab countries accredited in Portugal. Only later, in September 1977, a piece of land on Avenida José Malhoa was ceded.

The laying of the first stone took place in January 1979 and the inauguration of the first phase of construction took place on March 29, 1985. By then, the community was already estimated at more than four thousand people (1981 Census), mostly from the former Portuguese colonies. According to the 1991 census recorded by

Instituto Nacional de Estatística (the National Statistical Institute of Portugal), there were 9,134 Muslims in Portugal, about 0.1% of the total population. As of 2021, the community is estimated at 65 thousand people (many from the Maghreb and the Middle East, notably from Syria and Iraq, as well as from Afghanistan and Bangladesh among other countries) and spreads over several parts of Portugal, most prominently within the Lisbon Metropolitan Area, Porto Metropolitan Area, and Algarve.

Shia Imami Ismaili Muslims

The Aga Khan Development Network has been present in Portugal since 1983. Agreements were established between the Ismaili Imamat and Portugal, particularly the Protocol of Cooperation with the Portuguese Government signed in 2005 as well as the Protocol of International Cooperation with the Ministry of Foreign Affairs which was signed in 2008.

In 2015, Lisbon was chosen to be the global seat of the Nizari Isma'ili community, the second largest Shia denomination in the world. On July 11, 2018 the Aga Khan decided to move his global headquarters along with his official residence to Portugal. On June 3, 2015 Portugal's Minister of State and Foreign Affairs Rui Machete and His Highness the Aga Khan signed a landmark Agreement between the Republic of Portugal and the Ismaili Imamat for the establishment of a formal Seat of the Aga Khan in Portugal. The accord, which was approved by Portugal's Parliament and the President of Portugal, will result in intensified cooperation between Portugal and the Aga Khan Development Network in attempting to support research and the knowledge society as well as attempting to improve the quality of life of Portugal's inhabitants.

The Aga Khan recently acquired the Henrique de Mendonça Palace, a 12-million-euro estate he has renamed the "Diwan of the Ismaili Imamat", to take place as the new Global Headquarters and serve as an administrative structure to coordinate the Aga Khan Development Network. Rui Machete told the Portuguese daily national newspaper Público, "It is natural that an institution with an annual budget of between €600-€900 million will bring something to Portugal." The Aga Khan stated that he also has goals to, "plough money into health and social protection services in Portugal." The Aga Khan is followed by more than 15 million Muslims worldwide, of which 15,000 who live in Portugal.

The Aga Khan Development Network moving its headquarters to Lisbon, Portugal allows there to be a connection between Lisbon and the rest of the world in which the Aga Khan Development Network is affiliated. The international organization has many ties to Lisbon, not only because the Ismaili population is one of the biggest there, but also because most funding is coming from private sector partners which are located within Lisbon. Through various programs and initiatives, The Aga Khan Development Network is drastically changing the quality of life in Portugal in ways that are beneficial to people living there. The Aga Khan Development Network has been present in Portugal since 1983 focusing on research and innovative direct intervention in the areas of early childhood education, social exclusion and urban poverty. The activities in Portugal operate within the framework of the agreements established between the Aga Khan Development Network and the Protocol of Cooperation with the Portuguese Government.

Chapter 13

United Kingdom

Islam is the second-largest religion in the United Kingdom, with results from the 2011 Census giving the population as 4.4% of the total UK population, while results from the 2021 Census recorded a population of 6.5% in England and Wales. London has the greatest population of Muslims in the country. The vast majority of Muslims in the United Kingdom adhere to Sunni Islam, while smaller numbers are associated with Shia Islam.

During the Middle Ages, there was some general cultural exchange between Christendom and the Islamic world. Nonetheless, there were no Muslims in the British Isles; however, a few Crusaders did convert in the East, such as Robert of St. Albans. During the Elizabethan age, contacts became more explicit as the Tudors made alliances against Catholic Habsburg Spain, including with Morocco and the Ottoman Empire. As the British Empire grew, particularly in India, Britain came to rule territories with many Muslim inhabitants; some of these, known as the lascars, are known to have settled in Britain from the mid-18th century onwards. In the 19th century, Victorian Orientalism spurred an interest in Islam and some British people, including aristocrats, converted to Islam. Marmaduke Pickthall, an English writer and novelist, and a convert to Islam, provided the first complete English-language translation of the Qur'an by a British Muslim in 1930.

Under the British Indian Army, a significant number of Muslims fought for the United Kingdom during the First and the Second World Wars (a number of whom were awarded the Victoria Cross, Britain's highest honour). In the decades following the latter conflict and the Partition of India in 1947, many Muslims (from what is today Bangladesh, India and Pakistan) settled in Britain itself. To this day, South Asians constitute the majority of Muslims in Britain in terms of ethnicity, although there are significant Turkish, Arab and Somali communities, as well as up to 100,000 British converts of multiple ethnic backgrounds. Islam is the second largest religion in the United Kingdom and its adherents have the lowest average age out of all the major religious groups. Between 2001 and 2009, the Muslim population increased almost 10 times faster than the non-Muslim population.

History

Early history

Although Islam is generally thought of as a recent arrival in the UK, Muslims have been trading and exchanging ideas with the British for centuries.

The earliest evidence of Islamic influence in England dates to the 8th century, when Offa, the Anglo-Saxon king of Mercia, minted a coin with an Arabic inscription, largely a copy of coins issued by a contemporary Abbasid ruler, Caliph Al-Mansur. In the 16th century, Muslims from North Africa, the Middle East and Central Asia were present in London, working in a range of roles, from diplomats and translators to merchants and musicians.

Interactions under British Empire

Bengal was annexed by the East India Company from the quasi-independent Nawabs of Bengal following the Battle of Plassey in 1757. The manufactured goods produced in Bengal directly contributed to the Industrial Revolution in Britain, with the textiles produced in Bengal being used to support British industries such as textile manufacturing, aided by the invention of devices such as the spinning jenny. With the establishment of Crown control in India after 1857, the British Empire came to rule over a large Muslim population. The first educated South Asian to travel to Europe and live in Britain was I'tisam-ud-Din, a Bengali Muslim cleric, munshi and diplomat to the Mughal Empire who arrived in 1765 with his servant Muhammad Muqim during the reign of King George III. He wrote of his experiences and travels in his Persian book, Shigurf-nama-i-Wilayat (or 'Wonder Book of Europe').

In South Asia, specifically, the British ruled over one of the largest Muslim populations in the world. Upon coming into contact with such a population, the British authorities forged a uniquely Muslim identity for the local believers. This was, in part, due to the way British historians periodized South Asian history into an "ancient" Hindu one and a "medieval" Muslim one. Under the system, the colonial period was classified as "modern". Debate rages on concerning the utility and legitimacy of these labels themselves. Problems with these labels range from the connotations coupled with the word 'medieval' to the implications related to labelling the colonial era as "modern". The term medieval itself is quite controversial. Historians writing in journals relating to the time period have asked whether the term is a "tyrannous construct" or an "alien conceptual hegemony". This is because the label was originally developed during the study of European history to mark the period in between the fall of the Roman Empire and the fall of Constantinople.

Such classifications done by British historians throughout their long period of rule paved the way for a more cohesive Muslim identity. In the eighteenth century, this seemed unlikely. Muslims who hailed from Afghan, Turk, Persian, or Arab roots did not find their Muslim identities especially salient. Mughal courts divided not into Hindu or Muslim factions but Persian and Turkish ones. Converts to the religion outside of courtly life, the majority of the Muslim population in the Subcontinent, too were more focused on their regional and lingual cultural identities-whether that be Bengali, Punjabi, Sindhi, or Gujarati.

The first group of Muslims to come to Great Britain in significant numbers, in the 18th century, were lascars (sailors) recruited from the Indian subcontinent, largely from the Bengal region, to work for the East India Company on British ships, some of whom settled down and took local wives. Due to the majority being lascars, the earliest Muslim communities were found in port towns. Naval cooks also came, many of them from the Sylhet district of British Bengal (now in Bangladesh). One of the most famous early Asian immigrants to England was the Bengali Muslim entrepreneur Sake Dean Mahomet, a captain of the East India Company who in 1810 founded London's first Indian restaurant, the Hindoostanee Coffee House.

Between 1803 and 1813, there were more than 10,000 lascars from the Indian subcontinent visiting British port cities and towns. By 1842, 3,000 lascars visited the UK annually, and by 1855, 12,000 lascars were arriving annually in British ports. In 1873, 3,271 lascars arrived in Britain. Throughout the early 19th century lascars visited Britain at a rate of 1,000 every year, which increased to a rate of 10,000 to 12,000 every year throughout the late 19th century. A prominent English convert of the 19th century was Henry Stanley, 3rd Baron Stanley of Alderley, who became a Muslim in 1862. Although not a convert himself, the Victorian Age adventurer, Sir Richard Francis Burton visited Mecca in disguise, documented in The Book of the Thousand Nights and a Night. At the beginning of World War I, there were 51,616 South Asian lascars working on British ships, the majority of whom were of Bengali descent. In 1932, the Indian National Congress survey of 'all Indians outside India' (which included modern Pakistani and Bangladeshi territories) estimated that there were 7,128 Indians living in the United Kingdom.

By 1911, the British Empire had a Muslim population of 94 million, larger than the empire's 58 million Christian population. By the 1920s, the British Empire included roughly half of the world's Muslim population. More than 400,000 Muslim soldiers of the British Indian Army fought for Britain during World War I, where 62,060 were killed in action. Muslim soldiers of the British Indian Army later fought for Britain against the Nazis in World War II, where Muslim soldiers accounted for up to 40% of the 2.5 million troops serving the British Indian Army. David Lloyd George, British Prime Minister from 1916 to 1922, stated: "we are the greatest Mahomedan power in the world and one-fourth of the population of the British Empire is Mahomedan. There have been no more loyal adherents to the throne and no more effective and loyal supporters of the Empire in its hour of trial." This statement was later reiterated by Gandhi in 1920. Winston Churchill also stated in 1942: "We must not on any account break with the Moslems, who represent a hundred million people, and the main army elements on which we must rely for the immediate fighting."

The Shah Jehan Mosque in Woking was the first purpose-built mosque in Britain, and was built in 1889. In the same year, Abdullah Quilliam installed a mosque in a terrace in Liverpool, which became the Liverpool Muslim Institute. The first mosque in London was the Fazl Mosque, established in 1924, commonly called the London mosque.

Quran translators Yusuf Ali and Marmaduke Pickthall, who authored The Meaning of the Glorious Koran: An Explanatory Translation in 1930, were both trustees of the Shah Jehan Mosque in Woking and the East London Mosque.

Other aristocratic British converts included Sir Archibald Hamilton, 5th Baronet, Rowland Allanson-Winn, 5th Baron Headley, St John Philby and Zainab Cobbold (the first Muslim woman born in Britain to perform the pilgrimage to Mecca).

Immigration and post-World War II

Large-scale immigration of Muslims to Britain began after World War II, as a result of the destruction and labour shortages caused by the war. Muslim migrants from former British colonies, predominantly India, Pakistan, and Bangladesh, were recruited in large numbers by government and businesses to rebuild the country. Large numbers of doctors recruited from India and Pakistan, encouraged by health minister Enoch Powell in the early 1960s, also played a key role in the establishment of the National Health Service.

British Asians (both Muslim and non-Muslim) faced increased discrimination following Powell's Rivers of Blood speech and the establishment of the National Front in the late 1960s. This included overt racism in the form of "Paki bashing", predominantly from white power skinheads, the National Front, and the British National

Party, throughout the 1970s and 1980s. Drawing inspiration from the civil rights movement, the black power movement, and the anti-apartheid movement, young British Pakistani and British Bangladeshi activists began a number of anti-racist Asian youth movements in the 1970s and 1980s, including the Bradford Youth Movement in 1977, the Bangladeshi Youth Movement following the murder of Altab Ali in 1978, and the Newham Youth Movement following the murder of Akhtar Ali Baig in 1980.

The majority of mosques founded after World War II in Britain are reflective of the major strands of Sunni Islam predominating in the Indian subcontinent; namely Deobandi and Barelvi (the latter of which is more Sufi-orientated). There are also a smaller number of Salafi-oriented mosques, inspired by Abul A'la Maududi and Jamaat-e-Islami, are representative of the Arab mainstream or are associated with the UK Turkish Islamic Trust. In addition to this there are Twelver Shia Mosques. The Murabitun World Movement founded by Abdalqadir as-Sufi (born Ian Dallas) in 1968 is a branch of the Sufi Darqawi-Shadhili-Qadiri tariqa which was run out of Achnagairn in the Scottish Highlands.

Martin Lings, an English Muslim scholar, published a biography of Muhammad in 1983 entitled Muhammad: His Life Based on the Earliest Sources. The publication of Salman Rushdie's novel The Satanic Verses in 1988 caused major controversy. A number of Muslims in Britain condemned the book for blasphemy. On 2 December 1988, the book was publicly burned at a demonstration in Bolton attended by 7,000 Muslims, followed by a similar demonstration and book-burning in Bradford on 14 January 1989.

Recently, several wars in the Balkans, Middle East and North Africa have led to many Muslims migrating to the United Kingdom.

In 1992, with the outbreak of the Bosnian War, a large number of Bosniaks who fled the ethnic cleansing and genocide ended up settling in Britain. Their numbers currently exist at between 10,000 and 15,000 including their descendants. Just over three years later, an insurgency in Kosovo beginning in 1995, eventually evolving into the Kosovo War in 1998, would see 29,000 Kosovo Albanians flee their homes and settle in Britain. It is commonly believed that many Albanians from Albania moved to the United Kingdom at this time, posing as refugees from Kosovo, in search of a better life in the UK.

A mere decade later, the Arab Spring (and later Arab Winter) brought a wave of Muslim refugees fleeing civil war in Syria, war in Iraq, two wars in Libya, war in Yemen and countless other insurgencies by political groups and other terrorist organisations which exerted control over vast swathes of territory in the Middle East. Britain took on 20,000 refugees from Syria and 11,647 from Iraq.

The growing number of Muslims resulted in the establishment of more than 1,500 mosques by 2007.

Demographics

The Muslim population of England and Wales has grown consistently since World War II. Sophie Gilliat-Ray attributes the recent growth to "recent immigration, the higher than average birth rate, some conversion to Islam".

According to the 2021 United Kingdom census, Muslims in England and Wales numbered 3,868,133, or 6.5% of the population.

Census Year	Number of Muslims	Population of England and Wales	Muslim (% of population)	Registered mosques	Muslims per mosque
1961	50,000	46,196,000	0.11	7	7,143
1971	226,000	49,152,000	0.46	30	7,533
1981	553,000	49,634,000	1.11	149	3,711
1991	950,000	51,099,000	1.86	443	2,144
2001	1,600,000	52,042,000	3.07	614	2,606
2011	2,706,000	56,076,000	4.83	1,500	1,912
2021	3,868,133	59,597,542	6.5	–	–

According to a 2017 projection the Muslim population in the UK in the year 2050 is likely to number around 13 million.

Several large cities have one area that is a majority Muslim even if the rest of the city has a fairly small Muslim population. In addition, it is possible to find small areas that are almost entirely Muslim: for example, Savile Town in Dewsbury.

Initial limited mosque availability meant that prayers were conducted in small rooms of council flats until the 1980s when more and larger facilities became available. Some synagogues and community buildings were turned into mosques and existing mosques began to expand their buildings. This process has continued down to the present day with the East London Mosque recently expanding into a large former car park where the London Muslim Centre is now used for prayers, recreational facilities and housing. Most people regard themselves as part of the ummah, and their identity is based on their religion rather than their ethnic group.

The 2001 census recorded that there were 179,733 Muslims who described themselves as 'white'. 65% of white Muslims described themselves as "other white", and would likely have originated from locations such as Bosnia and Herzegovina, Kosovo, Adygea, Chechnya, Albania, Turkey, Bulgaria, the region of East Macedonia and Thrace in Northern Greece, and North Macedonia. The remainder of white Muslims are converts and mostly identified themselves as White British and White Irish.

Islam is the third-largest religious group of British Indian people, after Hinduism and Sikhism. 8% of UK Muslims are of Indian descent, principally those whose origins are in Gujarat, West Bengal, Telangana and Kerala. Gujarati Muslims from the Surat and Bharuch districts started to arrive from the 1940s when India was under British colonial rule, settling in the towns of Dewsbury and Batley in Yorkshire and in parts of Lancashire.

South Asian

Pakistanis

The single largest group of Muslims in the United Kingdom are of Pakistani descent. Pakistanis were one of the first South Asian Muslim communities to permanently settle in the United Kingdom, arriving in England first in the late 1940s. Immigration from Mirpur in Pakistan grew from the late 1950s, accompanied by immigration from other parts of Pakistan especially from Punjab, particularly from the surrounding Punjab villages of Faisalabad, Sahiwal, Sialkot, Jhelum, Gujar Khan and Gujarat, in addition to from the north-west Punjab including the chhachhi Pathans and Pashtuns from Attock District, and some from villages of Ghazi, Nowshera and Peshawar. There is also a fairly large Punjabi community from East Africa found in London. People of Pakistani extraction are particularly notable in West Midlands, West Yorkshire, London, Lancashire/Greater Manchester and several industrial towns such as Luton, Slough and High Wycombe in the Home Counties. There are smaller numbers of Sindhis in Greater London. Pakistanis were traditionally working class but are slowly progressing into a Metropolitan middle class; they continue to face social integration issues.

Bangladeshis

People of Bangladeshi descent are the second largest Muslim community (after Pakistanis), 15% of Muslims in England and Wales are of Bangladeshi descent, one of the ethnic groups in the UK with the largest proportion of people following a single religion, being 92% Muslim. The majority of these Muslims come from the Sylhet Division of Bangladesh. Many mosques opened by the British Bangladeshi community are often named after Shah Jalal and other Sufi saints who took part in the Islamic conquest of Sylhet in 1303. British Bangladeshi Muslims are mainly concentrated in London (Tower Hamlets and Newham), Luton, Birmingham and Oldham. The Bangladeshi Muslim community in London forms 24% of the Muslim population, larger than any other ethnic group. Other smaller Bangladeshi Muslim communities are present in Newcastle upon Tyne, Bradford, Manchester, Sunderland, Portsmouth, and Rochdale.

There are groups which are active throughout Bangladeshi communities such as The Young Muslim Organisation. It is connected to the Islamic Forum Europe, associated with the East London Mosque and the London Muslim Centre – all of which have connections with the Bangladeshi political party, the Jamaat-e-Islami. Other large groups include another Sunni movement, the Fultoli (founded in Sylhet), and the Tablighi Jamaat – which is a missionary and revival movement, and avoids political attention. The Hizb ut-Tahrir calls for the Khilafah (caliphate) and influences by publishing annual magazines, and lectures through mainly political concepts, and the other which is a movement within Sunni Islam is the Salafi – who view the teachings of the first generations after Muhammed as the correct teachings, and appeals to younger Muslims as a way to differentiate themselves towards their elders. All these groups work to stimulate Islamic identity among local Bengalis or Muslims and particularly focus on the younger members of the communities. The British Bangladeshi community has held a strong point in Islam, often opening large mosques such as East London Mosque and Brick Lane Masjid, as well as opening madrassas and Islamic TV channels.

Indians

There are large numbers of Gujarati Muslims in Dewsbury, Blackburn (including Darwen), Bolton, Preston, Nottingham, Leicester, Nuneaton, Gloucester and London (Newham, Waltham Forest and Hackney).

Middle Eastern

Kurds

The UK has a significant Iraqi Kurdish population. Iraqi Kurds are mostly Sunni Muslims.

According to the Department for Communities and Local Government, the Iraqi Kurds make up the largest group of Kurds in the country, exceeding the numbers from Turkey and Iran.

Arabs

People of Arab origin in Britain are the descendants of Arab immigrants to Britain from a variety of Arab states, including Yemen, Syria, Iraq, Lebanon, Jordan, Egypt and Palestine. Most British Arabs are Sunni Muslim, although some – such as those of Iraqi and Lebanese origin – are Shi'ite. The main Arab Muslim communities in the UK live in the Greater London area, with smaller numbers living in Manchester, Liverpool, and Birmingham. There are also sizable and very long-established communities of Muslim Yemenis in the United Kingdom in among other places Cardiff and the South Shields area near Newcastle.

The 2001 UK Census recorded 32,236 Iraqi-born residents, and the Office for National Statistics estimates that, as of 2009, this figure had risen to around 65,000. According to estimates by the

Iraqi embassy, the Iraqi population in the UK is around 350,000–450,000.

Turks

Turks in the United Kingdom represent a unique community in the country because they have emigrated not only from the Republic of Turkey but also from other former Ottoman regions; in fact, the majority of British Turks are Turkish Cypriots who migrated from the island of Cyprus from the British colonial period onwards. The second largest Turkish community descend from Turkey. There has also been ethnic Turkish migration waves from Arabic-speaking countries (such as Iraq and Syria) as well as the Balkans (including Bulgaria, Greece, and Romania). A report published by the Home Affairs Committee in 2011 claimed that there were 500,000 British Turks, made up of approximately 150,000 Turkish nationals, 300,000 Turkish Cypriots, and the remainder from other countries. As of 2013, there was a growing number of ethnic Turks from the modern diaspora in Western Europe; for example, Turks with German and Dutch citizenship (i.e. Turkish Germans and Turkish Dutch) had also immigrated to Britain in accordance with the freedom of movement under EU law.

Turkish Cypriots first began to migrate to the United Kingdom in 1917. At the time, the British Empire had already annexed Cyprus and the residents of Cyprus became subjects of the Crown. Migration continued through the 1920s; during the Second World War, the number of Turkish-run cafes increased from 20 in 1939 to 200 in 1945 – creating a demand for more Turkish Cypriot workers. However, due to the Cyprus conflict, many Turkish Cypriots began to leave the island for political reasons in the 1950s, with the numbers increasing significantly after the intercommunal violence of late 1963. With the subsequent division of the island in 1974 (followed by the declaration of the Turkish Republic of Northern Cyprus in 1983) an economic embargo against the Turkish Cypriots by the Greek Cypriot controlled Republic of Cyprus, caused a further 130,000 Turkish Cypriots to leave the Island for the United Kingdom.

Migrant workers from the Republic of Turkey began to arrive in large numbers in the 1970s, followed by their family members in the late 1970s and 1980s. Many of these workers were recruited by Turkish Cypriots who had already established businesses such as restaurants. These workers were required to renew their work permits every year until they became residents after living in the country for five years. By the 1980s, intellectuals, including students, and highly educated professionals arrived in the country, most of which received support from the Turkish Cypriot community. Mainland Turks settled in similar areas of London in which the Turkish Cypriots lived in; however, many have also moved to the outer districts, such as Essex.

The Turkish community have established several mosques in the country. The first was Shacklewell Lane Mosque, established by the Turkish Cypriot community in 1977. There are numerous other Turkish mosques in London, mainly in Hackney, including the Aziziye Mosque and Suleymaniye Mosque. Notable Turkish mosques outside London include Selimiye Mosque in Manchester, Hamidiye Mosque in Leicester, and Osmaniye Mosque in Stoke-on-Trent.

Turks from the same districts from their homeland tend to congregate in the same quarters in the UK. The majority live in capital city of London, particularly in Hackney, Haringey, Enfield, Lewisham, Lambeth, Southwark, Croydon, Islington, Kensington,

Waltham Forest, and Wood Green. Outside London there are smaller Turkish communities in Birmingham, Hertfordshire, Luton, Manchester, Sheffield and the East Midlands.

African

Maghrebis

Although data is short, findings indicate Maghrebis make up a substantial community in Europe and the United Kingdom. Britain has long ties with Maghrebis, through contact with the Maghrebis. Nevertheless, Britain has a far lower count of Maghrebis in comparison to France, the Netherlands and Spain, where the majority of Muslims are Maghrebi.

Nigerians

A 2009 government paper estimated the Nigerian Muslim community at 12,000 to 14,000 people. The community is concentrated in London.

Nigerian Muslims in the UK are represented by several community organizations including the Nigeria Muslim Forum.

Somalis

The United Kingdom, with 43,532 Somalia-born residents in 2001, and an estimated 101,000 in 2008, is home to the largest Somali community in Europe. A 2009 estimate by Somali community organisations puts the Somali population figure at 90,000 residents. The first Somali immigrants were seamen and traders who arrived in small numbers in port cities in the late 19th century, although most Somalis in the UK are recent arrivals. Further more Somali

European such as from Holland or Denmark have been emigrating in recent years. Established Somali communities are found in Bristol, Cardiff, Liverpool and London, and newer ones have formed in Leicester, Manchester and Sheffield.

White European

The history of native British Muslims has a long presence in the country. The earliest known Englishman to convert to Islam was John Nelson of the 16th century. Thomas Keith was a Scottish soldier who converted to Islam and became the governor of Medina. Abdullah Quilliam was a 19th-century Englishman who converted to Islam and built what is argued to be the first mosque in the country in Liverpool. He was known locally for his work advocating trade unionism and divorce law reform and persuaded more people in Liverpool to convert but they faced abuse from the wider society.

Branches

An August 2017 survey by the Bertelsmann Stiftung foundation found that among British Muslims, 75% were Sunni and 8% were Shia. A September 2017 survey by the Institute for Jewish Policy Research found that among British Muslims, 77% were Sunni, 5% were Shia, 1% were Ahmadiyya, and 4% were members of other denominations. 14% of British Muslims said they did not know or refused to answer the survey.

The denominational or theme breakdown of mosques and prayer rooms in the UK in 2017 with a sum total of more than 5% were as follows: 41.2% Deobandi, 23.7% Barelvi, 9.4% Salafi, and 5.9% Shia (Twelver, Bohra, Ismaili). 7.4% were non-denominational prayer rooms.

Sunni

In 2015, The Economist stated that were 2.3 million Sunnis in the UK.

Among British Sunnis in 2017, 66.7% were just non-denominational Sunni, 5.9% were Barelvi, 5.0% were Salafis, 4.1% were Deobandi, and 18.3% adhered to another Sunni Islam denomination.

The majority of British mosques are Sunni, including Deobandi, Barelvis and Salafi. In 2010 the affiliation of the mosques was: 44.6% Deobandi, 28.2% Barelvi and other Sufi, 5.8% Salafi, 2.8% Maudoodi-inspired; of the remainder many were part of other Sunni traditions or unaffiliated, while 4.2% were Shi'a (4%). The majority of mosque managers are of Pakistani and Bangladeshi origin, with many Gujarati, and fewer Arab, Turkish and Somali managed entities.

Shia

In 2015, The Economist stated that were 400,000 Shias in the UK.

Shia mosques are usually Twelvers but also cater for Zaydis and the 50,000-strong Ismaili community; they usually include facilities for women. Various Shia mosques include the Husseini Islamic Centre in Stanmore, Harrow which acts as one of the main Shia Muslim mosques in Britain as well as Masjid-e-Ali in Luton, one of the largest Imam Bargah/community centres in the UK, and the Islamic Centre of England in Maida Vale, also a large multi-ethnic community centre. Others include Al Masjid ul Husseini in Northolt, Ealing, and Imam Khoei Islamic Centre in Queens Park, Brent. Across the country Manchester, Birmingham and London have the most Shia residents.

Ahmadiyyat

The Ahmadiyya Muslim Community (AMC) established itself in the UK in 1912 and is thus the longest-standing Muslim community in the UK. The UK and worldwide headquarters of the AMC are currently situated on the grounds of 'The Blessed Mosque' (Masjid Mubarak), inaugurated on 17 May 2019 by Mirza Masroor Ahmad, the fifth caliph of the Ahmadiyya movement, in Tilford, Surrey. The AMC also has the largest Muslim youth organisation, the Ahmadiyya Muslim Youth Association (Majlis Khuddamul Ahmadiyya) in the UK (membership of 7,500) and the largest Muslim women's organisation, the Ahmadiyya Muslim Women's Association (Lajna Ima'illah), in the UK (membership of 10,000).

Sectarian relations

There has also been discrimination by orthodox Sunni Muslims against Ahmadi Muslims. In 2014, on the 125 anniversary of the establishment of the Ahmadiyya Muslim Community, the Community published an advertisement in the Luton on Sunday. Following a written complaint from Dr Fiaz Hussain, co-ordinator of the Preservation of Finality of Prophethood Forum (PFPF), stating that the Ahmadiyya community should not be called "Muslim" because it rejected some of the basic principles of Islam, the paper received a delegation of 'Community Leaders' and shortly afterwards printed an apology disassociating itself from the Ahmadiyya advertisement. Tell MAMA responded by identifying attempts to intimidate or discriminate against Ahmadiyya Muslims "as anti-Muslim in nature".

Society

Economics

In a 2010 aggregate study published by the Government Equalities Office, Muslims in the United Kingdom had the lowest median hourly salary and held the least wealth amongst religious groups. They also held the lowest employment rates amongst religious groups, at 24% for Muslim women and 47% for Muslim men. The study noted that Muslim women who worked earned more than Muslim men and that Muslim men were more likely to be in self employment compared to the general population of men. Muslim men also had the smallest proportion with degrees, at 18%. More than two-fifths of Muslim men and women have no qualification beyond level 1 (equivalent to grades D-G at GCSE). According to analysis based on the 2011 census, Muslims in the United Kingdom faced poor standards of housing and were more vulnerable to long-term illness.

According to a 2013 assessment from the Muslim Council of Britain, it was estimated that there were more than 10,000 Muslim millionaires and 13,400 Muslim-owned businesses in London, creating more than 70,000 jobs and representing just over 33 per cent of Small to Medium Enterprises in London.

Amongst the economically active population in England and Wales, 19.8% of the Muslim population were in full-time employment compared to 34.9% of the overall population. Data from the ONS for England and Wales in 2020 indicated that across religious groups, Muslims continue to hold the lowest earnings, lowest rates of employment, highest rates of economic inactivity, least likely to work in high-skilled occupations, least likely to hold managerial positions, and most likely to report holding no qualifications. However, there had been progress in these metrics. The 2021 United Kingdom census for England and Wales found that the Muslim population had consistently lower rates of employment across every age group compared to the general population. Between the ages of 25–54, the employment rate for Muslims was typically 60% compared to around 80% across the whole population. Overall, 48.6% of working aged British Muslims were in employment, with the employment rate of Muslim women improving to 37%. Muslim women were 3.5 times more likely to report economic inactivity due to looking after family or home compared to the general population of women.

Education

In 2018, 34 per cent of British Muslims had degree level qualifications, compared to 30 per cent of Christians and 35 per cent of those with no religion. 13 per cent of Muslims had no qualifications, higher than every other religious group.

In 2006, it was found that approximately 53% of British Muslim youth chose to attend university. This was higher than the figure for Christians (45%) and the non-religious (32%) but lower than for Hindus (77%) and Sikhs (63%).

There are around 184 Muslim faith schools in the UK, 28 of them being state-funded. In 2008, 86.5% of pupils attending Muslim schools achieved five GCSEs, compared to a figure of 72.8% of Roman Catholic schools and 64.5% of secular schools.

In 2019, four Islamic schools were in the top ten ranking for secondary schools in England, including Tauheedul Islam Girls High School in first place.

In 2018, the Crown Prosecution Service brought its first prosecution in England & Wales against an unregistered school, the Islamic faith school Al-Istiqamah Learning Centre in Southall, London where nearly 60 children aged 5–11 were being taught. Head teacher Beatrix Bernhardt and director Nacerdine Talbi were convicted as running a school not registered with the Department for Education violates the Education and Skills Act 2008. They received fines and a curfew.

Politics

Muslims are playing an increasingly prominent role in political life. Nineteen Muslim MPs were elected in the December 2019 general election, and there are nineteen Muslim peers in the House of Lords.

The majority of British Muslims vote for the Labour Party, however there are some high-profile Conservative Muslims, including former Minister for Faith and Communities and former Co-chairman and the Conservative Party Sayeeda Warsi, described by The Guardian as a 'rising star' in the Tory party. The Guardian stated that "The treasury minister is highly regarded on the right and would be the Tories' first Muslim leader." Salma Yaqoob is the former leader of the left-wing Respect Party. Sayeeda Warsi, who was the first Muslim to serve in a British cabinet, was appointed by David Cameron in 2010 as a minister without portfolio. She was made a senior minister of state in 2012. In August 2014 she resigned over the government's approach to the 2014 Israel-Gaza conflict.

Muslim political parties in Britain have included the People's Justice Party (UK), a Pakistani and Kashmiri party that won city council seats in Manchester in the 2000s, and the unsuccessful

Islamic Party of Britain, an Islamist party in Bradford in the 1990s. In 2023, the Electoral Commission rejected an application to set up a new political party named 'Party of Islam'.

In the 2017 general election, 15 Muslim MPs (12 Labour and 3 Conservative) were elected, up from 13 Muslim MPs in 2015 general election. In the 2019 general election, a record number of 19 Muslim MPs were elected (15 Labour and 4 Conservative).

Survey data analysed by UK in a Changing Europe showed that Labour (72 per cent) led Conservatives (11 per cent) by 61 points amongst Muslim voters in 2019. Further analysis showed that many minorities were "necessity liberals" who voted for Labour not because they were social liberals, but because Labour represented a broader political package and distrusted the Conservatives on identity matters. British Pakistani and British Bangladeshi voters in particular, by a margin of 20–30 points, believed that LGBT rights had gone too far.

Law

Although sharia is not part of the British legal system, several British establishment figures have supported its use in areas of dispute resolution in Islamic communities. For example, in February 2008 Rowan Williams the Archbishop of Canterbury (the head of the Church of England) lectured at the Royal Courts of Justice on Islam and English law. In this lecture he spoke of the possibility of using sharia in some circumstances:

[...] it might be possible to think in terms of [...] a scheme in which individuals retain the liberty to choose the jurisdiction under which they will seek to resolve certain carefully specified matters, so that 'power-holders are forced to compete for the loyalty of their shared constituents'.

—Rowan Williams, 2008

Several months later, Lord Phillips, then Lord Chief Justice of England and Wales supported the idea that sharia could be reasonably employed as a basis for "mediation or other forms of alternative dispute resolution", and explained that "It is not very radical to advocate embracing sharia law in the context of family disputes, for example, and our system already goes a long way towards accommodating the archbishop's suggestion."

In March 2014, The Law Society issued guidance on how to draft sharia-compliant wills for the network of sharia courts which has been established to deal with disputes between Muslim families. The guidance was withdrawn later in 2014 following criticism by solicitors and by Chris Grayling, the Justice Secretary.

In 2016–2018 an independent panel commissioned by the UK government investigated the practices of sharia councils operating in England and Wales. The councils have no legal status and no legal jurisdiction in the UK. Estimates for their number range between 30 and 85. The investigation found that most people consulting the councils are women seeking an Islamic divorce. The review concluded that "there is unanimous agreement among the sharia councils themselves that discriminatory practices do occur in some instances within the councils in England and Wales" and made legislative and administrative recommendations to remedy the abuses. The panel was not aware of any sharia councils operating in Scotland.

According to Kaveri Qureshi, while women educate themselves and follow Islamic norms and values referring to colonial era Islamic advice literature about marriage not for continuation but to end their marriages and for justification of remarriages contrary to original intention of authors of the literature.

Media and culture

There are several Islamic television channels operating in the UK, including British Muslim TV, Muslim Television Ahmadiyya International (MTA International), Ummah Channel, Ahlebait TV, and Fadak.

British Muslims are represented in various media positions across different organisations. Notable examples include Mehdi Hasan, the political editor of the UK version of The Huffington Post and the presenter of Al Jazeera English shows The Café and Head to Head, Mishal Husain, a British news presenter for the BBC, currently appearing on BBC World News and BBC Weekend News, Rageh Omaar, special correspondent with ITV and formerly Senior Foreign Correspondent with the BBC and a reporter/presenter for Al Jazeera English, and Faisal Islam, economics editor and correspondent for Channel 4 News.

In 2013, there were 40 Muslim players in the English Premier League, up from one in 1992. Man of the Match awardees were awarded bottles of champagne, which is forbidden in Islam, and after Muslim player Yaya Toure refused the award, champagne was phased out for small trophies instead. Children playing football have been seen falling to their knees as if in prayer after scoring a goal, a common practice of Muslim footballers.

Associations

- Ahmadiyya Muslim Association
- Association of British Muslims, the oldest organisation of British Muslims, created in 1889 as the English Islamic Association by Abdullah Quilliam.
- Association of Muslim Lawyers
- British Muslim Forum
- Civil Service Islamic Society
- Daru-Al-Moameneen
- Islamic Forum of Europe
- Islamic Party of Britain
- Islamic Society of Britain
- Minhaj-ul-Quran UK
- Mosques & Imams National Advisory Board
- Muslim Association of Britain
- Muslim Council of Britain
- Muslim Educational Trust
- Muslim Parliament of Great Britain
- Muslim Public Affairs Committee UK
- Muslim Safety Forum
- Sufi Muslim Council
- The Young Muslims UK
- UK Islamic Mission
- World Islamic Mission
- Young Muslim Organisation

Practice

Proselytization

It is estimated that 5,200 Britons convert to Islam annually, with a total of about 100,000 converts in 2013. For men, prisons have proven a fertile ground for conversions. About 18% of the British prison population, or over 14,000 prisoners, are Muslims, disproportionately higher than the general population. The proportion of Muslims in the UK prison population rose from 8% in 2002 to 15% in 2016. According to the UK prison officers' union in 2013, some Muslim prisoners in the UK had allegedly forcibly converted fellow inmates to Islam in prisons. There have been multiple cases of non-Muslim prisoners threatened with violence with "convert or get hurt" being a commonly used phrase by Muslim gangs according to an independent report published by the government. A 2010 report by the Chief Inspector of Prisons stated that 30% of the Muslim prisoners interviewed had converted to Islam while in prison, some of whom were "convenience Muslims" who adopted the religion in order to get benefits available only to Muslims. Mosques in the country are sometimes seen as ethnic clubs which are not welcoming of new converts but there have also been recent convert led mosques. A study in 2023 found that amongst some schools, there were tensions between Hindu and Muslims pupils. Hindu students were labelled as "kaffirs" and threatened to either convert or face "hell for disbelievers".

Extremist ideology

In June 2017, Jeremy Corbyn, leader of the Labour Party, said that difficult conversations are needed, starting with Saudi Arabia and other Gulf states that have funded and fuelled extremist ideology. Tom Brake, Liberal Democrat, foreign affairs spokesman has said that Saudi Arabia provides funding to hundreds of mosques in the UK, espousing a very hardline Wahhabist interpretation of Islam.

The French political scientist Olivier Roy argues that the majority of Islamic terrorists are radicals first and are drawn to fundamentalist Islam as a result, whereas fellow political scientist Gilles Kepel argues that terrorists are radicalized by Salafi ideology before choosing violence. Roy has also argued that the burkini bans and secularist policies of France provoked religious violence in France, to which Kepel responded that Britain has no such policies and still suffered several jihadist attacks in 2017 while there were no major attacks in France.

Some preachers in London's mosques look for Muslim boys who lack clear direction, and set them on the path to radicalisation and terror.

According to Gilles de Kerchove in 2017, the UK had the highest number of Islamist radicals in the EU numbering between 20-25,000. Of those, 3000 were considered a direct threat by MI5 and 500 were under constant surveillance. Among those known to security services but not considered an immediate threat were the terrorists of three ISIS-linked attacks in 2017 which killed 35 victims in the UK.

In July 2017, a report by the Henry Jackson Society, a neo-conservative think tank, claimed that Middle Eastern nations are providing financial support to mosques and Islamic educational institutions that have been linked to the spread of extremist material with "an illiberal, bigoted Wahhabi ideology". The report said that the number of Salafi and Wahhabi mosques in Britain had increased from 68 in 2007 to 110 in 2014.

Hardline groups, including Hizb-ut-Tahrir, use accusations of Islamophobia to silence legitimate debate about extremism. While they in general are opposed to Western-style human rights, they use human rights to promote an Islamist ideology. The Independent Reviewer for the government's anti-terror programme, Sir William Shawcross, has stated that there was a reluctance to investigate Islamist threats due to fears of being labelled Islamophobic or racist.

A report published in 2020 found that of the 43,000 extremists on MI5's watchlist, around nine-tenths on the list are Islamist extremists. Islamic terrorism represented 67% of attacks since 2018, 75% of MI5's caseload, and 64% of those in custody for terrorism-connected offences according to the 2023 CONTEST report.

In March 2024, Communities Secretary Michael Gove announced that five organisations would be assessed against the government's new definition of extremism. Three of these organisations, named as Cage, Muslim Association of Britain, and Muslim Engagement and Development, were of concern due to their Islamist orientation and views. The latter two groups threatened to sue after the announcement.

Relations with wider society

Attitudes of British Muslims

According to the 2006 Pew Global Attitudes Survey, around 81% of Muslims think of themselves as Muslim first. This is consistent with Muslims living in Muslim-majority countries, who also tend to think of themselves as Muslim first rather than identifying with nation states (for example 87% of Pakistanis identify themselves as Muslim first rather than Pakistani). However, around 83% of

Muslims are proud to be a British citizen, compared to 79% of the general public, 77% of Muslims strongly identify with Britain while only 50% of the wider population do, 86.4% of Muslims feel they belong in Britain, slightly more than the 85.9% of Christians, 82% of Muslims want to live in diverse and mixed neighbourhoods compared to 63% of non-Muslim Britons. In polls taken across Europe 2006, British Muslims hold the most negative view of westerners out of all Muslims in Europe, whilst overall in Britain 63% of British hold the most favourable view of Muslims out of all the European countries (down from 67% the year before).

In the wake of the cartoon depiction of Mohammed in Danish newspapers and the 7/7 attacks, a 2006 ICM Research poll found that 97% of British Muslims believed it was wrong to show Muhammad with 86% of respondents feeling personally offended by the depiction. 96% believed it was wrong for Muslims to have bombed London during 7/7, although 20% had sympathy with the feelings and motives of the attackers. 40% of those surveyed also supported the introduction of Sharia law in Muslim-majority areas of Britain. Another poll by GfK revealed that 28% of British Muslims hoped that Britain would one day become an Islamic state, while 52% disagreed, and 20% did not venture an opinion either way.

On religious issues, a 2007 poll reported that 36% of 16- to 24-year-olds believed if a Muslim converted to another religion they should be punished by death, compared to 19% of 55+ year old Muslims. A poll reported that 59% of Muslims would prefer to live under British law, compared to 28% who would prefer to live under sharia law. 61% of respondents agreed with the statement that homosexuality is wrong and should be illegal. This appeared to be borne out by a Gallup poll in 2009 of 500 British Muslims, none of whom believed that homosexuality was morally acceptable. Such polls suggest that British Muslims have strongly conservative views on issues relating to extra-marital and/or homosexual sexual acts compared with their European Muslim counterparts – who are markedly more liberal.

A survey by Gallup in 2009 found that the Muslim community claimed to feel more patriotic about Britain than the general British population as a whole, while another survey found that Muslims assert that they support the role of Christianity in British life more so than British Christians themselves.

However, a poll conducted by Demos in 2011 reported that a greater proportion of Muslims (47% – slightly higher than the 46.5% of Christians who agreed with the statement) than other religions agreed with the statement "I am proud of how Britain treats gay people", with less than 11% disagreeing. On 18 May 2013, just as the bill to legalise same-sex marriages was being prepared to pass into law, over 400 leading Muslims including head teachers and senior representatives of mosques across the country, published an open letter opposing the bill on the grounds that "Muslim parents will be robbed of their right to raise their children according to their beliefs, as homosexual relationships are taught as something normal to their primary-aged children". A face-to-face survey conducted in 2015 by ICM Research for Channel 4 found that 18 per cent of British Muslims agreed with the statement that homosexuality should be legal in Britain, while 52 per cent disagreed, and 22 per cent neither agreed or disagreed.

A 2016 report by the centre-right think tank Policy Exchange in conjunction with ICM Research found that 93 per cent of British Muslims hold fairly or very strong attachment to Britain, 53 per cent wanted to "fully integrate with non-Muslims in all aspects of life" and British Muslims were found to be more likely to condemn terrorism than the general population. The report, which was co-authored by Khalid Mahmood MP, also found that British Muslims had "separatist" tendencies and were inclined to believe in conspiracy theories to do with 9/11 and plots to "do down Muslims". When asked what they would do if someone they knew was involved with supporters of terrorism in Syria, only 52% said they would report them to the police.

A survey carried out by J.L. Partners in 2024 reported that 52 per cent of British Muslims wanted to make it illegal to show a picture of Mohammed, 32 per cent wanted to see Sharia law implemented in the UK and 46 per cent believed Jews have too much power over UK government policy. The survey was conducted between February and March during the Israel–Hamas war with 46 per cent of British Muslims surveyed sympathising with Hamas and just 24 per cent believing that Hamas committed murder and rape in Israel on October 7th. Younger and more educated Muslims were more likely to hold these beliefs.

Attitudes towards British Muslims

The British media has been criticised for propagating negative stereotypes of Muslims and fueling Islamophobic prejudice. In 2006, several British cabinet ministers were criticised for helping to "unleash a public anti-Muslim backlash" by blaming the Muslim community over issues of integration despite a study commissioned by the Home Office on white and Asian-Muslim youths demonstrating otherwise: that Asian-Muslim youths "are in fact the most tolerant of all" and that white youths "have far more intolerant attitudes," concluding that the attitudes held by members of the white community was a greater "barrier to integration."

In January 2010, the British Social Attitudes Survey found that the general public "is far more likely to hold negative views of Muslims than of any other religious group," with "just one in four" feeling "positively about Islam," and a "majority of the country would be concerned if a mosque was built in their area, while only 15 per cent expressed similar qualms about the opening of a church." The "scapegoating" of British Muslims by the media and politicians in the 21st century has been compared in the media to the rise of antisemitism in the early 20th century.

A 2013 survey by YouGov indicated that immigrants from Muslim countries were perceived as integrating less well into British society than immigrants from other countries were. Another YouGov poll conducted in 2015 found that 55% of the British public believed there was a fundamental clash between Islam and the values of British society. Only 22% believed British values and Islam were generally compatible.

A survey conducted in 2017 by Chatham House revealed widespread opposition to Muslim immigration across the UK. 47% were opposed to further Muslim immigration meanwhile 23% disagreed with stopping further migration from mainly Muslim countries. This opposition figure was lower than other European countries, Austria: 65%; Belgium: 64%; France: 61%; Germany: 53%; Italy: 51%, and lower than the European average of 55%.

In 2019, a survey conducted by the Pew Research Center found that 78% of Britons had a favourable view of Muslims, while 18% had an unfavourable view of Muslims. This was the most favourable in Europe.

A 2021 study published by the University of Birmingham found that Muslims are the British public's second 'least liked' group, after Gypsy and Irish Travellers with 25.9% of the British public holding negative views towards Muslims and 23.5% holding a positive view. People from middle and upper-class backgrounds were more likely to hold prejudiced views about Islam compared to those from working-class backgrounds. 71% of respondents named Islam as having a more negative impact on society compared to other religions with 18.1% of those surveyed supported banning all Muslim migration to the UK.

Islamophobia

A survey conducted in 2024 by Opinium for Hope not Hate found that 30 per cent of the British public believed that Islam was a threat to the British way of life and the existence of 'no-go' zones for non-Muslims in European cities. Conservative party members were more likely to hold these views, with 58% believing Islam was a threat and 52% believing in the existence of 'no-go' zones.

There have been cases of threats, one fatal attack, and non-fatal attacks on Muslims and on Muslim targets, including attacks on Muslim graves and mosques. In January 2010, a report from the University of Exeter's European Muslim Research Centre noted that the number of anti-Muslim hate crimes has increased, ranging from "death threats and murder to persistent low-level assaults, such as spitting and name-calling," for which the media and politicians have been blamed with fueling anti-Muslim hatred. However, Met Police figures showed an 8.5 per cent fall in anti-Muslim crimes between 2009 and 2012, with a spike in 2013 due to the murder of Lee Rigby. In the four months following the 2023 Israel-Gaza conflict, Tell MAMA reported a more than three-fold increase in Islamophobic incidents to 2,010, with Muslim women targeted in two-thirds of incidents.

The emergence of the English Defence League resulted in demonstrations in English cities with large Muslim populations. The EDL was a right wing, anti Islam street protest movement which opposed what it considers to be a spread of Islamism, Sharia law and Islamic extremism in the United Kingdom. The EDL has been described by The Jewish Chronicle as Islamophobic. The group has faced confrontations with various groups, including supporters of Unite Against Fascism (UAF) and Anonymous.

Sikh relations

In 2018, a report by a Sikh activist organisation, Sikh Youth UK, entitled "The Religiously Aggravated Sexual Exploitation of Young Sikh Women Across the UK" made allegations of similarities between the case of Sikh women and the Rotherham child sexual exploitation scandal. However, in 2019 this report was criticised by researchers and an official UK government report led by two Sikh academics for false and misleading information. It noted: "The RASE report lacks solid data, methodological transparency and rigour. It is filled instead with sweeping generalisations and poorly substantiated claims around the nature and scale of abuse of Sikh girls and causal factors driving it. It appealed heavily to historical tensions between Sikhs and Muslims and narratives of honour in a way that seemed designed to whip up fear and hate". Another investigation by another Sikh scholar, Katy Sian of the University of York, also found no truth to the allegations and instead found it was an allegation being pushed by extremist Sikh groups.

Antisemitism

According to British Muslim journalist Mehdi Hasan, "anti-Semitism isn't just tolerated in some sections of the British Muslim community; it's routine and commonplace". A 2016 survey of

5,446 adult Britons, part of a report titled Anti-Semitism in contemporary Great Britain conducted by the London-based Institute for Jewish Policy Research found that the prevalence of antisemitic views among Muslims was two to four times higher than the rest of the population, that 55% of British Muslims held at least one antisemitic view (compared to 30% of the general population), and that there was a correlation between Muslim religiosity and antisemitism. A 2020 poll by Hope not Hate found that 45% of British Muslims held a generally favourable view of British Jews, and 18% held a negative view. A 2024 poll by a polling and research firm J.L. Partners ordered by Henry Jackson Society found that "Muslims in the South East are the most likely to hold antisemitic views, while Scottish Muslims are the least antisemitic."

In March 2024, the Civil Service Muslim Network (CSMN) was suspended by the Deputy Prime Minister, Oliver Dowden due to widespread use of antisemitic remarks and tropes. The network hosted webinars during working hours to coach civil servants on how to "lobby" and "petition" senior officials to change government policy on Israel, encouraged others to take up "resistance" against the government's stance, and taught members how to be "strategic and smart" in avoiding disciplinary action. This included using mental health facilities to "advocate" for Palestinian positions so that any advocacy would be done from a wellbeing perspective. The CSMN has also been criticised for promoting homophobic websites as guidance for government officials.

Notable Muslims

Media and entertainment

- Asad Ahmad, BBC News presenter
- Riz Ahmed, Academy Award winning actor
- Mishal Hussain, BBC News presenter
- Riz Lateef, BBC News presenter

Politics

- Waqar Azmi OBE, EU Ambassador of Intercultural Dialogue
- Sadiq Khan, Labour Party mayor of London
- Humza Yousaf, First Minister of Scotland and Leader of the SNP
- Sayeeda Warsi, Conservative and Unionist Life Peer and former Cabinet Minister

Sport

- Moeen Ali, England cricketer
- Mo Farah, runner and four-time Olympic gold medalist
- Amir Khan, world champion boxer
- Adil Rashid, England cricketer

Religious

- Syed Abdul Qadir Jilani, Pakistani Sunni scholar and jurist
- Allama Qamaruzzaman Azmi, Leader of World Islamic Mission
- Shaykh Muhammad al-Ya'qoubi of Al-Mustafa Centre

- Muhammad Arshad Misbahi Imam of Manchester Central Mosque
- Sheikh Abdul Qayum, Chief Imam of East London Mosque
- Abu Yusuf Riyadh ul Haq, khateeb of Birmingham Central Mosque
- Faiz-ul-Aqtab Siddiqi, principal of Hijaz College
- Ajmal Masroor, imam and politician
- Haitham al-Haddad, Britain Muslim television host
- Ibrahim Mogra, Leicester imam
- Joel Hayward, New Zealand-born British Islamic scholar
- Timothy Winter, Dean of Cambridge Muslim College and Director of Studies at Cambridge University

Philanthropy

- Muhammad Abdul Bari, secretary of Muslim Aid

Military

- Ashfaq Ahmed Malik MBE - Warrant Officer in the Royal Air Force 1980-2012,

Notable mosques

- Shah Jahan Mosque, Woking – Britain's first mosque
- Cambridge Central Mosque, Europe's first eco-friendly mosque and the first purpose-built mosque within the city of Cambridge
- Ghamkol Shariff Masjid, Birmingham
- Manchester Central Mosque, Manchester
- Madina Mosque (Sheffield), Sheffield
- Green Lane Masjid, Birmingham

- Markazi Mosque, Dewsbury – Headquarters of the Tablighi Jama'at
- Al-Rahma Mosque, Liverpool
- Jamea Masjid, Preston
- Birmingham Central Mosque
- East London Mosque, London
- Leeds Grand Mosque, Leeds
- Finsbury Park Mosque, London
- Abbey Mills Mosque, London
- Glasgow Central Mosque, Glasgow

Chater 14

Australia & New Zealand

AUSTRALIA

Islam is the second largest religion in Australia. According to the 2021 Census in Australia, the combined number of people who self-identified as Muslims in Australia, from all forms of Islam, constituted 813,392 people, or 3.2% of the total Australian population. That total Muslim population makes Islam, in all its denominations and sects, the second largest religious grouping in Australia, after all denominations of Christianity (43.9%, also including non-practicing cultural Christians).

Demographers attribute Muslim community growth trends during the most recent census period to relatively high birth rates, and recent immigration patterns. Adherents of Islam represent the majority of the population in Cocos (Keeling) Islands, an external territory of Australia.

The vast majority of Muslims in Australia are Sunni, with significant minorities belonging to the Shia denomination. The followers of each of these are further split along different Madhhab (schools of thought within Islamic jurisprudence for the interpretation and practice of Islamic law) and Sub-Sect. There are also practitioners of other smaller denominations of Islam such as Ibadi Muslim Australians of Omani descent, and approximately 20,000 Druze Australians whose religion emerged as an offshoot of Islam which arrived in Australia with the immigration of Druze mainly from Lebanon and Syria. There are also Sufi (Islamic mysticism) minorities among Muslim practitioners in Australia.

While the overall Australian Muslim community is defined largely by a common religious identity, Australia's Muslims are not a monolithic community. The Australian Muslim community has traditional sectarian divisions and is also extremely diverse racially, ethnically, culturally and linguistically. Different Muslim groups within the Australian Muslim community thus also espouse parallel non-religious ethnic identities with related non-Muslim counterparts, either within Australia or abroad.

History

Prior to 1860

Islam has been in Australia since the 1700s when Makassar traders were long-term visitors to Arnhem land (now Northern Territory). A dance among the Warramiri people refers to a dreamtime creational being is given the name, Walitha Walitha, which is an adaptation of the Arabic phrase Allah ta'ala (God, the exalted). The 'Dreaming' creation figure, Walitha' walitha, is also known as Allah. In the Warramiri tradition, Walitha' walitha descends from heaven to re-establish order from infighting and violence between different groups in Arnhem land. Indigenous Australians share this ceremony, known as the Wurramu, with the people of Macassar Indonesia, but the Aboriginal version is a mortuary ritual. Aboriginal elders explain on an 'outside' level' the dance performance is about the new world introduced to Aborigines in pre-colonial times as a result of this first contact experience, but on an 'inside' level, they focus on the Aboriginal deaths that occurred as a consequence of contact with these fishing peoples from the north of Australia. The 'inside' meaning of the ritual relates to the passage of the soul of the deceased to a heavenly paradise above, the abode of Allah.

Indonesian Muslims trepangers from the southwest corner of Sulawesi visited the coast of northern Australia, "from at least the eighteenth century" to collect and process trepang, a marine invertebrate prized for its culinary and medicinal values in Chinese markets. Remnants of their influence can be seen in the culture of some of the northern Aboriginal peoples. Regina Ganter, an associate professor at Griffith University, says, "Staying on the safe grounds of historical method... the beginning of the trepang industry in Australia [can be dated] to between the 1720s and 1750s, although this does not preclude earlier, less organised contact." Ganter also writes "the cultural imprint on the Yolngu people of this contact is everywhere: in their language, in their art, in their stories, in their cuisine." According to anthropologist John Bradley from Monash University, the contact between the two groups was a success: "They traded together. It was fair - there was no racial judgement, no race policy." Even into the early 21st century, the shared history between the two peoples is still celebrated by Aboriginal communities in Northern Australia as a period of mutual trust and respect.

Others who have studied this period have come to a different conclusion regarding the relationship between the Aboriginal people and the visiting trepangers. Anthropologist Ian McIntosh has said that the initial effects of the Macassan fishermen were "terrible", which resulted in "turmoil" with the extent of Islamic influence being "indeterminate". In another paper McIntosh concludes, "strife, poverty and domination. . is a previously unrecorded legacy of contact between Aborigines and Indonesians." A report prepared by the History Department of the Australian National University says that the Macassans appear to have been welcomed initially, however relations deteriorated when, "aborigines began to feel they were being exploited . . leading to violence on both sides".

A number of "Mohammedans" were listed in the musters of 1802, 1811, 1822, and the 1828 census, and a small number of Muslims arrived during the convict period. Beyond this, Muslims generally are not thought to have settled in large numbers in other regions of Australia until 1860.

Muslims were among the earliest settlers of Norfolk Island while the island was used as a British penal colony in the early 19th century. They arrived from 1796, having been employed on British ships. They left following the closure of the penal colony and moved to Tasmania. The community left no remnants; only seven permanent residents of the island identified themselves as "non-Christian" in a 2006 census.

1860 onward: cameleers and pearlers

Among the early Muslims were the "Afghan" camel drivers who migrated to and settled in Australia during the mid to late 19th century. Between 1860 and the 1890s a number of Central Asians came to Australia to work as camel drivers. Camels were first imported into Australia in 1840, initially for exploring the arid interior, and later for the camel trains that were uniquely suited to the demands of Australia's vast deserts. The first camel drivers arrived in Melbourne, Victoria, in June 1860, when eight Muslims and Hindus arrived with the camels for the Burke and Wills expedition. The next arrival of camel drivers was in 1866 when 31 men from

Rajasthan and Baluchistan arrived in South Australia with camels for Thomas Elder. Although they came from several countries, they were usually known in Australia as 'Afghans' and they brought with them the first formal establishment of Islam in Australia.

Cameleers settled in the areas near Alice Springs and other areas of the Northern Territory and inter-married with the Indigenous population. The Adelaide, South Australia to Darwin, Northern Territory, railway is named The Ghan (short for The Afghan) in their memory.

The first mosque in Australia was built in 1861 at Marree, South Australia. The Great Mosque of Adelaide was built in 1888 by the descendants of the Afghan cameleers. The Broken Hill Mosque at North camel camp was built by the cameleers between 1887 and 1891.

During the 1870s, Muslim Malay divers were recruited through an agreement with the Dutch to work on Western Australian and Northern Territory pearling grounds. By 1875, there were 1800 Malay divers working in Western Australia. Most returned to their home countries. One of the earliest recorded Islamic festivals celebrated in Australia occurred on 23 July 1884 when 70 Muslims assembled for Eid prayers at Albert Park, Melbourne. The Auckland Star noted the ceremony's calm demeanor, stating: "During the whole service the worshippers wore a remarkably reverential aspect."

20th century

Most of the cameleers returned to their countries after their work had dried up, but a few had brought wives and settled in Australia with their families, and others settled either on their own (some living at the Adelaide Mosque), or married Aboriginal or European women. Halimah Schwerdt, secretary to Mahomet Allum, a former cameleer who established himself as herbalist, healer and philanthropist in Adelaide, became first European woman in Australia to publicly embrace Islam. She was engaged to Allum in 1935-37, but there is no record of a wedding. He married Jean Emsley in 1940, who converted to Islam later. Allam also published pamphlets and articles about Islam.

From 1901, under the provisions of the White Australia policy, immigration to Australia was restricted to persons of white European descent (including white Europeans of the Muslim faith). Meanwhile, persons not of white European heritage (including most Muslims) were denied entry to Australia during this period, and those already settled were not granted Australian citizenship.

Notable events involving Australian Muslims during this early period include what has been described either as an act of war by the Ottoman Empire, or the earliest terrorist attack planned against Australian civilians. The attack was carried out at Broken Hill, New South Wales, in 1915, in what was described as the Battle of Broken Hill. Two Afghans who pledged allegiance to the Ottoman Empire shot and killed four Australians and wounded seven others before being killed by the police.

In the 1920s and 1930s Albanian Muslims, whose European heritage made them compatible with the White Australia Policy, immigrated to the country. The Albanian arrival revived the Australian Muslim community whose ageing demographics were until that time in decline and Albanians became some of the earliest post-colonial Muslim groups to establish themselves in Australia. Some of the earliest communities with a sizable Albanian Muslim population were Mareeba, Queensland and Shepparton in Victoria.

Post-war migration

The perceived need for population growth and economic development in Australia led to the broadening of Australia's immigration policy in the post-World War II period. This allowed for the acceptance of a number of displaced white European Muslims who began to arrive from other parts of Europe, mainly from the Balkans, especially from Bosnia and Herzegovina. As with the Albanian Muslim immigrants before them, the European heritage of these displaced Muslims also made them compatible with the White Australia Policy.

Albanians partook in the revival of Islamic life within Australia, in particular toward creating networks and institutions for the community. Albanian Muslims built the first mosque in Shepparton, Victoria (1960), first mosque in Melbourne (1969) and another in 1985, and a mosque in Mareeba, Far North Queensland (1970).

With the increase in immigration of Muslims after the war from countries such as Bosnia, Albania and Kosovo, the Islam in Australia developed its characteristic plurality. The move proved enriching for Muslim migrants, who "met Muslim fellows from many different ethnic, racial, cultural, sectarian and linguistic backgrounds" and "found Islam more pluralistic and more sophisticated" than their countries of origin.

Later, between 1967 and 1971, during the final years of the step-by-step dismantling of the White Australia policy, approximately 10,000 Turkish citizens settled in Australia under an agreement between Australia and Turkey. From the 1970s onwards, there was a significant shift in the government's attitude towards immigration, and with the White Australia policy now totally dismantled from 1973 onwards, instead of trying to make newer foreign nationals assimilate and forgo their heritage, the government became more accommodating and tolerant of differences by adopting a policy of multiculturalism.

Larger-scale Muslim migration of non-White non-European Muslims began in 1975 with the migration of Lebanese Muslims, which rapidly increased during the Lebanese Civil War from 22,311 or 0.17% of the Australian population in 1971, to 45,200 or 0.33% in 1976. Lebanese Muslims are still the largest and highest-profile Muslim group in Australia, although Lebanese Christians form a majority of Lebanese Australians, outnumbering their Muslim counterparts at a 6-to-4 ratio.

1990s

Trade and educational links have been developed between Australia and several Muslim countries. Muslim students from countries such as Malaysia, Indonesia, India, Bangladesh and Pakistan, are among the thousands of international students studying in Australian universities.

A number of Australian Arabs experienced anti-Arab backlash during the First Gulf War (1990–91). Newspapers received numerous letters calling for Arab Australians to "prove their loyalty" or "go home", and some Arab Australian Muslim women wearing hijab head coverings were reportedly harassed in public. The Australian government's Human Rights and Equal Opportunity Commission included accounts of racial harassment experienced by some Australian Arabs in their 1991 report on racism in Australia.

21st century

By the beginning of the 21st-century, Muslims from more than sixty countries had settled in Australia. While a very large number of them come from Bosnia, Turkey, and Lebanon, there are Muslims from Indonesia, Malaysia, Iran, Fiji, Albania, Sudan, Somalia, Egypt, the Palestinian territories, Iraq, Afghanistan, Pakistan and Bangladesh, among others. At the time of the 2011 census, 476,000 Australians (representing 2.2 percent of the population) reported Islam as their religion.

On a few occasions in the 2000s and 2010s, tensions have flared between Australian Muslims and the general population. The Sydney gang rapes formed a much-reported set of incidents in 2000; a group of Lebanese men sexually assaulted non-Muslim women. In 2005, tensions between Muslims and non-Muslims in the Cronulla area of Sydney led to violent rioting; the incident resulted in mass arrests and criminal prosecution. In 2012, Muslims protesting in central Sydney against Innocence of Muslims, an anti-Islam film trailer, resulted in rioting. There was an increase in anti-Muslim sentiment in the aftermath of the Sydney hostage crisis on 15–16 December 2014, including a threat made against a mosque in Sydney. However, the Muslim community also received support from the Australian public through a social media campaign.

The founding president of the Australian Federation of Islamic Councils has said that with moderate Muslims being sidelined by those promoting more fundamentalist views, there is a need to be more careful in regard to potential Australian immigrants. Keysar Trad has said moderate Muslims need to take back control.

An article in The Australian in May 2015 opined, "Most Muslims want the peace and prosperity that comes from an Islam that coexists with modernity; it is a fanatical fringe that seeks to impose a fabricated medieval Islam". It describes Dr Jamal Rifi as a brave insider who is working to assist "the cause of good Muslims who are struggling for the soul of Islam".

Islamic denominations in Australia

Most Australian Muslims are Sunni, with Shia, Sufi and Ahmadiyya as minorities.

Sunni

In Sydney, adherents of the Sunni denomination of Islam are concentrated in the suburb of Lakemba and surrounding areas such as Punchbowl, Wiley Park, Bankstown and Auburn.

In Australia there are also groups associated with the "hardline" Salafi branch of Sunni Islam, including the Islamic Information and Services Network of Australasia and Ahlus Sunnah Wal Jamaah Association (Australia) (ASWJA). While their numbers are small, the ASWJA is said to "punch above its weight".

There are communities of NSW Muslims who adhere to Tablighi Jamaat form of Islam and worship at the Granville, Al Noor Masjid, which is led by Sheik Omar El-Banna. Similarly many Bangladeshi Tablighi Jamaat, Muslims worship at mosques in Seaton, NSW and in Huntingdale Victoria.

Dawateislami, which is a "non-political Islamic organisation based in Pakistan", has adherents in Australia.

In 2015, Wikileaks cables released information that Saudi Arabia closely monitors the situation of Islam and Arab community in Australia, whilst at the same time spending considerately to promote its fundamentalist version of Sunni Islam within the country.

Shia

The Shi'a denomination of Islam is centred in the St George, Campbelltown, Fairfield, Auburn and Liverpool regions of Sydney, with the al-Zahra Mosque, built in Arncliffe in 1983, and the Al-Rasool Al-A'dham Mosque serves the region in Bankstown. In 2008, the mainstream Shia community numbered 30,000 followers nationally.

In October 2004 Sheikh Mansour Leghaei established the Imam Hasan Centre in Annangrove, NSW.

In November 2014, up to 3,000 Shi'a Muslims marched in Sydney on the annual Ashura Procession to mark the death of the prophet's grandson. In November 2015 there was Ashura march in Sydney and a Victorian school observed Muharram.

Others

There are also others from smaller non-mainstream sects of Islam, including approximately 20,000 Alawites from Turkish, Syrian and Lebanese backgrounds. They have at least one school called Al Sadiq College, with campuses in the Sydney suburbs of Yagoona and Greenacre. There is also a population of the related, though distinct, Alevis.

There is also an Ismaili population of unspecified size. While Dawoodi Bohra, a small Ismaili Shia sect has its Sydney Jamaat located in Auburn NSW.

Additionally, the Druze, who practice Druzism, a religion that began as an offshoot of 11th-century Ismaili Islam, are reported to have around 20,000 followers living in Australia.

Sufi

The study of the history of Sufism in Australia is a fledgling discipline. Initial examination indicates that the Sufis have played an important part in Muslim engagement with Australia and its peoples. There are many reported instances of Sufism amongst the cameleers, though the best available evidence of this to date exists within a hand written manuscript at the historic Broken Hill mosque, providing at least one instance of Qadiri Sufis amongst the cameleers.

Baron Friedrich von Frankenberg, who was inspired by the man who first brought to the West, Inayat Khan, moved to Australia from Germany with his family in 1927. The baron and his Australian wife were well-liked, and students would study Sufism under von Frankenberg at their home in Camden, New South Wales. In 1939 he organised the visit of a renowned Sufi leader, or Murshida, and devotee of Khan, known as Murshida Rabia Martin. Born Ada Ginsberg, the daughter of Russian Jewish immigrants to the US, Martin's visit was of great significance because of her link to Khan. After the baron's death in 1950, the poet and artist Francis Brabazon, student of Meher Baba, another early spiritual teacher took up a leadership role. However, there is some contention regarding the extent to which this group adhered to Islamic practice, limiting the extent to which this group can be considered a representation of Islam in Australia.

Currently there are communities representing most of the major Sufi Orders within Australia, including, but not limited to the Mevlevi, Rifaii, Naqshbandiyya, and Burhaniyya. Amongst these Sufi communities, it is estimated there are at least 5,000 adherents.

Sectarian tensions

Conflict between religious groups in the Middle East are reflecting as tensions within the Australian community and in the schools.

Religious life

The Australian Muslim community has built a number of mosques and Islamic schools, and a number of imams and clerics act as the community's spiritual and religious leaders. In 1988, the Australian Federation of Islamic Councils (AFIC) appointed Sheikh Taj El-Din Hilaly as the first Grand Mufti of Australia and New Zealand. In 2007, Hilaly was succeeded by Fehmi Naji in June 2007 who was succeeded by the current Grand Mufti, Ibrahim Abu Mohamed in September 2011.

Fatwas, edicts based on Islamic jurisprudence which aim to provide "guidance to Muslim Australians in the personal, individual and private spheres of life", are issued by various Australian Islamic authorities.

Organisations

A number of organisations and associations are run by the Australian Islamic community including mosques, private schools and charities and other community groups and associations. Broad community associations which represent large segments of the Australian Muslim public are usually termed "Islamic councils". Some organisations are focused on providing assistance and support for specific sectors within the community, such as women.

Two organisations with strong political emphasis are Hizb ut-Tahrir which describes itself as a, "political party whose ideology is Islam" and Ahlus Sunnah Wal Jamaah Association (ASWJA).

A number of financial institutions have developed Sharia-compliant finance products, with university courses leading to Islamic financial qualifications also being established. Other Australian Islamic organisations have been set up to manage sharia-compliant investments, superannuation, Islamic wills and zakat management.

Halal certification

There are close to two dozen Halal certification authorities in Australia. Halal meat and meat product exports to the Middle East and Southeast Asia have greatly increased from the 1970s onwards; this expansion was due in part to efforts of the AFIC. Halal certification has been criticised by anti-Halal campaigners who argue that the practice funds the growth of Islam, results in added costs, a requirement to officially certify intrinsically-halal foods and with consumers required to subsidise a particular religious belief.

An inquiry by an Australian Senate committee, which concluded in December 2015, found the current system is "lacklustre" and made recommendations for improvement. It found there was no evidence to support claims that the profits of halal certification are used to fund terrorism. The report recognised that halal certification has economic benefits for Australia because of increased export opportunities. It recommended that the federal government increase its oversight of halal certifiers to address fraudulent conduct, with halal products to be clearly labelled and for meat products sourced from animals subject to religious slaughter, to be specifically labelled. It said that it had heard, "credible reports suggesting that the lack of regulation has been unscrupulously exploited". In tabling the report, committee chairman Sam Dastyari said, "Some certifiers are nothing more than scammers." The committee recommended a single halal certification authority. The committee in recommending clearer labelling, specifically referred to the need for meat processors to label products sourced from animals subject to religious slaughter.

Demography

Historical population

Historical population		
Year	Pop.	±%
1981	76,792	—
1991	147,487	+92.1%
2001	281,578	+90.9%
2011	476,291	+69.2%
2016	604,235	+26.9%
2021	813,392	+34.6%

During the 1980s the Australian Muslim population increased from 76,792 or 0.53% of the Australian population in 1981, to 109,523 or 0.70% in 1986. In the 2011 Census, the Muslim population was 479,300 or 2.25%, an increase of 438% on the 1981 number.

The general increase of the Muslim population in this decade was from 147,487 or 0.88% of the Australian population in 1991, to 200,885 or 1.12% in 1996.

In 2005 the overall Muslim population in Australia had grown from 281,600 or 1.50% of the general Australian population in 2001, to 340,400 or 1.71% in 2006. The growth of Muslim population at this time was recorded as 3.88% compared to 1.13% for the general Australian population. From 2011-2016, Muslim population grew by 27% from 476,291 to 604,200 with majority residing in New South Wales.

The following is a breakdown of the country of birth of Muslims in Australia from 2001:

There were 281,578 Muslims recorded in this survey; in the 2006 census the population had grown to 340,392. 48% of Australian-born Muslims claimed Lebanese or Turkish ancestry.

The distribution by state of the nation's Islamic followers has New South Wales with 50% of the total number of Muslims, followed by Victoria (33%), Western Australia (7%), Queensland (5%), South Australia (3%), ACT (1%) and both Northern Territory and Tasmania sharing 0.3%.

The majority of people who reported Islam as their religion in the 2006 Census were born overseas: 58% (198,400). Of all persons affiliating with Islam in 2006 almost 9% were born in Lebanon and 7% were born in Turkey.

According to the 2016 census, the Muslim population numbered 604,235 individuals, of whom 42% live in Greater Sydney, 31% in Greater Melbourne, and 8% in Greater Perth. The states and territories with the highest proportion of Muslims are New South

Wales (3.58%) and Victoria (3.32%), whereas those with the lowest are Queensland (0.95%) and Tasmania (0.49%).

4.2% of people in Greater Melbourne are Muslim. Many Muslims living there are Bosnian and Turkish. Melbourne's Australian Muslims live primarily in the northern suburbs surrounding Broadmeadows, (mostly Turkish), Coburg, Brunswick, Epping (mostly Lebanese) and Truganina, Tarneit (mostly Indian). They also form communities in outer south-eastern suburbs such as Dandenong and Hallam (mostly Afghan and Pakistani).

Very few Muslims live in rural areas with the exceptions of the sizeable Albanian and Turkish communities in Shepparton, which has Victoria's oldest mosque, and Malays in Katanning, Western Australia. A community of Iraqis have settled in Cobram on the Murray River in Victoria. An Albanian Muslim community resides in Mareeba who established Queensland's second oldest mosque.

Perth also has a Muslim community focussed in and around the suburb of Thornlie, where there is a mosque. Perth's Australian Islamic School has around 2,000 students on three campuses.

Mirrabooka and Beechboro contain predominantly Bosnian communities. The oldest mosque in Perth is the Perth Mosque on William Street in Northbridge. It has undergone many renovations although the original section still remains. Other mosques in Perth are located in Rivervale, Mirrabooka, Beechboro and Hepburn.

There are also communities of Muslims from Turkey, the Indian subcontinent (Pakistan, India and Bangladesh) and South-East Asia, in Sydney and Melbourne, the Turkish communities around Auburn, New South Wales and Meadow Heights and Roxburgh Park and the South Asian communities around Parramatta. Indonesian Muslims, are more widely distributed in Darwin.

Communities

Muslim population by country of origin

Australia (36%)

Lebanon (10%)

Turkey (8%)

Bosnia-Herzegovina (3.6%)

Afghanistan (3.5%)

Pakistan (3.2%)

Indonesia (2.9%)

Iraq (2.8%)

Bangladesh (2.7%)

Iran (2.3%)

Fiji (2%)

Other (23%)

It is estimated that Australian Muslims come from 63 different backgrounds, with "loose associations" between them.

Aboriginal Muslims

According to Australia's 2011 census, 1,140 people identify as Aboriginal Muslims, almost double the number of Aboriginal Muslims recorded in the 2001 census. Many are converts and some are descendants of Afghan cameleers or, as in the Arnhem Land people, have Macassan ancestry as a result of the historical Makassan contact with Australia. In north east Arnhem Land, there is some Islamic influence on the songs, paintings, dances, prayers with certain hymns to Allah and funeral rituals like facing west during prayers, roughly the direction of Mecca, and ritual prostration reminiscent of the Muslim sujud. As a result of Malay indentured laborers, plenty of families in Northern Australia have names like Doolah, Hassan and Khan. Notable Aboriginal Muslims include the boxer Anthony Mundine and Rugby League footballer Aidan Sezer. Many indigenous converts are attracted to Islam because they see a compatibility between Aboriginal and Islamic beliefs, while others see it as a fresh start and an aid against common social ills afflicting indigenous Australians, such as alcohol and drug abuse.

Some academics who have studied these issues have come to less positive conclusions regarding the relationship between the Aboriginal people and the visiting trepangers.

Albanian Muslims

In the late twentieth century, 80% of Albanian speakers in Australia followed Islam. In the twenty first century, the largest Albanian communities in Australia, Shepparton and Melbourne's suburb of Dandenong in Victoria are mostly Muslims. Muslim Albanian communities exist in Western Australia, South Australia, Queensland, New South Wales and the Northern Territory.

As Islam is the dominant religion among Albanian Australians, it has given the community a sense of unity and the capacity and resources to construct their own mosques. They have symbolised the Albanian community's permanent settlement in Australia. Mosques serve as important centres for community activities and are pivotal toward retaining the religious identity of Albanian Australians. Albanian representatives serve in most federal Islamic organisations, with some in senior positions. In the few areas of concentrated Albanian settlement, their small numbers shaped local areas through the construction of their first mosques or becoming a sizable proportion of the school Muslim population. The foundations created by Albanian Australians have attracted future Muslim migrants to areas which have an existing mosque or services assisting with settlement.

Albanians perform certain Muslim practices. Muslim head coverings are worn mainly by a few older women, Ramadan fasts are adhered to by some people and in Shepparton, Islam is influenced by Sufi Bektashism from Albania.

Bangladeshi Muslims

According to the 2016 Australian Census, Bangladeshi origin population were around 55,000; among them about 33,000 were living in NSW. Bangladeshi Muslims are located primarily in Rockdale, Lakemba, Bankstown and many suburbs in Western Sydney region with a mosque in Sefton and in the south-east of Melbourne, with a mosque at Huntingdale. The Sefton Mosque has been linked to the Tablighi Jamaat School of Islam and has hosted Hizb ut-Tahrir. For Bangladeshi Muslims attending the Huntingdale Mosque, all Islamic lunar months, such as Ramadan are observed using local moon-sightings, rather than being based on Middle-Eastern, or other, timings. According to the 2016 Australian census, 81.2% of the Bangladesh-born population in Australia was Muslim by faith.

Bosnian Muslims

Bosnian Muslims have predominantly arrived in Australia after 1992, with most of the community living in the south east of

Melbourne and in the south west of Sydney. There are Bosnian run mosques in Deer Park, Noble Park, Penshurst and Smithfield. According to the 2016 Australian census, 23.2% of the Bosnia and Herzegovina-born population in Australia was Muslim by faith.

Egyptian Muslims

Egyptian Muslims in Sydney are represented by The Islamic Egyptian Society. The Society has managed the Arkana College in Kingsgrove since 1986. It is reported that enrolments for its 203 co-educational places are booked out until 2020. According to the 2016 Australian census, 15.6% of the Egypt-born population in Australia was Muslim by faith.

Indonesian Australians

Though Islam is the majority religion in Indonesia, Muslims are the minority among Indonesians in Australia. In the 2006 Australian Census, only 8,656 out of 50,975 Indonesians in Australia, or 17%, identified as Muslim. However, in the 2011 census, that figure rose to 12,241 or 19.4%, 18.9% in 2016, and 19.3% in 2021.

Iraqi Australians

Iraqi Muslims mainly came to the country as a refugees after the Iran–Iraq War, failed 1991 uprisings in Iraq, and then post-2003. They predominately settled in the western suburbs of Sydney, such as Fairfield and Auburn. According to the 2016 Australian census, 31.4% of the Iraqi-born population in Australia was Muslim by faith.

Kurdish Muslims

Kurdish Muslims have predominantly arrived in Australia since the second half of the 1980s, with most of the community settling in Melbourne and Sydney. Although the large majority of the Kurdish Australians are Muslims, there are no registered Kurdish run mosques in Australia.

Lebanese Muslims

Lebanese Muslims form the core of Australia's Muslim Arab population, particularly in Sydney where most Arabs in Australia live. Approximately 3.4% of Sydney's population are Muslim. Approximately 4.2% of residents in Greater Melbourne are Muslim, and Sydney Road in Brunswick and Coburg is sometimes called 'Little Lebanon'.

In November 2016, Immigration Minister, Peter Dutton said that it was a mistake of a previous administration to have brought out Lebanese Muslim immigrants. Foreign Minister, Julie Bishop said Mr Dutton was making a specific point about those charged with terrorism offences. "He made it quite clear that he respects and appreciates the contribution that the Lebanese community make in Australia".

According to the 2016 Australian census, 43.5% of the Lebanon-born population in Australia was Muslim by faith.

Somali Muslims

Although the first Somali community in Victoria was established in 1988, most Somalis began to settle in the country in the early 1990s following the civil war in Somalia. Somalis are active in the wider Australian Muslim community, and have also contributed significantly to local business. According to the 2016 Australian census, 93.4% of the Somalia-born population in Australia was Muslim by faith.

Turkish Muslims

Turkish Muslims are a significant segment of the Australian Muslim community. Melbourne has the largest Turkish community in Australia, with the majority of Turkish Muslims living around Broadmeadows and other northern suburbs. The majority of Turkish Muslims in Sydney are from Auburn, Eastlakes and Prestons. Despite still having a large Turkish population in Auburn and Eastlakes, According to the 2016 Australian census, 64.0% of the Turkey-born population in Australia was Muslim by faith.

Malay Muslims

According to the 2016 Australian census, only 5.2% of the Malaysia-born population in Australia was Muslim by faith.

Discrimination

According to some scholars, a particular trend of anti-Muslim prejudice has developed in Australia since the late 1980s. Since the 2001 World Trade Center attacks in New York, and the 2005 Bali bombings, Islam and its place in Australian society has been the subject of much public debate.

A report published in 2004 by the Human Rights and Equal Opportunity Commission pointed to many Muslim Australians who felt the Australian media was unfairly critical of, and often vilified their community due to generalisations of terrorism and the emphasis on crime. The use of ethnic or religious labels in news reports about crime was thought to stir up racial tensions.

After the White Australia immigration laws were replaced with multicultural policies the social disadvantage of Muslims was thought to have been alleviated. Some sources, however, note that Muslims now face some disadvantages on account of their religion. At times there has been opposition to the construction of new mosques in Australia. A 2014 report from the Islamic Sciences and Research Academy, University of Western Sydney, on mosques in New South Wales found that 44 percent of mosques in the state had "experienced resistance from the local community when the mosque was initially proposed". In around 20 percent of these cases opposition was from a small number of people.

According to Michael Humphrey, a professor of sociology at the University of Sydney, much of Islamic culture and organisation in Australia has been borne of the social marginalisation experiences of Muslim working class migrants. This "immigrant Islam" is often viewed by the host society as a force of "cultural resistance" toward the multicultural and secular nature of the general Australian culture. Muslim practices of praying, fasting and veiling appear as challenging the conformity within public spaces and the values of gender equality in social relationships and individual rights. The immigrant Muslims are often required to "negotiate their Muslimness" in the course of their encounters with Australian society, the governmental and other social institutions and bureaucracies.

A poll of nearly 600 Muslim residents of Sydney released in November 2015 found that the respondents were three to five times more likely to have experienced racism than the general Australian population. However, approximately 97 per cent of the Muslim respondents reported that they had friendly relations with non-Muslims and felt welcome in Australia.

In an Australia-wide survey published in November 2015, which was based on 1,573 interviews, which asked, "Are Muslims that live in Australia doing enough to integrate into the Australian community, or should they be doing more?", only 20% of respondents thought Muslims are currently "doing enough".

A poll conducted by the University of South Australia's International Centre for Muslim and non-Muslim Understanding which was released in 2016 found that 10 per cent of Australians have hostile attitudes towards Muslims. The accompanying report concluded that "the great majority of Australians in all states and regions are comfortable to live alongside Australian Muslims".

A Council for the Prevention of Islamophobia Inc has been established. An Australian speaking tour by Ayaan Hirsi Ali, was proposed for April 2017. Because of her alleged Islamophobia, the Council for the Prevention of Islamophobia told organisers that there would be 5,000 protesters outside the Festival Hall in Melbourne if she was to speak at that venue. Her Australian tour was cancelled. It is likely that Australian Muslims are facing up to six times exclusion from the society.

Views on homosexuality

In line with the views of most Islamic scholars worldwide, Islamic leaders in Australia generally believe that homosexuality is not permitted by their faith.

In June 2016, the president of the Australian National Imams Council (ANIC), Sheikh Shady Alsuleiman participated in an Iftar dinner at Kirribilli House hosted by the Prime Minister. The Prime Minister said he would not have been invited Alsuleiman had he known of his position regarding homosexuals. The sheikh had previously spoken about the "evil actions" of homosexuality. Australia's Grand Mufti, Ibrahim Abu Mohamed has defended Alsuleiman, saying Islam has a, "longstanding" position on homosexuality" which "no person can ever change". He said that any attempt to call out its teachings could lead to radicalisation. ANIC treasurer Imam Mohamed Imraan Husain said, "Islam prevents lesbianism and being gay." Uthman Badar spokesman for Hizb ut-Tahrir (Australia), said that Mr Turnbull was condemning the "normative Islamic position on homosexuality".

Yusuf Peer, president of the Council of Imams Queensland, in referring to the sharia law death penalty for homosexuality said, "that is what Islam teaches and that will never change." The Imam of Australia's largest mosque, located in Lakemba, NSW, Shaykh Yahya Safi has said, "In Islam we believe it's a major sin to have such relations between men and men, a sexual relation. We don't discuss this because it's obvious."

In August 2017 the National Imams Council issued a statement opposing the proposed introduction of same-sex marriage in Australia, and several individual religious leaders have also argued against same-sex marriage. However, some Australian Muslims support same-sex marriage, and the Muslims for Progressive Values and Muslims for Marriage Equality groups have campaigned in favour of such a reform. As of September 2017, there was no polling data on the Australian Islamic community's views on this issue.

Employment, education and crime

As of 2007, average wages of Muslims were much lower than those of the national average, with just 5% of Muslims earning over $1000 per week compared to the average of 11%. Unemployment rates amongst Muslims born overseas were higher than Muslims born in Australia. Muslims are over-represented in jails in New South Wales, at 9% to 10% of the prison population, compared to less than 3% within the NSW population.

In literature and film

There are a number of notable works in Australian literature that discuss the Muslims during the "Afghan period" (1860-1900).

- The Camel in Australia, by Tom L. McKnight

- Fear and Hatred, by Andrew Markus

- Afghans in Australia, by Michael Cigler

- Tin Mosques and Ghantowns, by Christine Stevens

- Ali Abdul v The King, by Hanifa Deen

- Australia's Muslim Cameleers: Pioneers of the inland, 1860s–1930s, by Dr Anna Kenny

Veiled Ambition is a documentary created by Rebel Films for the SBS independent network following a Lebanese-Australian woman named Frida as she opens a shop selling fashionable clothing for Muslim women on Melbourne's Sydney Road. The documentary follows Frida as she develops her business in Melbourne while juggling a husband and home in Sydney and a pregnancy. Veiled Ambition won the Palace Films Award for Short Film Promoting Human Rights at the 2006 Melbourne International Film Festival.

Ali's Wedding is an Australian film based on a true story of an Iraqi Shia immigrant family. It depicts some of the religious and social practices of the Shia community in Australia.

Notable figures

- Randa Abdel-Fattah, novelist
- Aziza Abdel-Halim, female political activist
- Yassmin Abdel-Magied, mechanical engineer
- Mohammad Hussein al-Ansari, Ayatollah for Shia Islam
- Fawad Ahmed, cricket player
- Ameer Ali, academic and political activist
- Mahomet Allum (c. 1858–1964), Adelaide herbalist and healer, former Afghan cameleer
- Shady Alsuleiman, senior Muslim cleric
- Waleed Aly, radio and television presenter
- Ed Husic, trade unionist, politician
- Anne Aly, academic, politician
- Sam Dastyari, former politician
- Mehreen Faruqi, politician
- Wassim Doureihi, spokesman for Hizb ut-Tahrir
- Ahmed Fahour, former CEO of Australia Post
- Mamdouh Habib, former Guantanamo Bay detainee, anti-war activist
- Abu Hamza, community activist
- Taj El-Din Hilaly, Sunni Imam and Mufti
- Bachar Houli, former Australian rules footballer
- Adem Yze, former Australian rules footballer
- Nazeem Hussain, comedian
- Rabiah Hutchinson, convert, wife of Mustafa Hamid

- John Ibrahim, businessman
- John Ilhan, businessman
- Usman Khawaja, cricket player
- Mansour Leghaei, Shia sheikh
- Rashid Mahazi, soccer player
- Hazem El-Masri, rugby league player
- Ibrahim Abu Mohamed, Grand Mufti of Australia
- Feiz Mohammad, Muslim preacher
- Anthony Mundine, boxer and former professional rugby league footballer
- Fehmi Naji, Muslim Imam and Mufti
- Mohammed Omran, ASWJA Sheikh
- Aamer Rahman, comedian
- Jamal Rifi, General Practitioner and community leader
- Osamah Sami, actor
- Keysar Trad, community and political activist
- Mariam Veiszadeh, lawyer and community advocate
- Samina Yasmeen, academic
- Waqar Younis, former Pakistani fast bowler
- Irfan Yusuf, author
- Samier Dandan, President of Lebanese Muslim Association

New Zealand

Islam in New Zealand is a religious affiliation representing about 1.3% of the total population. Small numbers of Muslim immigrants from South Asia and Eastern Europe settled in New Zealand from the early 1900s until the 1960s. Large-scale Muslim immigration began in the 1970s with the arrival of Fiji Indians, followed in the 1990s by refugees from various war-torn countries.

The first Islamic centre in New Zealand opened in 1959 and there are now several mosques and two Islamic schools. The majority of Muslims in New Zealand are Sunni, with significant Shia and Ahmadiyya minorities. The Ahmadiyya Community has translated the Qur'an into the Māori language.

History

Historical population		
Year	Pop.	±%
1945	67	—
1951	205	+206.0%
1956	200	−2.4%
1961	260	+30.0%
1966	551	+111.9%
1971	779	+41.4%
1976	1,415	+81.6%

1981	2,004	+41.6%
1986	2,544	+26.9%
1991	5,772	+126.9%
1996	13,545	+134.7%
2001	23,631	+74.5%
2006	36,072	+52.6%
2013	46,149	+27.9%
2018	57,276	+24.1%

Early migration, 19th century

The earliest Muslim presence in New Zealand dates back to the late 19th century. The first Muslims in New Zealand were an Indian family who settled in Cashmere, Christchurch, in the 1850s. The 1874 government census reported 15 Chinese Muslim gold diggers working in the Dunstan gold fields of Otago in the 1870s. The first Muslim to be buried in New Zealand was a Javanese sailor named Mohamed Dan, who died in Dunedin in 1888. The anthropologist Erich Kolig also speculates that a few Muslim sailors from Southeast Asia and South Asia may have settled in New Zealand during that period.

Most of the early Muslim migrants settled in major centres like Auckland and Christchurch. In 1890, a group of Punjabi Muslim migrants including Sheik Mohamed Din settled in Christchurch. Other notable migrants including the Turkmen Saleh Mohamed and his father Sultan (who both settled in Christchurch in 1905), the Gujarati immigrant Ishamel Ahmed Bhikoo (who became a shopkeeper in Auckland), Essop Moosa, and Muhammad Suleiman Kara (who settled in Christchurch). According to Kolig, Bhikoo and Moses also brought relatives to New Zealand.

Modern migration, 20th and 21st centuries

In 1920, New Zealand adopted a restrictive immigration policy that limited Asian immigration. The Muslim population remained less than a hundred until after the Second World War. In 1945, there were 67 recorded Muslims in New Zealand. In 1951, the refugee boat SS Goya brought over 60 Muslim men from Albania and Yugoslavia, boosting the Muslim population to 205.

Between 1961 and 1971, the Muslim population increased from 260 to 779. The Muslim community in New Zealand continued to grow during the 1970s and 1980s, reaching around 2,000 by 1979 and 2,500 by 1986. Large-scale Muslim immigration began with the arrival of mainly working class Indo-Fijians in the 1970s. They were followed by professionals after the first Fiji coup of 1987. During the 1990s many migrants were admitted under New Zealand's refugee quota, from war zones in Somalia, Bosnia, Afghanistan, Kosovo and Iraq. There are also a significant number of Muslims from Iran who live in New Zealand.

Religious life and institutions

New Zealand has several mosques and Islamic centres and trusts in the major centres, and two Islamic schools (Al Madinah and Zayed College for Girls) in Auckland. Auckland alone has about 15 Islamic centres, mosques, and trusts.

Organisations

The Federation of Islamic Associations of New Zealand (FIANZ) is the national umbrella organisation that represents the Muslim community in New Zealand. FIANZ is affiliated with seven regional organisations, trusts, and most mosques and Islamic centres in New Zealand. FIANZ was founded in April 1979 by Mazhar Krasniqi, who brought together the three regional Muslim organisations of Canterbury, Wellington and Auckland. He was honoured for his efforts by the New Zealand government in 2002, receiving a Queens Service Medal.

Later Hajji Ashraf Choudhary served as President (1984–85) before pursuing a political career and entering the New Zealand Parliament in 1999. (However, Choudhary would separate his religion from politics, in line with New Zealand secularism). In 2008, FIANZ established the Harmony Awards "as part of Islam Awareness Week to recognise the contributions of New Zealanders to improving understanding and relationships between Muslims and the wider community".

The FIANZ is affiliated with seven regional associations including the New Zealand Muslim Association (NZMA), the South Auckland Muslim Association (SAMA), the Waikato Muslim Association (WMA), the Manawatu Muslim Association (MMA), the International Muslim Association of New Zealand (IMAN), the Muslim Association of Canterbury (MAC), and the Otago Muslim Association. Other Muslim organisations have included the predominantly Fijian Indian Anjuman Himayat al-Islam, the University of Otago's Muslim Student Association (MUSA), the Ahmadiyya Jama'at New Zealand, and the Southland Muslim Association.

Demography

The number of Muslims in New Zealand according to the 2018 census is 57,276, up 24% from 46,149 in the 2013 census. The majority of New Zealand Muslims are Sunnis but there is a large number of Shias who live in New Zealand, concentrated mainly in Auckland (the largest city of New Zealand). In recent years Shia Muslims have become active holding Ashura commemoration programmes in Auckland parks. The first of these was conducted by the Fatima Zahra Charitable Association on 19 January 2008.

There are significant communities of Muslims from the Middle East (Turkey and Lebanon), South Asia (Pakistan, India and Bangladesh) and Southeast Asia. There is also a large Indo-Fijian Muslim community and an equally substantial Somali minority in New Zealand. Contrary to popular assertions from various community leaders, no one single ethnic group can claim to contribute more than half of the New Zealand Muslim population. The majority of Muslims in New Zealand are concentrated in the major cities of Auckland, Hamilton, Wellington, and Christchurch.

From the mid-1990s, an influx of Malay students from Malaysia and Singapore has increased the proportion of Muslims in some other centres, notably the university city of Dunedin. Dunedin is home to a mosque called Al-Huda mosque, which is run by the Otago Muslim Association. As of 2019, the southernmost mosque in New Zealand is the Southland Muslim Association Masjid/Community Centre in Invercargill.

Māori Muslims

Islam was estimated to be the fastest growing religion among the Māori, however recently there is only a growth of 39 individuals in 12 years between 2006 and 2018. Census figures showing the number of Muslims of Māori ethnicity increasing from 99 to 708 from 1991 to 2001. The Māori Muslim population thereafter virtually stabilised from 1,077 in 2006 to 1,083 in 2013 to 1,116 in 2018. Te Amorangi Izhaq Kireka-Whaanga, leader of the Aotearoa Maori Muslim Association, views tino rangatiratanga as a form of jihad, and Islam as "the perfect vehicle for Māori nationalism". The leader of the AMMA, Sheikh Eshaq Te Amorangi Morgan Kireka-Whaanga was identified in 2010 among the top 500 most influential Muslims. In 2004 Sheikh Eshaq led the Quran Tilawat at the "National Islamic Converts Conference" at the Canterbury mosque in Christchurch. The Ahmadiyya Community has translated the Qur'an into the Māori language, Te Reo.

Pacific Islanders

While New Zealand's overall Pacific Islander community grew 15% according to census data from 2001 to 2006, Muslim Pacific Islanders grew 87.43%. According to 2013 census data, there were 1,536 Muslims among the Pacific islander community (a little under 3.5% of New Zealand's Muslim population). It increased to 1,866 Muslims in 2018.

One Muslim from this community is a rugby player and heavyweight boxer, Sonny Bill Williams, as well as fellow All Black player Ofa Tu'ungafasi.

Europeans

According to 2013 census data, there were 4,353 Muslims (about 9.5% of the total Muslim population) among the European community (Pākehā). It decreased to 3,693 Muslims in 2018 Census.

Issues

Muhammad cartoons controversy

In 2006, two newspapers in New Zealand decided to republish controversial Danish cartoons depicting Muhammad, the prophet of Islam. The Muslim community registered its displeasure through press statements and a small peaceful march in Auckland. The editors said they did not mean offence but would not back down. Prime Minister Helen Clark and opposition leader Don Brash both made statements that the cartoons were not appreciated if they deeply offended members of the New Zealand community, but that such decisions were for editors to make, not politicians. Muslim leaders and the editors got together with the Race Relations office, and Jewish and Christian representatives in Wellington. As a result of this meeting the editors said they would not apologise but in good faith would refrain from publishing the offending images again. The New Zealand Muslim leadership, through the Federation of Islamic Associations of New Zealand (FIANZ), then proceeded in good faith to consider the matter closed, and drafted letters to 52 Muslim countries reversing their earlier stance and asking that New Zealand products not be boycotted.

Further controversies

In November 2016, Mohammad Anwar Sahib, the Imam of the Al-Taqwa mosque in Manukau, Auckland and a religious adviser to the FIANZ, drew controversy when he made offensive remarks about Jews, Christians, and women in a series of speeches that were posted by the right-wing blogger Cameron Slater on YouTube. Sahib's comments were condemned by a wide range of figures and groups in New Zealand society including the FIANZ's President Hazim Arafeh, the Islamic Women's Council of New Zealand (IWCNZ), the Race Relations Commissioner Dame Susan Devoy, the Ethnic Communities Minister Sam Lotu-Iiga, the ACT party David Seymour, the New Zealand First leader Winston Peters, the New Zealand Jewish Council, and the Ahmadiyya community. In response to negative publicity, Sahib was dismissed from his advisory position at the FIANZ. Sahib denied accusations of racism and issued a statement claiming his statements had been taken out of context.

In late October 2017, it was reported in the media that the first secretary of the Iranian Embassy Hormoz Ghahremani, the visiting Iranian cleric Hojatoleslam Shafie, and community elder Sayed Taghi Derhami had made remarks denying the Holocaust and attacking Israel at the Shia Islamic Ahlulbayt Foundation in Pakuranga, Auckland during a meeting to commemorate Quds Day in June. A video of the speeches had been posted on the Foundation's YouTube channel. These remarks were criticised by the New Zealand Jewish Council and the pro-Israel think tank the Israel Institute of New Zealand, who advocated Ghahremani's expulsion. Ghahremani later clarified that his actions represented the Iranian government's official position on Israel. Race Relations Commissioner Devoy also condemned the trio's anti-Semitic statements. The opposition New Zealand National Party's foreign affairs spokesperson Gerry Brownlee also urged the incumbent Labour-New Zealand First-Green coalition government to expel Ghahremani. In response, Foreign Minister Winston Peters countered that the incident had occurred under the previous National government's watch. Peters indicated that the Ministry of Foreign Affairs and Trade had summoned Ghahremani to express its disapproval.

Christchurch mosque shootings

On 15 March 2019, a terrorist attacked worshippers at two mosques in Christchurch, killing 51 people, including 42 at the Al Noor Mosque in Riccarton, 7 at the Linwood Islamic Centre, and 2 who died in hospital. The attacks took place on a Friday afternoon, when worshippers inside the mosques were gathering for Jumu'ah. The accused perpetrator of the attack was an Australian described as a white supremacist who intended to create an "atmosphere of fear" against Muslims.

However, a week after the attack, a nationwide moment of silence was observed in New Zealand on Friday – ushered in by the Muslim call to prayer. The prayer and two-minute reflection were broadcast live on national media outlets and came as an estimated 20,000 people, including Prime Minister Jacinda Ardern, gathered metres from the Al Noor mosque in the city of Christchurch for Muslim Friday prayers. Gamal Fouda, an imam who survived the attack at Al Noor mosque, said "last Friday I stood in this mosque and saw hatred and rage in the eyes of the terrorist, but today from the same place I look out and I see the love and compassion in the eyes of thousands of New Zealanders and human beings from around the globe". Speaking to mourners in the crowd, Prime

Minister Ardern said "New Zealand mourns with you. We are one". Quoting Muhammad, she said: "The believers in their mutual kindness, compassion, and sympathy are just like one body. When any part of the body suffers, the whole body feels pain." The horrific bloody event was condemned world wide. New Zealand businesses and community has come together to combat discrimination among Muslims.

Queenstown mosque vandalism

On 23 December 2020, six posters depicting Muhammad taken from the French satirical magazine Charlie Hebdo and hostile messages were plastered on the Queenstown Islamic Centre, which had opened on 11 December. The Mayor of Queenstown-Lakes Jim Boult condemned the incident and apologised on behalf of Queenstown to the Muslim community. An 18-year-old teenager was subsequently arrested in connection to the incident and also charged with possessing a knife.

Notable New Zealand Muslim figures

- Abdul Rahim Rasheed, activist.

- Ahmed Bhamji, politician and businessman.

- Anjum Rahman, community leader and human rights activist.

- Ashraf Choudhary, politician.

- Atta Elayyan was a Jordanian-New Zealand futsal player, coach, businessman, and developer. As a futsal player, Elayyan played on the New Zealand national futsal team and coached for the Christchurch Boys' High School. As a businessman and developer, he founded several businesses including Lazyworm

Applications and LWA Solutions. He was murdered in the Christchurch mosque shootings.

- Ibrahim Omer was a Member of Parliament for the Labour Party from 2020 to 2023.

- Joel Hayward, scholar, writer and poet. Kirkus Reviews said that Hayward "is undeniably one of academia's most visible Islamic thinkers". The National newspaper called Hayward "eminent' and a "distinguished historian of warfare and military strategy". He is considered to be one of "the world's five hundred most influential Muslims," with his listing in the 2023 and 2024 editions of The Muslim 500 stating that "he weaves together classical Islamic knowledge and methodologies and the source-critical Western historical method to make innovative yet carefully reasoned sense of complex historical issues that are still important in today's world."

- Mazhar Krasniqi was a New Zealand Muslim and Albanian community leader of Kosovar Albanian descent, businessman and human rights activist. He was both the first president of the New Zealand Albanian Civic League and Federation of Islamic Associations of New Zealand (FIANZ).

- Naila Hassan, police officer.

- Ofa Tu'ungafasi, rugby player.

- Sonny Bill Williams is a heavyweight boxer, and a former professional rugby league and rugby union player. He is only the second person to represent New Zealand in rugby union after first playing for the country in rugby league, and is one of only 43 players to have won the Rugby World Cup twice.

Chapter 15

Latin America

Latin American Muslims are Muslims from countries in Latin America. A survey conducted by the Pew Research Center in 2010 found that Muslims make up 0.1% of all of Latin America's population.

History

Some believe that the first Muslims that came to Latin America came under Portuguese and Spanish armies.

Quoted from "Muslims in Latin America" by Muhammad Yusuf Hallar - "According to statistics, the number of Muslims in Latin America is over four million, serving as an example 700,000 (seven hundred thousand) in Argentina and more than 1,500,000 (one point five million) in Brazil." Based on other estimates, there are 100,000 Muslims in Latin America, mainly concentrated in Brazil, Mexico, Jamaica and Argentina, with smaller concentrations in Venezuela, Haiti, Colombia and Paraguay. Most of these Latin American Muslims are from either Lebanese, Syrian and some convert origin.

A survey conducted by the Pew Research Center in 2010 found that the number of Muslims in Latin America and Caribbean is around 840,000. According to the International Religious Freedom Report in 2015, the actual size of Argentina's Muslim community is estimated to be around 1% of the total population (400,000 to 500,000 members). And according to the 2010 census, the number of Muslims in Brazil, was 35,207 out of a population of approximately 191 million people.

Suriname has the highest percentage of Muslims in its population for the region, with 13.9% or 75,053 individuals, according to its 2012 census. Islam came to Suriname with immigrants from Indonesia (Java) and South Asia (today India, Pakistan and Bangladesh).

Organizations

Many Muslim organizations exist in Latin America, such as the Islamic Organization of Latin America and the Caribbean (OIPALC). OIPALC is considered the most active organization in Latin America in promoting Islamic affiliated endeavors.

There are 33 countries in Latin America and the Caribbean today, according to the United Nations. The full list is shown in the table below, with current population and subregion (based on the United Nations official statistics).

Not included in this total of "countries" and listed separately are:

- Dependencies (or dependent territories, dependent areas) or Areas of Special Sovereignty (autonomous territories)

#	Country	Population (2023)	Subregion
1	Brazil	**216,422,446**	South America
2	Mexico	**128,455,567**	Central America
3	Colombia	**52,085,168**	South America
4	Argentina	**45,773,884**	South America
5	Peru	**34,352,719**	South America
6	Venezuela	**28,838,499**	South America
7	Chile	**19,629,590**	South America
8	Ecuador	**18,190,484**	South America
9	Guatemala	**18,092,026**	Central America
10	Bolivia	**12,388,571**	South America
11	Haiti	**11,724,763**	Caribbean

#	Country	Population (2023)	Subregion
12	Dominican Republic	**11,332,972**	Caribbean
13	Cuba	**11,194,449**	Caribbean
14	Honduras	**10,593,798**	Central America
15	Nicaragua	**7,046,310**	Central America
16	Paraguay	**6,861,524**	South America
17	El Salvador	**6,364,943**	Central America
18	Costa Rica	**5,212,173**	Central America
19	Panama	**4,468,087**	Central America
20	Uruguay	**3,423,108**	South America
21	Jamaica	**2,825,544**	Caribbean
22	Trinidad and Tobago	**1,534,937**	Caribbean

#	Country	Population (2023)	Subregion
23	Guyana	**813,834**	South America
24	Suriname	**623,236**	South America
25	Bahamas	**412,623**	Caribbean
26	Belize	**410,825**	Central America
27	Barbados	**281,995**	Caribbean
28	Saint Lucia	**180,251**	Caribbean
29	Grenada	**126,183**	Caribbean
30	St. Vincent & Grenadines	**103,698**	Caribbean
31	Antigua and Barbuda	**94,298**	Caribbean
32	Dominica	**73,040**	Caribbean
33	Saint Kitts & Nevis	**47,755**	Caribbean

Dependencies or other territories

#	Territory	Population (2023)	Dependency of
1	Puerto Rico	**3,260,314**	U.S.A.
2	Guadeloupe	**395,839**	France
3	Martinique	**366,981**	France
4	French Guiana	**312,155**	France
5	Curaçao	**192,077**	Netherlands
6	Aruba	**106,277**	Netherlands
7	U.S. Virgin Islands	**98,750**	U.S.A.
8	Cayman Islands	**69,310**	U.K.
9	Turks and Caicos	**46,062**	U.K.
10	Sint Maarten	**44,222**	Netherlands
11	British Virgin Islands	**31,538**	U.K.
12	Caribbean Netherlands	**27,148**	Netherlands
13	Anguilla	**15,899**	U.K.
14	Montserrat	**4,386**	U.K.
15	Falkland Islands	**3,791**	U.K.

Chapter 16

Africa

Islam in Africa is the continent's second most widely professed faith behind Christianity. Africa was the first continent into which Islam spread from Southwest Asia, during the early 7th century CE. Almost one-third of the world's Muslim population resides in Africa. Muslims crossed current Djibouti and Somalia to seek refuge in present-day Eritrea and Ethiopia during the Hijrah ("Migration") to the Christian Kingdom of Aksum. Like the vast majority (90%) of Muslims in the world, most Muslims in Africa are also Sunni Muslims; the complexity of Islam in Africa is revealed in the various schools of thought, traditions, and voices in many African countries. Many African ethnicities, mostly in North, West and East Africa consider Islam their Traditional religion. The practice of Islam on the continent is not static and is constantly being reshaped by prevalent social, economic, and political conditions. Generally Islam in Africa often adapted to African cultural contexts and belief systems forming Africa's own orthodoxies.

It was estimated in 2002 that Muslims constituted 40% of the population of Africa, a fraction which has slightly decreased in the meantime due to high birth rates in predominantly Christian Sub-Saharan Africa. Islam is the main religion of North Africa, the Horn of Africa, Sahel, the Swahili Coast, and West Africa, with minority immigrant populations in South Africa.

History

The presence of Islam in Africa can be traced to the 7th century CE, when in Rajab 8 BH, or May 614 CE, Muhammad advised a number of his early disciples, who were facing persecution by the polytheistic inhabitants of the Mecca, to seek refuge across the Red Sea in Axum. In the Muslim tradition, this event is known as the first hijrah, or migration. Twenty-three Muslims migrated to Abyssinia where they were protected by its king, Armah An-Najāshī, who later accepted Islam. They were followed by 101 Muslims later in the same year. Most of those Muslims returned to Medina in 7 AH / 628 CE but some settled in the neighboring Zeila (current day Somalia) which was at that time part of Bilād al-Barbar ("Land of the Berber(s)"). Once in Zeila, they built the Masjid al-Qiblatayn ("Mosque of the two Qiblahs") in 627 CE. This mosque has two Qiblas because it was built before the Prophet switched the Qiblah from Jerusalem to Mecca. They also reportedly built Africa's oldest mosque, that is the Mosque of the Companions in the Eritrean city of Massawa. This qibla of this mosque in Massawa points towards Jerusalem as well, though now defunct, occasional prayers are still held in this mosque with qibla correction towards Mecca.

In 20 H / 641 CE, during the reign of Caliph Umar ibn al-Khattab, Muslim troops took over current Egypt and conquered current Libya the following year. Muslims then expanded to current Tunisia in 27 H / 647 CE, during the reign of the third Muslim Caliph Uthman Ibn Affan. The conquest of North Africa continued under the Umayyad dynasty, which annexed parts of Algeria around 61 H/680 CE and Morocco the following year.

From the latter Muslim troops crossed the Strait of Gibraltar to Europe in 92 H/711 CE. Islam gained momentum during the 10th century in West Africa with the start of the Almoravid dynasty movement on the Senegal River and as rulers and kings embraced Islam. Islam then spread slowly in much of the continent through trade and preaching. During this period these Muslims from North and West Africa came to be known by Europeans at large as Moors. By the 9th century, Muslim Sultanates started being established in the Horn of Africa, and by the 12th century, the Kilwa Sultanate had spread as far south as Mozambique. Islam only crossed deeper into Malawi and Congo in the second half of the 19th century under the Zanzibar Sultanate. Then the British brought their labor force from India, including some Muslim-Indian nationals, to their colonies in Africa towards the end of the nineteenth and beginning of the twentieth century.

Islam was introduced to the northern Somali coast early on from the Arabian peninsula, shortly after the hijra. Zeila's two-mihrab Masjid al-Qiblatayn dates to the 7th century, and is the oldest mosque in the city. In the late 9th century, Al-Yaqubi wrote that Muslims were living along the northern Somali seaboard. He also mentioned that the Adal kingdom had its capital in the city, suggesting that the Adal Sultanate with Zeila as its headquarters dates back to at least the 9th or 10th century. According to I.M. Lewis, the polity was governed by local dynasties, who also ruled over the similarly-established Sultanate of Mogadishu in the littoral Benadir region to the south. Adal's history from this founding period forth would be characterized by a succession of battles with neighboring Abyssinia.

In the following centuries, the consolidation of Muslim trading networks, connected by lineage, trade, and Sufi brotherhoods, had reached a peak in West Africa, enabling Muslims to wield tremendous political influence and power. During the reign of Umar II, the then governor of Africa, Ismail ibn Abdullah, was said to have won the Berbers to Islam by his just administration. Other early notable missionaries include Abdallah ibn Yasin, who started a movement which caused thousands of Berbers to accept Islam.

The History of Islam in Africa and accounts of how the religion spread, especially in North and the Horn of Africa, has always been contentious. Head of Awqaf Africa London, Sheikh Dr. Abu-Abdullah Adelabu has written in his Movements of Islam in face of the Empires and Kingdoms in Yorubaland claims about the early arrival of Islam in southwestern Nigeria. He seconded the Arab anthropologist Abduhu Badawi on the argument that the early Muslim missionaries had benefited their works from the fall of Kush in northern Sudan and the prosperity of the politically multicultural Abbasid period in the continent which, according to him, had created several streams of migration, moving west in the mid-9th century into Sub-Saharan Africa. Adelabu pointed at the popularity and influences of the Abbasid Dynasty (750–1258), the second great dynasty with the rulers carrying the title of 'Caliph' as fostering peaceful and prosperous migration of the intercultural Muslims from the Nile Valley to Niger as well as of the Arab traders from the desert to Benue. Some argue that adoption of Islam was motivated by the desire to enhance trade, as Islam provided a moral code of conduct to regulate commercial activities, especially with respect to credit and security.

Similarly, in the Swahili coast, Islam made its way inland – spreading at the expense of traditional African religions. This expansion of Islam in Africa not only led to the formation of new communities in Africa, but it also reconfigured existing African communities and empires to be based on Islamic models. Indeed, in the middle of the 11th century, the Kanem Empire, whose influence extended into Sudan, converted to Islam. At the same time but more toward West Africa, the reigning ruler of the Bornu Empire embraced Islam. As these kingdoms adopted Islam, their subjects thereafter followed suit. In praising the Africans' zealousness to Islam, the 14th-century explorer Ibn Battuta stated that mosques were so crowded on Fridays, that unless one went very early, it was impossible to find a place to sit.

In the 16th century, the Ouaddai Empire and the Kingdom of Kano embraced Islam, and later toward the 18th century, the Nigeria based Sokoto Caliphate led by Usman dan Fodio exerted considerable effort in spreading Islam.

Today, Islam is the predominant religion of the northern half of Africa, mainly concentrated in North Africa, the Horn of Africa and the Sahel, as well as West Africa.

Characteristics

Islam has been in Africa for so long, since its emergence on the Arabian peninsula, that some scholars have argued that it is a traditional African religion.

Although the majority of Muslims in Africa are non-denominational Muslims, Sunni or Sufi, the complexity of Islam in Africa is revealed in the various schools of thought, traditions, and voices that constantly contend for dominance in many African countries. Islam in Africa is not static and is constantly being reshaped by prevalent social, economic and political conditions.

Islam in Africa is often adapted to local cultural contexts and belief systems, thereby forming the continent's own orthodoxies. Different societies in Africa have generally appropriated Islam in both more inclusive ways, or in the more radical ways, as with the Almoravid movement in the Maghreb and Sahara.

Additionally, Islam in Africa has both local and global dimensions. On the local level, experts assert that Muslims (including African Muslims) operate with considerable autonomy and do not have an international organization that regulates their religious practices. This fact accounts for the differences and varieties in Islamic practices throughout the African continent. On the global level, Muslims in Africa are also part of the Ummah (Islamic community worldwide), and follow global issues and current events that affect the Muslim world with keen interest. With globalization and new initiatives in information technology, Muslims in Africa have developed and maintained close connections with the wider Muslim world.

Analysts argue that Muslims in Africa, like other Muslims in Asia, the Middle East and the rest of the world, seem to be locked into an intense struggle regarding the future direction of Islam. At core of the struggle are questions about the way in which Muslims should practice their faith. The scholars assert that the majority seems to prefer to remain on the moderate, tolerant course that Islam has historically followed. However, a relatively small, but growing group would like to establish a stricter form of the religion, one that informs and controls all aspects of society.

Shari'ah

The Sharī'ah of Islam broadly influences the legal code in most Islamic countries, but the extent of which its impact varies widely. In Africa, most states limit the use of Sharia to "personal-status law" for issues such as marriage, divorce, inheritance and child custody. With the exception of northern Nigeria in West Africa, secularism does not seem to face any serious threat in Africa, even though the new Islamic revival is having a great impact upon segments of Muslim populations. Cohabitation or coexistence between Muslims and non-Muslims remains, for the most part, peaceful.

Nigeria is home to Africa's largest Muslim population. In 1999, Nigeria's northern states adopted the Sharia penal code, but punishments have been rare. In fact, dozens of women convicted of adultery and sentenced to stoning to death have later been freed. Egypt, one of the largest Muslim states in Africa, claims Sharia as the main source of its legislation, yet its penal and civil codes are based largely on French law.

Sects

Muslims in Africa mostly adhere to the Sunni Islam, with sizable Ibadi adherents. In addition, Sufism, the mystical dimension of Islam, has a very big presence. The Maliki madh'hab is the dominant school of jurisprudence amongst most of the continent's Sunni communities, while the Shafi'i madh'hab is prevalent in the Horn of Africa, eastern Egypt, and the Swahili Coast. The Hanafi fiqh is also followed in western Egypt.

Quranists

Quranism is an umbrella term denoting a strand within Islam that endorses a Quran-oriented form of Islam and often eschews hadiths. There are many forms of Quranism and they may not all agree on practical tenets.

Nondenominational Muslims

According to a survey by Pew, there are thirteen countries in Africa wherein at least twenty percent of the Muslim population adheres to a non-denominational form of Islam, i.e. are non-denominational Muslims. These countries, as well as the percentages of the Muslim populations who fall under this bracket include, Mali (55%), Nigeria (42%), Cameroon (40%), Tunisia (40%), Guinea Bissau (36%), Uganda (33%), Morocco (30%), Senegal (27%), Chad (23%), Ethiopia (23%), Liberia (22%), Niger (20%), and Tanzania (20%).

Sufism

Sufism, which focuses on the mystical elements of Islam, has many orders as well as followers in West Africa and Sudan, and, like other orders, strives to know God through meditation and emotion. Sufis may be nondenominational Muslim, Sunni or Shi'ite, and their ceremonies may involve chanting, music, dancing, and meditation.

Many Sufis in Africa are syncretic where they practise Sufism with traditional folklore beliefs. Salafis criticize the folklorists Sufis, who they claim have incorporated "un-Islamic" beliefs into their practices, such as celebrating the several events, visiting the shrines of "Islamic saints", dancing during prayer (the whirling dervishes). West Africa and Sudan have various Sufi orders regarded skeptically by the more doctrinally strict branches of Islam in the Middle East. Most orders in West Africa emphasize the role of a spiritual guide, marabout or possessing supernatural power, regarded as an Africanization of Islam. In Senegal and Gambia, Mouridism Sufis claim to have several million adherents and have drawn criticism for their veneration of Mouridism's founder Amadou Bamba. The Tijani is the most popular Sufi order in West Africa, with a large following in Mauritania, Mali, Niger, Senegal and Gambia.

Salafism

Recently, Salafism has begun spreading in Africa, as a result of many Muslim Non-Governmental Organizations (NGOs) such as the World Muslim League, the World Assembly for Muslim Youth, and the Federation of Mab and Islamic Schools primarily funded by Salafi governments in the Arab states of the Persian Gulf. These Salafist organizations, often based out of Saudi Arabia, promote a form of conservative reformism and regard Sufism as "heterodox" and contrary to their interpretation of traditional Islam. Such NGOs have built Salafi-dominated mosques and Islamic centers in Africa, and many are staffed by puritanical African Muslims, often trained in the Middle East. Academic scholarships to study in Islamic universities in the Middle East are also offered to further Salafism.

On the other hand, Africanist scholars trace the popularity of Salafi ideals to local cultural factors and the social efforts of prominent African Salafi scholars, reformists, organisations and intellectuals and their religious ties with various Islamic scholars across the Muslim World.

Notable kingdoms and sultanates

Harla Kingdom (500 - 1500)

Wadai Sultanate (1501-1911)

Kanem Empire (700 - 1376)

Idrisid dynasty (789 - 974)

Sultanate of Mogadishu (c. 900 - 16th century)

Maghrawa dynasty (987 - 1070)

Kingdom of Kano (1000 - 1805)

Almoravid dynasty (1073 – 1147)

Kilwa Sultanate (12th century – 1505)

Almohad dynasty (1147 – 1269)

Mali Empire (1230s – 1600s)

Marinid dynasty (1258 – 1420)

Ajuran Sultanate (13th century - 17th century)

Ifat Sultanate (1285 - 1415)

Songhai Empire (1340 - 1591)

Bornu Empire (1369 - 1893)

Adal Sultanate (1415 - 1555)

Hiraab Imamate (17th century - 1874)

Isaaq Sultanate (17th century - 1884)

Wattasid dynasty (1420 – 1554)

Sennar Sultanate (1502 - 1821)

Saadi dynasty (1554 – 1659)

Dendi Kingdom (1591 - 1901)

Sultanate of Darfur (1603 - 1874)

Alaouite dynasty (1666 - current)

Kong Empire (1710 - 1894)

Majeerteen Sultanate (mid-18th century – early 20th century)

Imamate of Futa Jallon (1727 - 1896)

Almamyate of Futa Toro (1776 - 1861)

Sokoto Caliphate (1804 - 1903)

Kingdom of Gomma (early 19th century – 1886)

Kingdom of Jimma (1830 – 1932)

Kingdom of Gumma (1840 – 1902)

Wassoulou Empire (1878 - 1898)

Sultanate of Hobyo (1880s - 1920s)

Dervish State (1896 - 1920)

Emirate of Harar (967-1887)

Makhzumi dynasty (896-1286)

Muslim population in Africa by country

According to the Pew Research Center, three of the ten countries with the largest Muslim populations in 2015 were in Africa: Nigeria (where there were an estimated 90.02 million Muslims, accounting for 50% of the total population), Egypt (83.87 million; 95.1%) and Algeria (37.21 million; 97.9%).

Estimated Muslim population by country, 2010[25]

	Muslim population	Total population	Percentage Muslim
Algeria	34,730,000	35,470,000	97.9
Angola	40,000	19,080,000	<1.0
Benin	2,110,000	8,850,000	23.8
Botswana	<10,000	2,010,000	<1.0
Burkina Faso	10,150,000	16,470,000	61.6
Burundi	230,000	8,380,000	2.8
Cameroon	3,590,000	19,600,000	18.3
Cape Verde	<10,000	500,000	<1.0
Central African Republic	370,000	4,400,000	8.5
Chad	6,210,000	11,230,000	55.3

Estimated Muslim population by country, 2010[25]

	Muslim population	Total population	Percentage Muslim
Comoros	720,000	730,000	98.3
Congo	50,000	4,040,000	1.2
Democratic Republic of the Congo	970,000	65,970,000	1.5
Djibouti	860,000	890,000	96.9
Egypt	76,990,000	81,120,000	94.9
Equatorial Guinea	30,000	700,000	4.0
Eritrea	1,920,000	5,250,000	36.6
Ethiopia	28,680,000	82,950,000	34.6
Gabon	170,000	1,510,000	11.2
Gambia	1,640,000	1,730,000	95.1
Ghana	3,860,000	24,390,000	15.8
Guinea	8,430,000	9,980,000	84.4
Guinea-Bissau	680,000	1,520,000	45.1

Estimated Muslim population by country, 2010[25]

	Muslim population	Total population	Percentage Muslim
Ivory Coast	7,390,000	19,740,000	42.5
Kenya	3,920,000	40,510,000	9.7
Kingdom of Morocco	32,460,000	32,460,000	99.0
Lesotho	<10,000	2,170,000	<1.0
Liberia	480,000	3,990,000	12.0
Libya	6,140,000	6,360,000	96.6
Madagascar	620,000	20,710,000	3.0
Malawi	1,930,000	14,900,000	13.0
Mali	14,510,000	15,370,000	94.4
Mauritania	3,430,000	3,460,000	99.0
Mauritius	220,000	1,300,000	17.3
Mayotte	200,000	200,000	98.6
Mozambique	4,200,000	23,390,000	18.0
Namibia	<10,000	2,280,000	<1.0

Estimated Muslim population by country, 2010[25]

	Muslim population	**Total population**	**Percentage Muslim**
Niger	15,270,000	15,510,000	98.4
Nigeria	80,300,000	158,420,000	50.8
Reunion	40,000	850,000	4.2
Rwanda	190,000	10,620,000	1.8
St. Helena	<10,000	<10,000	<1.0
Sao Tome and Principe	<10,000	170,000	<1.0
Senegal	11,980,000	12,430,000	96.4
Seychelles	<10,000	90,000	1.1
Sierra Leone	4,580,000	5,870,000	78.0
Somalia	9,310,000	9,330,000	98.0
South Africa	860,000	50,130,000	1.7
South Sudan	2,316,000	11,580,000	20
Sudan	45,480,000	46,880,000	97
Swaziland	<10,000	1,190,000	<1.0

Estimated Muslim population by country, 2010[25]

	Muslim population	Total population	Percentage Muslim
Tanzania	15,770,000	44,840,000	35.2
Togo	840,000	6,030,000	14.0
Tunisia	10,430,000	10,480,000	99.0
Uganda	3,840,000	33,420,000	11.5
Zambia	70,000	13,090,000	<1.0
Zimbabwe	110,000	12,570,000	<1.0

Chapter 17

Islamic World

The terms Muslim world and Islamic world commonly refer to the Islamic community, which is also known as the Ummah. This consists of all those who adhere to the religious beliefs, politics, and laws of Islam or to societies in which Islam is practiced. In a modern geopolitical sense, these terms refer to countries in which Islam is widespread, although there are no agreed criteria for inclusion. The term Muslim-majority countries is an alternative often used for the latter sense.

The history of the Muslim world spans about 1,400 years and includes a variety of socio-political developments, as well as advances in the arts, science, medicine, philosophy, law, economics and technology during the Islamic Golden Age. Muslims look for guidance to the Quran and believe in the prophetic mission of the Islamic prophet Muhammad, but disagreements on other matters have led to the appearance of different religious schools of thought and sects within Islam. The Islamic conquests, which culminated in the Arab empire being established across three continents (Asia, Africa, and Europe), enriched the Muslim world, achieving the economic preconditions for the emergence of this institution owing to the emphasis attached to Islamic teachings. In the modern era, most of the Muslim world came under European colonial domination. The nation states that emerged in the post-colonial era have adopted a variety of political and economic models, and they have been affected by secular as well as religious trends.

As of 2013, the combined GDP (nominal) of 60 Muslim majority countries was US$ 5.7 trillion. As of 2016, they contributed 8% of the world's total. In 2020, the Economy of the Organisation of Islamic Cooperation which consists of 57 member states had a combined GDP(PPP) of US$ 24 trillion which is equal to about 18% of world's GDP or US$ 30 trillion with 5 OIC observer states which is equal to about 22% of the world's GDP.

As of 2020, 1.8 billion or more than 25% of the world population are Muslims. By the percentage of the total population in a region considering themselves Muslim, 91% in the Middle East-North Africa (MENA), 89% in Central Asia, 40% in Southeast Asia, 31% in South Asia, 30% in Sub-Saharan Africa, 25% in Asia, 1.4% in Oceania, 6% in Europe, and 1% in the Americas.

Most Muslims are of one of two denominations: Sunni Islam (87–90%) and Shia (10–13%). However, other denominations exist in pockets, such as Ibadi (primarily in Oman). Muslims who do not belong to, do not self-identify with, or cannot be readily classified under one of the identifiable Islamic schools and branches are known as non-denominational Muslims. About 13% of Muslims live in Indonesia, the largest Muslim-majority country; 31% of Muslims live in South Asia, the largest population of Muslims in the world; 20% in the Middle East–North Africa, where it is the dominant religion; and 15% in Sub-Saharan Africa and West Africa (primarily in Nigeria). Muslims are the overwhelming majority in Central Asia, the majority in the Caucasus, and widespread in Southeast Asia. India has the largest Muslim population outside Muslim-majority countries. Pakistan, Bangladesh, Iran, and Egypt are home to the world's second, fourth, sixth and seventh largest Muslim populations respectively. Sizeable Muslim communities are also found in the Americas, Russia, India, China, and Europe. Islam is the fastest-growing major religion in the world partially due to their high birth rate, according to the same study, religious switching has no impact on Muslim population, since the number of people who embrace Islam and those who leave Islam are roughly equal. China has the third largest Muslim population outside Muslim-majority countries, while Russia has the fifth largest Muslim population. Nigeria has the largest Muslim population in Africa, while Indonesia has the largest Muslim population in Asia.

The history of the Islamic faith as a religion and social institution begins with its inception around 610 CE, when the Islamic prophet Muhammad, a native of Mecca, is believed by Muslims to have received the first revelation of the Quran, and began to preach his message. In 622 CE, facing opposition in Mecca, he and his followers migrated to Yathrib (now Medina), where he was invited to establish a new constitution for the city under his leadership. This migration, called the Hijra, marks the first year of the Islamic calendar. By the time of his death, Muhammad had become the political and spiritual leader of Medina, Mecca, the surrounding region, and numerous other tribes in the Arabian Peninsula.

After Muhammad died in 632, his successors (the Caliphs) continued to lead the Muslim community based on his teachings and guidelines of the Quran. The majority of Muslims consider the first four successors to be 'rightly guided' or Rashidun. The conquests of the Rashidun Caliphate helped to spread Islam beyond the Arabian Peninsula, stretching from northwest India, across Central Asia, the Near East, North Africa, southern Italy, and the Iberian Peninsula, to the Pyrenees. The Arab Muslims were unable to conquer the entire Christian Byzantine Empire in Asia Minor during the Arab–Byzantine wars, however. The succeeding Umayyad Caliphate attempted two failed sieges of Constantinople in 674–678 and 717–718. Meanwhile, the Muslim community tore itself apart into the rivalling Sunni and Shia sects since the killing of caliph Uthman in 656, resulting in a succession crisis that has never been resolved. The following First, Second and Third Fitnas and finally the Abbasid Revolution (746–750) also definitively destroyed the political unity of the Muslims, who have been inhabiting multiple states ever since. Ghaznavids' rule was succeeded by the Ghurid Empire of Muhammad of Ghor and Ghiyath al-Din Muhammad, whose reigns under the leadership of Muhammad Bakhtiyar Khalji extended until the Bengal, where Indian Islamic missionaries achieved their greatest success in terms of dawah and number of converts to Islam. Qutb ud-Din Aibak conquered Delhi in 1206 and began the reign of the Delhi Sultanate, a successive series of dynasties that synthesized Indian civilization with the wider commercial and cultural networks of Africa and Eurasia, greatly increased demographic and economic growth in India and deterred Mongol incursion into the prosperous Indo-Gangetic Plain and enthroned one of the few female Muslim rulers, Razia Sultana. Notable major empires dominated by Muslims, such as those of the Abbasids, Fatimids, Almoravids, Gao Empire, Seljukids, largest contiguous Songhai Empire (15th-16th centuries) of Sahel, West Africa, southern North Africa and western Central Africa which dominated the centers of Islamic knowledge of Timbuktu, Djenne, Oualata and Gao, Ajuran, Adal and Warsangali in Somalia, Mughals in the Indian subcontinent (India, Bangladesh, Pakistan e.t.c), Safavids in Persia and Ottomans in Anatolia, Massina Empire, Sokoto Caliphate of northern Nigeria, Toucouleur Empire, were among the influential and distinguished powers in the world.

19th-century colonialism and 20th-century decolonisation have resulted in several independent Muslim-majority states around the world, with vastly differing attitudes towards and political influences granted to, or restricted for, Islam from country to country. These have revolved around the question of Islam's compatibility with other ideological concepts such as secularism, nationalism, socialism, democracy, republicanism, liberalism and progressivism, feminism, capitalism and more.

Gunpowder empires

Scholars often use the term Age of the Islamic Gunpowders to describe period the Safavid, Ottoman and Mughal states. Each of these three empires had considerable military exploits using the newly developed firearms, especially cannon and small arms, to create their empires. They existed primarily between the fourteenth and the late seventeenth centuries. During the 17th–18th centuries, when the Indian subcontinent was ruled by Mughal Empire's sixth ruler Muhammad Auranzgeb through sharia and Islamic economics, India became the world's largest economy, valued 25% of world GDP.

Great Divergence

"Why do the Christian nations, which were so weak in the past compared with Muslim nations begin to dominate so many lands in modern times and even defeat the once victorious Ottoman armies?"…"Because they have laws and rules invented by reason."

Ibrahim Muteferrika, Rational basis for the Politics of Nations (1731)

The Great Divergence was the reason why European colonial powers militarily defeated preexisting Oriental powers like the

Mughal Empire, starting from the wealthy Bengal Subah, Tipu Sultan's Kingdom of Mysore, the Ottoman Empire and many smaller states in the pre-modern Greater Middle East, and initiated a period known as 'colonialism'.

Beginning with the 15th century, colonialism by European powers profoundly affected Muslim-majority societies in Africa, Europe, the Middle East and Asia. Colonialism was often advanced by conflict with mercantile initiatives by colonial powers and caused tremendous social upheavals in Muslim-dominated societies.

A number of Muslim-majority societies reacted to Western powers with zealotry and thus initiating the rise of Pan-Islamism; or affirmed more traditionalist and inclusive cultural ideals; and in rare cases adopted modernity that was ushered by the colonial powers.

The only Muslim-majority regions not to be colonized by the Europeans were Saudi Arabia, Iran, Turkey, and Afghanistan. Turkey was one of the first colonial powers of the world with the Ottoman empire ruling several states for over 6 centuries.

In the 20th century, the end of the European colonial domination has led to creation of a number of nation states with significant Muslim populations. These states drew on Islamic traditions to varying degree and in various ways in organizing their legal, educational and economic systems. The Times first documented the term "Muslim world" in 1912 when describing Pan-Islamism as a movement with power importance and cohesion born in Paris where Turks, Arabs and Persians congregated. The article considered The position of the Amir; the effect of the

Tripoli Campaign; Anglo-Russian action in Persia; and "Afghan Ambitions".

A significant change in the Muslim world was the defeat and dissolution of the Ottoman Empire (1908–1922), to which the Ottoman officer and Turkish revolutionary statesman Mustafa Kemal Atatürk had an instrumental role in ending and replacing it with the Republic of Turkey, a modern, secular democracy. The secular values of Kemalist Turkey, which separated religion from the state with the abolition of the Caliphate in 1924, have sometimes been seen as the result of Western influence.

In the 21st century, after the September 11 attacks (2001) coordinated by the Wahhabi Islamist terrorist group Al-Qaeda against the United States, scholars considered the ramifications of seeking to understand Muslim experience through the framework of secular Enlightenment principles. Muhammad Atta, one of the 11 September hijackers, reportedly quoted from the Quran to allay his fears: "Fight them, and God will chastise them at your hands/ And degrade them, and He will help you/Against them, and bring healing to the breasts of a people who believe", referring to the ummah, the community of Muslim believers, and invoking the imagery of the early warriors of Islam who lead the faithful from the darkness of jahiliyyah.

By Sayyid Qutb's definition of Islam, the faith is "a complete divorce from jahiliyyah". He complained that American churches served as centers of community social life that were "very hard [to] distinguish from places of fun and amusement". For Qutb, Western society was the modern jahliliyyah. His understanding of the "Muslim world" and its "social order" was that, presented to the Western world as the result of practicing Islamic teachings, would impress "by the beauty and charm of true Islamic ideology". He argued that the values of the Enlightenment and its related precursor, the Scientific Revolution, "denies or suspends God's sovereignty on earth" and argued that strengthening "Islamic character" was needed "to abolish the negative influences of jahili life."

Islam by country

As the Muslim world came into contact with secular ideals, societies responded in different ways. Some Muslim-majority countries are secular. Azerbaijan became the first secular republic in the Muslim world, between 1918 and 1920, before it was incorporated into the Soviet Union. Turkey has been governed as a secular state since the reforms of Mustafa Kemal Atatürk. By contrast, the 1979 Iranian Revolution replaced a monarchial semi-secular regime with an Islamic republic led by the Ayatollah, Ruhollah Khomeini.

Some countries have declared Islam as the official state religion. In those countries, the legal code is largely secular. Only personal status matters pertaining to inheritance and marriage are governed by Sharia law. In some places, Muslims implement Islamic law, called sharia in Arabic. The Islamic law exists in a number of variations, called schools of jurisprudence. The Amman Message, which was endorsed in 2005 by prominent Islamic scholars around the world, recognized four Sunni schools (Hanafi, Maliki, Shafi'i, Hanbali), two Shia schools (Ja'fari, Zaidi), the Ibadi school, and the Zahiri school.

Government and religion

Islamic states

Eight Islamic states have adopted Islam as the ideological foundation of state and constitution.

- Afghanistan

- Brunei

- Iran

- Mauritania

- Oman

- Pakistan

- Saudi Arabia

- Yemen

State religion

The following nineteen Muslim-majority states have endorsed Islam as their state religion, and though they may guarantee freedom of religion for citizens, do not declare a separation of state and religion:

- Algeria

- Bahrain

- Bangladesh

- Comoros

- Djibouti

Egypt

Iraq

Jordan

Kuwait

Libya

Malaysia

Maldives

Morocco

Palestine

Qatar

Somalia

Syria

Tunisia

United Arab Emirates

Secular states

Twenty-two Secular states in the Muslim world have declared separation between civil/government affairs and religion.

Albania

Azerbaijan

Bosnia and Herzegovina

Burkina Faso

Chad

Gambia

Guinea

Guinea-Bissau

Indonesia (except Aceh province)

Kazakhstan

Kosovo

Kyrgyzstan

Mali

Niger

Nigeria

Senegal

Sierra Leone

Sudan

Tajikistan

Turkey

Turkmenistan

Uzbekistan

Others

Lebanon

Muslim-minority states

According to the Pew Research Center in 2015 there were 50 Muslim-majority countries, which are shown in the Government and religion section above in the article. Apart from these, large Muslim populations exist in some countries where Muslims are a minority, and their Muslim communities are larger than many Muslim-majority nations:

- India: 200 million Muslims (14.6%)

- Ethiopia: 34.7 million Muslims (31.3%)

- China: 25–40 million Muslims (2–3%)

- Tanzania: 19.4 million Muslims (35.2%)

- Russia: 14–20 million Muslims (10–14%)

- Ivory Coast: 12 million Muslims (42%)

- DR Congo: 10 million Muslims (15%)

- Philippines: 8–9 million Muslims (9–10%)

During much of the 20th century, the Islamic identity and the dominance of Islam on political issues have arguably increased during the early 21st century. The fast-growing interests of the Western world in Islamic regions, international conflicts and globalization have changed the influence of Islam on the world in contemporary history.

Islamism

Islamism (also often called political Islam) is a religio-political ideology. The advocates of Islamism, also known as "al-Islamiyyun", are dedicated to realizing their ideological interpretation of Islam within the context of the state or society. The majority of them are affiliated with Islamic institutions or social mobilization movements, often designated as "al-harakat al-Islamiyyah." Islamists emphasize the implementation of sharia, pan-Islamic political unity, the creation of Islamic states, (eventually unified), and rejection of non-Muslim influences—particularly Western or universal economic, military, political, social, or cultural.

In its original formulation, Islamism described an ideology seeking to revive Islam to its past assertiveness and glory, purifying it of foreign elements, reasserting its role into "social and political as well as personal life"; and in particular "reordering government and society in accordance with laws prescribed by Islam" (i.e. Sharia). According to at least one observer (author Robin Wright), Islamist movements have "arguably altered the Middle East more than any trend since the modern states gained independence", redefining "politics and even borders".

Central and prominent figures in 20th-century Islamism include Sayyid Rashid Riḍā, Hassan al-Banna (founder of the Muslim Brotherhood), Sayyid Qutb, Abul A'la Maududi, Ruhollah Khomeini (founder of the Islamic Republic of Iran), Hassan Al-Turabi. Syrian Sunni cleric Muhammad Rashid Riḍā, a fervent opponent of Westernization, Zionism and nationalism, advocated Sunni internationalism through revolutionary restoration of a pan-Islamic Caliphate to politically unite the Muslim World. Riḍā was a strong exponent of Islamic vanguardism, the belief that Muslim community should be guided by clerical elites (ulema) who steered the efforts for religious education and Islamic revival. Riḍā's Salafi-Arabist synthesis and Islamist ideals greatly influenced his disciples like Hasan al-Banna, an Egyptian schoolteacher who founded the

Muslim Brotherhood movement, and Hajji Amin al-Husayni, the anti-Zionist Grand Mufti of Jerusalem.

Al-Banna and Maududi called for a "reformist" strategy to re-Islamizing society through grassroots social and political activism. Other Islamists (Al-Turabi) are proponents of a "revolutionary" strategy of Islamizing society through exercise of state power, or (Sayyid Qutb) for combining grassroots Islamization with armed revolution. The term has been applied to non-state reform movements, political parties, militias and revolutionary groups.

At least one author (Graham E. Fuller) has argued for a broader notion of Islamism as a form of identity politics, involving "support for [Muslim] identity, authenticity, broader regionalism, revivalism, [and] revitalization of the community." Islamists themselves prefer terms such as "Islamic movement", or "Islamic activism" to "Islamism", objecting to the insinuation that Islamism is anything other than Islam renewed and revived. In public and academic contexts, the term "Islamism" has been criticized as having been given connotations of violence, extremism, and violations of human rights, by the Western mass media, leading to Islamophobia and stereotyping.

Following the Arab Spring, many post-Islamist currents became heavily involved in democratic politics, while others spawned "the most aggressive and ambitious Islamist militia" to date, such as the Islamic State of Iraq and the Levant (ISIL).

Demographics

More than 24.1% of the world's population is Muslim, with an estimated total of approximately 1.9 billion. Muslims are the majority in 49 countries, they speak hundreds of languages and come from diverse ethnic backgrounds. The city of Karachi has the largest Muslim population in the world.

Geography

Because the terms 'Muslim world' and 'Islamic world' are disputed, since no country is homogeneously Muslim, and there is no way to determine at what point a Muslim minority in a country is to be considered 'significant' enough, there is no consensus on how to define the Muslim world geographically. The only rule of thumb for inclusion which has some support, is that countries need to have a Muslim population of more than 50%.

In 2010, 73% of the world's Muslim population lived in countries where Muslims are in the majority, while 27% of the world's Muslim population lived in countries where Muslims are in the minority. India's Muslim population is the world's largest Muslim-minority population in the world (11% of the world's Muslim population). Jones (2005) defines a "large minority" as being between 30% and 50%, which described nine countries in 2000, namely Eritrea, Ethiopia, Guinea-Bissau, Ivory Coast, Nigeria, North Macedonia, and Tanzania.

Religion

Islam

The two main denominations of Islam are the Sunni and Shia sects. They differ primarily upon of how the life of the ummah ("faithful") should be governed, and the role of the imam. Sunnis believe that the true political successor of Muhammad according to the Sunnah should be selected based on **Shura** (consultation), as was done at the Saqifah which selected Abu Bakr, Muhammad's father-in-law, to be Muhammad's political but not his religious successor. Shia, on the other hand, believe that Muhammad designated his son-in-law Ali ibn Abi Talib as his true political as well as religious successor.

The overwhelming majority of Muslims in the world, between 87 and 90%, are Sunni. Shias and other groups make up the rest, about 10–13% of overall Muslim population. The countries with the highest concentration of Shia populations are: Iran – 89%, Azerbaijan – 65%, Iraq – 60%, Bahrain – 60%, Yemen – 35%, Turkey – 10%, Lebanon – 27%, Syria – 13%, Afghanistan – 10%, Pakistan – 10%, and India – 10%.

Non-denominational Muslims make up a majority of the Muslims in seven countries (and a plurality in three others): Albania (65%), Kyrgyzstan (64%), Kosovo (58%), Indonesia (56%), Mali (55%), Bosnia and Herzegovina (54%), Uzbekistan (54%), Azerbaijan (45%), Russia (45%), and Nigeria (42%). They are found primarily in Central Asia. Kazakhstan has the largest number of non-denominational Muslims, who constitute about 74% of the population. Southeastern Europe also has a large number of non-denominational Muslims.

The Kharijite Muslims, who are less known, have their own stronghold in the country of Oman holding about 75% of the population.

The major Sunni madhhabs are Hanafi, Maliki, Shafi'i, and Hanbali.

The major Shi'a branches are Twelver (Imami), Ismaili (Sevener) and Zaidi (Fiver). Isma'ilism later split into Nizari Ismaili and Musta'li Ismaili, and then Mustaali was divided into Hafizi and Taiyabi Ismailis. It also gave rise to the Qarmatian movement and the Druze faith, although Druzes do not identify as Muslims. Twelver Shiism developed Ja'fari jurisprudence whose branches are Akhbarism and Usulism, and other movements such as Alawites, Shaykism and Alevism.

Similarly, Kharijites were initially divided into five major branches: Sufris, Azariqa, Najdat, Adjarites and Ibadis.

Among these numerous branches, only Hanafi, Maliki, Shafi'i, Hanbali, Imamiyyah-Ja'fari-Usuli, Nizārī Ismā'īlī, Alevi, Zaydi, Ibadi, Zahiri, Alawite, Druze and Taiyabi communities have survived. In addition, new schools of thought and movements like Quranist Muslims and Ahmadi Muslims later emerged independently.

Other religions

There are sizeable non-Muslim minorities in many Muslim-majority countries, includes, Christians, Jews, Hindus, Buddhists, Bahai's, Druzes, Yazidis, Mandaeans, Yarsanis and Zoroastrians.

The Muslim world is home to some of the world's most ancient Christian communities, and some of the most important cities of the Christian world—including three of its five great patriarchates (Alexandria, Antioch, and Constantinople). Scholars and intellectuals agree Christians have made significant contributions to Arab and Islamic civilization since the introduction of Islam, and they have had a significant impact contributing the culture of the Middle East and North Africa and other areas. Pew Research Center estimates indicate that in 2010, more than 64 million Christians lived in countries with Muslim majorities (excluding Nigeria). The Pew Forum study finds that Indonesia (21.1 million) has the largest Christian population in the Muslim world, followed by Egypt,

Chad and Kazakhstan. While according to Adly A. Youssef and Martyn Thomas, in 2004, there were around 30 million Christians who lived in countries with Muslim majorities, with the largest Christian population number lived in Indonesia, followed by Egypt. Nigeria is divided almost evenly between Muslims and Christians, with more than 80 million Christians and Muslims.

In 2018, the Jewish Agency estimated that around 27,000 Jews live in Arab and Muslim countries. Jewish communities have existed across the Middle East and North Africa since the rise of Islam. Today, Jews residing in Muslim countries have been reduced to a small fraction of their former sizes, with the largest communities of Jews in Muslim countries exist in the non-Arab countries of Iran (9,500) and Turkey (14,500); both, however, are much smaller than they historically have been. Among Arab countries, the largest Jewish community now exists in Morocco with about 2,000 Jews and in Tunisia with about 1,000. The number of Druze worldwide is between 800,000 and one million, with the vast majority residing in the Levant (primarily in Syria and Lebanon).

In 2010, the Pew Forum study finds that Bangladesh (13.5 million), Indonesia (4 million), Pakistan (3.3 million) and Malaysia (1.7 million) has a sizeable Hindu minorities. Malaysia (5 million) has the largest Buddhist population in the Muslim world. Zoroastrians are the oldest remaining religious community in Iran.

Literacy and education

The literacy rate in the Muslim world varies. Azerbaijan is in second place in the Index of Literacy of World Countries. Some members such as Iran, Kuwait, Kazakhstan, Tajikistan and Turkmenistan have over 97% literacy rates, whereas literacy rates are the lowest in Mali, Afghanistan, Chad and other parts of Africa. Several Muslim-majority countries, such as Turkey, Iran and Egypt have a high rate of citable scientific publications.

In 2015, the International Islamic News Agency reported that nearly 37% of the population of the Muslim world is unable to read or write, basing that figure on reports from the Organisation of Islamic Cooperation and the Islamic Educational, Scientific and Cultural Organization. In Egypt, the largest Muslim-majority Arab country, the youth female literacy rate exceeds that for males. Lower literacy rates are more prevalent in South Asian countries such as in Afghanistan and Pakistan, but are rapidly increasing. In the Eastern Middle East, Iran has a high level of youth literacy at 98%, but Iraq's youth literacy rate has sharply declined from 85% to 57% during the American-led war and subsequent occupation. Indonesia, the largest Muslim-majority country in the world, has a 99% youth literacy rate.

A 2011 Pew Research Center showed that at the time about 36% of all Muslims had no formal schooling, with only 8% having graduate and post-graduate degrees. The highest of years of schooling among Muslim-majority countries found in Uzbekistan (11.5), Kuwait (11.0) and Kazakhstan (10.7). In addition, the average of years of schooling in countries in which Muslims are the majority is 6.0 years of schooling, which lag behind the global average (7.7 years of schooling). In the youngest age (25–34) group surveyed, Young Muslims have the lowest average levels of education of any major religious group, with an average of 6.7 years of schooling, which lag behind the global average (8.6 years of schooling). The study found that Muslims have a significant amount of gender inequality in educational attainment, since Muslim women have an average of 4.9 years of schooling, compared to an average of 6.4 years of schooling among Muslim men.

Refugees

According to the UNHCR, Muslim-majority countries hosted 18 million refugees by the end of 2010.

Since then Muslim-majority countries have absorbed refugees from recent conflicts, including the uprising in Syria. In July 2013, the UN stated that the number of Syrian refugees had exceeded 1.8 million. In Asia, an estimated 625,000 refugees from Rakhine, Myanmar, mostly Muslim, had crossed the border into Bangladesh since August 2017.

Culture

Throughout history, Muslim cultures have been diverse ethnically, linguistically and regionally. According to M. M. Knight, this diversity includes diversity in beliefs, interpretations and practices and communities and interests. Knight says perception of Muslim world among non-Muslims is usually supported through introductory literature about Islam, mostly present a version as per scriptural view which would include some prescriptive literature and abstracts of history as per authors own point of views, to which even many Muslims might agree, but that necessarily would not reflect Islam as lived on the ground, 'in the experience of real human bodies'.

Classical culture

The term "Islamic Golden Age" has been attributed to a period in history during which science, economic development and cultural works in most of the Muslim-dominated world flourished. The age is traditionally understood to have begun during the reign of the Abbasid caliph Harun al-Rashid (786–809) with the inauguration of the House of Wisdom in Baghdad, where scholars from various parts of the world sought to translate and gather all the known world's knowledge into Arabic, and to have ended with the collapse of the Abbasid caliphate due to Mongol invasions and the Siege of Baghdad in 1258. The Abbasids were influenced by the Quranic injunctions and hadiths, such as "the ink of a scholar is more holy than the blood of a martyr," that stressed the value of knowledge. The major Islamic capital cities of Baghdad, Cairo, and Córdoba became the main intellectual centers for science, philosophy, medicine, and education. During this period, the Muslim world was a collection of cultures; they drew together and advanced the knowledge gained from the ancient Greek, Roman, Persian, Chinese, Vedic, etc.

Egyptian, and Phoenician civilizations.

Ceramics

Between the 8th and 18th centuries, the use of ceramic glaze was prevalent in Islamic art, usually assuming the form of elaborate pottery. Tin-opacified glazing was one of the earliest new technologies developed by the Islamic potters. The first Islamic opaque glazes can be found as blue-painted ware in Basra, dating to around the 8th century. Another contribution was the development of fritware, originating from 9th-century Iraq. Other centers for innovative ceramic pottery in the Old world included Fustat (from 975 to 1075), Damascus (from 1100 to around 1600) and Tabriz (from 1470 to 1550).

Literature

The best known work of fiction from the Islamic world is One Thousand and One Nights (In Persian: hezār-o-yek šab > Arabic:

ʔalf-layl-at-wa-l'-layla= One thousand Night and (one) Night) or *Arabian Nights, a name invented by early Western translators, which is a compilation of folk tales from Sanskrit, Persian, and later Arabian fables. The original concept is derived from a pre-Islamic Persian prototype Hezār Afsān (Thousand Fables) that relied on particular Indian elements. It reached its final form by the 14th century; the number and type of tales have varied from one manuscript to another. All Arabian fantasy tales tend to be called Arabian Nights stories when translated into English, regardless of whether they appear in The Book of One Thousand and One Nights or not. This work has been very influential in the West since it was translated in the 18th century, first by Antoine Galland. Imitations were written, especially in France. Various characters from this epic have themselves become cultural icons in Western culture, such as Aladdin, Sinbad the Sailor and Ali Baba.

A famous example of Arabic poetry and Persian poetry on romance (love) is Layla and Majnun, dating back to the Umayyad era in the 7th century. It is a tragic story of undying love. Ferdowsi's Shahnameh, the national epic of Greater Iran, is a mythical and heroic retelling of Persian history. Amir Arsalan was also a popular mythical Persian story.

Ibn Tufayl (Abubacer) and Ibn al-Nafis were pioneers of the philosophical novel. Ibn Tufail wrote the first Arabic novel Hayy ibn Yaqdhan (Philosophus Autodidactus) as a response to Al-Ghazali's The Incoherence of the Philosophers, and then Ibn al-Nafis also wrote a novel Theologus Autodidactus as a response to Ibn Tufail's Philosophus Autodidactus. Both of these narratives had protagonists (Hayy in Philosophus Autodidactus and Kamil in Theologus Autodidactus) who were autodidactic feral children living in seclusion on a desert island, both being the earliest examples of a desert island story. However, while Hayy lives alone with animals on the desert island for the rest of the story in Philosophus Autodidactus, the story of Kamil extends beyond the desert island setting in Theologus Autodidactus, developing into the earliest known coming of age plot and eventually becoming the first example of a science fiction novel.

Theologus Autodidactus, written by the Arabian polymath Ibn al-Nafis (1213–1288), is the first example of a science fiction novel. It deals with various science fiction elements such as spontaneous generation, futurology, the end of the world and doomsday, resurrection, and the afterlife. Rather than giving supernatural or mythological explanations for these events, Ibn al-Nafis attempted to explain these plot elements using the scientific knowledge of biology, astronomy, cosmology and geology known in his time. Ibn al-Nafis' fiction explained Islamic religious teachings via science and Islamic philosophy.

A Latin translation of Ibn Tufail's work, Philosophus Autodidactus, first appeared in 1671, prepared by Edward Pococke the Younger, followed by an English translation by Simon Ockley in 1708, as well as German and Dutch translations. These translations might have later inspired Daniel Defoe to write Robinson Crusoe, regarded as the first novel in English. Philosophus Autodidactus, continuing the thoughts of philosophers such as Aristotle from earlier ages, inspired Robert Boyle to write his own philosophical novel set on an island, The Aspiring Naturalist.

Dante Alighieri's Divine Comedy, derived features of and episodes about Bolgia from Arabic works on Islamic eschatology: the Hadith and the Kitab al-Miraj (translated into Latin in 1264 or shortly before as Liber scalae Machometi) concerning the ascension to Heaven of Muhammad, and the spiritual writings of

Ibn Arabi. The Moors also had a noticeable influence on the works of George Peele and William Shakespeare. Some of their works featured Moorish characters, such as Peele's The Battle of Alcazar and Shakespeare's The Merchant of Venice, Titus Andronicus and Othello, which featured a Moorish Othello as its title character. These works are said to have been inspired by several Moorish delegations from Morocco to Elizabethan England at the beginning of the 17th century.

Philosophy

One of the common definitions for "Islamic philosophy" is "the style of philosophy produced within the framework of Islamic culture." Islamic philosophy, in this definition is neither necessarily concerned with religious issues, nor is exclusively produced by Muslims. The Persian scholar Ibn Sina (Avicenna) (980–1037) had more than 450 books attributed to him. His writings were concerned with various subjects, most notably philosophy and medicine. His medical textbook The Canon of Medicine was used as the standard text in European universities for centuries. He also wrote The Book of Healing, an influential scientific and philosophical encyclopedia.

One of the most influential Muslim philosophers in the West was Averroes (Ibn Rushd), founder of the Averroism school of philosophy, whose works and commentaries affected the rise of secular thought in Europe. He also developed the concept of "existence precedes essence".

Another figure from the Islamic Golden Age, Avicenna, also founded his own Avicennism school of philosophy, which was influential in both Islamic and Christian lands. He was also a critic of Aristotelian logic and founder of Avicennian logic, developed the concepts of empiricism and tabula rasa, and distinguished between essence and existence.

Yet another influential philosopher who had an influence on modern philosophy was Ibn Tufail. His philosophical novel, Hayy ibn Yaqdhan, translated into Latin as Philosophus Autodidactus in 1671, developed the themes of empiricism, tabula rasa, nature versus nurture, condition of possibility, materialism, and Molyneux's problem. European scholars and writers influenced by this novel include John Locke, Gottfried Leibniz, Melchisédech Thévenot, John Wallis, Christiaan Huygens, George Keith, Robert Barclay, the Quakers, and Samuel Hartlib.

Islamic philosophers continued making advances in philosophy through to the 17th century, when Mulla Sadra founded his school of Transcendent theosophy and developed the concept of existentialism.

Other influential Muslim philosophers include al-Jahiz, a pioneer in evolutionary thought; Ibn al-Haytham (Alhazen), a pioneer of phenomenology and the philosophy of science and a critic of Aristotelian natural philosophy and Aristotle's concept of place (topos); Al-Biruni, a critic of Aristotelian natural philosophy; Ibn Tufail and Ibn al-Nafis, pioneers of the philosophical novel; Shahab al-Din Suhrawardi, founder of Illuminationist philosophy; Fakhr al-Din al-Razi, a critic of Aristotelian logic and a pioneer of inductive logic; and Ibn Khaldun, a pioneer in the philosophy of history.

Sciences

Muslim scientists placed far greater emphasis on experiment than the Greeks. This led to an early scientific method being developed in the Muslim world, where progress in methodology was made, beginning with the experiments of Ibn al-Haytham (Alhazen) on optics from circa 1000, in his Book of Optics. The most important development of the scientific method was the use of experiments to distinguish between competing scientific theories set within a generally empirical orientation, which began among Muslim scientists. Ibn al-Haytham is also regarded as the father of optics, especially for his empirical proof of the intromission theory of light. Jim Al-Khalili stated in 2009 that Ibn al-Haytham is 'often referred to as the "world's first true scientist".' al-Khwarzimi's invented the log base systems that are being used today, he also contributed theorems in trigonometry as well as limits. Recent studies show that it is very likely that the Medieval Muslim artists were aware of advanced decagonal quasicrystal geometry (discovered half a millennium later in the 1970s and 1980s in the West) and used it in intricate decorative tilework in the architecture.

Muslim physicians contributed to the field of medicine, including the subjects of anatomy and physiology: such as in the 15th-century Persian work by Mansur ibn Muhammad ibn al-Faqih Ilyas entitled Tashrih al-badan (Anatomy of the body) which contained comprehensive diagrams of the body's structural, nervous and circulatory systems; or in the work of the Egyptian physician Ibn al-Nafis, who proposed the theory of pulmonary circulation. Avicenna's The Canon of Medicine remained an authoritative medical textbook in Europe until the 18th century. Abu al-Qasim al-Zahrawi (also known as Abulcasis) contributed to the discipline of medical surgery with his Kitab al-Tasrif ("Book of Concessions"), a medical encyclopedia which was later translated to Latin and used in European and Muslim medical schools for centuries. Other medical advancements came in the fields of pharmacology and pharmacy.

In astronomy, Muḥammad ibn Jābir al-Ḥarrānī al-Battānī improved the precision of the measurement of the precession of the Earth's axis. The corrections made to the geocentric model by al-Battani, Averroes, Nasir al-Din al-Tusi, Mu'ayyad al-Din al-Urdi and Ibn al-Shatir were later incorporated into the Copernican heliocentric model. Heliocentric theories were also discussed by several other Muslim astronomers such as Al-Biruni, Al-Sijzi, Qutb al-Din al-Shirazi, and Najm al-Din al-Qazwini al-Katibi. The astrolabe, though originally developed by the Greeks, was perfected by Islamic astronomers and engineers, and was subsequently brought to Europe.

Some most famous scientists from the medieval Islamic world include Jābir ibn Hayyān, al-Farabi, Abu al-Qasim al-Zahrawi, Ibn al-Haytham, Al-Biruni, Avicenna, Nasir al-Din al-Tusi, and Ibn Khaldun.

Technology

In technology, the Muslim world adopted papermaking from China. The knowledge of gunpowder was also transmitted from China via predominantly Islamic countries, where formulas for pure potassium nitrate were developed.

Advances were made in irrigation and farming, using new technology such as the windmill. Crops such as almonds and citrus fruit were brought to Europe through al-Andalus, and sugar cultivation was gradually adopted by the Europeans. Arab merchants dominated trade in the Indian Ocean until the arrival of the Portuguese in the 16th century. Hormuz was an important center for this trade. There was also a dense network of trade routes in the Mediterranean, along which Muslim-majority countries traded with each other and with European powers such as Venice,

Genoa and Catalonia. The Silk Road crossing Central Asia passed through Islamic states between China and Europe. The emergence of major economic empires with technological resources after the conquests of Timur (Tamerlane) and the resurgence of the Timurid Renaissance include the Mali Empire and the India's Bengal Sultanate in particular, a major global trading nation in the world, described by the Europeans to be the "richest country to trade with".

Muslim engineers in the Islamic world made a number of innovative industrial uses of hydropower, and early industrial uses of tidal power and wind power. The industrial uses of watermills in the Islamic world date back to the 7th century, while horizontal-wheeled and vertical-wheeled water mills were both in widespread use since at least the 9th century. A variety of industrial mills were being employed in the Islamic world, including early fulling mills, gristmills, paper mills, hullers, sawmills, ship mills, stamp mills, steel mills, sugar mills, tide mills and windmills. By the 11th century, every province throughout the Islamic world had these industrial mills in operation, from al-Andalus and North Africa to the Middle East and Central Asia. Muslim engineers also invented crankshafts and water turbines, employed gears in mills and water-raising machines, and pioneered the use of dams as a source of water power, used to provide additional power to watermills and water-raising machines. Such advances made it possible for industrial tasks that were previously driven by manual labour in ancient times to be mechanized and driven by machinery instead in the medieval Islamic world. The transfer of these technologies to medieval Europe had an influence on the Industrial Revolution, particularly from the proto-industrialised Mughal Bengal and Tipu Sultan's Kingdom, through the conquests of the East India Company.

Arts

The term "Islamic art and architecture" denotes the works of art and architecture produced from the 7th century onwards by people who lived within the territory that was inhabited by culturally Islamic populations.

Architecture

Islamic architecture comprises the architectural styles of buildings associated with Islam. It encompasses both secular and religious styles from the early history of Islam to the present day. The Islamic world encompasses a wide geographic area historically ranging from western Africa and Europe to eastern Asia. Certain commonalities are shared by Islamic architectural styles across all these regions, but over time different regions developed their own styles according to local materials and techniques, local dynasties and patrons, different regional centers of artistic production, and sometimes different religious affiliations.

Early Islamic architecture was influenced by Roman, Byzantine, Iranian, and Mesopotamian architecture and all other lands which the early Muslim conquests conquered in the seventh and eighth centuries. Further east, it was also influenced by Chinese and Indian architecture as Islam spread to South and Southeast Asia. Later it developed distinct characteristics in the form of buildings and in the decoration of surfaces with Islamic calligraphy, arabesques, and geometric motifs. New architectural elements like minarets, muqarnas, and multifoil arches were invented. Common or important types of buildings in Islamic architecture include mosques, madrasas, tombs, palaces, hammams (public baths), Sufi hospices (e.g. khanqahs or zawiyas), fountains and sabils, commercial buildings (e.g. caravanserais and bazaars), and military fortifications.

Islamic architecture

Dome of the Rock in Jerusalem

Taj Mahal in Agra city of India was constructed during the Mughal Empire

Menara Kudus Mosque in Kudus, Indonesia with pre-Islamic Javanese style architecture

Sultan Ahmed Mosque in Istanbul, Turkey

Sultan Salahuddin Abdul Aziz Mosque in Selangor, Malaysia

Great Mosque of Córdoba in Spain is a Moorish-style mosque.

The Charminar in Hyderabad, India

"Tower of Introspection" at the Great Mosque of Xi'an, China

The design of Faisal Mosque in Islamabad, Pakistan is inspired by Bedouin's tent.

Moscow Cathedral Mosque in Moscow, Russia

Lagos Central Mosque in Lagos, Nigeria

Shah Mosque in Tehran, Iran

Aniconism

No Islamic visual images or depictions of God are meant to exist because it is believed that such artistic depictions may lead to idolatry. Muslims describe God by the names and attributes that, according to Islam, he revealed to his creation. All but one sura of the Quran begins with the phrase "In the name of God, the Beneficent, the Merciful". Images of Mohammed are likewise prohibited. Such aniconism and iconoclasm can also be found in Jewish and some Christian theology.

Arabesque

Islamic art frequently adopts the use of geometrical floral or vegetal designs in a repetition known as arabesque. Such designs are highly nonrepresentational, as Islam forbids representational depictions as found in pre-Islamic pagan religions. Despite this, there is a presence of depictional art in some Muslim societies, notably the miniature style made famous in Persia and under the Ottoman Empire which featured paintings of people and animals, and also depictions of Quranic stories and Islamic traditional narratives. Another reason why Islamic art is usually abstract is to symbolize the transcendence, indivisible and infinite nature of God, an objective achieved by arabesque. Islamic calligraphy is an omnipresent decoration in Islamic art, and is usually expressed in the form of Quranic verses. Two of the main scripts involved are the symbolic kufic and naskh scripts, which can be found adorning the walls and domes of mosques, the sides of minbars, and so on.

Distinguishing motifs of Islamic architecture have always been ordered repetition, radiating structures, and rhythmic, metric patterns. In this respect, fractal geometry has been a key utility, especially for mosques and palaces. Other features employed as motifs include columns, piers and arches, organized and interwoven with alternating sequences of niches and colonnettes. The role of domes in Islamic architecture has been considerable. Its usage spans centuries, first appearing in 691 with the construction of the Dome of the Rock mosque, and recurring even up until the 17th century with the Taj Mahal. And as late as the 19th century, Islamic domes had been incorporated into European architecture.

Girih

Girih (Persian: گره, "knot", also written gereh) are decorative Islamic geometric patterns used in architecture and handicraft objects, consisting of angled lines that form an interlaced strapwork pattern.

Girih decoration is believed to have been inspired by Syrian Roman knotwork patterns from the second century. The earliest girih dates from around 1000 CE, and the artform flourished until the 15th century. Girih patterns can be created in a variety of ways, including the traditional straightedge and compass construction; the construction of a grid of polygons; and the use of a set of girih tiles with lines drawn on them: the lines form the pattern. Patterns may be elaborated by the use of two levels of design, as at the 1453 Darb-e Imam shrine. Square repeating units of known patterns can be copied as templates, and historic pattern books may have been intended for use in this way.

The 15th century Topkapı Scroll explicitly shows girih patterns together with the tilings used to create them. A set of tiles consisting of a dart and a kite shape can be used to create aperiodic Penrose tilings, though there is no evidence that such a set was used in medieval times. Girih patterns have been used to decorate varied materials including stone screens, as at Fatehpur Sikri; plasterwork, as at mosques and madrasas such as the Hunat Hatun Complex in Kayseri; metal, as at Mosque-Madrassa of Sultan Hassan in Cairo; and in wood, as at the Mosque–Cathedral of Córdoba.

Islamic calligraphy

Islamic calligraphy is the artistic practice of handwriting and calligraphy, in the languages which use Arabic alphabet or the alphabets derived from it. It includes Arabic, Persian, Ottoman, and Urdu calligraphy. It is known in Arabic as khatt Arabi (خط عربي), which translates into Arabic line, design, or construction.

The development of Islamic calligraphy is strongly tied to the Qur'an; chapters and excerpts from the Qur'an are a common and almost universal text upon which Islamic calligraphy is based. Although artistic depictions of people and animals are not explicitly forbidden by the Qur'an, pictures have traditionally been limited in Islamic books in order to avoid idolatry. Although some scholars dispute this, Kufic script was supposedly developed around the end of the 7th century in Kufa, Iraq, from which it takes its name. The style later developed into several varieties, including floral, foliated, plaited or interlaced, bordered, and square kufic. In the ancient world, though, artists would often get around the aniconic prohibition by using strands of tiny writing to construct lines and images. Calligraphy was a valued art form, even as a moral good. An ancient Arabic proverb illustrates this point by emphatically stating that "Purity of writing is purity of the soul."

However, Islamic calligraphy is not limited to strictly religious subjects, objects, or spaces. Like all Islamic art, it encompasses a diverse array of works created in a wide variety of contexts. The prevalence of calligraphy in Islamic art is not directly related to its non-figural tradition; rather, it reflects the centrality of the notion of writing and written text in Islam.

Islamic calligraphy developed from two major styles: Kufic and Naskh. There are several variations of each, as well as regionally specific styles. Arabic or Persian calligraphy has also been incorporated into modern art, beginning with the post-colonial period in the Middle East, as well as the more recent style of calligraffiti.

Calendar

Two calendars are used all over the Muslim world. One is a lunar calendar that is most widely used among Muslims. The other one is a solar calendar officially used in Iran and Afghanistan.

Islamic lunar calendar

The Hijri calendar (Arabic: ٱلتَّقْوِيم ٱلْهِجْرِيّ, romanized: al-taqwīm al-hijrī), or Arabic calendar also known in English as the Muslim calendar and Islamic calendar, is a lunar calendar consisting of 12 lunar months in a year of 354 or 355 days. It is used to determine the proper days of Islamic holidays and rituals, such as the annual fasting and the annual season for the great pilgrimage. In almost all countries where the predominant religion is Islam, the civil calendar is the Gregorian calendar, with Syriac month-names used in the Levant and Mesopotamia (Iraq, Syria, Jordan, Lebanon and Palestine) but the religious calendar is the Hijri one.

This calendar enumerates the Hijri era, whose epoch was established as the Islamic New Year in 622 CE. During that year, Muhammad and his followers migrated from Mecca to Medina and established the first Muslim community (ummah), an event commemorated as the Hijrah. In the West, dates in this era are usually denoted AH (Latin: Anno Hegirae, lit. 'In the year of the Hijrah'). In Muslim countries, it is also sometimes denoted as H from its Arabic form (سَنَة هِجْرِيَّة, abbreviated ه). In English, years prior to the Hijra are denoted as BH ("Before the Hijra").

Since 19 July 2023 CE, the current Islamic year is 1445 AH. In the Gregorian calendar reckoning, 1445 AH runs from 19 July 2023 to approximately 7 July 2024.

Solar Hijri calendar

The Solar Hijri calendar is a solar calendar and one of the various Iranian calendars. It begins on the March equinox as determined by the astronomical calculation for the Iran Standard Time meridian (52.5°E, UTC+03:30) and has years of 365 or 366 days.

It is the modern principal calendar in Iran and Afghanistan and is sometimes also called the Shamsi calendar and Khorshidi calendar. It is abbreviated as SH, HS or, by analogy with AH, AHSh.

The ancient Iranian Solar calendar is one of the oldest calendars in the world, as well as the most accurate solar calendar in use today. Since the calendar uses astronomical calculation for determining the vernal equinox, it has no intrinsic error. It is older than the Lunar Hijri calendar used by the majority of Muslims (known in the West as the Islamic calendar); though they both count from the Hijrah, the journey of the Islamic prophet Muhammad and his followers from Mecca to Medina in the year 622, one uses solar years and the other lunar years.

Each of the twelve months corresponds with a zodiac sign, and in Afghanistan the names of the zodiacal signs were used for the months; elsewhere the month names are the same as in the Zoroastrian calendar. The first six months have 31 days, the next five have 30 days, and the last month has 29 days in common years but 30 days in leap years.

The ancient Iranian New Year's Day, which is called Nowruz, always falls on the March equinox. While Nowruz is celebrated by communities in a wide range of countries from the Balkans to Mongolia, the Solar Hijri calendar itself remains only in official use in Iran.

Women

According to Riada Asimovic Akyol while Muslim women's experiences differs a lot by location and personal situations such as family upbringing, class and education; the difference between culture and religions is often ignored by community and state leaders in many of the Muslim majority countries, the key issue in the Muslim world regarding gender issues is that religious texts constructed in highly patriarchal environments and based on biological essentialism are still valued highly in Islam; hence views emphasizing on men's superiority in unequal gender roles are widespread among many conservative Muslims (men and women). Orthodox Muslims often believe that rights and responsibilities of women in Islam are different from that of men and sacrosanct since assigned by the God. According to Asma Barlas patriarchal behaviour among Muslims is based in an ideology which jumbles sexual and biological differences with gender dualisms and inequality. Modernist discourse of liberal progressive movements like Islamic feminism have been revisiting hermeneutics of feminism in Islam in terms of respect for Muslim women's lives and rights. Riada Asimovic Akyol further says that equality for Muslim women needs to be achieved through self-criticism.

Muslims

Projected Global Muslim Population, 2010-2050

	POPULATION ESTIMATE	% OF WORLD'S POPULATION
2010	1,599,700,000	23.2%
2020	1,907,110,000	24.9
2030	2,209,270,000	26.5
2040	2,497,830,000	28.1
2050	2,761,480,000	29.7

Source: The Future of World Religions: Population Growth Projections, 2010-2050 Population estimates are rounded to the nearest 10,000. Percentages are calculated from unrounded numbers.

PEW RESEARCH CENTER

The number of Muslims around the world is projected to increase rapidly in the decades ahead, growing from about 1.6 billion in 2010 to nearly 2.8 billion in 2050. Muslims are expected to grow twice as fast as the overall global population. Consequently, Muslims are projected to rise from 23% of the world's population in 2010 to 30% in 2050.

Chapter 18

Islamist Terrorist Attacks

Islamism (also often called political Islam) is a religio-political According to Fondapol, a French think tank, between 1979 and May 2021, at least 48,035 Islamist terrorist attacks took place worldwide, causing the deaths of at least 210,138 people. During this period, each Islamist attack resulted in the death of about 4.4 persons on average. The most common type of weapon used are explosives (43.9%). The main target of these attacks is the military (31.7%), followed by civilians (25.0%) and police forces (18.3%). Afghanistan was the country most affected by Islamist terrorism, followed by Iraq and Somalia. With at least 82 Islamist attacks and 332 deaths, France remains the country most affected by Islamist terrorism within the European Union. The majority of Islamist attacks (89.5%) were in Muslim countries and the victims were mainly Muslims, in the same proportions.

2001

Location	Date	Description	Deaths	Injuries
United States	September 11	A series of four coordinated terrorist attacks by al-Qaeda involving the hijacking and crashing of passenger jet airliners.	2,996	25,000+

2002

Location	Date	Description	Deaths	Injuries
Indonesia	October 12	2002 Bali bombings in the tourist district of Kuta on the island of Bali.	202	240

2003

Location	Date	Description	Deaths	Injuries
Saudi Arabia	May 12	Riyadh compound bombings; Al-Qaeda attackers drove three car bombs into residential compounds housing Westerners and others. Nine bombers and another 3 insurgents also died.	27	160

2004

Location	Date	Description	Deaths	Injuries
Spain	March 11	Madrid train bombings.	193	2,050

2005

Location	Date	Description	Deaths	Injuries
United Kingdom	July 7	7 July 2005 London bombings - Four suicide bombers attacked London Underground trains and a double decker bus during the morning rush hour.	52	~784
Egypt	July 23	2005 Sharm El Sheikh bombings - Bombing attacks through shopping and hotel areas in the Red Sea resort of Sharm el-Sheikh.	88	~150
Indonesia	October 29	2005 Tentena market bombings. Three attacks in crowded markets and a bus.	60	180+
Jordan	November 9	2005 Amman bombings. A series of coordinated suicide attacks on hotels in Amman. Four attackers including a husband and wife team were involved.	60	115+

2006

Location	Date	Description	Deaths	Injuries
Egypt	April 24	2006 Dahab bombings - Bomb attacks on the resort city of Dahab.	23	~ 80
India	July 11	2006 Mumbai train bombings: Seven bomb blasts over a period of 11 minutes on the Suburban Railway in Mumbai.	209	700+

2008

Location	Date	Description	Deaths	Injuries
India	May 13	Nine synchronized blasts in Jaipur, claimed by the Indian Mujahideen, suspected to be carried out by the Harkat-ul-Jihad al-Islami.	80	216

Location	Date	Description	Deaths	Injuries
India	July 26	2008 Ahmedabad bombings	56	200+
India	November 26	A series of coordinated attacks on Mumbai. The Indian government blamed Pakistan-based militant group Lashkar-e-Taiba and stated that the attackers were citizens of Pakistan, which the Pakistani government first rejected but then accepted when given proof. One of the attackers, Ajmal Kasab, was caught alive.	166+	300+

2009

Location	Date	Description	Deaths	Injuries
Pakistan	March 3	A bus carrying Sri Lankan cricketers was fired upon by 12 gunmen, believed to be members of Lashkar-e-Jhangvi, near Gaddafi Stadium in Lahore. Six members of the Sri Lanka national cricket team were wounded and six Pakistani policemen and two civilians were killed.	8	9

2010

Location	Date	Description	Deaths	Injuries
Russia	March 29	Moscow Metro bombings. Caucasus Emirate claimed responsibility	40	102

Location	Date	Description	Deaths	Injuries
Pakistan	May 28	2010 Ahmadiyya mosques massacre Tehrik-i-Taliban Pakistan claimed attacks on two mosques belonging to the Ahmadiyya Muslim Community	86	45+
Pakistan	July 1	July 2010 Lahore bombings, anti-Sufi attack.	42+	175+

2012

Location	Date	Description	Deaths	Injuries
France	March 11 – 22	Toulouse and Montauban shootings – Mohammed Merah, a French citizen of Algerian extraction, attacked French soldiers and later children and a teacher from a Jewish school in Montauban and Toulouse.	7	5

Location	Date	Description	Deaths	Injuries
Russia	May 3	Makhachkala attack carried out by the Caucasus Emirate.	14	130

2013

Location	Date	Description	Deaths	Injuries
United States	April 15	Boston Marathon bombing – Two brothers, Tamerlan and Dzhokhar Tsarnaev, planted two bombs near the finish line of the Boston Marathon in Massachusetts.	3	183
United Kingdom	May 22	Murder of Lee Rigby in Woolwich, London	1	0

Location	Date	Description	Deaths	Injuries
▌France	May 25	2013 La Défense attack – A Muslim convert attacked a French soldier with a knife while on patrol in La Defense, Hauts-de-Seine, Île-de-France.	0	1
▌Kenya	September 21	Westgate shopping mall attack in Nairobi	67	175

2014

Location	Date	Description	Deaths	Injuries
▌Nigeria	February 14	Borno Massacre	200+	

Location	Date	Description	Deaths	Injuries
Iraq	June 10	Badush prison massacre; The Islamic State of Iraq and the Levant (ISIL) killed at least 670 Shia prisoners in an attack on the Badush prison. ISIL first separated the Sunni inmates before executing the remaining prisoners.	670	
Iraq	June 12	The Camp Speicher massacre occurred when ISIL attacked Camp Speicher in Tikrit. At the time, there were between 5,000 and 10,000 unarmed cadets in the camp, and ISIL fighters selected the Shias and non-Muslims for execution.	1,095+	
Australia	September 23	2014 Endeavour Hills stabbings. Numan Haider, an Afghan Australian stabbed two counter terrorism officers in Melbourne. He was then shot dead.	1	2

Location	Date	Description	Deaths	Injuries
Russia	October 5	2014 Grozny bombing	6	12
Canada	October 22	2014 shootings at Parliament Hill, Ottawa. Lone attacker shot a soldier at a war memorial and attacked Parliament.	1	3
United States	October 23	Zale H. Thomson, also known as Zaim Farouq Abdul-Malik, attacked four New York City policemen in the subway with a hatchet, severely injuring one in the back of the head and injuring another policeman in the arm before being shot to death by the remaining officers, who also shot a civilian.	0	5

Location	Date	Description	Deaths	Injuries
Nigeria	November 28	Kano bombing	120	260

Country	Date	Event		
Russia	December 4	2014 Grozny clashes	26	
Australia	December 15–16	Lindt Cafe siege	3	4
Pakistan	December 16	2014 Peshawar school massacre	140	
Yemen	December 16	2014 Radda bombings Two suicide car bombers rammed their vehicles into a Shiite rebel checkpoint.	26	
Nigeria	December 18	2014 Gumsuri kidnappings. Boko Haram insurgents also kidnapped at least 185 women and children.	32	
France	December 20	2014 Tours police station stabbing. A man yelling Allahu Akbar attacked a police office with a knife. He was killed and three police officers were injured.	1	3

Iraq	August 2014	Genocide of Yazidis by the Islamic State. An estimated 7,000 women and girls were also forced into sex slavery, according to the United Nations.	5,000	4,200–10,800

2015

Location	Date	Description	Deaths	Injuries
France	January 7	Two brothers, Saïd and Chérif Kouachi, forced their way into the offices of the French satirical weekly newspaper Charlie Hebdo in Paris and opened fire.	12	11
Nigeria	January 8	Boko Haram attacked the town of Baga. Another 2,000 were missing.	200+	–

Location	Date	Description	Deaths	Injuries
France	February 3	2015 Nice stabbing – A man wielding a knife named Moussa Coulibaly attacked three soldiers guarding a Jewish community center in Nice.	0	2
Denmark	February 14–15	2015 Copenhagen shootings. A gunman opened fire at the Krudttoenden café and later at the Great Synagogue in Copenhagen.	2	5
Tunisia	March 18	Bardo National Museum attack. Militants linked to ISIL attacked the Bardo National Museum with guns.	21	50+
Yemen	March 20	2015 Sana'a mosque bombings. Bombings on several Shia mosques by ISIL.	142	351

Location	Date	Description	Deaths	Injuries
Libya	March 25	ISIL affiliates, the Shura Council of Benghazi Revolutionaries carried out suicide bombings in Benghazi.	12	25
Kenya	April 2	Garissa University College attack by Al-Shabaab.	148	79
Saudi Arabia	April 8	In Riyadh, two policemen were shot dead in an attack blamed on ISIL.	2	
Iraq	April 17	A series of bombings by ISIL in Baghdad.	40+	59+
Iraq	April 17	A car bomb exploded at the entrance of the US consulate in Erbil. ISIL took credit for the attack.	3	5
Afghanistan	April 18	A suicide bomb detonated in front of a bank in Jalalabad. ISIL claimed responsibility.	33	100+

Location	Date	Description	Deaths	Injuries
Somalia	April 20	A minivan of UN workers was bombed by Al-Shabaab in the Puntland region.	9	4
Bosnia and Herzegovina	April 27	A radical Islamist opened fire at a police station in Zvornik. A police officer was killed, two others were injured, and the attacker was killed by police.	2	2
Iraq	May 3	Two car bombs were detonated ten minutes apart in Baghdad. ISIL claimed responsibility for the attacks.	19	
United States	May 3	Two gunmen attacked the Curtis Culwell Center during a 'Draw Muhammad' cartoon art exhibit in Garland, Texas.	2	1
Afghanistan	May 3	Taliban militants overran checkpoints in Warduj, killing 17 policemen.	17	

Location	Date	Description	Deaths	Injuries
Afghanistan	May 4	A government bus was attacked by a suicide bomber in Kabul.	1	15
Iraq	May 10	Two car bombs were detonated ten minutes apart in Baghdad and the surrounding towns of Taji and Tarmiyah. ISIL claimed responsibility.	14	30
Afghanistan	May 10	A bus carrying government employees was attacked in Kabul by a suicide bomber. The Taliban claimed responsibility.	3	10
Pakistan	May 13	A bus carrying Shia Muslims was attacked by six armed gunman who rode up in motorcycles. Several Islamist groups claimed responsibility.	45	13

Location	Date	Description	Deaths	Injuries
Afghanistan	May 14	A hotel hosting a cultural event was attacked by Taliban fighters in Kabul leaving 14 dead including an American, an Italian, and 4 Indians.	14	
Afghanistan	May 17	A Taliban suicide attack near the entrance of Hamid Karzai International Airport targeting a European police training vehicle.	3	18
Afghanistan	May 19	A suicide car bombing detonated in the parking lot of a Justice Ministry building in the diplomatic section of Kabul.	4	42
Libya	May 21	A suicide bomber detonated his explosives at a military checkpoint outside of Misrata killing himself and two guards.	3	

Location	Date	Description	Deaths	Injuries
Saudi Arabia	May 22	A suicide bomber attacked a Shia mosque during prayer in al-Qadeeh village. ISIL claimed responsibility.	21	90+
Afghanistan	May 25	Taliban militants killed 19 policemen and six soldiers during a siege at a police compound in Nawzad District.	25	
Kenya	May 26	Al-Shabaab militants attacked two police patrols north of Garissa, 5 police officers were injured but were able to kill both of the attackers.	2	5
Iraq	May 28	Two car bombs were set off minutes apart targeting the Cristal Grand Ishtar Hotel and the Babylon.	10	30

Location	Date	Description	Deaths	Injuries
Saudi Arabia	May 29	A suicide bomber attacked a Shia mosque in Dammam detonating the bomb in the parking lot.	4	
Iraq	June 1	Three suicide bombers in Humvees attacked a police station in the Tharthar region in Al Anbar Governorate.	41	63
Turkey	June 5	2015 Diyarbakır rally bombings – Twin bombing of a Peoples' Democratic Party (HDP) rally.	4	100+
Iraq	June 13	Four suicide SUV car bombs went off in a police station in Hajjaj near Tikrit and Baiji.	11	27
France	June 26	Saint-Quentin-Fallavier attack – Beheading in a factory near Lyon, head marked with Arabic writing and Islamist flags. Gas canisters set off a fire.	1	11

Location	Date	Description	Deaths	Injuries
Tunisia	June 26	2015 Sousse attacks – A gunman named Seifeddine Rezgui attacked a hotel targeting European tourists staying there.	38	39
Nigeria	June 26–30	Boko Haram killed attacked and bombed villages, mosques, and other public spaces.	200	
Nigeria	July 7	A bomb exploded in a government office in Zaria.	20	
Cameroon	July 13	Two suicide bombers exploded in a bar in Fotokol and killed 13 people, including a soldier from Chad who was killed in the second explosion.	15	
United States	July 16	A civilian opened fire on two military installations in Chattanooga, Tennessee, killing 5 military personnel.	5	

Location	Date	Description	Deaths	Injuries
Nigeria	July 17	Two towns were attacked by two suicide bombers.	62	
Turkey	July 20	2015 Suruç bombing in Kurdish majority city of Suruç. ISIL claimed responsibility.	33	104
Nigeria	July 22	A series of explosions at two bus stations in Gombe.	40	
Cameroon	July 26	A suicide bomber detonated at a popular nightclub in Maroua.	15	

Location	Date	Description	Deaths	Injuries
India	July 27	2015 Gurdaspur attack Three Islamic terrorists of Pakistani origin from Indian-administrated Kashmir disguised in army uniforms attacked the Dina Nagar police station in Gurdaspur District of Punjab. The attack killed 3 policemen, 4 civilians and 15 others were injured. All 3 attackers were killed by security forces.	10	15
Nigeria	August 11	Explosions at a crowded market in Sabon Gari.	47	
Iraq	August 13	August 2015 Baghdad bombing. A truck bomb in a market.	70+	200

Location	Date	Description	Deaths	Injuries
France	August 21	2015 Thalys train attack. Shooting and stabbing in train traveling from Amsterdam to Paris. The incident was believed by French police to be an Islamist terrorist attack.	0	5
Nigeria	August 28–30	Boko Haram members attacked three villages. 68 alone were killed in the village of Baanu.	79	
Nigeria	September 10	Explosion at a refugee camp for people fleeing Boko Haram.	2	
Iraq	September 17	Two suicide bombings in Baghdad. ISIL claimed responsibility.	12	55
Nigeria	September 21	Multiple explosions.	54	

Location	Date	Description	Deaths	Injuries
Yemen	September 24	A bomb attack on a Shia mosque in Sana'a during prayers for the Muslim holiday of Eid al-Adha. Claimed by ISIL.	25	
Bangladesh	September 29	Three men on a motorbike shot and killed an Italian aid worker. The attack was claimed by ISIL.	1	
Nigeria	October 1	Multiple suicide bombings by Boko Haram.	14	39
Israel	October 1	Gunmen opened fire on a car near Nablus on the northern West Bank, killing a man and woman. Four of their children were also in the car and witnessed the attack, but were uninjured. The attackers were praised by Hamas.	2	

Location	Date	Description	Deaths	Injuries
Australia	October 2	2015 Parramatta shooting. A NSW Police Force civilian employee was shot dead outside NSW Police Force headquarters on Charles Street, Parramatta, Sydney by a 15-year-old lone gunman. The gunman then engaged with NSW Police Special Constables in a shootout before being killed.	2	
Bangladesh	October 3	A Japanese man was shot and killed. The attack was claimed by ISIL.	1	
Iraq	October 3	Two suicide bombings in Shiite majority neighbourhoods in Baghdad. Attack claimed by ISIL.	20	61
Afghanistan	October 5	Two suicide bombings in Kabul targeted an intelligence centre. Claimed by the Taliban.	2	3

Location	Date	Description	Deaths	Injuries
Somalia	October 7	Al-Shabaab militants ambushed and killed the nephew of Somali president Hassan Sheikh Mohamud.	2	
Turkey	October 10	2015 Ankara bombings. ISIL is suspected.	109	500+
Chad	October 10	Multiple suicide bombings blamed on Boko Haram.	33	51
Afghanistan	October 11	A bomb attack in Kabul, targeting a British military convoy injured 7 Afghan civilians. The attack was claimed by the Taliban.	0	7
Nigeria	October 22	Boko Haram attack in Borno State.	20	
Nigeria	October 23	Two separate mosques were attacked by suicide bombers.	42	

Location	Date	Description	Deaths	Injuries
Niger	October 28	Boko Haram militants attacked a village, allegedly burning down houses and cars during the rampage.	13	
Egypt	October 31	Bomb on board a Russian jet brought it down in the Sinai peninsula.	224	
Lebanon	November 12	Twin suicide bombings in Beirut.	42	
France	November 13	A series of terrorist attacks in Paris involving a series of coordinated attacks which consisted of mass shootings and suicide bombings. This incident was the deadliest event on French soil since World War II.	137	416
Iraq	November 13	Suicide attack at a Shia funeral.	21	

Location	Date	Description	Deaths	Injuries
Philippines	November 17	A Malaysian national was beheaded by Abu Sayyaf.	1	
Nigeria	November 17	A suicide attack at a market in Yola blamed on Boko Haram.	30+	80+
Bosnia and Herzegovina	November 18	A lone wolf Islamist killed two soldiers and injured civilians in Sarajevo.	3	5
Nigeria	November 18	Two explosions blamed on Boko Haram struck a phone market in Kano.	15	100+
Iraq	November 20	A suicide bomber detonated inside a Shiite mosque.	11	5
Cameroon	November 21	Suicide bombing blamed on Boko Haram.	10	

Location	Date	Description	Deaths	Injuries
Nigeria	November 22	Suicide bombing.	8	
Tunisia	November 24	2015 Tunis bombing. ISIL claimed responsibility for an attack on a bus transporting members of the Presidential Guard.	14	11
Egypt	November 24	November 2015 Sinai attack. A day after the second round of parliamentary elections closed, militants attacked a hotel housing election judges in the provincial capital of al-Arish in North Sinai.	7	10+
Niger	November 25	Boko Haram attacked a village, shot residents and fired rockets.	18	
Nigeria	November 27	Boko Haram suicide attack on a Shia procession.	22	

Location	Date	Description	Deaths	Injuries
Egypt	November 28	Islamist gunmen killed four security personnel in an attack at a police checkpoint in Saqqara.	4	
Mali	November 28	Militants fired rockets on a MINUSMA peacekeeping forces base. Ansar Dine claimed responsibility.	3	20
United States	December 2	In the 2015 San Bernardino attack, married couple Rizwan Farook and Tashfeen Malik opened fire in an office.	14	22
Chad	December 5	Four female suicide bombers from Boko Haram attacked the island of Koulfoua on Lake Chad.	19	130+
Yemen	December 6	The governor of Aden, Jaafar Mohammed Saad, was killed in a car bomb attack claimed by ISIL.	1	

Location	Date	Description	Deaths	Injuries
Afghanistan	December 8	In the 2015 Kandahar Airport attacks several Taliban members attacked Kandahar Airport and surrounding areas.	70+	35
Egypt	December 8	An explosive device by Islamists targeting a military convoy went off in Rafah.	4	4
Iraq	December 9	A suicide bomber detonated in the doorway of a Shiite mosque.	11+	20
Afghanistan	December 11	In the 2015 Spanish Embassy attack in Kabul, Taliban militants detonated a car bomb and stormed a guesthouse near the embassy.	6	
Syria	December 11	Tell Tamer bombings. Three truck bombs set off by ISIL in Tell Tamer.	60	80

Location	Date	Description	Deaths	Injuries
Iraq	December 12	A militant detonated his explosives in a truck at an Iraqi position near the Saudi border.	6	14
Nigeria	December 13	Boko Haram attacked the villages of Warwara, Mangari, and Bura-Shika.	30	20
Afghanistan	December 21	A suicide bomber on a motorcycle detonated near Bagram Airfield.	7	3
Nigeria	December 26	Boko Haram gunmen raided Kimba village, opening fire on residents and torching their homes.	14+	
Afghanistan	December 28	A Taliban suicide bomber detonated on a road near a school close to Kabul International Airport.	2	33

Location	Date	Description	Deaths	Injuries
Nigeria	December 28	Fourteen Islamist female suicide bombers aged 12–18 attempted to simultaneously attack Maiduguri. Seven of the bombers were shot dead by security forces while three managed to escape and detonate themselves in Baderi and near a mosque, killing 36 people and wounding another 85.	36	85
Pakistan	December 29	A suicide bomber detonated in the entrance of an office of the National Database and Registration Authority in Mardan.	27	50+
Russia	December 29	A gunman opened fire on a group of residents who were visiting a viewing platform at the fortress in Derbent, Dagestan. ISIL claimed responsibility.	1	11

2016

Location	Date	Description	Deaths	Injuries
Afghanistan	January 1	A Taliban suicide bomber detonated himself in a French restaurant in Kabul.	2	15
India	January 2	In the 2016 Pathankot attack suspected Jaish-e-Mohammed militants attacked an air base killing 7 security force members.	7	
Iraq	January 3	Five Islamist suicide bombers attacked a military base.	15	22
Libya	January 7	In the Zliten truck bombing, Islamist militants detonated a truck bomb at the al-Jahfal police training camp in Zliten.	50+	100+

Location	Date	Description	Deaths	Injuries
France	January 7	In the January 2016 Paris police station attack an Islamist from Morocco wearing a fake explosive belt attacked police officers with a meat cleaver. He was shot dead.	1	0
Libya	January 7	Car bombing at a checkpoint in the oil port of Ras Lanuf.	7	11
Egypt	January 8	In the 2016 Hurghada attack two militants armed with a melee weapon and a signal flare stormed the Bella Vista Hotel.	0	3
France	January 11	A 15-year-old Turkish ISIL supporter attacked a teacher from a Jewish school in Marseille with a machete.	0	1
Iraq	January 11	ISIL gunmen detonated suicide vests in a shopping mall.	20	40+

Location	Date	Description	Deaths	Injuries
Turkey	January 12	In the 2016 Istanbul bombing an ISIL suicide bomber detonated in the historical centre of Istanbul.	11	15
Indonesia	January 14	2016 Jakarta attacks which were orchestrated by ISIL.	2	24
Somalia	January 15	In the El Adde attack, Al-Shabaab militants attacked an African Union Kenyan army base in El-Adde.	63+	
Burkina Faso	January 15	In the 2016 Ouagadougou attacks Islamist gunmen armed with heavy weapons attacked the Cappuccino restaurant and the Splendid Hotel in Ouagadougou.	20+	15+
Pakistan	January 21	Bacha Khan University attack. The Taliban claimed responsibility for the attack.	22	

Location	Date	Description	Deaths	Injuries
Somalia	January 22	Al-Shabab attack on beachside restaurant.	20	
Cameroon	January 25	Suspected Boko Haram insurgents blew themselves up in a market.	25	62
Nigeria	January 30	Boko Haram gunmen raided a village.	65	136
Uruguay	March 10	A 35-year-old man called Carlos Omar Peralta López from Paysandú repeatedly stabbed to death a Jewish merchant while screaming "Allah is great!" some months after his supposed conversion to Islam and assuming the identity of "Abdullah Omar". The victim's son was injured while trying to stop the attack.	1	1

Location	Date	Description	Deaths	Injuries
Ivory Coast	March 13	In the 2016 Grand-Bassam shootings, Al-Qaeda gunmen stormed 3 hotels in Grand-Bassam.	18	
Turkey	March 19	March 2016 Istanbul bombing; carried out by an ISIL member	5	36
Iraq	March 20	In Anbar, ISIL suicide bombers attacked a municipal building	24	
Belgium	March 22	2016 Brussels bombings. Two suicide bombings in Brussels Airport and one bombing in the Brussels Metro.	35	300+
Yemen	March 25	Three ISIL suicide bombers struck security checkpoints in Aden.	29	

Location	Date	Description	Deaths	Injuries
Iraq	March 25	A suicide bomber blew himself up at a football stadium in Iskandariya, south of Baghdad. ISIL claimed responsibility for the attack.	30	95
Pakistan	March 27	The 2016 Lahore suicide bombing targeted Christians who had gathered on Easter in Gulshan-e-Iqbal Park. The blast was orchestrated by Jamaat-ul-Ahrar, a Pakistani Taliban faction.	70	300
Afghanistan	April 19	The April 2016 Kabul attack targeted a security team responsible for protecting government VIPs in Kabul. It was the Taliban's biggest attack on an urban area since 2001.	64	347

Location	Date	Description	Deaths	Injuries
Bangladesh	April 23	Attackers hacked a university professor to death in Rajshahi. ISIL claimed responsibility for the attack stating that they assassinated him "for calling to atheism".	1	
Bangladesh	April 25	Two gay rights activists were hacked to death in Dhaka. An Al-Qaeda affiliated group claimed responsibility for the attacks.	2	
Iraq	May 11	Car bomb attack on a market in Baghdad. ISIL claimed responsibility.	40	60
United States	June 12	Mass shooting at a nightclub in Orlando, Florida. The shooter, Omar Mateen, pledged allegiance to ISIL by specifically calling police and journalists several times during the incident.	49	53

Location	Date	Description	Deaths	Injuries
France	June 14	A police officer and his wife were stabbed to death in Magnanville by a man swearing his allegiance to ISIL.	2	
Jordan	June 21	An ISIS militant attacked a refugee camp at an army post near Rukban. ISIL later claimed responsibility.	6	14
Pakistan	June 22	Assassination of Amjad Sabri, claimed by a splinter group of the Pakistani Taliban who accused him of blasphemy.	1	
Turkey	June 28	A simultaneous terrorist attack, consisting of shootings and suicide bombings at the international terminal of Terminal 2 of Istanbul Atatürk Airport.	45	230

Location	Date	Description	Deaths	Injuries
Bangladesh	July 1	Gunmen killed 20 hostages in the affluent Gulshan Thana neighborhood of Dhaka. Thirteen hostages were rescued; two police officers and six attackers were killed. One attacker was taken into custody. ISIL claimed responsibility, but according to Bangladeshi officials, the attack was carried out by homegrown militant group Jamaat-ul-Mujahideen Bangladesh. On August 27, Bangladeshi police killed three militants whom they accused of perpetrating the Dhaka attack, including Tamim Ahmed Chowdhury, a 30-year-old Canadian citizen born in Bangladesh, who was described as "one of the main suppliers of funds and arms for several recent attacks".	26	

Location	Date	Description	Deaths	Injuries
Iraq	July 3	July 2016 Baghdad bombings Two coordinated bomb attacks.	341+	246
Indonesia	July 4	A suicide bomber attacked a police station in Central Java, killing himself and injuring a police officer.	1	1
Iraq	July 7	A coordinated attack involving suicide car bombers, suicide bombers on foot, and gunmen against the mausoleum of Muhammad ibn Ali al-Hadi, a Shi'ite holy site in Baghdad. ISIL claimed responsibility.	56	75
France	July 14	2016 Nice truck attack.	87	450+
Germany	July 18	A 17-year-old Afghan refugee went on a stabbing spree inside a train near Würzburg. The attacker was shot dead when he attacked the arriving police officers.	1	5

Location	Date	Description	Deaths	Injuries
Germany	July 24	A suicide bombing outside a wine bar in Ansbach, in which a bomber tried to bomb a large music festival going on at the time. Many videos were discovered of him pledging allegiance to ISIL and Abu Bakr al-Baghdadi. The bomber was the only fatality.	1	15
France	July 26	A priest's throat was slit and four nuns were taken hostage in a church in Rouen. ISIL claimed responsibility for the attack. The two attackers were shot dead by authorities. One of the men was known to the French intelligence services and was on the French government's terror watch-list.	3	
Pakistan	August 8	77 people were killed and over 100 injured by a suicide bombing at a government hospital in Quetta.	77	100+

Location	Date	Description	Deaths	Injuries
United States	September 17–19	2016 New York and New Jersey bombings - three bombs exploded and several unexploded ones were found in the New York metropolitan area. The perpetrator was subsequently charged with attempting to radicalize fellow jail inmates to espouse violent jihadist beliefs.	0	31
India	September 18	2016 Uri attack – Four armed militants attacked an army brigade headquarters in Uri area of Baramulla district in Jammu and Kashmir State. 18 soldiers were killed and 19 were injured.	18	19

Location	Date	Description	Deaths	Injuries
United States	November 28	Ohio State University attack. Car ramming attack and mass stabbing at Ohio State University. The perpetrator, Abdul Razak Ali Artan, was a Muslim Somali refugee and legal permanent resident of the United States.	0	11
Pakistan	November 12	Bombing at the Shah Noorani shrine in Balochistan. More people were killed and injured during the stampede that resulted from people fleeing the blast. ISIL claimed responsibility.	56	102
Egypt	December 11	A suicide bomber killed 27 people and injured 47 others at St. Peter and St. Paul's Church (commonly known as El-Botroseya Church) in Cairo. ISIL claimed responsibility.	29	47

Location	Date	Description	Deaths	Injuries
Germany	December 19	2016 Berlin truck attack during which a truck was driven into the Christmas market next to the Kaiser Wilhelm Memorial Church at Breitscheidplatz in Berlin.	12	56

2017

Location	Date	Description	Deaths	Injuries
Turkey	January 1	An ISIL gunman opened fire on a crowd of people in the Reina Nightclub in Istanbul.	39	70
Iraq	January 2	A suicide bomber with a truck full of explosives attacked a predominantly Shia market in Baghdad. ISIL took responsibility for the attack.	36	52

Location	Date	Description	Deaths	Injuries
Afghanistan	February 8	ISIL militants attacked a convoy of aid workers of the Red Cross.	6	0
Afghanistan	February 11	Taliban suicide car bomber killed seven people outside a bank in Lashkargah.	7	21
Pakistan	February 16	During the Sehwan suicide bombing a suicide bomber entered the main hall of the Shrine of Lal Shahbaz Qalandar in Sehwan and detonated his payload amid dozens of worshippers.	91+	300+

Location	Date	Description	Deaths	Injuries
Iraq	February 19	Two suicide bombings that hit districts recently retaken from ISIL in eastern Mosul. The first attack targeted an army checkpoint, killing three soldiers, and the second a gathering of civilians in the commercial district known as "My Fair Lady," killing two.	5	0
Pakistan	February 21	Three militants threw hand grenades and opened fire as they launched an assault in Tangi, near the border with Afghanistan. Two of the men blew themselves up during the 20-minute gun battle with security forces at the gate, while the third was shot dead by police before he could detonate his explosive vest.	7	22

Location	Date	Description	Deaths	Injuries
Egypt	February 22	Two Coptic Christians were found killed in Al-Arish. The two were believed to have been kidnapped by militants from the ISIL-affiliated group "Sinai Province."	2	0
Afghanistan	February 28	Twelve policemen were killed in an "insider attack" in Lashkar Gah after a Taliban infiltrator allowed militants into the outpost.	12	0
Afghanistan	March 8	Gunmen dressed as medics attacked a military hospital in Kabul in an assault claimed by ISIL.	40+	50+
Iraq	March 8	Two suicide bombers blew themselves up at a wedding party in Hajaj, near Tikrit. ISIL claimed responsibility.	26	67

Location	Date	Description	Deaths	Injuries
United Kingdom	March 22	A man drove a car into pedestrians on the south side of Westminster Bridge.	6	49
Russia	April 3	A suicide bomber blew himself up on the St. Petersburg metro. The bomber was born in Kyrgyzstan and had ties to radical Islamists.	5	15
Sweden	April 7	2017 Stockholm truck attack – A rejected Uzbek asylum seeker stole a beer truck and drove onto a crowded high street to mow down as many pedestrians as possible. According to his testimony he wanted to pressure Sweden into ending its support for the fight against ISIL.	5	15

Location	Date	Description	Deaths	Injuries
Egypt	April 9	Palm Sunday church bombings on Christian churches in Tanta and Alexandria.	47	100+
France	April 20	Three police officers and a bystander were shot by an attacker wielding an AK-47 rifle on the Champs-Élysées in Paris. The attacker was shot dead. He had a note defending ISIL, and had previously attempted to communicate with its fighters in Iraq and Syria.	2	3
United Kingdom	May 22	The Manchester Arena bombing - an Islamist extremist suicide bomber detonated a shrapnel-laden homemade bomb as people were leaving the Manchester Arena following a concert by American singer Ariana Grande.	22	1,017 (112 hospitalised)

Location	Date	Description	Deaths	Injuries
Egypt	May 26	A gunman opened fire on a convoy carrying Coptic Christians traveling from Maghagha in Minya Governorate.	28	22
United Kingdom	June 3	The 2017 London Bridge attack was an incident where an attacker ran over multiple pedestrians on London Bridge. On Borough Market the occupants of the van stabbed multiple people before being shot by police.	11	48
France	June 6	2017 Notre Dame attack – A lone wolf carrying knives in his rucksack used a hammer to attack an officer guarding Notre-Dame de Paris. A video pledging allegiance to ISIL was later found.	0	2

Location	Date	Description	Deaths	Injuries
Iran	June 7	2017 Tehran attacks – In the first attacks orchestrated by ISIL in Iran, Tehran was targeted by suicide bombers and teams of gunmen when they stormed Iran's parliament and the nearby shrine of Ruhollah Khomeini. All 4 attackers at the parliament were killed.	22	43
Iraq	June 9	Suicide bombing in Karbala. The attack was claimed by ISIL.	30	36
Egypt	July 14	2017 Hurghada attack – An attacker with a knife stabbed foreign tourists.	2	4

Location	Date	Description	Deaths	Injuries
Pakistan	August 7	A truck carrying explosive material accidentally went off at Band Road in Lahore. A few hours after the attack, a clash erupted between 7 militants and the CTD team in which 4 militants were shot dead while 3 others managed to escape. The militants were identified as from the Pakistani Taliban.	2	35
Spain	August 17–18	2017 Barcelona attacks – Three separate attacks in Barcelona.	15	120

Location	Date	Description	Deaths	Injuries
✝ Finland	August 18	2017 Turku attack – Stabbing attack in Turku by an eighteen-year-old Moroccan asylum seeker named Abderrahman Bouanane. According to the police he was a radicalized lone wolf influenced by ISIS. The attacker was shot in the leg by police and was arrested. Police later discovered that the attacker had also planned attacks at different sites. Three other suspects, all Moroccans, were remanded in custody in connection with the attack. He was convicted for terrorism and murder. It was the first time a Finnish court has decreed that a crime was a terrorist act. Finland's prime minister described the stabbings as the country's first terrorist attack in history.	2	8

Location	Date	Description	Deaths	Injuries
United Kingdom	September 15	A bomb wrapped in a plastic grocery bag concealed in a bucket exploded at the height of the morning rush at the London Underground. ISIL claimed responsibility for the bombing.	0	29
United States	October 31	2017 New York City truck attack – A man drove a pickup truck into cyclists and runners along about 1 mile (2 km) of a bicycle path in Lower Manhattan, New York City. After leaving the vehicle, the driver wielded two guns (later found to be a paintball gun and a pellet gun); he was shot in the abdomen by police and arrested. An ISIL flag and a document that read either "It will endure." or "Islamic State will endure forever." in Arabic were found in the truck.	8	12

Location	Date	Description	Deaths	Injuries
Egypt	December 29	A gunman opened fire outside a church in Cairo before attempting to storm the building, at least seven people were killed. He had earlier shot at a store, killing two people inside. The Interior Ministry said that the shop was owned by a Copt and that the two dead were Christian men. ISIL claimed responsibility for the attacks.	at least 9	0

2018

Location	Date	Description	Deaths	Injuries
Iraq	January 15	2018 Baghdad bombings.	38	105

Location	Date	Description	Deaths	Injuries
Afghanistan	January 20	2018 Inter-Continental Hotel Kabul attack.	40	22
Afghanistan	January 24	Save the Children Jalalabad attack	6	27
Afghanistan	January 27	Kabul ambulance bombing.	103	235
Russia	February 18	Kizlyar church shooting	6	5
Somalia	February 18	February 2018 Mogadishu attack.	45	36
Burkina Faso	March 2	2018 Ouagadougou attacks	30	85
Afghanistan	March 21	March 2018 Kabul suicide bombing	33	65
France	March 23	Carcassonne and Trèbes attack - Hostage crisis	5	15

Location	Date	Description	Deaths	Injuries
Somalia	April 1	2018 African Union base attack in Bulo Marer.	59 (+30)	Unknown
Afghanistan	April 22	22 April 2018 Kabul suicide bombing	69	120
Afghanistan	April 30	30 April 2018 Kabul suicide bombings	29	50
Nigeria	May 1	2018 Mubi suicide bombings	86	58
Libya	May 2	2018 attack on the Libyan High National Elections Commission	16	20
Netherlands	May 5	Stabbing attack in The Hague.	0	3
France	May 12	2018 Paris knife attack	2	4
Indonesia	May 13	2018 Surabaya bombings	25	55
Belgium	May 29	2018 Liège attack	4	4

Location	Date	Description	Deaths	Injuries
Afghanistan	July 1	July 2018 Jalalabad suicide bombing	20	20
Pakistan	July 10	2018 Peshawar suicide bombing	22	75
Pakistan	July 13	2018 Mastung and Bannu bombings	154	223
Syria	July 25	2018 As-Suwayda attacks – A string of suicide bombings and gun attacks that took place in and around As-Suwayda. The attacks were committed by ISIL.	258 (+63 attackers)	180
Tajikistan	July 29	Terrorist attack against cyclists in Tajikistan – Assailants rammed American and European cyclists with a car in the Khatlon region, then attacked them with knives and an axe.	4	2

Location	Date	Description	Deaths	Injuries
Jordan	August 12	An explosion near a police van in Fuheis. Officials claimed that the attackers supported ISIL, but did not have links to the organisation.	5	26+
Netherlands	August 31	2018 Amsterdam stabbing attack - A 19-year-old Afghans with a German residence permit, stabbed two American tourists with a knife at Amsterdam central station. After the attack he was shot by police in his lower body and arrested.	0	2
Iran	September 22	2018 Ahvaz military parade attack - Militants wearing khaki uniforms shot at a military parade in Ahvaz. ISIL claimed the attack.	24+	20

Location	Date	Description	Deaths	Injuries
Egypt	November 2	Islamic militants ambushed three buses carrying Christian pilgrims returning from a remote Coptic Christian monastery and opened fire. ISIL claimed responsibility.	7	19
Australia	November 9	2018 Melbourne stabbing attack – A man of Somali origin set a car on fire and stabbed multiple people in Melbourne. He was shot dead after confronting officers on a busy street. ISIS claimed responsibility for the attack, but authorities said he was only inspired by the group and there did not appear to be direct links.	1	2

Location	Date	Description	Deaths	Injuries
Morocco	December 17	Murders of Louisa Vesterager Jespersen and Maren Ueland - Two female Scandiniavian tourists, a Danish and a Norwegian, were killed (one beheaded) near Imlil in the Atlas Mountains; the murderers filmed their action while branding the two women 'enemies of God' and saying their actions were God's will. Four suspects were arrested and Moroccan authorities said that they had pledged allegiance to the ISIL beforehand.	2	0

2019

Location	Date	Description	Deaths	Injuries
Kenya	January 15	Nairobi DusitD2 complex attack - Al-Shabaab militants attacked the DusitD2 hotel in Nairobi.	21+	0
India	February 14	A man rammed his car full of explosives into a convoy of soldiers. The attack was claimed by Pakistan-based terrorist organization, Jaish-e-Mohammed.	40 (+ 1, the suicide bomber)	35
Philippines	January 27	2019 Jolo Cathedral bombings - Two bombs exploded at the Our Lady of Mount Carmel Cathedral, Jolo, as worshipers gathered for Sunday Mass. ISIL claimed responsibility.	20+	102

Location	Date	Description	Deaths	Injuries
Sri Lanka	April 21	2019 Sri Lanka Easter bombings - on Easter Sunday, three churches across the country and three luxury hotels in Colombo were bombed. Later that day, there were smaller explosions at a housing complex and a guest house. Authorities confirmed that the bombers were Sri Lankan citizens associated with National Thowheed Jamaath (NTJ), a local militant radical Islamist group, but foreign links were suspected.	269 (+8 bombers)	500+
Sri Lanka	April 27	April 2019 Kalmunai shootout - Security forces and militants from NTJ allegedly linked to ISIL clashed after the security forces raided a militant safe house, upon which three suicide bombers blew themselves up.	16	2

Location	Date	Description	Deaths	Injuries
France	May 24	2019 Lyon bombing - Explosion outside a bakery in the center of Lyon. The suspect, a migrant from Algeria possessing jihadist propaganda, his parents and sibling were arrested.	-	13
Philippines	May 26	Abu Sayyaf militants attacked a group of soldiers in Jolo Island.	7	2
Afghanistan	August 17	17 August 2019 Kabul bombing - A suicide bomber detonated a bomb in a wedding hall.	92	142
United Kingdom	November 29	2019 London Bridge stabbing - Convicted Islamist terrorist Usman Khan stabbed members of the public on London Bridge before being wrestled to the floor by pedestrians and then shot dead by police.	2	3

2020

Location	Date	Description	Deaths	Injuries
Afghanistan	March 25	Kabul gurdwara attack –ISIL gunmen attacked a Sikh religious gathering and took dozens of hostages. At least 25 people were killed. After six hours of fighting 80 hostages were rescued.	25	—
Philippines	August 24	2020 Jolo bombings – A motorcycle bomb exploded on a busy street in Jolo, Sulu. As police and the military responded, a female suicide bomber detonated a second bomb, killing at least 14 people and wounding 75. ISIL is suspected of being behind the bombings.	14	75

Location	Date	Description	Deaths	Injuries
France	October 16	Murder of Samuel Paty – A middle-school teacher was attacked and beheaded by an 18 year-old Chechen. The teacher had previously shown Charlie Hebdo-Cartoons depicting Muhammad during class. The culprit forewarned of his intentions using his Twitter account.	1	
Afghanistan	October 24	October 2020 Afghanistan attacks - A suicide bombing outside an educational centre in Kabul. The ISK claimed responsibility for the attack.	30+	70+
France	October 29	2020 Nice stabbing – Stabbing attack in Notre-Dame de Nice, one of the victims was beheaded.	3	

Location	Date	Description	Deaths	Injuries
Austria	November 2	2020 Vienna attack – Shooting in Stadttempel, Vienna. The Vienna Police Department confirmed that the attacker was an ISIL sympathizer, and that the attack was motivated by Islamic extremism.	4	15
Mozambique	November 10	ISIL-linked militants attacked a village and turned a football pitch into an "execution site", where they beheaded and dismembered residents. State media reported that several more people were beheaded in another village. Executions and beheadings reportedly continued for two days.	50+	Unknown

Location	Date	Description	Deaths	Injuries
Syria	December 30	An assault targeted a bus with personnel from president Bashar al-Assad's elite Fourth Brigade returning from their posts in Deir ez-Zor. The bus was ambushed in a well-planned operation near the village of Shula by jihadists who set up a false checkpoint to stop the convoy and detonated bombs before opening fire. ISIL claimed responsibility.	40	

2021

Location	Date	Description	Deaths	Injuries
Pakistan	January 3	2021 Machh attack - ISIL claimed responsibility for killing miners in Machh, Balochistan, after kidnapping them and taking them to the mountains.	11	—
Iraq	January 21	January 2021 Baghdad bombings - ISIL targeted Shia muslims in a clothing market in Tayaran Square.	32	110
Iraq	July 19	Near the eve of Eid al-Adha, an ISIL suicide bomber detonated his vest in a crowded market in the densely populated neighbourhood of Sadr City. Some shops burned down as a result of the explosion.	30	50

Location	Date	Description	Deaths	Injuries
Afghanistan	August 26	2021 Kabul airport attack; ISIL claimed two suicide attacks near Hamid Karzai International Airport. 13 US service members and at least 170 Afghans were killed in the attacks.	183	200
New Zealand	September 3	2021 Auckland supermarket stabbing: An ISIL supporter stabbed multiple people before being shot by police in Auckland.	1	6

2022

Location	Date	Description	Deaths	Injuries
Norway	June 25	2022 Oslo shooting - Shooting in a busy nightlife district.	2	21

Location	Date	Description	Deaths	Injuries
India	June 28	Murder of Kanhaiya Lal – A Hindu tailor was murdered by two Muslim assailants in Udaipur. The assailants captured the attack on camera and circulated the video online. In a second video (taken after the attack), the assailants boasted about the murder to avenge the insult to Islam and also made threats against Prime Minister Narendra Modi.	1	
United States	August 12	Stabbing of Salman Rushdie – The Satanic Verses author Salman Rushdie was stabbed 33 years after a 1989 fatwa by Ayatollah Khomeini, condemning him for the book's allegorical presentation of the possible validity of the so-called Satanic Verses content of the Quran.		2

Location	Date	Description	Deaths	Injuries
Egypt	August 30	A Christian father and son, Salama Waheeb and his son Hany, were shot dead in Gelbana, 20 kilometres east of El Qantara by ISIL militants. They were working in their fields at the time.	2	
Afghanistan	September 30	September 2022 Kabul school bombing - A suicide bombing suspected to be carried out by ISK at a tutorial centre during a mock exam for both men and women in a Hazara neighbourhood.	25	36
France	October 7	In Chateau-Thierry, a Muslim man stabbed his mother and younger brother and then went on a stabbing spree along the street before being apprehended by police while making Islamic prayers at the roadside.		6

2023

Location	Date	Description	Deaths	Injuries
India	January 1-2	2023 Rajouri attacks - The first attack was a shooting which killed 4 people and injured 9. The second attack was an IED which killed 5 and injured 3.	9	12
Pakistan	July 30	2023 Khar bombing - ISK carried out a suicide bombing at a Jamiat Ulema-e-Islam (F) rally in Khar, Bajaur District, Khyber Pakhtunkhwa. and injuring over 200 others.	63+	200+
France	October 13	Arras school stabbing - A teacher was stabbed to death and two other people were wounded. The attacker shouted "Allahu akbar" according to police.	1	2

Location	Date	Description	Deaths	Injuries
Afghanistan	October 13	2023 Pul-i-Khumri bombing - During prayer, there was an explosion in the Imam Zaman mosque. Some of the injuries were treated at Pul-i-Khumri Hospital while others were transferred to Kunduz hospital for treatment. The Islamic State – Khorasan Province claimed responsibility for the attack, identifying the attacker as "Sayfullah al-Muwahhid".	7	17
Belgium	October 16	2023 Brussels shooting - Two Swedish nationals were shot dead and a third person injured in the attack. In a video posted on social media, a man identifying himself as the gunman claimed "to be inspired by the Islamic State".	2	1

2024

Location	Date	Description	Deaths	Injuries
Iran	January 3	2024 Kerman bombings – ISIS-K carried out a suicide bombing on a commemorative ceremony for assassinated Iranian general Qasem Soleimani at his grave in eastern Kerman.	96	284
Turkey	January 28	2024 Istanbul church shooting – Two gunmen entered the Church of Santa Maria in Istanbul during Sunday mass and shot and killed a man before leaving. Islamic State claimed responsibility for the attack.	1	1
Russia	March 22	2024 Crocus City Hall attack - ISIS-K carried out an attack at a concert hall in Moscow, killing 145. Russian officials at first attempted to associate the attack with Ukraine, but it was later admitted to be the work of Islamic terrorists.	145	551

Chapter 19

Concluding Remarks

Some important points to be remembered are

- Peaceful coexistence is important for the development of any region.

- Face is the identity of the person. Any person covering the face in the public places, gives rise to the feeling of insecurity in the minds of the other people.

There are many Islamic terrorist groups.

Some of them are

1. The Islamic State (IS), also known as the Islamic State of Iraq and the Levant (ISIL), the Islamic State of Iraq and Syria (ISIS) and by its Arabic acronym Daesh, is a transnational Salafi jihadist group and a former unrecognised quasi-state.

2. HAMAS – the acronym for Harakat al-Muqawama al-Islamiya (Islamic Resistance Movement)

3. Houthi terrorist group

4. Hezbollah terrorist organization

5. And many more......

These are not the armies of any country.

How can these organizations prosper without the support - financial, military etc. from any country?

This makes the things complicated.

If it is tried to spread Islam very aggressively, it is going to affect the peace.

We have seen in India, Love Jihad is resorted to.

And Taqiyyah at many other places.

What is Taqiyyah in Islam?

1. What is the meaning of "Taqiyyah"?

Its literal meaning is to safeguard; to defend; to fear; piety (because it saves one from the displeasure of Allah).

2. What is its significance in Islamic terminology?

In Islamic terminology it means "to save life, honor. or property (either one's own or of other believers) by hiding one's belief or religion"

Spreading Islam aggressively is like a war to gain supremacy over others. This might continue for centuries in the whole world.

Even if Islam wins, there cannot be the complete peace in the world.

Again there could be fighting for superiority between Sunni and the Rest.

It is left to the God to decide.

Om Shanti.

9 7 9 8 8 9 4 7 5 3 5 6 0